NOTICE: If any part of these contents is lost or damaged, the Patron will be charged for the total cost of all items.

_____ Disk	_____ Video
_____ Cassette	____|____ CD
____|____ Text	_____ Other

CIRCULATING WITH THE LISTED PROBLEM(S):

Using 3D Studio MAX, Painter, and Poser

Missing CD

5-1-04 $cb

NOV 8 2000

Using 3D Studio MAX, Painter, and Poser

An Introduction to Computer-Assisted Design for the Theatre

L. J. DeCuir

HEINEMANN

PORTSMOUTH, NH

Heinemann
A division of Reed Elsevier Inc.
361 Hanover Street
Portsmouth, NH 03801–3912
www.heinemanndrama.com

Offices and agents throughout the world

The author and publisher wish to thank those who have generously given permission to reprint borrowed material:

Screen shots reprinted by permission of MetaCreations Corp.

In the accompanying CD-ROM:

Photograph "Taiwan Dark Green, Taiwan" courtesy of Casatelli Marble & Tile Imports.

Image from *Surfaces: Visual Research for Artists, Architects, and Designers* by Judy A. Juracek. Copyright © 1996 by Judy A. Juracek. Reprinted by permission of W. W. Norton & Company, Inc.

Library of Congress Cataloging-in-Publication Data
DeCuir, L. J.
    Using 3D Studio MAX, Printer, and Poser : an introduction to computer-assisted design for the theatre / L. J. DeCuir.
        p. cm.
    Includes bibliographical references and index.
    ISBN 0-325-00222-3
    1. Theaters—Stage-setting and scenery—Computer programs.
    I. Title.
    PN2091.S8 D36 2000
    792'.025'0285—dc21   99-036491

Editor: Lisa A. Barnett
Production: Elizabeth Valway
Cover design: Monty Lewis
Technology coordinator: Dan Breslin
Manufacturing: Louise Richardson

Printed in the United States of America on acid-free paper
04 03 02 01 00   RRD   1 2 3 4 5

CONTENTS

ACKNOWLEDGMENTS

A book such as this one never gets written without a lot of help, and that is certainly the case here. Writing about all that help, however, is always a difficult task for the author. One cannot list every single person who has been of assistance, and inevitably, someone does get left out. So, I'll start this off with a big thank-you to all of those who have not been mentioned directly. Everyone's help has been appreciated, whether you are mentioned here or not.

The number one acknowledgment for helping this work actually make it into print has got to go to my wife, Mari. She's the one who struggled through the proofing of the early copies, kept track of the expenses necessary to keep the IRS happy, put up with my mumbling to myself at the dinner table about "commands" and "formatting," and has generally had to pick up the slack while I spent hour after hour pounding keys at the computer. Thank you, my dear!

After Mari there is a whole list of folks whose input and support have also been essential: Lisa Barnett at Heinemann, who has offered intelligent and down-to-earth advice; The Innovative Technologies Center at the University of Tennessee, which provided the grant that gave me the first hardware and software necessary to work with these programs; The Student Technology Fee at the University of Tennessee, which provided the grants that have created a functioning computer laboratory for our students and the opportunities to test out the ideas in this book in practice; The Department of Theatre at the University of Tennessee, which supported me both with time to write and the facilities necessary to see if many of the ideas in this book really work in practice; the students in my classes, who served as guinea pigs to ensure that the instructions are actually comprehensible when one is sitting in front of the computer trying to figure out how to make a program work; Marianne Custer, who let me use some of her designs for the exercises in this book; and Judy Juracek, who let me use some of the files from her own *Surfaces* book. Thanks to all of you as well.

The emotional support that is necessary for an author to keep going day after day has come from Mari as well, but also from Raphael, Rocky, Belle, and Nellie. These are our four English Bulldogs, who have all put in time snoring on the doggy bed next to the computer, giving me an affectionate nuzzle, and providing a friendly head to pat while I was puzzling over a problem.

My thanks to all of you,

L. J.

INTRODUCTION

With the explosion of computer use in all of our lives over the past few years it was inevitable that the rapid expansion of applications to the theatrical design process would quickly follow. By now most of us in the area of theatrical design have seen examples of computer-aided designs either in practice, at conventions, or on the World Wide Web, and many designers and technicians who have not yet begun to use computer programs in their work have at least started to wonder about the process and exactly what is required to begin.

Lighting designers were among the first to utilize the computer as an aid, primarily with such "drafting" tools as AutoCAD, Mini-CAD, etc. They recognized that computer-assisted drafting greatly sped up the process of modifying, refining, and changing drawings that is so much a part of the theatrical process. These computer-assisted "drafting" programs also had the capability of three-dimensional "drawing" that would let one, after creating a ground plan, quickly turn it into a perspective view of the scenery from any viewpoint desired. While these perspective views could be highly detailed, they usually lacked the capability of being turned into artistic visions without returning back to the drawing board or painter's easel.

There were already on the market a number of programs for the artist that would let one create artistic visions on the computer, but it was still extremely difficult if not impossible to work back and forth between the draftings necessary to communicate the vision to the lighting and scenery crews and the "renderings" that communicated the vision to the other designers and the director of a production. With the advent of a number of new programs, it is now possible to do exactly that.

This book and its companion are intended to serve as aids in understanding several computer programs that the designers on a theatrical production can use both in the creation of a rendering of their artistic vision and in the communication of that vision to the technicians responsible for transforming it into wood, plastic, metal, fabric, and lighting instruments. I have specifically chosen four programs that I have found to be highly useful to the scenic designer, lighting designer, costume designer, and technical director in this process. In addition to offering instruction in the basic understanding and use of these programs, I have further attempted here to deal with the integration of these four programs into the entire design process. Using these four programs, the set designer can begin with a simple ground plan, a rough "thumbnail" sketch, or a 3-D model on the computer and turn it into a rendering that is as detailed or open to interpretation as desired. The set designer can also, as a part of the same process on the computer, create the draftings necessary for the construction of the scenery or turn that part of the process over to the technical director. The costume designer can begin working from a "figure model" that is in whatever suitably dramatic pose or body type desired for a character or even begin working from a photo of the actor who will be playing the character in the actual production. The lighting designer can work from the renderings of the scenic designer and then experiment with lighting applications on top of that or start drafting the lighting plot from a highly accurate ground plan or 3-D model created by the scenic designer or technical director. At any part of the design process the three designers can also exchange information. The costume "sketches" can be imported into the scenic rendering for presentation to the director, for example, or the lighting designer's ideas can be expressed in the same 3-D model in which the scenic designer is working. By working together in these four programs all of the designers on a production can greatly enhance both their communication with one another and their visual communication with the rest of the production staff.

None of these four programs was originally designed for use in a theatrical application. As such they do have some shortcomings when adapted to our needs. Unfortunately, the theatrical market for computer programs has not yet expanded to the point where someone has attempted to create a single integrated program that fulfills all of the requirements and desires listed in the previous paragraph. Maybe sometime that will actually happen, but until that time we shall have to continue to adapt the best available programs to our own uses. The four programs covered in this book and its companion volume currently form one of the best groups of programs that will satisfy as many of these needs and desires as possible and offer the closest integration of all three design areas. All four are available for PC-based computers, which is the most widely distributed format today. Three of them are also available for Mac-based computers, the second most widely distributed format.

The four programs that I have chosen for this work are AutoCAD, 3D Studio MAX, Poser, and Painter. AutoCAD is the premier program currently on the market for both two-dimensional and three-dimensional drafting. The previous volume was intended primarily as an introduction to the use of AutoCAD for the theatrical designer and technician. This volume covers 3D Studio MAX,

Poser, and Painter. There are many other works currently available that explore each program in a great deal more depth and breadth if you are interested in further applications of this program. See the Bibliography for a listing of the works that I have found to be especially useful in working with AutoCAD as well as the other programs. One of AutoCAD's greatest virtues for us in theatrical design, however, is its ability to export both individual objects and entire three-dimensional views into other programs such as 3D Studio MAX or Painter. These objects and/or views can then serve as the basis for a highly detailed three-dimensional computer model in 3D Studio MAX or a rough sketch for a rendering in Painter. Once a model has been created in 3D Studio MAX or a rendering has been created in Painter, a variety of lighting techniques can be applied in these programs to create visions of individual scenes. It is a relatively easy matter to work between these three programs. The fourth program, Poser, is extremely easy to learn and can be used to make human figures for the renderings created in Painter or the 3-D models and drawings of 3D Studio MAX and AutoCAD. In Painter these figures can be used as the underlying figures in a costume rendering that can then be imported into a set rendering created in Painter. Using these four programs together as a part of the overall design process can enable the designers on a production to quickly and easily exchange ideas and information both among themselves and with the other members of the production staff.

The purpose of this book and its companion volume is to introduce these four programs in their theatrical applications. My hope is that this will form the basis of your own exploration of the possibilities inherent in these and other programs to your own design process. None of the sections on the individual programs is intended to be the definitive work on all possible aspects of the program's uses, but rather to offer you a beginning for understanding how the program works and how to integrate the four programs with one another in the theatrical design process. Above all, I have also attempted to use simple English in all of the instructions in this book. Anyone in theatre not already highly skilled in the areas of computers who has attempted to learn almost any computer program is only too familiar with the difficulties of doing so from the usual instruction manual supplied. Highly important steps in the use of the program seem invariably to be entirely left out or "assumed" to be already at your command. I have done my best to avoid those pitfalls in this work so that it can truly be accessible to even those with the most rudimentary of computer skills. Throughout the book I have tried to focus on the commands in each program that will be most useful to theatrical artists and to give detailed instructions on how to import and export files from one program to another. These import and export instructions along with your own imagination are the key to integrating the four programs with one another and the theatrical production process.

One final word of caution is necessary. One must remember that a computer is nothing more than a tool to assist you in your own artistic process. If you can't already draw, you won't be magically transformed into an artist by using a computer. If you don't understand the construction of scenery, drafting it on a computer will not suddenly turn a physically weak or poorly supported platform or step unit into one that will hold elephants. The computer will not turn a poor designer into a good one. Whatever your own levels of skills with a paintbrush or drafting board already are, they will remain the same. Once mastered, however, the computer programs covered in this book and its companion will allow you to utilize those skills, talents, and knowledge in ways that previously may not have been possible and often to do so at a great savings of both time and difficulty.

Using 3D Studio MAX, Painter, and Poser

THE PROGRAMS, HARDWARE, AND DRIVE BASICS

The Programs

AUTOCAD

AutoCAD, produced by AutoDesk, is one of the first sophisticated drawing programs that found widespread use in theatrical applications. As has been usual with computer applications in the theatre, the lighting designers were the first to make use of this program. The lighting designer probably now thinks of this program primarily as a drafting tool that allows one to quickly create and rapidly modify lighting plots, and the use of AutoCAD in this way will indeed be covered in this book. Included on the accompanying CD-ROM, for example, is a complete instrument library that one can simply import into one's hard drive and then use, as is, in creating lighting plots.

Following quickly on the heels of the lighting designers came the technical directors in finding uses for AutoCAD. They also realized that this program, once learned, offered them the opportunity to rapidly create and modify technical drawings for use in the scene shop, prop shop, etc. These uses of AutoCAD will also be covered in this book with particular attention to some of the commands that the technical director will find especially useful.

It is only more recently that many scenic designers have come to realize that AutoCAD is a tool that they can utilize also in more creative ways than simply drafting ground plans. The three-dimensional aspects of AutoCAD allow the scenic designer to create not just a ground plan, but an entire "virtual" 3-D model of a set and all of it's components. These models can then be exported from AutoCAD into Painter to create a rendering. The components can be exported into 3D Studio MAX and have textures added to create a 3-D model that can then have lighting applied so that the setting can be realistically viewed under a variety of different lighting conditions.

For the costume designer, the applications of AutoCAD are probably a bit more limited. He or she might find it useful, however, as the basis for yet another program that will allow him or her to quickly draft and resize patterns.

AutoCAD is available in a variety of versions for different platforms. The oldest version is for MS-DOS and operates primarily from keyboard commands. Release 12 was the first version that was available for Windows and will operate in Windows 3.1, Windows95, WindowsNT, and Windows98. Release 13 is available for both Windows and Macs. The latest version, Release 14, is only available for Windows95, NT, and 98. There are also inexpensive versions of AutoCAD called AutoCAD Lite, or LT, that are very similar in operation to the full versions, and because of their cost they are finding widespread use in theatrical applications but are only available for Windows. AutoCAD LT2 is extremely similar to R12. LT95 is similar to R13 and LT98 is similar to R14. If you have any of the versions of AutoCAD Lite or LT, refer to the AutoCAD sections dealing with the full version to which it is similar. You will find that most of the commands covered in this book work exactly the same in the Lite or LT versions. There are a few commands that you will not be able to use in Lite or LT, and these will be noted in the text.

AutoCAD is an expensive program. If you are affiliated with a college or university, check with your computer center about its arrangements for securing site licenses from AutoDesk and you will find that you should be able to buy copies at a considerable discount. If you are not connected with a college or university then you might seriously look into one of the older releases or AutoCAD Lite versions for your use. These will cover the needs of the vast majority of theatrical situations. There actually are very few "new" commands in R13 and R14. The biggest difference between these and R12 is a lot more graphics and a bit more "user-friendly" layout. All of the exercises in this book and all of the integration of work between AutoCAD and 3D Studio MAX, Painter, and Poser can be done with any of the AutoCAD releases or versions.

3D STUDIO MAX

3D Studio MAX is one of the most capable programs available today for the creation of simulated three-dimensional modeling on the computer. You can create your 3-D features directly in 3D Studio MAX or more accurately create them in AutoCAD and then import them into 3D Studio MAX. This second method allows you to save considerable time in the process because the features created in AutoCAD can also be turned directly into working drawings for the shop. The scenic designer can easily manipulate the components of the set in the program and move them around to try out different configurations. The basic components are easily "covered" with a wide variety of textures available in the program or imported from outside so that one can quickly change the color and texture of walls, furniture, etc. to try out different looks. Once a virtual model of the setting is created, the lighting designer can apply lighting "instruments" to it in the program that can be controlled for spread, intensity, color, and edge. You can also create gobos or patterns for use in the program. This is a program that really allows the set designer, the lighting designer, and the technical director to work together in the creation of the scenery and lighting requirements for a production.

Like AutoCAD, 3D Studio MAX is from AutoDesk. Unlike AutoCAD, which has a fairly steep learning curve, 3D Studio MAX is more "user-friendly" and is accompanied by a number of extremely helpful tutorials. At this time it is available only for Windows95, Windows98, and WindowsNT.

3D Studio MAX is an expensive program that is usually available for academic use through site licenses secured through your college or university at a considerably reduced cost. This program will represent a serious investment for the freelance theatrical artist or for theatrical companies without academic affiliations.

3D Studio MAX has so far gone through two releases with a number of smaller changes within those releases. This work covers both R1 and R2. For the sake of an introductory manual, the differences between the two programs are minor. The biggest difference is that R2 can read R1 files, but R1 cannot read R2 files. R2 can also accept files directly from AutoCAD R14.

PAINTER

Painter is one of the easiest to learn of the "rendering" programs available today for the traditionally trained theatrical artist. In conception and terminology it closely approximates all of the familiar techniques used in creating pencil, ink, watercolor, acrylic, oil, etc. work by hand with some greatly appreciated extras like the ability to use watercolor that doesn't dry until you tell it to. All of the rendering skills that you have spent years developing are available to you when you work in Painter. The scenic designer can easily import realistic-looking perspective views from AutoCAD or 3D Studio MAX and then create all the mood, atmosphere, and feeling that he or she would in a traditional rendering. The costume designer can import a figure from Poser, import a pencil sketch, or start with a photograph of an actor and create a costume rendering that will be as photo-realistic or stylized as he or she desires. There are a limited number of lighting effects available as well, but nothing like the more sophisticated control available in 3D Studio MAX. Painter can also be used to create textures, gobos, etc. that can be exported for use in 3D Studio MAX and Poser.

Painter is available from MetaCreations, formerly Fractal Design, for all Windows and Mac platforms. The latest version is Painter 5 and it comes packaged in a clever gallon paint bucket. As of this writing, there is also a 5.5 "Web Edition" upgrade available. While there are cheaper rendering programs out there, there are few that are as well conceived, offer as much variety of technique, and are as easy to use as Painter. Painter is at its most effective when it is used in combination with a graphic tablet such as a Wacom ArtPad, since this tool will allow you to control your stroke in a manner similar to a brush or pencil.

POSER

Poser is a program with applications in all three of the others. An extremely simple program to master, Poser allows you to create a wide variety of human figures that can then be imported into Painter, 3D Studio MAX, or AutoCAD for use with renderings or drawings. The basic figure is available in a large number of different sizes and body types—everything from giant figures to adults to children from svelte to obese. The program also literally lets you control the dimensions of specific parts of the figure to match a particular body type or actor. The figures can be covered with a simple wireframe, exposed muscle, or skin as desired and can be moved into any simulated three-dimensional pose that you wish. You can also control the lighting of the figure from up to three directions in both intensity and color. It has basic animation capabilities for the figures and the ability to import props and backgrounds.

Poser is made by MetaCreations, formerly Fractal Design, and is available for all Windows and Mac platforms. The latest version is Poser 4, which is an expanded version of Poser 3. While this book primarily covers Poser 3, the procedures and operations of Poser 4 are identical. The major difference in the two programs are in the size of the figure and other libraries that are available within the program. You will have no difficulties working with Poser 4 using the instructions in this book. Both Poser 4 and Poser 3, however, represent a radical change in layout, graphics, and operation from Poser 2. If you should have Poser 2, there are files on the CD-ROM that accompany this book that contain instructions for working with this older version of the program. You can print out one of these files or work with it directly from the CD-ROM if you like. One file, Poser/Poser2.wpd, is a WordPerfect 6.1 file. The second file, Poser/Poser2.txt, is the same text, but in a .txt format. The file Poser/Poser2.doc is in a Word format and the file Poser/Poser2.rtf is in a Rich Text format.

Hardware Requirements

Processor: For this group of programs I would recommend a computer with a minimum processor speed of 200 MHz. More important than processor speed, however, is the RAM of the computer.

RAM: Random access memory will keep these programs from turning into slow-motion exercises on you. Ignore what the manufacturers of the programs say here. An absolute minimum 64 MB of RAM is really necessary to run these programs properly, especially with modern operating systems, and the more you can get, the better.

Hard Drive: The size of hard drive necessary can vary considerably from one user to another, but many of the files created in these programs can get rather large. I would recommend a minimum of at least 4 to 6 GB of hard drive, and if you can afford an 8 GB drive, that would be preferred. It is always better to get a much larger hard drive than you think you will need so that you can easily add more programs and files at a later date without having to delete ones that are already there.

Video Card: The video card in the computer will determine the quality of color that your monitor will be able to display. For a larger size monitor such as is recommended for graphics work, a 2 MB video card will display 64,000 colors, which is OK for general use, but if you really want photo-realistic color resolution you will need a 4 MB video card to be able to handle 16.7 million colors.

Tape Backup Systems or Zip Drives: Many of the files that you will be creating may be so large that they cannot fit on a "floppy" disk, which has 1.0 to 1.4 MB capacity. A tape backup system, a Zip drive, or a large-capacity disk system—100 MB or greater—will allow you to transfer these files to storage other than your hard drive as well as move them from your computer to another. Seriously consider one of these as an option.

Modem or Ethernet Capability: Depending upon your location and linkage with other computers, either a modem or an Ethernet card will allow you to transfer files between your computer and others as well over the Internet. The resources available to the designer on the Internet are already numerous and are increasing daily. Check with your network server for information on what kind of Ethernet or network card is recommended for your system. If you are using a modem to connect to the Internet, then a modem of 33.6 K bps or above is strongly suggested. Again, check with your server for details on a modem.

CD-ROM: CD-ROM drives are now standard on almost all computers. Be sure that your computer does come with a CD-ROM drive as well as a 3.5-inch "floppy" drive. There is a considerable amount of design material available to you today on CD-ROMs.

Audio Card, Wavetable MIDI, Speakers, etc.: If the computer is going to be used by your sound person, talk to him or her about what you should be getting here. If it's just going to be used for graphics, don't even worry about it. Take the basics that come with the system and put your extra money into one of the other items above.

Accessories

Monitor: When using a computer for theatrical graphics, buying the largest monitor that you can afford is a real plus. The 14- or 15-inch monitor that comes with most computers becomes a problem when dealing with large draftings or details on drawings, forcing you to constantly zoom or adjust your viewpoint. A 17-inch monitor is the basic size I would recommend for this kind of work. Unfortunately, the price of monitors goes up rapidly after they get larger than 17 inches in diagonal screen size. Larger sizes are nice, but they can get quite costly. By the time that this book actually goes into print, however, much of that may have changed, considering how quickly the prices of computers and their accessories are dropping. So, buy the largest monitor that you think you can afford.

When considering a monitor, look at dot pitch, resolution, and refresh rate in addition to screen size. The smaller the dot pitch the better, with .28 mm being the largest you would want. Small differences in dot pitch, however, are really not that noticeable. The higher the resolution, the more detail being displayed, with $1,024 \times 768$ being minimal and $1,280 \times 1,024$ preferred. Don't be tempted, however, by a cheaper monitor with a high resolution and a slow refresh rate. The refresh rate will keep the screen from flickering at you and driving you crazy. The faster the refresh rate the better, with 75 Hz being the slowest you would want and a 85 Hz rate preferable.

Printer/Plotter: A good-quality color printer is a must for doing any kind of rendering work with your computer. If you are interested in printing on different kinds of papers, then one with a paper path that flows almost straight through the printer is necessary rather than one with a paper path that reverses itself. If possible, try to compare different printers for color and sharpness before buying. In an ink-jet printer, look for a minimum resolution of 600 dpi. Laser printers can give you a considerably higher resolution but are much more expensive. Do not even consider a dot-matrix printer.

If you are going to be using the computer for drafting work, then a plotter is a recommended accessory. While these are considerably more expensive than printers, it can be a godsend to have your own plotter in the theatre rather than having to wait for a commercial operator to do your plots for you. For most theatrical applications a plotter that can handle paper at least 36 inches wide is necessary.

Scanner: A good-quality flatbed scanner—300×600 dpi resolution or better—is a must for working with these programs. This will allow you to convert almost anything that you desire from a photograph or a flat image directly into a file that can be used by the programs. Scanner prices have now also dropped to the point where almost anyone who can afford a computer can easily afford a scanner as well. Be sure that you get a flatbed scanner rather than the kind that has a flow-through path. Another option to consider is a slide scanner. These will allow you to scan a 35 mm slide and turn it into a computer image. However, they are usually more costly than a flatbed scanner.

Graphic Tablet: A graphic tablet or "artpad" is a must for use with Painter. When drawing with a mouse, you will only be able to achieve one density of "line." A graphic tablet allows you to use the pen that accompanies it much as you would use a paintbrush, pen, or pencil. You will be able to taper, flare, and control the density of your strokes in the same way. The most useful size for theatrical work is probably a 6 × 8-inch or 9 × 11-inch size. They are available in smaller sizes at quite reasonable prices or larger sizes at considerably more cost.

Digital Camera: While rather expensive, a digital camera can be an extremely useful tool to combine with your computer. It will allow you to "photograph" an actor, an object, or an image directly as a digital image that can be used by the computer. If you have found a texture that you want to apply to the set, for example, you can shoot it with the digital camera and then apply it directly to the rendering of the set in the computer. A costume designer could also take a digital image of an actor and then create a costume rendering in Painter over the image of the actor.

Drive Basics

In order to integrate and work between the above programs it is necessary that you understand the drive system of your computer. If you do not already understand the layout and use of your hard drive, floppy drive, CD-ROM drive, and Zip or other drives, now is the time to learn. I strongly recommend that you find someone familiar enough with your computer to explain the use of these systems to you in detail. I will try to cover the basics behind them here, but the exact layout of any particular system will vary from computer to computer and you need to be familiar with your own.

The drive system of the computer organizes programs, files, etc. so that the computer and you can access them. These are the storage systems of the computer and how they are laid out. Today, most computers have at least three drive systems: a hard drive, or "permanent" storage; a 3.5-inch "floppy" drive, for storage on small disks with 1.0 to 1.4 MB capacity; and a CD-ROM drive, usually used to hold programs and large amounts of data. There are also a number of other drive systems that are now being offered for use such as Zip or auxiliary drives that offer you the option of external data storage in capacities of 100 MB or larger. Somewhere on your computer there is a program that will let you examine these drives to see how they are organized and what they contain. In Windows 3.1 this program is called File Manager. In Windows95 and Windows98 one program is called Explorer or Windows Explorer and a second is called My Computer. On Macs this is your Hard Drive and Floppy or A: drive icons. Before you continue with this book, become familiar with the program used on your computer and how to use it to navigate around your drive system. Many of the instructions in this book assume that you already know how to get around on your drive system. If you don't, you will quickly end up losing files and getting quite lost yourself.

On most computers today the "floppy" drive is referred to as the A: drive. If you want to read a file from a 3.5-inch disk or save one to it, you have to select the A: drive. The CD-ROM drive that lets you read what is on a CD-ROM is referred to by different letters on different computers. Depending upon your computer this may be the D:, E:, or F: drive. Find out how to access the CD-ROM drive on your particular computer. For most computers the hard drive is the C: drive. It may also be referred to by a name or a number. The hard drive is divided up into sections called folders or directories. When you install a program it is usually placed into a folder or directory that is created by the installation part of the program. It is important to know what folder or directory these programs have been placed in so that you can access them later. When you install a program, it will usually ask you if you want it to create a folder or directory with a particular name similar to the name of the program or the program's manufacturer. Remember the name of this folder or directory. You can also create folders or directories yourself to help you organize your files and make them easier to find. When I'm working on a show, for example, I may create a folder using the name of the show and place all of the files that I create in that folder so that it will be easier for me to find them later. I highly recommend this procedure so that you will not have to search all over your hard drive to find a particular file. You can also create subfolders and subdirectories under folders and directories. Learn how to create folders, subfolders, etc. so that you can organize your files. It will save you vast amounts of time in the long run.

The other important part of learning to use the drive system on your computer is learning to use your "floppy" A: drive to back up and/or save any files that you create. Hard drives crash, and when they do any material that is on them will usually be lost. Hours, months, or even years of work can be completely destroyed this way. I cannot say this too strongly: *BACK UP EVERY-THING THAT YOU PUT ON YOUR HARD DRIVE!* If you save a file onto the hard drive, save it onto a disk as well. Some people even recommend that you do a double backup and save it onto two separate disks. The 3.5-inch disks can go bad, too. If that happens, anything on that disk is lost. I would recommend saving important files onto two different disks. When I was writing this book I had it saved onto two different hard drives on two different computers and also onto a separate set of 3.5-inch disks and onto a Zip disk. When it comes to backup, the old "suspenders and belt" philosophy is a good idea.

The problem with 3.5-inch disks is that they will hold only about 1.0 to 1.4 MB of storage. When you start creating graphics files, you'll find this is not a lot of space. As a result, a number of different kinds of tape and large disk systems have been introduced with storage capacity of 100 MB to 4 to 8 GB. If you have one of these systems, often called tape drives or Zip drives, you can use it to back up large files or large groups of files so that you don't have to deal with ten to twenty 3.5-inch disks for a particular group of files.

Files that you create using these programs can also be saved only to 3.5-inch disks, tapes, or large disks in order to save room on your hard drive. If you have a small hard drive, you may find that it has very little room left on it after you install all the programs. You will then have to save your files to one of these storage systems because there is not enough room left on the hard drive. It is quicker and easier to get at files from the hard drive than it is from one of these external storage systems, but eventually if everything is saved to the hard drive you will run out of storage space. When I'm working on a show I usually save the files to the hard drive and back them up on an external drive, and then when that show is over I delete the work from the hard drive and just keep it on the external disk(s) or tapes. If it is an important project, I will normally have two copies of the external disk(s) or tape(s) on which the project has been saved. Following this practice can prevent you from having to replicate hours or weeks of work from scratch if a disaster happens. When you're working with computers there is always the possibility that something can go wrong . . . go wrong . . . go wrong! *Always* back up your work!

3D STUDIO MAX

INTRODUCTION

3D Studio MAX is a "3-D" modeling program that has much more sophisticated capabilities than AutoCAD and, while quite complex, is considerably more "user-friendly" and easier to learn. This program will allow you to import objects from AutoCAD, add textures and colors to them, move them around, add lighting effects, and thus create a rendering of the set that you have been drawing in AutoCAD. In 3D Studio MAX, you can also create and modify objects such as trees, bushes, snowy landscapes, etc., that are considerably more "free-form" than is easily possible in AutoCAD and these objects can be exported back to AutoCAD for the construction of working drawings. Another exciting capability of 3D Studio MAX for the theatrical designer is the ability to use the animation function to work out lighting cues, scenery changes, and other effects. By working in combination with AutoCAD, the set designer can integrate his or her work with the technical director and the lighting designer on the show. Files can be traded back and forth, which the technical director can use to make ground plans and working drawings and the lighting designer can use to create the light plot and his or her own lighting renderings of various scenes in the show. The cooperative capability that these two programs have when used in combination is one of their most intriguing aspects. For years we in the theatre have talked about the importance of collaboration. Now with the computer, we have some tools that can make that collaboration easier and faster for everyone involved. The scenic and lighting renderings created in 3D Studio MAX can along with the costume renderings also be exported to Painter, creating views involving all three design areas to help give the director an even better idea of how all the designs will work together in the final production. If this work is done in the computer before the construction is begun, modifications and changes become less time-consuming and expensive.

This section is intended to be an introduction to 3D Studio MAX. As such, it certainly does not cover everything that is possible for you to do with the program. It is, for example, well within the range of 3D Studio MAX to create much more complex objects than the simple examples that are covered in the exercises here. While the regular manuals for the program are still unfortunately written in language that can be difficult to comprehend, there is an excellent set of tutorials that accompany the program. Pull the manual titled *Tutorials* out of the large stack that came with 3D Studio MAX and keep it by your computer. After you have finished with the present book, start working through these tutorials with the program. If you have a question about a more complex procedure in 3D Studio MAX that is not covered in this book, try to find the answer in the *Tutorials* manual before you look at the rest of the 3D Studio MAX manuals. It doesn't cover everything that the program can do either, but it does provide answers in a format that is easy to understand and follow.

This book has been written to cover both Release 1 and Release 2 of the program. For the purposes of introduction, these two versions do not vary considerably. Differences between the versions are noted in the text.

This section, like all of the sections of this book and its companion, has been written in a carefully considered sequence. Follow the text and do the exercises in the order in which they appear to get the most out of the book. Each section and exercise is built upon the previous material. To do Exercise No. 3, for example, you will already need to know the material covered in Exercises No. 1 and No. 2. If you skip around you will have missed commands or procedures and will probably end up getting confused.

INSTALLING THE PROGRAM

You will quickly find that 3D Studio MAX is considerably easier to deal with than AutoCAD, and the installation of the program is no exception. Depending upon the version that you have, you may find a number of CD-ROMs and disks in your package. Many of these are for other aspects of the program that you will want to learn about eventually but which need not concern you immediately. The ones that you are interested in right now are the CD-ROM labeled 3D Studio MAX KINETIX and possibly a 3.5-inch disk labeled the same and also labeled as the Initialization Disk. These plus your Authorization Number are what you will need to install the basic program. In later versions of the program, you may only need the CD-ROM and the Authorization Number.

Insert the CD-ROM in your computer. Under My Computer in Windows95 or WindowsNT, double click on Control Panel, then double click on Add/ Remove Programs. Click on Install and follow your on-screen instructions from there. At some point in the process you will be prompted to insert the

Initialization Disk if it is required. Do so when instructed. When the installation is complete you will also have to authorize your copy before it can be used. Before you start the program, click on the Start button in Windows95 or NT. Then click on Programs, then on Kinetix, then on authorize 3DS Max. Enter the Authorization Number that you have been given with the program.

Before you can use the program there is one other thing that you probably must do. You will probably have received a Hardware Lock or "Key" along with the program package. If you did, it must be installed on the parallel port (printer port) of your computer. Disconnect the printer cable from the back of your computer. Install the Hardware Lock in that connector and then install the printer cable into the back of the Hardware Lock. I would also strongly recommend that you make a backup copy of your Initialization Disk if you have one. You might also want to create a shortcut to 3D Studio MAX on your desktop so that the program can be started from there rather than from the Start/Programs/Kinetix path.

Now you are ready to start 3D Studio MAX. Configuration such as you did with AutoCAD is not necessary. There will be a number of preferences that you will want to set, but those will be covered as they come up in the text.

BECOMING FAMILIAR WITH THE WORK SPACE

When you start 3D Studio MAX, the screen is somewhat intimidating, as with most programs that you have not used before. There are lots of buttons and icons that don't mean anything yet and you don't even know where to begin. Open the program and locate the parts of the screen that are described below and illustrated in the figure labeled The Opening Screen on the next page. This will get you familiar with the layout of the screen and what the icons represent.

THE PULL DOWN MENUS

You should already be familiar with the idea of pull down menus from other programs. Clicking on a word on the pull down menu bar at the top of the screen will open a list directly below it with other words that will activate commands when clicked on. Some of the important items located in these pull down menus are described below.

File:

New: This command creates a new drawing space.

Open: This displays the Open File box, which you can use to open drawings that you have already created.

Save: This command saves changes that you have made in a drawing to the same location from which it was opened.

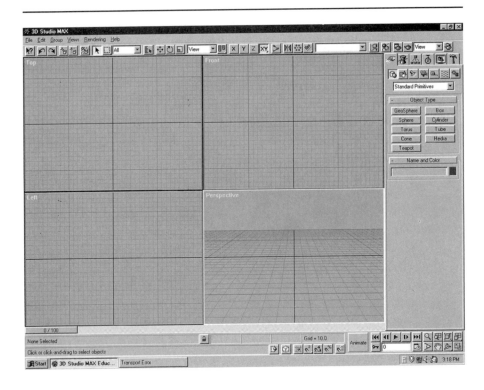

Save As: This command saves changes that you have made in a drawing to a new location or name. You also use it to save a drawing for the first time and give it a name and location.

Import: This command is used to bring in a drawing from AutoCAD or other source.

Export: This command is used to export a drawing as a .dwg (AutoCAD) or .dxf file.

Preferences: This command opens the Preference Settings box. This box allows you to determine your own settings for eight categories of items: General, Rendering, Inverse Kinematics, Animation, Keyboard, Files, Gamma, and Viewports. For the time being, do not change any of these settings. I will cover how to use them later in the book.

Edit:

Select by: This allows you to select objects by their name or color after these have been assigned.

Region: This lets you choose between window and crossing selection options. There is also a button on the status bar at the bottom of the screen that controls this choice.

Views:

Units Setup: This opens the Units Setup box. This is where you decide what measurement units you would like the program to use. For theatrical applications you would most likely want to click first in the circle next to US Standard, then on the arrow below it to select Feet w/Fractional Inches, and then on the arrow next to that to select how small of a fractional inch—for theatre, usually 1/16". Change these settings before you start working in the program.

Viewport Configuration: This opens the Viewport Configuration box. This lets you choose from a number of different viewport setups for the program.

Rendering:

Render: This command is used to create a rendering of a view on the working screen that can be saved as a file for use in other programs such as Painter.

Make Preview: This sets the parameters for a preview of the rendering. Previews load much faster than renderings. These can be used to get a quick view to decide if you want to do a full rendering or change something first.

View Preview: This shows you a preview of a scene rather than a rendering.

Help:

Topics (R1) or Online Reference (R2): This opens the Help box, where you can search for help by topic. The Help Mode button on the toolbar will also open Help for a particular item on the screen.

THE TOOLBAR

The toolbar is just below the pull down menus. This contains many of the tools that are most useful in 3D Studio MAX. If you pause the cursor just over a button, a caption will appear with the name of the button, and a longer description of what it does will appear in the prompt line at the lower left-hand corner of the screen. Working from left to right on the screen, some of the most important of these buttons are:

The Help Mode Button: Click on this button, then click on something on the screen, and it will open an information box on that subject.

The Undo Button: Click on this button to remove the effect of the last command. The program allows you to undo up to twenty steps. This is also available in the Edit pull down menu, which will tell you the name of the function to be undone.

The Redo Button: Click on this button to restore what was undone by the last undo command. This is also available in the Edit pull down menu, which will tell you the name of the function to be redone.

 The Select and Link Button: Click on this button to link two or more objects together as a child and parent. Click on the object you want to be the child, and then drag a line to the parent. Whatever is done to the parent such as rotate or move also affects the child, but not vice versa.

 The Unlink Button: Click on this button to unlink two linked objects. Select the objects that you want to unlink and then click on this button.

 The Bind to Space Warp Button: Click on this button to bind or link an object to another object that has a space warp attached to it. Space warps affect the appearance of objects by generating ripples, waves, or explosions. They can be used to create snow, rain, and water effects.

 The Select Object Button: Click on this button and then select a single object for an operation such as move, rotate, etc.

 The Selection Region Button: Click and hold on this button to display three choices: rectangle, circle, or fence. Click to draw a rectangle, circle, or irregular shape. Anything within the area defined is selected. You can use this to select multiple objects at once.

 The Selection Filters Window: Click on the arrow to choose a selection filter. When a filter is active, the selection tool will only be able to select that kind of object. This option can help sort out a specific type of object from a busy drawing.

 The Select by Name Button: This lets you select an object from a list of all of the objects in the window.

 The Select and Move Button: Choose this option, then click on an object to select it and drag it to move it. If you click outside of an object, you can drag the mouse to create a selection window. Then you can move all of the objects in the selection window. If you click on one of the X, Y, and Z buttons further to the right on the toolbar, it will restrict the movement of the object to that axis.

 The Select and Rotate Button: This button operates like the Select and Move button, but it rotates objects instead.

The Select and Scale Button: Click and hold on this button to activate one of three options: Uniform Scale, which scales an object larger or smaller on all three axes; Non-Uniform Scale, which scales an object only on the X, Y, or Z axis selected; or Squash, which "squashes" an object on the axis selected, meaning that a decrease or increase in size on one axis will be translated into an increase or decrease on another.

 The Transformation Coordinate System Window: Click on the arrow to select the coordinate system—View, Screen, World, etc.—on which you want a transformation such as move, rotate, etc. to take place. The world and screen coordinate systems of 3D Studio MAX are similar in some ways to the WCS and UCS systems of AutoCAD. Luckily, you don't usually need to work with this in 3D Studio MAX the way that you do in AutoCAD.

 The Use Pivot Point Selection Tool: Click on this button to select one of three points around which an object can be rotated or scaled. The Pivot Point option starts as the object's center of mass. The Selection Center option uses the object's geometric center. The Transform Coordinate Center option rotates or scales the object around the current center of the coordinate system. Note that the pivot point and selection center may often be the same, but the pivot point can be changed.

 The Restrict to X, Y, or Z Buttons: These restrict movement or change of an object to just the X, Y, or Z axis if selected.

 The Restrict to Plane Button: This restricts movement or change of an object to just the X,Y or other plane if selected. Click on button to select plane.

 The Inverse Kinematics Button: When toggled on, this button will cause the parent object to follow a moving or rotating child object. When the button is toggled off, moving or rotating a child object will not affect the parent object.

 The Mirror Button: This button lets you mirror an object. Select the object and click this button. It will open a Mirror dialogue box with options for axis of rotation, distance from the original, and whether the object is to be cloned.

 The Array/Snapshot Button: Select an object and click and hold on this button to select array or snapshot. Snapshot clones the currently selected object. Array creates a series of clones in a geometric pattern.

 The Align/Align Normals/Place Highlight Button: Click and hold to select one of these buttons. The Align button aligns the object already selected with another. The Align Normals button aligns the faces of the object already selected with another. The Place Highlight button lets you align an object or light with another object so that its highlights can be positioned.

 The Named Selection Set Box: This box allows you to select a group of objects and give it a name by clicking in this box and then typing in the name you would like. You can recall the selection set later with the box.

Note: If you have set a screen resolution of less than 1,024 × 768 pixels, the next five items may not appear on your toolbar. You will still be able to access most of these commands via the pull down menu.

 The Track View Button: This function gives you access to animation time parameters. It is also available via Edit / Track View.

 The Materials Editor Button: This function gives you access to materials and maps. It is also available via Edit / Material Editor.

 The Render Scene Button: This button opens the dialogue box to set parameters for rendering the selected view. The function is also available via Rendering/Render.

 The Quick Render Button: This renders the selected view without using the last set of render parameters, but using simple parameters.

 The Render Modifier Window: Use this to specify the portion of the scene that you want to render.

 The Render Last Button: This repeats the last render.

THE COMMAND PANEL

Just below the toolbar on the right-hand side of the screen there is a group of six buttons that make up the top part of the command panel. Clicking on any of these buttons will change the options open in the part of the screen below the six buttons. These options permit you to make detailed choices about the objects, effects, textures, colors, etc. that make up the basis of the scene that you are creating. They will be covered in more detail later.

As you start using these options, you will find that some of them are so large that they will not fit in the space allocated to the command panel. When this happens you will see only the top part of the options available. At that

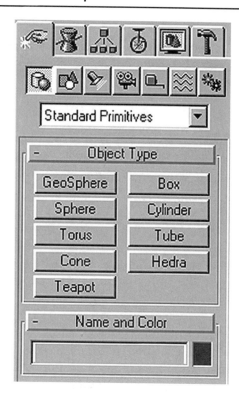

point when you place the cursor over any part of the command panel that is not clickable, you will see a hand appear. Click and drag with the mouse to scroll the command panel options up and down to find the one that you want. Pop-up menus are another aspect of the command panel. The bars that run all the way across the command panel such as **Object Type** or **Name and Color** on the create panel are pop-up menus. A + on the left-hand side of the bar indicates that there is a menu underneath. If you click on the pop-up menu bar, the hidden menu will appear and the + will change to a −. The six buttons at the top of the command panel are:

 The **Create Panel** Button: This opens the options to let you create objects in the scene such as shapes, lights, cameras, etc. When the **Create Panel** button is clicked, the display on the command panel looks like the figure labeled The Create Panel.

 The **Modify Panel** Button: This accesses the options used in changing objects. Here you can make more serious modifications to objects than just moving, rotating, cloning, etc.

 The **Hierarchy Panel** Button: This lets you change the linkages between objects.

The Motion Panel Button: This provides access to the controls for the motion of objects within the scene.

The Display Panel Button: This button accesses the tools used in controlling the display of objects. It lets you hide and unhide and freeze and unfreeze objects. This is also where you can control the display of color, links, and other aspects of objects.

The Utilities Panel Button: This accesses plug-ins that may be purchased separately from the basic program. It also provides access to the Color clipboard.

The seven lower buttons on The Create Panel are:

The Standard Primitives Button: This lets you create basic geometric shapes such as box, sphere, cylinder, tube, torus, cone, hedra, and teapot.

The Splines or Shapes Button: This gives you the tools to create shapes, which are spline-based objects. A spline is a collection of vertices and connecting segments that form a line. By adjusting the vertices and segments you can make portions of the line straight or curved. Splines can then be rotated or extruded to create shapes.

The Lights Button: This tool is used to create lighting instruments.

The Camera Button: Here is where you create cameras to view the scene that you have drawn.

The Helper Button: This creates a variety of helper tools such as a dummy, grid, point, or tape.

The Space Warp Button: This controls space warps in the program. Space warps are modifiers that create special effects such as bomb, wave, gravity, wind, deflector, ripple, and displace.

The Systems Button: This provides access to plug-in systems.

VIEWPORTS

Four large, gridlike areas take up the major portion of the screen. These are the viewports that will display your scene from different angles and through different methods if you prefer. The viewports can be modified in a number of different ways. Until you get more familiar with 3D Studio MAX though, I would not recommend making any major changes here. Only one viewport can be active at any time. To make a viewport active, right click in that viewport or click on the name of the viewport in the upper left-hand corner. Left clicking in the viewport activates the viewport, but it will also perform an action in that viewport such as selecting an object or starting the creation of a new one.

Viewport Configuration

The viewport configuration controls different aspects of how the viewports look and work. To open the Viewport Configuration box, click on View/Viewport Configuration. The Viewport Configuration box will open with tabs at the top that let you access boxes for Rendering Method, Layout, Safe Frames, Adaptive Degradation, and Regions.

Rendering Method

The Rendering Method box lets you choose from a variety of rendering appearances from Smooth & Highlight to Wireframe. You will want to familiarize yourself with the various rendering options available. They control the look of the final rendering that you will be creating. After you create your first scene in 3D Studio MAX, take some time to try rendering it with each of the different options so that you will know how they work.

Layout

The Layout box offers you a variety of different screen layouts for your viewports besides the four-view standard that opens the program.

Changing the View Displayed in a Viewport

If you right click on the name of the viewport displayed in the upper left-hand corner of that viewport, a shortcut box opens that lets you change aspects of the viewport such as what view is displayed there. By choosing some of the options in the box that opens, you can:

- change the rendering method for that viewport
- toggle the grid, background, and safe frame display on and off
- disable the view
- click on View and change the view displayed in the viewport to Grid, Perspective, User, Front, Back, Top, Bottom, Left, Right, Track, or Shape
- change layouts
- open the Viewport Configuration box

STATUS BAR CONTROLS

The status bar runs all the way across the bottom of the screen. This has a number of controls on it as well as windows that display current information. The following buttons and windows are on the status bar.

Viewport Navigation Controls

The viewport navigation controls are located in the lower right-hand corner of your screen on the status bar. These let you change the way that you view a scene in a viewport. They modify the view of the scene, not the objects themselves. Most of these controls are concerned with zooming and panning and will change depending upon the type of viewport that is currently active.

 The Min/Max Toggle Button: Click on this button to make the active viewport go to a full screen size. Click again and you restore the multiscreen setup.

 The Zoom Button: Click on the Zoom button to activate the Zoom Function, then click and drag vertically in the active screen. The view will zoom in and out. Note that when you click on the Zoom button it turns green. This tells you that you are in the Zoom command. To turn off the Zoom button, either right click in the active window or click on another button.

 The Zoom Extents Button: Click on this button to make the window zoom so that the objects just fill it.

 The Zoom All Button: Click on the button and then click and drag vertically in the active window. All windows will zoom in and out.

 The Zoom Extents All Button: Click here to make all windows zoom so that the objects fill them.

 The Pan Button: Click on the button and then click in the active viewport and drag to move the view from side to side or up and down.

 The Arc Rotate Button: Click on the button. A green circle appears in the active viewport. If you click and drag inside the circle, the view will rotate around the X and Y axes, depending upon the direction in which you drag. If you click and drag outside the circle, the view will rotate around the Z axis. There are also two tags on the circle labeled Y and two tags labeled X. Click and drag vertically on one of the X tags and the view will rotate only around the X axis. Click and drag horizontally on one of the Y tags and the view will rotate only around the Y axis.

 The Field of View Button: The Field of View button only appears when a perspective view is active. This button changes the perspective, making it wider or narrower. This can increase or decrease distortion in the viewport.

 The Region Zoom Button: This button replaces the Field of View button when you're in any view but a perspective. This acts like zoom window in

AutoCAD. Click on a corner, move the mouse, and then click on the other corner to select a rectangular view.

Animation Controls

Just to the left of the viewport navigation controls on the status bar are the animation controls. These are the controls that let you create and control the animation features of 3D Studio MAX. You can easily set up and replay a simple animation sequence using these controls. This can be a useful tool for the theatrical designer. The lighting designer can set up light cue sequences and watch them happen on the computer, adjusting the time, intensity, etc. of the cue to get an idea of what he or she wants to do before creating it in the theatre. A set designer can pan around the audience space checking sight lines and the effect of the scenery from all of the seats in the house. The technical director can set up scenery movement and work out the coordination and timing of a scene change. These are the animation controls:

The **Animate** Button: This button turns key framing on and off. Key frames or keys mark the beginning and end of each animation sequence. Each change is marked as a key frame when this button is on. When this button is off, each change is applied to frame 0.

The **Key Mode** Button: When the **Key Mode** button is toggled on, each move forward or backward in the frames is to a key frame. A key frame is one in which a change begins. The frames in between key frames are skipped.

The **Time Configuration** Button: This button lets you control the settings for frame rate and timing in animation.

The **Frame** Window: This displays the current frame number. Click in the window, hit **Backspace**, type in a frame number, hit **Enter**, and you will go to that frame number.

The **Frame** and **Play/Stop** Buttons: These buttons let you move backward and forward in the frames that you have created, and play and stop the animation sequence. From left to right they are:

1. **Go to Start:** This moves the time slider to the first frame in a sequence.
2. **Previous Frame:** This moves the time slider back one frame, or key frame if **key mode** is on.
3. **Play/Stop:** Click here and hold for two options:
   A. **Play/Stop:** Click here to start an animation sequence, click again to stop it.

B. Play Selected: Select an object and then click this option. The animation sequence for only this object will play. Click again to stop.

4. Next Frame: This moves the time slider forward one frame, or key frame if key mode is on.

5. Go to End: This moves the time slider to the last frame in a sequence.

Window, Degradation, Snap, and Spinner Settings

To the left of the animation controls is another group of seven buttons that control the way that a number of different functions of 3D Studio MAX operate. Working from left to right in the group, they are:

 The Window/Crossing Toggle Button: This switches between a window and crossing option when you click on the button. In the window option, objects must be completely inside the window you draw to be selected. For the crossing option, objects are selected if the window that you draw touches them. This affects how the Selection Region button up on the toolbar operates. You then click and drag in the active viewport to select by region.

 The Degradation Override Button: While you are working, the program will automatically lower the rendering level to a display that speeds up your working time. To stop this function, toggle this button off. This function overcomes some of the time delays that will occur if your video memory isn't large enough to handle complex rendering methods at the same speed you are working. If you do toggle this button off and your video memory isn't sufficient, you will find much of your work going into slow motion on you. If that happens, toggle it back on.

 The Snap Control Buttons: This group of four buttons controls how the snap function of the program operates. Working from left to right:

1. The Relative/Absolute Snap Button: When this button is on, absolute snap is activated, and you will snap to grid lines. When this button is off, relative snap is activated and you can use the snap spacing feature, but without having to snap to grid lines.

2. 2-D, 2.5-D, 3-D Snap Button: Click and hold to display the three options:

    A. 2-D Snap: You can only snap to the grid—X,Y plane—not to the Z axis.

    B. 2.5-D Snap: You can snap to the grid—X,Y plane—or to parts of an object that project above or below the grid.

    C. 3-D Snap (default): This snaps directly to any geometry in 3-D space.

3. The Angle Snap Button: This controls what kind of increments the angle of rotation of an object will move in. Right click on the button to set a snap angle. Then a left click on the button activates it. Rotation commands will only move in the angle specified when angle snap is activated.

4. The Percent Snap Button: This controls the increments of scaling. A right click on the button lets you set a scale percentage. A left click on the button activates it. Any scaling up or down in size will then be only by the percentage specified when percent snap is activated.

 The Spinner Snap Button: Many parameters in 3D Studio MAX are controlled by what the program calls "spinners." A spinner is a box with a number in it and up and down arrows to the side. Click on the up arrow to increase the number, or value, in the box and on the down arrow to decrease it. Right click on the Spinner Snap button to set the up and down increment for all spinners. Left click on this button to activate that increment value. The fastest way to reset the value in a spinner, however, is not to use the arrows, but to double click in the box with the number, type in the new value, and then hit Enter. You can also click behind the number in the box and drag the mouse forward to highlight the whole number and then enter a new value.

Grid and Coordinate Display Windows

Just above the Snap Control buttons is the Grid Setting Display window. This shows you the grid increment in the active viewport. As you zoom in or out, this will change to smaller or larger values. To the left of the Grid Setting Display are the Coordinate Display windows. These show you the current position of the cursor in X, Y, and Z values. Move the cursor around in the active viewport, and you will see these values change. The left window is the X value. The middle window is the Y value. The right window is the Z value.

 ### Lock Selection Button

To the left of the Coordinate Display windows on the status bar is the Lock Selection button. This turns selection locking on and off. After you have selected an object in a viewport you can keep it selected by turning the Lock Selection button on. Then it will stay selected while you switch to a different viewport. This is useful with small objects or complex objects with a lot of parts.

Status and Prompt Lines

To the left of the Lock Selection button is the status line. This displays the name and category of selected object(s). Immediately underneath the status line is the prompt line. This is a help system to tell you what the program expects next or what you can do next in an operation. It will change depending upon the cursor location and your current activity.

Time Slider

Above the prompt and status lines and below the viewports is the time slider. When the program opens, the slider is all the way to the left and displays 0/100. The time slider is used with animation sequences. It shows the current frame value, followed by a backslash (\), followed by the total number of frames in the sequence. If you are running an animation sequence, it will move from left to right displaying the current frame number as it moves. If you would like to work on a specific frame in a sequence, you can click on it and drag it left or right until the frame number that you desire is active.

MODIFYING THE OPENING SCREEN

There are a number of settings for the 3D Studio MAX opening screen that can be changed from the initial view that you see when you first start the program. If you would like to save these settings so that the program always opens with the settings that you prefer, you can do so by creating or re-creating a file named maxstart.max in the scenes folder of the 3dsmax directory. You must do this when the program first opens before you open, import, draw, or create anything else. You can change the settings for maxstart.max anytime that you open the program.

For example, say that you would like the program to always open with the units set up as US Standard/Feet w/Fractional Inches. When the program initially opens, click on the changes that you would like such as View, then Units Setup, and then select US Standard/Feet w/Fractional Inches. When all of the modifications to the opening screen have been made, click on File/Save As. The Save File As box opens. In the File name: window, type in maxstart.max. In the Save as type: window, be sure that the 3D Studio MAX (*.max) file type is selected. In the Save in: window, be sure that the scenes folder is open.

Note: You should not have to change the selection in either the Save as type: or the Save in: windows—just be sure that the selections there are correct. Click on the Save button. Whatever settings changes that you have made will now apply anytime that you open 3D Studio MAX. If you would like to change these settings to something else as you become more familiar with the program, just repeat these procedures anytime that you open the program.

Exercise No. 1: Navigating the Work Space: Viewing, Selecting, Moving, and Other Commands

This exercise will familiarize you with some of the basic tools for 3D Studio MAX including the ones that you use to view a scene, select objects in the scene, and move objects around. You will need knowledge of these basic tools when you start importing or creating objects in the program. There is a sample scene already created for you on the CD-ROM that accompanies this book that will help you with this exercise. Open 3D Studio MAX and click on **File/Open**. The **Open File** box appears. Click on the arrow next to the **Look in:** window. Locate your CD-ROM drive and double click on it. Then find the folder 3dstudio on the CD-ROM and double click on it. Locate the file Proj1.max in this folder and click on it. The name Proj1.max should appear in the small window next to **Look in:**. Click on **Open**. The scene will appear on your screen. You cannot save to the CD-ROM.

Note: Some of the exercises in this section may be too long for you to do all in one sitting. If you need to leave the exercise and come back to it at a later time, use the **Save As** command under **File** to save where you are in the exercise. Give it a file name of **Exer1.max** or Exer2, etc. Make sure **Save as type:** says 3D **Studio MAX (*.max)**, and in the **Save in:** area, select a location on your hard drive or save it to a 3.5-inch disk (a: drive), then click on the **Save** button. You can then return to where you were in the Exercise later by opening that file from the location where it was saved.

Viewing the Work Space

1. Activating a viewport: When the file opens, take a close look at the four viewports on the screen. One viewport has a white line around it. This indicates that it is the active viewport. To activate another viewport, simply right click in that viewport or click on the name of the viewport. Activate all of the viewports one at a time, finishing with the **Perspective** viewport active.

2. Changing the rendering options for a viewport: The rendering options for a viewport control how the objects appear in that viewport. To change them, right click on the name of the viewport in the upper left-hand corner of the viewport. Activate the rendering options for the Perspective viewport. In the box that opens, you should notice that **Smooth & Highlight** has been checked. I recommend that you check this option only for the Perspective viewport. If you check this option in the other viewports, the construction and modification of objects can take an excessive amount of time. Leave the other viewports set to **Wireframe**. You may want to turn off the **Show Grid** option in the Perspective viewport as well. You can do so by clicking on it in this box.

    Another option available by right clicking on the name of the viewport is to change the viewpoint shown in that viewport. If you click on **Views**, another box will open. Click on the appropriate name here to change that viewport from a left view to a right view or any of the other options.

3. In the lower right-hand corner of the screen are the viewport navigation controls. These buttons will let you change the size of the view and what part of the scene that you are seeing in the viewports. If you cannot remember what a particular button will do, hold the cursor over it for a moment without clicking. The name of the button will appear on the screen. If you would like to know more about a particular button, click on the **Help Mode** button on the extreme left of the toolbar, then click on the button on which you would like more information. A **Help** box will open on that button or group of buttons.

A. Click on the **Zoom** button. Move the cursor to the **Perspective** viewport. Click and drag the mouse *upward* in the viewport, and the view will zoom closer in. Click and drag the mouse *downward* in the viewport, and the view will zoom farther away. When you have finished zooming, return to the original view.

B. Click on the **Pan** button. Move the cursor to the Perspective viewport. Click and drag the mouse from one point to another in the viewport. You can pan the view up or down, and left or right without changing the zoom factor. When you have finished panning, return to the original view.

C. Click on the **Min/Max Toggle** button. The Perspective viewport will fill the screen. Remember, whichever viewport is currently active will be the viewport affected by this button. Click on the **Min/Max Toggle** button again to restore to the original viewport arrangement.

D. Click on the **Zoom All** button. Move the cursor to the Perspective viewport. Click and drag the mouse as you did when you were using the **Zoom** command. Notice, however, that instead of just the Perspective viewport changing, all of the viewports change.

E. Click and hold on the **Zoom Extents** button. Two pop-up buttons will appear. The one with the faces of the cube in grey is the **Zoom Extents** button. The one with the faces of the cube in white is the **Zoom Extents Selected** button. Move the cursor up to the **Zoom Extents** button and release the mouse button. Select the **Zoom** button and zoom in to a close-up view of the tabletop. Click on the **Zoom Extents** button. Notice that the view zooms back to one that shows all of the objects in the scene. If an object in the scene had been selected and you had clicked the **Zoom Extents Selected** button, it would have zoomed to a view of just that object.

F. Click and hold on the **Zoom Extents All** button. Two pop-up buttons will appear. The one with the faces of the cube in grey is the **Zoom Extents All** button. The one with the faces of the cube in white is the **Zoom Extents All Selected** button. Move the cursor up to the **Zoom Extents All** button and release the mouse button. Click on the **Zoom** button. Click and drag to a different zoom in each viewport. Click on the **Zoom Extents All** button. Notice that all of the viewports have gone to a view that shows all of the objects in the scene. If an object in the scene had been selected and you had clicked the **Zoom Extents All Selected** button, it would have zoomed to a view of just that object.

G. If you don't have the Perspective viewport active, click in that viewport. Click on the **Field of View** button. Click and drag in the Perspective viewport. It looks like you are zooming, but what you are actually doing is changing the perspective. If objects appear distorted in the Perspective viewport, change the field of view and then rezoom. The Field of View button only appears when the Perspective viewport is active. If another viewport is active, it is replaced by the Region Zoom button.

H. Click in another viewport besides Perspective. Notice that the **Region Zoom** button appears where the Field of View button was earlier. The Region Zoom button acts much like zoom window in AutoCAD. Click and hold to define one corner of a zoom window, drag the cursor to define the other corner of the zoom window, and release the mouse button to zoom to that window. Use region zoom to get into different views in the **Top**, **Front**, and **Left** viewports.

I. Click on the **Zoom Extents All** button to restore the original view.

J. Click and hold on the **Arc Rotate** button. Two pop-up buttons will appear. The one with the face of the circle in grey is the **Arc Rotate** button. The one with the face of the circle in white is the **Arc Rotate Selected** button. Move the cursor to the **Arc Rotate** button and release the mouse button. The Arc Rotate button rotates your viewpoint around the view. Click in the **Perspective** viewport. A "trackball" will appear on the screen. Click and drag inside the trackball and watch the view rotate around the viewing plane. Click and drag outside the trackball and watch the view rotate around an imaginary line from the center of the view perpendicular to the screen. Restore the Perspective view to something close to what it was when you began.

If you use the **Arc Rotate** command in any view other than Perspective, you will move out of that view into one called **User**. To restore the view that was formerly in that viewport, right click on the word **User**. In the box that opens, click on **Views**, then click on the name of the view desired.

With **Arc Rotate** selected, click in the **Top** viewport. Rotate the view to a new one. Notice that the name has changed to **User**. Right click on the word **User**. Click on **Views** and then click on **Top**.

The **Arc Rotate Selected** button works like the Arc Rotate button except that it will rotate the view around a selected object.

Selecting Objects in the Work Space

The toolbar at the top of the screen contains buttons that will let you select objects and then perform various operations on the selected objects. In order to move, rotate, scale, or do a number of other things to objects, you must select them first.

1. Activate the Select Object button: The Select Object button lets you point at an object and then select it. Click on the Select Object button. As you move the cursor around in any viewport, you will notice that it changes from an arrow to a white + as you approach objects in the scene. In the Top viewport, move the cursor to the edge of the circle that defines the blue floor underneath the table and chairs. When the arrow turns to a white +, click the mouse button. Notice that the blue circle turns white in color to indicate that it has been selected. Click on the Undo button to deselect the circle.

2. Deselecting multiple objects: If you have selected only one object or selected several objects at once by using the Select by Region command, then the quickest way to deselect is to click on the Undo button, as long as you have not issued any other command since the selection. However, if you have gone through several selection steps or have performed other commands since the selection, Undo will move you back through the whole process step by step including the other commands, which you may not want to undo. Then the fastest way to deselect everything selected at once is to click Edit/Select None. Also under Edit there is a Select All command for selecting everything in the scene and a Select Invert command that deselects what is currently selected and selects everything else.

3. Activate the Select by Region button: To the right of the Select Object button is the Select by Region pop-up. Click and hold on the Select by Region button. Three buttons will pop up. These are the Rectangular Selection Region, the Circular Selection Region, and the Fence Selection Region buttons. Move the cursor to the Rectangular Selection Region button and release the mouse button. This selects the button as active. Click, drag, and release to form a window around the wine bottle in the Top viewport. The wine bottle will turn white, indicating that it has been selected. Anything that the rectangle you formed with the cursor touches will be selected. It does not have to be completely enclosed by the rectangle. If you accidentally touched part of the wineglass next to the bottle, for example, in forming your selection window, it would be highlighted as selected also.

    The Circular Selection Region button works in a similar manner, with the initial click defining the center of a circle, the drag forming the radius of the circle, and the release performing the selection of everything touched by the circle.

The Fence Selection Region button works a little differently. It lets you draw a fence around the item(s) you would like to select. Click and drag to form the first line of the fence. When you get to the end of the first line, release the mouse button. Move the cursor to form the second line of the fence. When you get to the end of the second line, click the mouse button to define its end point. Move the cursor in a new direction to form the third line of the fence and click to establish its end point. Keep moving and clicking to define as many fence lines as you want. When you want to close the fence and select what it touches, move the cursor back to the start point of the first fence line. A black + will appear on the screen. Click the mouse button. The fence will be formed and anything that it touches will be selected.

Now deselect the selected object(s).

Another option with the Select by Region command is located under the Edit pull down menu. So far when you have been using this command, you have been employing a crossing window that selects anything that it touches. If you click on Edit/Region/Window, it will change the region to an enclosure window that only selects things that are completely enclosed within it. Try this option and then deselect the selected objects before moving on to step 4.

4. Use the Selection Filter window: If you keep getting more objects than you want in a selection, you might try using the Selection Filter window. Click on the arrow to the side of it and you can choose the type of objects that you want to select. Click on the kind of object you want to select and any of the selection processes above will ignore everything except that kind of object. Click on Shapes, for example, and you will not be able to select the wine bottle. Click on Geometry and you will. This brings up an interesting semantic point with this filter. The wine bottle, the glasses, and several other objects in the scene started out being created as shapes rather than geometry, but when they had thickness added by extruding or lathing, they became geometry. I will discuss this in more detail later.

5. Use the Select by Name button: To the right of the Selection Filter window is the Select by Name button. If you are having trouble selecting just one object or selecting the particular object that you want, this can be the button to use, *if* you remembered to name your objects when you created them and you can remember what the name of the desired object is. Click on this button, and the Select Objects box will open. Here you can select objects by name, type, or color. You can also select all, none, or invert your selection. Click on wineglass 1 and then on Select. You have selected the wineglass on the right-hand side of the scene. Select several more objects and then deselect all before you move on to the next section of the exercise.

Moving, Rotating, Scaling, and Mirroring Objects

Just to the right of the Select by Name button are the Select and Move, Select and Rotate, and Select and Scale buttons. These let you perform the operations named on objects.

1. The Select and Move button: As the name implies, this button lets you both select an object and move it to a new location.

   A. Click on the Select and Move button.

   B. Move the cursor in the Top viewport until it is over the top of the wine bottle. The arrow will turn into a white +. Click to select the wine bottle. A red X,Y axis will appear and the object will turn white. When the cursor is over the object capable of being moved, it turns into a black + with arrow points on all four ends. Click and drag to move the object. Move the wine bottle over next to the other wineglass.

   C. Using the Restrict to X, Y, or Z buttons: Further to the right on the toolbar there are four buttons labeled X, Y, Z, and XY. These buttons can be used to restrict movement to a specific plane.

      1. Click on the X button.

      2. Move the still selected wine bottle. You can only move it on the X axis.

      3. Click on the Y button.

      4. Move the wine bottle again. You can only move it on the Y axis.

      5. Click on the XY button.

      6. Move the wine bottle again. You can move it on both the X and Y axes.

      7. Notice the little tab at the corner of the XY button. This indicates that it is a pop-up button with more buttons underneath. Click and hold on the XY button, and the YZ and ZX buttons will also appear. You can move the cursor to one of these and release the mouse button to activate either of these options. Activate the YZ option.

         a. Try to move the wine bottle in the Top viewport. You will find that you cannot. In the Top viewport you can only move in the XY plane. The only viewport that you can use the YZ and the ZX buttons to move an object is the Perspective viewport. Click and drag on the wine bottle in the Perspective viewport and you will see that you can move it down off of the table and onto the floor. You can also move it on a line that runs from "upstage" to "downstage," but you can't move it "stage left" or "stage right."

         b. Activate the ZX option. Again, you will not be able to move the wine bottle in the Top, Front, or Left viewports. In the Perspective viewport you can move the wine bottle vertically and from "stage left" to "stage right," but not "upstage" or "downstage."

      c. Activate the XY option. In the Front viewport, move the wine bottle vertically up to the table and from side to side till it is next to the first wineglass. Notice over in the Top viewport, however, that the bottle is actually hanging in the air and really isn't on top of the table.

      d. Go to the Top viewport and move the wine bottle back to where it was originally, next to the first wineglass. Click on Edit/Select None to deselect the wine bottle.

D. Using the Region Select button: To the right of the Select arrow is the Region Select button. It is also a pop-up button with Rectangular, Circular, and Fence options. Select the Rectangular option. Click on Edit/Region/Crossing on the pull down menu.

    1. Working in the Top viewport, try to select both the wine bottle and the wineglass next to it without selecting anything else. Be careful to start forming your rectangle when the cursor is an arrow, not when it is a white +. Notice that the tabletop gets selected along with the wineglass and wine bottle. Deselect what you have selected.

    2. Click on Edit/Region/Window. You have now activated the Window option rather than the Crossing option that was active earlier. Again try to select just the wine bottle and the glass next to it. If you are careful in how you form your rectangle, you will be able to select just these two objects. Again take care to start forming the rectangle when the cursor is an arrow, not a white +.

    3. Click on Edit/Region/Crossing. The Crossing option is now active again. Click and hold on the Region Select button and choose the Fence option. Work in the Top viewport. Remember that you do not have to completely enclose the wine bottle and glass to select them when you form the fence. Use the fence to select just the wine bottle and the glass next to it:

      a. Start forming the fence at a point where the cursor is an arrow, not a white +. Click and drag to form the first line. Release the mouse button at the end of the first line.

      b. Move the cursor to form the second line. Click at the end of it.

      c. Move the cursor to form the third line. If the first two lines are in the right directions and long enough, you should be able to return to the start point with the third line. If not, then you may have to form a fourth line.

      d. When you think that you are ready to return to the start point, move the cursor until you are over the start point and a black + forms. Click the mouse button. If you have not selected both the wine bottle and the glass, deselect and try again.

   e. Move both the wine bottle and the glass—remember that you are
      going to have to click on the Select and Move button after you
      have used the fence to select—along the tabletop until they are
      next to the other wineglass. Deselect the wine bottle and glass.

2. The Select and Rotate button: Next to the Select and Move button is the
   Select and Rotate button. This lets you rotate objects about an axis. The
   Select and Rotate button acts much like the Select and Move button in that
   you can use it to both select objects and rotate them, or you can select the
   object(s) using one of the other selection methods and then use the Rotate
   button to rotate them.

   A. Click on the Select and Rotate button. Work in the Top viewport.

   B. Move the cursor until it is over the chair on the left side of the screen
      and the cursor arrow turns into a white +.

   C. Click the mouse button. The chair will turn white to indicate that it is
      selected. The cursor will turn into a circular arrow.

   D. Click and drag vertically to rotate the chair. If you drag *down* in the
      viewport, the chair will rotate *counterclockwise*. If you drag *up* in
      the viewport, the chair will rotate *clockwise*. Rotate the chair so that
      it is facing away from the table. Deselect the chair.

3. The Select and Scale button: Notice that the Select and Scale button
   has a tab on it. Click and hold on the button and three options will pop
   up; from top to bottom they are: Uniform Scale, Non-Uniform Scale, and
   Squash. Select Uniform Scale.

   A. In the Front viewport, zoom in to a closer view of the wine bottle.
      Don't get so close, however, that there won't be room in the view for
      the wine bottle to grow.

   B. Click on the Select and Uniform Scale button.
      1. Move the cursor over the wine bottle and a white + will appear.
         Click the mouse button.
      2. Notice that the wine bottle has turned white to indicate that it is
         selected and an X,Y axis appears in red. The cursor has turned into
         the Uniform Scale icon.
      3. Click and drag in the up direction to scale the bottle larger. Click
         and drag in the down direction to scale the bottle smaller. Return
         the bottle to its original size and deselect it.

   C. Select the Non-Uniform Scale button. This button works with one of
      the axis constraint buttons to scale up or down along a single axis.
      1. Click on the Y button on the toolbar.
      2. Click on the Select and Non-Uniform Scale button.
      3. Move the cursor over the wine bottle in the Front viewport until
         the white + forms and then click.

    4. The wine bottle will turn white to indicate that it is selected. The cursor will turn into the Non-Uniform Scale icon, but only the Y axis line appears red.

    5. Click and drag the cursor vertically. Move it up, and the bottle will grow only along the Y axis. Move it down, and the bottle will shrink only along the Y axis.

    6. Return the bottle to its original size and deselect it.

  D. Select the Squash button. This button also works with one of the axis constraint buttons to decrease the size along one axis while it increases the size along another axis.

    1. Click on the Y button on the toolbar.

    2. Click on the Squash button.

    3. Move the cursor over the wine bottle in the Front viewport until the white + forms and then click.

    4. The wine bottle will turn white to indicate that it is selected. The cursor will turn into the Squash icon, but only the Y axis line appears red.

    5. Click and drag the cursor vertically. Move it up, and the bottle will grow longer along the Y axis and thinner along the X axis. Move it down, and the bottle will grow shorter along the Y axis and fatter along the X axis.

    6. Return the bottle to its original size and deselect it.

4. The Mirror button: The Mirror button is located on the toolbar to the right of the axis constraint buttons. It creates a mirror image of an object along a selected axis. The object(s) have to be selected before you click on the button.

  A. In the Front viewport, select the bowl.

  B. Click on the Mirror button.

  C. The Mirror Screen Coordinates box opens:

    1. The Clone Selection section offers several options:

      a. No Clone: If this is checked, the object being mirrored will disappear.

      b. Copy: If this is checked, the object being mirrored will remain.

      c. Instance: If this is checked, you will be making a copy that is linked to the original and vice versa. Any changes made to the copy or the original will be reflected in the other. If you want to make changes in the copy that don't affect the original, do not check this.

      d. Reference: If this is checked, any changes made in the original will be reflected in the copy, but not vice versa.

    Check Copy. Do not check Instance or Reference.

2. The Offset window allows you to determine how far away the object will be mirrored.
   a. Enter an offset distance of 4'0".
3. The Mirror Axis section allows you to determine the axis or plane that the object will be mirrored along.
   a. Click on each of the selections and watch the screen. You will see how each of the different axes or plane selections changes the position of the white mirrored object.
   b. Select the Y axis.
4. Click on OK in the Mirror Screen Coordinates box.
5. You have just created a blue lampshade 4 feet above the bowl.
6. On the right-hand side of the screen in the command panel, under the bar labeled Name and Color, you will see the name bowl01 in a window and a small color box with the color blue in it.
7. Double click just to the right of the name bowl01 in the window. The name will highlight. Type in the word lampshade and hit Enter.
8. Double click on the blue color in the box to the right of the window with the name lampshade in it.
9. In the Object Color box that opens, click on the dark green color and then click on OK.
10. Deselect the green lampshade. You have just used mirror to create a new object and then given it a new name and color.

5. The Array/Snapshot button: The Array/Snapshot button has a tab on it that lets you select either the Array or the Snapshot command. It is located directly to the right of the Mirror button. The Snapshot command has to do with animation and will be saved for that section of the book. The Array button works much like the Mirror button in that you have to select the object(s) first and then activate the command.

A. In the Top viewport, select the green lampshade.

B. Click on the Array button. The Array box opens.
   1. In the Type of Object section, select Copy. Instance and Reference work like they do in Mirror.
   2. In the Total in Array section, you enter the number of copies that you want to make. Enter 4.
   3. The Array Transformation Screen Coordinates section has the following options:
      a. Move: Here you can choose the distance along the X, Y, and Z axes that each element of the array will be formed.
         1. Enter 3' in the X box and then click on OK. Take a look at the array that you have created. Click on Undo.

2. Click on the Array button again. Enter 3' in the Y box and then click on OK. Take a look at the array that you have created. Click on Undo.

   b. **Rotate:** Here you can enter how many degrees you want each element of the array to be rotated along a particular axis.

     1. Click on Array. In the X axis box, enter 90 degrees. Click on OK.

     2. Take a look at the array that you have created. Click on Undo.

   c. **Scale:** Here you can decide what percentage each element of the array will be scaled along a particular axis.

     1. Click on Array. In the X axis box, enter 150 percent. Click on OK.

     2. Take a look at the array that you have created. Click on Undo.

6. The Clone command: There is no button for cloning or copying an object, but the command can be activated in one of two ways:

- Method 1: Use Select and Move with the Shift key.

  A. Click on the Select and Move button.

  B. Hold down the Shift key and then move the cursor over the object to be cloned. Click and drag the clone away from the object.

  C. The Clone Options box will open. Here you can select:

    - the number of copies to be made,
    - the name for the copies, and
    - whether they are copies, instances, or references.

    These functions are the same as under Mirror or Array.

  D. Click on OK to make the copy or copies.

- Method 2: Click on Edit/Clone.

  A. Select the object to be cloned.

  B. Click on Edit/Clone.

  C. The Clone Options box will open. Here you can select:

    - whether it is a copy, instance, or reference and
    - a name for the copy.

  D. Click on OK to make the copy.

  E. The clone/copy is created in the same space as the object copied. Immediately click on the Select and Move button and move the clone out of the way. The original object will remain in the same place.

Choose method 1 or 2 to copy one of the wineglasses. Move it just to the side of the other two. Name it wineglass03.

7. The Delete command: If you would like to delete or eliminate an object, you have two options.
- Method 1:
  1. Select the object.
  2. Hit the Delete key on the keyboard.

Note: Method 1 may not work on some brands of computers, depending upon their keyboard layout.

- Method 2:
  1. Select the object.
  2. Click on Edit/Delete.

Choose method 1 or 2 and delete the copy of the wineglass that you just made.

8. Click on File/Save As. The Save File As box opens.
   A. Give your file the file name of Exer1.max.
   B. In the Save in: window, select the folder on your hard drive to which you would like to save the file, or the a: drive if you want to save it to a 3.5-inch disk.
   C. Click on Save to save the file.
   D. Compare what you have done to Proj1a.max on the CD-ROM.

IMPORTING, CREATING, AND EXPORTING OBJECTS

3D Studio MAX is an object-oriented program. The vast majority of the work that you will be doing deals with various aspects of creating, modifying, and positioning objects. In this way, working with the program is much like the way that we work in theatrical design. This section will deal with importing objects from AutoCAD, creating objects in 3D Studio MAX, and exporting those objects back to AutoCAD so that you can then do working drawings with them. Which way you want to work will depend primarily on the object involved. Most of your work in creating objects will probably be in AutoCAD. Those will then be imported into 3D Studio MAX as .dxf files. However, you will find that some objects will be easier to create in 3D Studio MAX and then export to AutoCAD. Generally speaking, any object with very complex curves may be easier to create in 3D Studio MAX rather than in AutoCAD. After you work with both programs for a while you will find that you start developing a feeling for which is the best way to handle a particular object.

IMPORTING OBJECTS FROM AUTOCAD

The first step in importing an object (file) from AutoCAD to 3D Studio MAX is to create that object in AutoCAD. This process is covered in the 3-D section of the AutoCAD book. When you have finished creating the objects and are ready to export them out of AutoCAD as a .dxf file, there are a few guidelines to keep in mind. Before anything is exported from AutoCAD R12 to 3D Studio MAX, be sure that it has been meshed. Even if the object isn't a solid, it can still be meshed and will work in 3D Studio MAX. If you are exporting an object from AutoCAD R13 or R14 it does not have to be meshed. 3D Studio MAX claims that AutoCAD R13 and R14 files can be imported directly as .dwg files. I have had indifferent success with this method and recommend that you export them as .dxf files before importing them into 3D Studio MAX. Next, be sure to export any objects that will have different textures or surface treatments as separate files. If, for example, you have created a window, the window frame and the window panes will have to be exported separately. The frame may get a wooden texture and color, while the panes will have a glass texture.

As you create each .dxf file for each object, give the file a name that will quickly identify it to you. The file name is how the object will be named in 3D Studio MAX. This will make it easier for you to locate it in the named lists for selection later. A complete set rendering in 3D Studio MAX may contain dozens of objects, and you can waste time just trying to figure out which one you want if you don't use a naming system that is easy to follow and remember. Instead of just naming the .dxf files Chair1, Chair2, etc. it may make it easier to locate if you call them SLChair, SRChair, and so on. In sets with many objects, it is a very good idea to keep a written list of exactly what object has what name. You could also print out a copy of a drawing or view of the set and label each object with its name.

Remember that while each object has to be imported into 3D Studio MAX as a separate .dxf file, that doesn't mean that you have to draw each of them as a separate file in AutoCAD. You can create as much or as little of your set as you want in one AutoCAD drawing. The parts of the set that need to be separate files can then be wblocked into separate files and you will still have a "master" drawing of the set. In some ways it is actually easier to work like this. If all of the parts of the set are created in the "master" drawing and wblocked with their insertion point as the origin, then when they are imported into 3D Studio MAX they will already be in the location desired and won't have to be moved around.

Once the .dxf file from AutoCAD is created, it is a simple process to insert it into 3D Studio MAX. It is usually best to begin importing objects (files) with something that will give you an overall orientation for everything else, such as the floor or platforming. You don't have to do it this way, it just makes it easier for you to keep yourself clear on relationships between objects.

To Import a .dxf File from AutoCAD

1. In 3D Studio MAX, click on File, then on Import.
2. The Select File to Import box opens:
   A. Under Files of Type: click on AutoCAD (*.DXF).
   B. Under Look In: locate the drive and directory that contains the file that you want to import. This could be in your hard drive, usually c:, or on a 3.5-inch disk, in the a: drive.
   C. Click on the file name so that it appears in the File name window.
   D. Click on Open.
      1. The Import DXF file box opens.
      2. Under the Derive Objects From section:
         a. If the object in the drawing is all in one layer and you want to import it all as one object, click on Layer. Different layers will be imported as different objects. Different entities within the same layer will be imported as one object. Since you will usually be creating one object in AutoCAD on a single layer, this is typically the circle that should have a dot in it.
         b. If you click Entity, every AutoCAD entity will be imported as a different object.
         c. If you click Color, every layer with the same color will be imported as the same object.
      3. Under the Weld Vertices section:
         a. Be sure there is a check in the box next to Weld. This will assure that different AutoCAD entities are imported as one object.
         b. If you find that something that you want to be one object has been imported as two or more objects, increase the weld threshold.
      4. Under the Auto-Smooth section:
         a. Be sure there is a check in the box next to Auto-Smooth.
         b. The smooth angle becomes important when importing objects with faces. Objects with angles between their faces that are greater than the smooth angle will appear faceted. Objects with angles between their faces that are less than the smooth angle will have the edge between the faces smoothed. Try using the default of 30 degrees. If the object doesn't appear the way that you would like, then come back and try changing the smooth angle.
      5. The Arc Degrees section: This section determines how many degrees there are between the vertices of an imported arc or circle. Generally speaking, if you want a smoother curve you should

lower the number of degrees in this section. Try the default 10 degrees first. Then if the object doesn't appear the way that you would like, decrease or increase the number of degrees in the **Degrees:** box.

    6. Under the **Miscellaneous** section:

        a. Have a check in all boxes.

  E. Click on **OK**.

3. The object will appear on the screen and in the command panel section to the right, the name of the object will appear. Notice that the **Create Objects** icon is selected.

4. Click on the **Modify Objects** icon in the command panel.

5. Under **Modifiers** below that in the command panel, click on **UVW** map. This will map the surface of the object being imported so that texture can be applied later.

6. Under the **Parameters** section below that, place a dot in the box next to one of the following. Select the shape that most closely fits the shape of the object being imported.

  A. **Planar:** Choose this for flat objects.

  B. **Cylindrical:** Choose this for roughly cylindrical or cone-shaped objects.

    1. **With Cap:** Choose this for solid cylinders.

    2. **W/O Cap:** Choose this for hollow cylinders.

  C. **Spherical:** Pick this for roughly spherical, ellipsoidal, or ball-shaped objects.

  D. **Shrink Wrap:** Choose this for very complex objects.

  E. **Box:** Choose this for rectangular or cube-shaped objects.

7. Under the **Alignment** section below that, click on **Fit**.

8. You can now apply a material or texture to the object or import another one.

CREATING OBJECTS IN 3D STUDIO MAX

3D Studio MAX has a number of different ways that you can create objects in the program itself in addition to importing them from AutoCAD. There are certain kinds of objects that are easier to create in 3D Studio MAX than they would be in AutoCAD. Objects that involve complex curves, for example, are much easier to form in 3D Studio MAX. This section will cover some of the basic ways that you can create objects in the program.

 Creating an object begins with the command panel. At the top left corner of the command panel is the button that opens the create panel. (See the figure to the left.)

In the next row of buttons immediately below the Create Panel button are the Geometry, or Standard Primitives, and the Shapes, or Splines, buttons.

The Geometry, or Standard Primitives, Button

One of the simplest ways to create objects in 3D Studio MAX is to use the options available in the command panel under the Geometry button. Click on the Create button, and immediately under it a row of seven other buttons appear. The one furthest to the left is the Geometry button. Click on it and in the window beneath it the words Standard Primitives will appear as well as a list of the shapes available under the Object Type bar. The basic shape options are: Geosphere, a geodesic sphere or hemisphere; Sphere; Torus, a donut, Cone; Teapot; Box; Cylinder; Tube; and Hedra, a polyhedron. To draw one of these basic shapes, follow the instructions below. **Note:** The exact sequence of the commands required will vary with the shape chosen.

Drawing a Tube

1. Activate the Top viewport by clicking in it.
2. Click on Tube. Prompt reads: Click and drag to begin creation process.
3. Click anywhere in the Top viewport, but do not release the mouse button. An X,Y,Z axis will appear at the creation point.
4. Move the mouse, and you will see a circle appear in the Top viewport. When the circle is the size that you want, release the mouse button. This forms the first wall of the tube or cylinder.
5. Move the mouse again, and you will see a second circle appear either inside or outside the first circle, depending upon which direction you move the mouse. When this is located where you would like, click the mouse button. This forms the second wall of the cylinder.
6. Move the mouse again vertically, and you will see the height of the tube being formed in the Left and Right viewports. When it is the height that you would like, click the mouse.
7. Now let's go back to the command panel.
8. Notice that under the Name and Color bar, the program has given this object the name Tube01 and assigned it a color.
   A. Double click in the name window to highlight the name. To change the name, type in a new name and hit Enter.
   B. Double click in the color window to open the Object Color box. If you would like to assign a new color, click on that color in the palette, and then click on OK.
9. The specifications for the tube that you have drawn are displayed under the Parameters bar. The easiest way to draw any of these standard primitives to a specific dimension is to just draw it to any

dimension as outlined above and then change the specifications in the Parameters section.

A. Double click in the Radius1 window to highlight the radius. To change that radius, type in a new figure and hit Enter.

B. Double click in the Radius2 window to highlight the radius. To change that radius, type in a new figure and hit Enter.

C. Double click in the Height window, and the height will be highlighted. To change the height, type in a new figure and hit Enter.

D. You can also change the following parameters:

1. Height Segments: This is important if you want to modify the tube. If you want to pinch, bend, or twist the tube, it will need more height segments than the default of 1. If you just want a straight tube, then leave the height segments at 1.

2. Cap Segments: The tube comes with a cap at each end. If you want to divide those caps up into segments that later can be modified, increase the cap segments.

3. Sides: This specification works with the Smooth box just below it. If the Smooth box is checked, you will get a smooth tube. If it isn't checked, you will get a polygon-shaped tube with the number of sides specified here.

    The smoothing will not appear initially on the screen, but will show up when you render the figure. You can also have the smoothing show up in the Perspective viewport by right clicking on the name—Top, Left, Right, or Perspective—of any of the viewports and then clicking on Smooth & Highlight in the selection box that opens.

10. The other standard primitives are drawn in a similar manner. The exact sequence is slightly different, depending upon the particular primitive chosen.

The Shapes, or Splines, Button

Another way to create objects in 3D Studio MAX with the create panel is to use the options available under the Shapes, or Splines, button. When you click on this button, the following options will appear under the Object Type bar: Line; Donut; Circle; Arc; Helix, a 3-D spiral, like a spring; Ngon, a polygon with N number of sides; Rectangle; Ellipse; Star; and Text. When you create any of these shapes, they will be 2-D objects unless they are extruded using the Modify button. To draw one of these shapes, follow the instructions below.

Drawing an Ellipse

1. With the Shapes button selected, click on Ellipse under the Object Type bar.

2. Move the cursor to the Top viewport and click and drag to form an ellipse.

3. Notice that under the **Name and Color** bar the program has given this the name of **Ellipse01** and assigned it a color. You can change these just like you changed the name and color of the tube earlier.

4. Under the **Parameters** bar you can change the length and width of the ellipse.

5. Using the **Modify** button, you can now extrude this shape into 3-D.

Other shapes are formed in a similar manner, but with different parameters, depending upon the object.

Drawing a Line

1. With the **Shapes** button selected, click on **Line** under the **Object Type** bar.

2. Move the cursor to the **Top** viewport and click to select the start point of the line.

3. Move the mouse to the next point in the line and click again.

4. Keep moving and clicking the mouse until you have drawn all of the parts of the line.

5. Right click to finish the line.

6. You can then use the **Modify** commands to change this line into a variety of shapes, including curves.

7. The **Modify** button will also let you extrude this shape into 3-D and change it in other ways as well, such as turning it on a lathe.

EXPORTING OBJECTS TO AUTOCAD

Earlier you learned how to create objects in AutoCAD and export them to 3D Studio MAX. This section will deal with the reverse process. It is also possible to create objects in 3D Studio MAX and then export them to AutoCAD. Many of the objects that can be created in 3D Studio MAX with complex curves can be much more difficult to create in AutoCAD. After a little experience with both programs, you will quickly learn which one is easier to use for what kind of object and can begin to work back and forth between the two.

Exporting an Object from 3D Studio MAX to AutoCAD

1. After you have drawn the object in 3D Studio MAX and given it a name, save it to a file name and directory using the **Save As** command under **File**. This is not part of the export process, just good working management so that the object doesn't get accidentally lost.

2. If you want to export an object that is part of a larger scene you will need to go through another step first. 3D Studio MAX will export the entire scene that is on the screen. If you just want to export one or a few of the

objects that are in the scene, you should save the objects that you want to export as a separate file from the scene file. You can do this using the File/Save Selected option under the pull down menu File:

A. Select the object(s) that you want to save in a separate file.

B. Click on File, then on Save Selected.

C. This opens the Save File As box. Give the new file a name and directory and click on Save.

D. Open the new file you have created.

3. Click on File, then on Export. The Save File to Export box opens.

Your next step will depend upon the version of AutoCAD that you are using. In the Save as type window at the bottom of the box, you can select 3D Studio Mesh (*.3DS), AutoCAD (*.DWG), or AutoCAD (*.DXF). For export to AutoCAD you will need to select either *.DWG or *.DXF depending upon your version of AutoCAD. Earlier editions of 3D Studio MAX export .dwg files as AutoCAD R13 and later editions export them as both R13 and R14. If you are using R13 or higher, you can export directly as a .dwg file. If you are using version 12 or AutoCAD LT2, you will need to export as a .dxf file and import the file into AutoCAD.

A. Click on the file type that you want.

B. Click in the File name window and give the file a name.

Note: It is important to give the file not just a name, but also the .dwg or .dxf extension in this window. What you type into the window should look like this: filename.dxf or filename.dwg. If you don't add the extension, you will get a message from 3D Studio MAX that tells you that it cannot create that file type.

C. In the Save in window, select the location where you want to create the file.

D. Click on Save.

4. Exporting a .dwg file: If you have selected a .dwg file type, the Export Options box will open.

A. In the Derive Layers by section your choices are:
1. Object: Each 3D Studio MAX object is placed on its own layer.
2. 1 Layer: All of the objects are placed on the same layer.
3. Color: Each 3D Studio MAX object of the same color is placed on the same layer.

B. In the Convert Groups to section, your choices are:
1. Layers: 3DS groups are placed on the same layer.
2. Groups: 3DS groups are brought into AutoCAD as a group.

Note: This section does not concern you unless you have created groups or selection sets in 3D Studio MAX.

C. In the General Options section, place a check mark by each of the options. These all concern more complex operations in 3D Studio MAX than you will be dealing with right now. If you'd like more information on these options, check out AutoCAD DWG Export under the Help Topics.

D. Click on OK, and the .dwg file will be exported to the location that you indicated.

E. You can now go into AutoCAD and open the file directly as you would any .dwg file.

5. Exporting a .dxf file: If you have selected a .dxf file type, the Export DXF File box will open. Under Save to Layers, you have three choices:

- 1 Layer: This is the simplest option. All of the objects will be brought into AutoCAD on a single layer.

- By Material: Each different material will be brought into AutoCAD on a different layer.

- By Object: Each object will be brought into AutoCAD on a different layer. This option can give you difficulties, however. Each object is brought in on a layer using its object name in 3D Studio MAX as its layer name. When you try to import the .dxf file into AutoCAD, you must already have layer names created in your drawing that match the object name in 3DS. If you want to use this option, write down all of the object names in 3D Studio MAX. Open the AutoCAD file in which you want to import the object(s), then create layer names in AutoCAD that match the object names from 3D Studio MAX.

A. After you have made one of the three choices above, click on OK.

B. You have just exported the object(s) as a .dxf file. To bring this into AutoCAD you must import it; it cannot be opened directly as a .dwg file can. Open the AutoCAD file in which you would like to import the object(s). Click on Import/Export/DXF in. . . . Locate the directory and file name that you want to import and click on OK.

Exercise No. 2: Importing, Creating, and Exporting Objects

Importing Objects from AutoCAD

1. Open AutoCAD. In AutoCAD, open the file crown.dwg from the 3dstudio folder of the CD-ROM.

2. Export this file as the .dxf file crown.dxf to a location on your hard drive or to a 3.5-inch disk.

3. Close AutoCAD.

4. Open 3D Studio MAX.

5. Under Views/Units Setup choose US Standard/Feet w/Fractional Inches.

6. Right click on the name of the Perspective viewport. Click on Smooth & Highlight to reset the rendering level.

Note: If you don't want to keep changing these settings every time that you open 3D Studio MAX, now might be a good time to change your maxstart.max file to make them part of your opening screen. See Modifying the Opening Screen (page 26) for instructions.

7. Click on File and then on Import. The Select File to Import box opens.

A. Under Files of type: select AutoCAD (*.DXF).

B. Click on the arrow next to the Look in: window and locate the crown.dxf file where you saved it in step 2 above. Click on it so that its name appears in the File name: window.

C. Click on Open.

D. The Import DXF file box opens. Click on OK.

8. The file crown.dxf has now been imported into 3D Studio MAX. This is a drawing of a 10-foot-long and 1-foot-high piece of crown molding that was done in AutoCAD. In the command panel to the right, change the name to Crown and the color to brown.

9. In the viewport navigation controls in the lower right-hand corner of the screen, click on the Arc Rotate button. Working in the Perspective viewport, move the mouse around until you get a good perspective view looking down the front of the molding at an angle. Then click on the Zoom and Pan buttons to frame the view so that the molding fills most of the Perspective viewport.

10. Save this file as crown.max to a location on your hard drive or to a 3.5-inch disk using the Save As command under File. Compare what you have done to the file crown1.max on the CD-ROM.

Creating Objects in 3D Studio MAX

Creating Objects Using Standard Primitives

1. If another file is open, reset the screen by clicking on File/Reset.

2. If you have not created a maxstart.max file with a Units Setup of US Standard/Feet w/Fractional Inches and a Rendering Level of Smooth & Highlight for the Perspective viewport, then reset these as well or create a maxstart.max file now.

3. Click on the Create Panel button.

4. Click on the Geometry button immediately below it. Standard Primitives should appear in the window below that.

5. Click on the Cylinder bar below the Object Type bar.

6. In the upper right-hand quadrant of the Top viewport, click and drag to form a circle. When the circle is the size that you want—somewhere around 6 inches in radius—release the mouse button, then drag the mouse button upward to form the height of the cylinder. The further upward that you drag, the greater the height that will be given to the cylinder. Click when you are at a height that you desire—somewhere around 30 inches.

Note: Do not worry if this is not exact. Do not even worry if you have no idea how large the cylinder is. You will be correcting it to be precisely what you desire. It is very difficult to control the size of the objects in 3D Studio MAX while you are creating them, but it is very easy to use the Parameters area to change them to precisely the size that you want. Therefore, throughout this and subsequent exercises in which you will be creating objects, the initial instructions will be imprecise about size. Create the objects any size that you want. Following the initial creation instructions will be another set of instructions telling you how to change the object to a precise size.

A. Under the Parameters bar, click on the right-hand side of the Radius window and drag the mouse across to the left. This should highlight the entire figure in the window. Type in a new radius of 6", and hit Enter.

B. Enter a new height of 30".

C. Enter a new value in the Height Segments area of 10. This will be used in a later exercise with the Modify command.

D. Sides should be 24 and the Smooth box should be checked.

E. Name the cylinder Table Base and color it a light tan.

7. Click on Cone under Object Type.

8. In the upper left-hand quadrant of the Top viewport, click and drag to form a circle. When the circle is the size you want—about twice the radius of the cylinder—release the mouse button. Move the mouse upward to form the height of the cone. When it is the height that you want—about a third taller than the cylinder—click. Move the mouse vertically to form the top of the cone. When it is the size that you want—about the same radius as the cylinder—click. Once again, none of these measurements have to be exact. You will change them to precise figures after the cone is created.

A. Under Parameters, change Radius1 to 1'.

B. Change Radius2 to 6".

C. Change the height to 4'.

D. Change the height segments to 10.

E. Check to see that sides is 24 and the Smooth box is checked.

F. Name the cone sculpture and color it a light gold.

Creating Objects Using Shapes

1. Click on the Shapes button next to the Geometry button. The window underneath should say Splines.

2. Click on the Ellipse button under Object Type.

3. Next to the cylinder in the upper right-hand quadrant of the Top viewport, click and drag to create an elliptical object. When it is the size that you want—about four times the radius of the base of the cone—release the mouse button.

   A. Under Parameters, give it a length of 4' and a width of 3'.

   B. Name it Table Top and give it a color of brown.

4. Click on the Star button.

5. In the lower left-hand quadrant of the Top viewport, click and drag to form a star-shaped object. When it is the size that you want—about twice the radius of the base of the cone—release the mouse button. Move the mouse button and you will see that the star can be formed inside or outside of the diameter you have chosen. When you have the star fully formed, click the mouse button.

   A. Under Parameters, change Radius1 to 2'.

   B. Change Radius2 to 1'.

   C. Change the points to 5.

   D. Leave the name as Star01, but change the color to light yellow.

6. Click on the Text button.

   A. In the Parameters box, change the text to read Exer 2.

   B. Change the size to 4'.

   C. Change the font to Times New Roman by clicking on the arrow next to the window with a font name in it and then scrolling up and down until you find the font you want.

   D. Click on the I button under the font name window for italic.

   E. In the lower right-hand corner of the Top viewport, click on the center of where you want the text to appear. If it doesn't appear instantaneously, wait just a second or two. It's coming.

   F. Name the text Title and give it a color of red.

Saving the Exercise

1. Click on File and then on Save As. The Save As box opens.
2. Give it a file name of Exer2.max, choose 3D Studio MAX (*.max) in the Save as type: window, and in the Save in: area, choose a location on your hard drive where you can find it later or save it to a 3.5-inch disk.
3. Compare what you have drawn to Proj2.max on the CD-ROM.

Exporting Objects from 3D Studio MAX to AutoCAD

1. Open 3D Studio MAX, or if it is still open, click on File and Reset.
2. In the command panel, click on the Create Panel button and then on Teapot.
3. In the Top viewport, click and drag to create a teapot.
4. Under Parameters, make the radius 1'.
5. Change the name to Teapot.
6. Click on File, then on Export.
   A. The Select File to Export box opens.
   B. In the File name: window, type in Teapot.dxf.
   C. In the Save as type: window, select AutoCAD (*.DXF).
   D. In the Save in: window, choose a directory on your hard drive where you can find the file or save to a 3.5-inch disk in the a: drive.
   E. Click on the Save button.
   F. The Export DXF File box opens.
   G. Select 1 Layer and click on OK.
7. Close 3D Studio MAX without saving the file and open AutoCAD.
8. Click on File, then on Import/Export, then on DXF In.
9. The Select DXF File box opens.
10. Under Drives and Directories, locate the file Teapot.dxf that you exported earlier from 3D Studio MAX.
11. When the file name Teapot.dxf appears in the larger window under File Name:, click once on it so that it appears in the small window under File Name:.
12. Click on OK.
13. The teapot appears on the AutoCAD screen as the file opens.
14. Go to several different views of the teapot, and you will see that you have imported a 3-D object.
15. In one or more of the views, type hide and hit Enter.
16. Save the file as Teapot.dwg in your hard drive or on a 3.5-inch disk.
17. Compare it with the file Teapot1.dwg located on the CD-ROM in the 3dstudio folder.

MODIFYING OBJECTS

While you can create a wide variety of objects in 3D Studio MAX, the modifications that you can make to them really make this program an excellent companion to AutoCAD. The objects that can be created by using the **modify panel** include many that would be extremely difficult if not impossible to create directly in AutoCAD. These objects can, however, be exported back to AutoCAD to create detailed working drawings. To use the modify panel you first must create an object using the create panel as you did in Exercise No. 2. You can either apply the modifications immediately when you have finished creating the object or you can wait until later, select the object, and then modify it. This section will cover some of the basic ways that you can modify objects using the program.

 In the command panel, the button just to the right of the Create Panel button is the **Modify Panel** button. If you open the modify panel with no object selected, you will see the **Modifier** bar and the **Modifier Stack** bar with very little displayed below them. Select an object first or when you have just finished creating an object, and the modify panel will display the following areas:

1. The name and color of the object selected will be displayed above the Modifier bar.

2. Below the Modifier bar are displayed the modifiers that are available with that object. Not all modifiers will be available for all objects. Modifiers include:

    A. **Bend:** The **Bend** modifier lets you place a uniform bend in an object's geometry. The bend can be limited to part of the object or all of it and can be applied along all three axes.

    B. **Twist:** The **Twist** modifier lets you twist all or part of an object like the threads of a screw.

    C. **Extrude:** The **Extrude** modifier acts much like adding thickness does in AutoCAD. It gives a 2-D shape a third dimension, creating a solid.

    D. **UVW Map:** The **UVW Map** modifier applies mapping coordinates to an imported object such as one from AutoCAD. You'll use this later when you will learn to apply textures to objects.

    E. **Edit Mesh:** The **Edit Mesh** modifier converts objects into triangular meshes. You can then edit the vertices, faces, and edges of the object. If you have an irregular shape that cannot be extrude, applying edit mesh can make it appear to be a solid object.

    F. **Taper:** The **Taper** modifier lets you scale one end, both ends, or the middle of an object in or out.

G. Noise: The Noise modifier creates random distortion effects. Fractal settings under this modifier create rippling or mountainous effects.

H. Lathe: The Lathe modifier rotates a 2-D shape around an axis to create a 3-D shape.

I. Edit Patch: The Edit Patch modifier converts the surfaces of an object into separate patches consisting of a lattice and a surface. By editing the lattice, you can change one surface of the original object without affecting the others.

J. Edit Spline: The Edit Spline modifier lets you change or edit shapes. Straight lines can be turned into curves, different corner treatments can be applied, etc. This is extremely useful in reshaping 2-D objects before they are lathed or extruded.

K. More: The More button accesses a list of other modifiers such as Skew, Ripple, Smooth, and Stretch.

L. Sets: The Sets button shows you a list of named button sets under Modify. The button to the right of the Sets button displays the Configure Button Sets dialogue box, which lets you change the buttons that appear and then give that new set of buttons a name. Any buttons that you take off of the button set will be shifted to the More list.

3. The Modifier Stack bar appears just below the modifiers. There are several more controls below the Modifier Stack bar.

A. The Modifier Stack window is just below the Modifier Stack bar. This window displays the history of modification to the object, with the last modification appearing in the window. Click on the arrow next to the window to see the history in the stack list. If you have modified an object, this window will let you access either the changes or the original object for further modifications. Click on the arrow and then on the name of the original object to make changes in the object. Click on the arrow and then on the name of the modifier to make changes in the modification.

B. Other controls under the Modifier Stack bar are:

1. The Pin Stack Button: This locks the modifier panel and the modifier stack to the currently selected object.

2. The Active/Inactive Modifier Button: This turns off the current modifier so you can see the effect without changing the parameters of the modifier. Click again to turn the modifier back on.

3. The **Show End Result** Button: When toggled on, the end result of applying all modifiers is shown. When toggled off, the result of the modification history up to the step currently in the Modifier Stack window is shown.

4. The **Make Unique** Button: If you are modifying an object with instanced copies, the modifications will be applied only to the currently selected copy.

5. The **Remove Modifier** Button: This removes the effect of a modifier on the selected object.

6. The **Edit Stack** Button: This allows you to edit the contents of the modifier stack by renaming, removing, making unique, or collapsing.

4. The **Parameters** section is below the modifier stack section. The choices available to you either for creating the modifier chosen or with the original object are displayed in this section. If the name of the original object appears in the Modifier Stack window, these are the parameters for it. If the name of the modification appears in the Modifier Stack window, these are its parameters. The parameters will change for each object and modification. Note that if it is a long list of parameters, some of them may disappear underneath the controls at the bottom of the screen. Move the cursor over part of the Parameters section that isn't clickable. If a hand appears instead of an arrow then some of the parameters are hidden underneath. Click and drag with the hand to see more parameters.

Exercise No. 3: Modifying an Object

This exercise is designed to give you practice in using the modifiers that are available with 3D Studio MAX. It will work you through the process of changing objects using some of these modifiers.

Modifying Existing Objects

1. Open the scene Exer2.max that you saved earlier.
2. Save this as Exer3.max to a location on your hard drive or a 3.5-inch disk.
3. In the **Front** viewport, select the brown cylinder.
4. Use the **Taper** modifier:
   A. Under **Modifier** bar, click on **Taper**. Notice that the word **Taper** has appeared in the modifier stack and the parameters have changed.

B. Click on the arrow next to the window where the word Taper appears. Notice that in the stack list that appears are both Taper and Cylinder. If you wanted to change the parameters of the original cylinder you would click on it so that Cylinder would appear in the Modifier Stack window. For now though, leave Taper in the Modifier Stack window so that you can apply a taper to the cylinder.

C. Apply a taper to the cylinder:

1. Under Parameters in the Taper section:
   a. Change the amount to -0.7 and hit Enter.
   b. Change the curve to -1.5 and hit Enter. The cylinder is now an inward-curving column.
   c. In the Front viewport, zoom in closer to the cylinder so that you can see the changes more easily.
   d. Change the amount to 2.0 and hit Enter.
   e. Change the curve to 2.0 and hit Enter. The cylinder has turned into a bowl-shaped object.

2. Use Limits: In the lower part of the Parameters box is the Limits section. You may have to use the hand to click and drag the Parameters box upward so that you can see all of the Limits section. The limits allow you to specify parts of the column where the Taper modifier *will not* be applied.
   a. The cylinder is 2 feet 6 inches high. Set the upper limit to 2'0".
   b. Click in the box next to Limit Effect.
   c. Notice that the upper 6 inches of the cylinder has straightened out and no longer has the Taper modifier applied to it.

3. Deselect the cylinder: Edit/Select None.

Creating a Box and Applying Multiple Modifiers

1. Click on the Create button. Click on the Geometry button and then on the Box bar.
2. Working in the upper left-hand quadrant next to the cone in the Top viewport, click and drag to create a rectangle.
3. Click to complete the rectangle, then move the cursor upward to add height to the rectangle and create a box. Click when you have the height that you want.
4. In the Name and Color area, change the name to Green Box and the color to dark green.
5. In the Parameters area, change the length to 1'0", width to 1'0", height to 8'0", and height segments to 20. Hit Enter after making each of the changes.
6. Zoom out in the Front viewport and then use the Region Zoom button to zoom down to a better view of the green box.

7. Click on the Modify button and then on Twist.
   A. Under Parameters, change the angle to 180 and hit Enter.
   B. Notice how the green box has twisted into a screwlike shape.
8. Click on the Bend button.
   A. Under Parameters, change the angle to 180 and hit Enter.
   B. Notice how the twisted green box has now bent into an arch.
9. Use the stack list to change parameters. Let's say that you have decided that what you have created is not quite right and you want to make some changes. This is where the stack list will let you access the various steps, or a history, that the object has gone through to get where it is.
   A. Go to the Modifier Stack window under Modifier Stack and click on the arrow. This will show the history of changes made to the original box. Click on Box so that you can make changes to the original box. The parameters of the original box appear.
      1. Change the height to 10'0" and hit Enter.
      2. Notice the change take place.
   B. Go back to the Modifier Stack window and click on the arrow. Click on Twist. Now you can make changes in the Twist modifier.
      1. Change the twist angle to 360 and hit Enter.
      2. Notice the change take place.
   C. Go back to the Modifier Stack window and click on the arrow. Click on Bend. Now you can make changes to the Bend modifier.
      1. Change the bend angle to 360 and hit Enter.
      2. Notice the change take place. You may need to pan the Front viewport to get a better view of the object at this point.
      3. If you look closely at the object you will see that the Bend modifier is having a little trouble bending this object into 360 degrees. It is not quite as smooth a bend as you might want. So let's change the height segments of the original object to give it more of them to work with in twist and bend. This will also give you an idea of how the segments of the original object work with the modifiers.
   D. Go back to the Modifier Stack window and click on the arrow. Click on Box. Again you can make changes to the original box.
      1. Change the height segments to 40 and click on Enter.
      2. You now have a little smoother bend and twist.
   E. Looking at the object, you may decide that you really don't like the bend at all and want to straighten it out. This is where the Remove Modifier button can come into play. Go back to the Modifier Stack window and click on Bend.
      1. Click on the Remove Modifier button underneath the window.
      2. The effect of the Bend modifier is now gone.

F. Now let's apply a new modifier to the green box. The **Skew** modifier is not on the current modifier panel, but it is still available. It is located under the **More** button.
1. Click on **More** and the **Modifier** box opens.
2. Click on **Skew** and then on **OK**. A whole new set of parameters appears.
3. Change the skew amount to 4' and hit **Enter**.
4. This would also be a good time to see the effect of the **Direction** window that you may have noticed earlier in some of the other modifier parameters. This changes the direction of the modification in degrees counterclockwise.
    a. Change the direction to 90 and hit **Enter**.
    b. Change the direction to 180 and hit **Enter**.
    c. Change the direction to 270 and hit **Enter**.

G. That should give you a good idea of how several of the modifiers operate and how to use the stack list to work with the history of the modifiers. Now let's work with some other modifiers.

Working with Other Modifiers

1. Earlier in Exercise No. 2 you created the text **Exer2**. Change that to **Exer3** and give it some thickness by extruding, using the following instructions.
    A. Click on the **Select** button.
        1. In the **Top** viewport, select the text **Exer2**.
        2. Under **Parameters**, click to the right of **Exer2** in the **Text:** box. Hit the **Backspace** and type **3** on the keyboard.
        3. Notice the text change.
    B. Next let's use the **Extrude** command to give it some thickness.
        1. Under **Modifiers**, click on **Extrude**.
        2. Under **Parameters**, change the amount to 1' and hit **Enter**.
    C. Then let's make it easier to see in the **Perspective** viewport.
        1. Click on the **Rotate** button.
        2. Working in the **Left** viewport, rotate the text so that it is upright in that viewport and easily readable in the **Perspective** viewport.
        3. Click on the **Select and Move** button.
        4. Working in the **Left** viewport, move the text so that it is sitting on the Perspective plane instead of being half underneath it.
        5. Deselect the text.
2. Use the **Extrude, Move,** and **Rotate** commands to:
    A. Extrude the ellipse to an amount of 1' and place it on top of the cone.
    B. Extrude the star to an amount of 6", rotate it upright, and move it on top of the ellipse.

Note: You will need to work in several different viewports to do this and will probably have to zoom, region zoom, and/or pan to do it precisely.

    C. Choose the Zoom Extents All command when you have finished and click on Edit/Select None.

Next you will learn to use the Create Line command and the Edit Spline and Lathe modifiers to create a beaker and a banister post.

Creating a Beaker

1. Use the Region Zoom button to zoom down to the blank space above the text in the Front viewport.
2. Use the Min/Max Toggle button to expand this viewport to full screen size.
3. Click on the Create button, then on the Shapes button, then on Line.
4. In the Creation Method section below Name and Color and Interpolation, select Corner for the initial type and Bezier for the drag type. This will let you control what is happening at the points that you select for the line by how you use your mouse. You will still be able to go back later and use the Edit Spline button to change it.

    A. With initial type as Corner, if you click on a point and release the mouse button, it will create a corner. You can then move the cursor to the next point in a straight line. Click on that corner and release the mouse button and you will have created another corner followed by a straight line.

    B. With a Bezier drag type, when you get to a point, click and hold down the mouse button. This creates a bezier at the point, or vertex, where you clicked. As you drag the cursor away from the vertex, a smooth, adjustable curve will be created through the vertex.

    C. You can alternate corners and beziers by clicking and releasing the mouse button for a corner and clicking and dragging the mouse button for a bezier to create straight lines and curves.

5. Now you are going to be drawing a figure that will later be modified using the Edit Spline command and then turned using the Lathe command to create a 3-D figure. While you work through these instructions, refer to the figure labeled Unedited Beaker Drawing on the next page. Click and release the mouse at a point near the lower center of the screen to create the point at the lower left-hand corner (A) shown in the figure. This will be the initial point for the object. Move the mouse to the right to the next corner of the figure (B). Click and release at this corner. Continue clicking at each corner, releasing the mouse button, and then

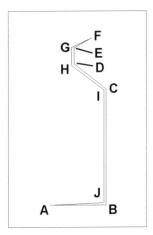

moving it to the next corner until you have drawn the complete figure. The last line drawn should return to the initial point (A). When you click again on the initial point, the **Spline** box will open, asking if you want to **Close Spline?** Click on **Yes**. This completes the figure.

6. Click on the **Modify** button and then on **Edit Spline**. Now you are going to add bezier corners to change the shape of the figure. While working, refer to the figure labeled Edited Beaker Drawing. Be sure that the **Select and Move** button is active and highlighted on the toolbar. Move the cursor over corner B. It will turn into a white +. Right click. A box opens that lets you change the corner type. Click on **Bezier Corner**. On the screen you will

**EDITED
BEAKER
DRAWING**

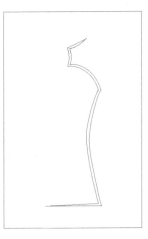

notice that there are two grey lines coming out of the corner with small green boxes on the end of them. These green boxes are the handles that let you change the shape of the corner. Click and drag on these boxes to change the shape of the corner and the lines coming into and out of it. If you click and drag directly on the corner itself, you can also move its position. You will need to turn C, D, E, H, and I into bezier corners and then manipulate them so the figure changes to look like the drawing in the figure.

7. Now you are going to lathe the figure to turn it into a 3-D beaker. Under **Modifiers**, click on **Lathe**. Notice that a new **Parameters** box has appeared. Move the cursor down into the Parameters area until it turns into a hand. Move the Parameters box up so that you can see the whole thing. You will notice that the figure doesn't look quite the way that you may have expected. Make sure that **Degrees** is set to **360**. In the **Align** area, click on **Min**. Now it should look more like you expected. The Align section determines what the figure is lathed around.

8. Go up to just below the command panel buttons where the name of the figure is given and the color is displayed. Change the name of the figure to **Beaker** and the color to a medium blue.

9. Click on the **Min/Max Toggle** button and the **Extents Zoom All** button to view the result.

10. Move the beaker down to the **Perspective** plane by working in the **Left** viewport. Then move it to the right of the cylinder that turned into a bowl and above the **Exer3** text by working in the **Perspective** window.

11. In the lathing process, your **Front** viewport may have become disabled. If it did the word **Disabled** will be displayed in the viewport next to its name. To reenable the viewport, right click on the name of the viewport. In the box that opens there will be a check next to **Disable View**. Click on **Disable View** to reenable the viewport.

12. Deselect the beaker.

Creating a Banister Post

The process for creating the banister post will be similar to the process for creating the beaker except that here you will be using beziers in addition to bezier corners and corners.

1. Use the **Region Zoom** button to zoom down to a blank area of the **Front** viewport and then the **Min/Max Toggle** button to toggle it to full screen.

2. Click on the **Create** button, the **Shapes** button, and the **Line** button.

3. Draw a figure that looks like the one in the figure labeled Post 1. The curves were created by using beziers. Remember that with the **Bezier**

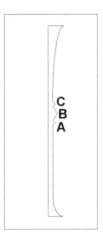

drag type selected, you click and hold to create a bezier, then drag past the point to create the curve. It may take a little practice to master the technique. If it starts looking like a real mess, right click to finish the line and hit the Undo button to start over again. You will still be able to use the Edit Spline command to reposition the location of all vertices, and you will be changing points A, B, and C into bezier corners. The last line should return to the point at which you started so that you can close the spline.

4. When the figure is drawn and the spline is closed, click on the Modify button and then on Edit Spline. Be sure that the Select and Move button on the toolbar is activated. Right click on point A and turn it into a bezier corner. Use the handles to turn corner A into a curve. Do the same for corners B and C. Take a look at the figure labeled Post 2 and try to make

your figure look like that. Remember that you can also use the Move command to move vertices until the figure is correct.

5. When all your editing is done, click on Lathe. Change align to Min.
6. Change the name of the object to Banister Post and the color to a brown.
7. Click on the Min/Max Toggle button to return to the four-viewport screen.
8. Click on Zoom Extents All to return all four viewports to a full view.
9. Move the banister post down to the Perspective plane in the Left viewport and then move it next to the beaker in the Perspective viewport.
10. Deselect the banister post.

Using the Noise Modifier

The Noise modifier can be used to create a number of random, ripple, and wave effects that can be quite interesting.

1. Click on the Create button, then on the Geometry button, and then on Box.
2. Working in the Top viewport, click and drag to draw a rectangle in the blank lower left-hand portion of the viewport. When it is the size that you want, click to establish the size of the rectangle and then move the cursor upward to form the height of the box. Click to set the height.
3. Change the name of the box to Noise Test and make its color light blue.
4. Change the length to 10', the width to 10', and the height to 1'.
5. Change the length segments to 40, the width segments to 40, and the height segments to 40.
6. Click on Zoom Extents All to get a good view of the whole scene. If something else is in the middle of the box, move that object out of the way.
7. Click on the Modify button and then on the Noise button. A new set of parameters will appear. You will probably have to use the hand function of the cursor to move the Parameters section upward so that you can see all of it.
   A. Work in the Strength section:
      1. Change the Z value to 10' and hit Enter.
      2. Change the Z value to 20' and hit Enter.
      3. Change the Z value to 0, the X value to 20', and hit Enter.
      4. Change the Z value to 10', the X value to 0, and hit Enter.
   B. In the Noise section:
      1. Click on the up arrow next to the Seed window one click at a time, increasing the value from 0 to 9 and observing what happens with each click.

2. Each number represents a different random noise pattern, not a progression. You will notice, though, that these are smooth curves.

3. Return the value in the Seed window to 0.

C. Check the Fractal box.

1. Click on the up arrow next to the Seed window one click at a time, increasing the value from 0 to 9 and observing what happens with each click.

2. Each number represents a different random fractal pattern, not a progression. You will notice, though, that these are jagged curves.

3. Find a fractal pattern that you like and leave it at that setting. Later when you compare your work to the sample on the CD-ROM you should notice that your pattern may not be the same even if the seed number is the same. The noise generator is random in nature. When you find a pattern that you like, record the setting. It could take some searching to find something like it again.

4. Deselect the Noise Test box.

8. Use the Save As command to save the scene that you have created as Exer3.max in a location on your hard drive or to a 3.5-inch disk.

9. Open Proj3.max from the CD-ROM and compare your work with it.

APPLYING MATERIALS AND MAPS: ADDING TEXTURES AND COLORS TO SURFACES

You have already learned the basics of getting around in 3D Studio MAX, importing drawings from AutoCAD, creating your own objects in 3D Studio MAX, and modifying and editing those objects. You have even learned how to color the objects in a simple way. To create realistic-looking scenes, however, you are going to need to apply much more complex textures and use color in a more sophisticated manner. That is what this section of the book is all about. Here you will learn how to use the textures and colors that are already available to you in the program and how to import an even wider variety of materials to use on the objects that you either import from AutoCAD or create in 3D Studio MAX.

The key to applying materials in 3D Studio MAX is learning to use the Material Editor.

THE MATERIAL EDITOR

 The Material Editor button is located on the toolbar, just to the left of the Render buttons. Clicking on this button will open the Material Editor. When first opened, it will look something like the figure labeled The Material Editor.

**THE MATERIAL
EDITOR**

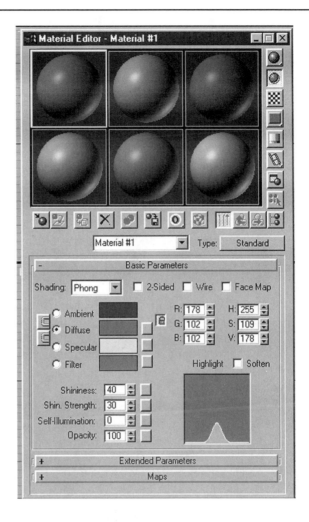

Parts of the Material Editor

The Material Editor has two sections that are divided by the Basic Parameters bar. The upper portion is always displayed, though some buttons may be active or inactive depending upon what you are doing. The lower portion will change with the material chosen and the level in that material on which you are working.

The sample slots are the six large windows on the upper left that display different colored spheres. These slots display the materials you have chosen as they will appear in the rendered scene, which may not be the same as they appear in the viewports. The active sample slot has a white border around it. You activate a sample slot by clicking in it.

The vertical toolbar runs down the right side of the sample slots. Most of these buttons change the display in the sample slots. From top to bottom, these buttons are:

 The **Sample Type** Button: Click and hold on this button to show the **Sphere, Cube,** and **Cylinder** pop-ups. Select one of these types to change the object displayed in the sample slot window.

 The **Backlight** Button: Click on this button to add a backlight to the display in the sample slot window. This is on unless you turn it off.

 The **Pattern Background** Button: This button changes the background in the window to a checkered pattern. This can be useful when you are working with translucent or transparent material.

 The **Sample UV Tiling** Button: Click and hold on this button to display the **Tile 1, 4, 9,** and **16** options. These affect the way that mapped material is displayed in the sample slot window. It does not affect the way that this mapped material will be displayed in the viewports or the final rendering.

 The **Video Color Check** Button: This checks the colors in the sample slot window for video compatibility.

 The **Make Preview** Button: Click and hold here to display the **Make Preview, Play Preview,** and **Save Preview** options. These options let you run a preview of the effect of animation on a material.

 The **Options** Button: This opens the **Material Editor Options** box. This box lets you change aspects of the way that materials are viewed in the sample window such as the **Ambient Light** and **Background** intensities.

 The **Select by Material** Button: This lets you select objects in the viewports on the basis of the material selected in the Material Editor. This button will display a list of all of the objects in the viewports and highlight the ones that have the selected material applied to them.

The horizontal toolbar runs along the bottom of the sample slots. These buttons let you move materials from material libraries to the sample slots and then to the scene. Other buttons here let you explore the various levels of materials and maps available. From left to right, these buttons are:

 The **Get Material** Button: This opens the **Material/Map Browser** for access to materials and maps.

The **Put Material in Scene** Button: This button is only active when a material has already been assigned to an object in a scene, you have taken that material and made a change in it, and you want to assign the changed material back to the object(s) in the scene. See the **Make Material Copy** button below.

 The **Assign Material to Selection** Button: This button is used to assign the material in the active sample window to an object in the scene that has already been selected.

 The **Clear Material Settings** Button: This button resets all values for the material in the active sample window.

 The **Make Material Copy** Button: This button copies the material to itself. It works with the **Put Material in Scene** button in the following way: If you have a material that is already assigned to an object in the scene, but you want to make a change in the settings (parameters) for that material, any changes that you make will appear immediately on the screen. This is referred to as the material being "hot." If you don't want those changes to appear in the scene until they are completed:

1. Activate the sample slot that holds the material.
2. Copy the material to itself using the **Make Material Copy** button. This makes the material "cold."
3. Make the changes using the Parameters section of the Material Editor.
4. Reassign the material back to the scene using the **Put Material in Scene** button. This once again makes the material "hot."

 The **Put to Library** Button: This button adds the currently selected and changed material to the current library. If you have brought up a material and made changes in it, you should use this button to save those changes under a new name so that you can bring up that material with all of those changes again.

 The **Material Effects Channel** Button: This button is used in creating videos to tag a material for a video post effect.

 The **Show Map in Viewport** Button: This shows mapped materials on the surfaces of objects.

 The **Show End Result** Button: When on, this button lets you see the end result of working with compound materials. When you are applying more than one material to the surface of an object, you can turn this button off to see the individual effect of each material or turn it on to see the end result of all of them.

The **Go to Parent** Button: If you are working with compound materials—more than one material on the surface of the same object—the top material in the list, which is the first material applied, is the parent material. If you are somewhere down in the list, this button will take you to the top material. If the button is off, you know that you are already at the top material or that you only have one material applied to the object.

 The **Go to Sibling** Button: If you are working with compound materials, they may be applied on layers. If there is more than one material on the same layer, this button will take you to those materials.

 The **Material/Map Navigator** Button: If you are working with compound materials, this opens the **Material/Map Navigator** box. This box lets you see the entire hierarchy of the materials displayed and lets you go to the level and material that you want by clicking on the icon next to it.

Just below the horizontal toolbar and above the Basic Parameters bar is the **Name Field** window and **Type:** button. The **Name Field** window displays the name of the currently selected material. It can also be used to rename materials. The **Type:** button displays the currently selected material type. When you click on the **Type:** button, you open the **Material/Map Browser**, where you can change the current type.

The lower section of the Material Editor contains the **Basic Parameters**, **Extended Parameters**, and **Maps** bars. On the left-hand side of each bar there will be either a + or a −. The − sign indicates that the information in the area is being displayed and not hidden. The + sign indicates that there is information there that is not being displayed. Click on the bar to close or open the information display. Even if the information is being displayed, you still may not be able to see all of it because it may be scrolled under the bottom or top of the box. Move the cursor over a nonclickable area of the box, and it will turn into a hand if there is some information scrolled underneath. You can then click and drag with the hand to raise and lower the box to display hidden information.

Exercise No. 4: Working with Materials

The following exercise is designed to help you understand how the Material Editor works. It will walk you through applying materials to objects, changing and saving materials, and setting the basic parameters.

Assigning Materials to Objects

In Exercise No. 3 you gave colors to the objects that you were modifying. These colors were not materials and could not be changed in the ways that materials can be changed. Let's start out by assigning some simple materials to objects in the scene that you created in Exercise No. 3.

1. Open Exer3.max from where you saved it earlier or open Proj3.max from the CD-ROM.

2. Use the Save As command to save this file as Exer4.max to the location you have chosen on your hard drive or to a 3.5-inch disk.

3. Select the beaker.

4. Open the Material Editor. The six sample slots are filled with sample materials.

5. Assign Material #5 to the beaker by clicking on the middle box in the bottom row and then on the Assign Material to Selection button. Notice that when you click on Material #5, the sample box outline turns white to indicate that it is selected. When you click on the Assign Material to Selection button, white triangles appear at the corners. These triangles indicate that the material is "hot"— that is, it has been assigned to an object in the scene. Click on Material #4, which is to the left of Material #5. The white outline indicates that Material #4 is the currently selected material. The white triangles remain around Material #5, however, to indicate that it is hot.

6. Changing the name of the material: When you have assigned a material to an object, it is a very good idea to change the name of the material so that you can more easily find it again after you have used a lot of different materials.

   A. Click on Material #5 in the sample box again so that its name appears in the Name Field window. Click to the right of the name in the window. The name will be highlighted. Type in a new name— Beaker Material—and again click on Material #5.

7. Assigning a material to two different objects: The Material Editor should have come up on the left side of your screen. You still should be able to see the Perspective and Front viewports and make selections in them. If you need to move the Material Editor to another part of the screen so that you can see a different viewport, click and drag on the blue bar at the top that says Material Editor. Do not click on the icon to the left of the words Material Editor or on the minimize and close boxes on the right side of the bar.

   A. Select the cylinder that you turned into a bowl-shaped object, named Cylinder01. Assign Material #4 to it and rename Material #4 Cyl & Star Material.

   B. Select the star. Assign Cyl & Star Material to the star.

8. Changing a material: Changing a material after it has been assigned to an object can be as simple as just calling the material up and making changes in the Basic Parameters section, but not necessarily. Remember those

white triangles that indicate that a material is hot. If you change the basic parameters of a hot material those changes will immediately appear in the scene. If you don't want them to appear in the scene until you have finished the changes then you have to "cool off" the material first, make the changes, and then reassign it back to the scene. Let's change a material using both methods.

A. Click on the sample box for the Cyl & Star Material. Notice the white triangles that indicate it is hot.

   1. In the **Basic Parameters** area, change the hue:

      a. Make sure there is a dot in the circle next to **Diffuse**.

      b. Change the values in the **R:** (red), **G:** (green), and **B:** (blue) boxes to create a new color. For all the non–lighting designers out there, these are your primaries. You are working in the additive color mixing system, not the subtractive system. The primaries are red, blue, and green. The secondaries are magenta, cyan (blue-green), and yellow. The complementaries are red and cyan, blue and yellow, and green and magenta. Complementaries mix to white, not black.

      c. You can also change the hue by changing the values in the **H:** spinner. Notice as it moves up and down in value the values in the R:, G:, and B: boxes change as well.

   2. Notice that the color of both the cylinder and the star change as you make the hue changes. You are working in a hot material.

B. Make sure that the sample box for **Cyl & Star Material** is selected.

   1. Click on the **Make Material Copy** button on the toolbar. Notice that the white triangles disappear. You have just cooled off the material. Now you can make changes in it that won't be reflected in the scene.

   2. Make changes in the **RGB** or **HSV** spinners to create a new color. The **H:** spinner changes the hue. The **S:** spinner changes the saturation of the color. The **V:** spinner changes the value—brightness, intensity. Notice that as you make the color changes, you can see them reflected in the sample box but not in the scene.

   3. Click on the **Put Material to Scene** button to assign the new color to both the cylinder and the star in the scene. This also turns the Cyl & Star Material hot again.

C. Other changes in the **Basic Parameters** area: There are a number of other changes that can be made to the material in the Basic Parameters area. Most of the following areas will be part of the basic parameters for nearly any material that you choose from the material library. You can use these parameters to create some highly unusual and in many cases extremely effective new materials. You can, for example, create wood grain that looks neon by making it both self-illuminating and translucent. Other of these effects can be so subtle as to be difficult to detect unless you know what to look for. Below I will try to give you some settings that will show you some of the extremes of each of these parameters so that you can get an idea of the range of effects available within each of them. In making the following changes, try to work by double clicking in a window when numbers are involved to highlight the number. Then enter the new number on the keyboard, and while watching the sample box, hit **Enter**. This should give you the quickest change, making it easiest to detect the difference. Click on the sample slot for **Material #6**.

1. Start with these basic parameters: Shading: Phong; 2-Sided, Wire, Face Map, and Soften: unchecked; Shinniness: 40; Shin. Strength: 30; Self-Illumination: 0; Opacity: 100; Ambient: R: 178, G: 102, B: 178; Diffuse: R: 255, G: 0, B: 252; Specular: H: 0, S: 0, V: 255; Filter: H: 0, S: 0, V: 255.

2. You have already seen that diffuse is the setting that determines the principal color of the material, but ambient, specular, and filter will also affect color. The diffuse color is the color reflected in direct light. The ambient color is the color reflected from the shadows on the material. The specular color is the color reflected from the highlights on the material. The filter color is the color as transmitted through a transparent or translucent material such as glass. After each change and restore below, hit the **Enter** key.

   a. Click on the circle next to **Ambient**, putting a dot in the circle. Change R: to 0. Restore R: to 178. Change B: to 0. Restore B: to 178.

   b. Click on the circle next to **Specular**, putting a dot in the circle. Watch the highlights, and change V: to 0.

   c. Click on the circle next to **Filter**, putting a dot in the circle. Watch carefully and change V: to 255. Change V: to 0. Restore V: to 128. Restore Specular V: to 255.

3. So far you have been changing colors by just using the RGB and HSV spinners. There is another way to change the diffuse, ambient, specular, and filter colors. This is using the Color Selector. Click in the colored box to the right of **Diffuse**. The **Color Selector** box will open. On the left side of the Color Selector box you will see the horizontal scale for hue with a small white triangle and the vertical scales for whiteness and blackness with a small white triangle. The triangles are sliders that you can click on and drag to change these values. Underneath the RGB and HSV scales there is a rectangle.

The left side of this rectangle shows the current color for diffuse, since that is where you clicked to activate the Color Selector. The right side of this rectangle shows the color that you are creating in the Color Selector box.

a. Click on the hue triangle and drag it left and right. Notice that the hue on the right side of the rectangle changes.

b. Click on the whiteness triangle and drag it up and down. Notice that the whiteness on the right side of the rectangle changes.

c. Click on the blackness triangle and drag it up and down. Notice that the blackness on the right side of the rectangle changes.

d. There is a colored + in the rainbow-colored square between the hue, whiteness, and blackness triangles that moves when you move the sliders. Try clicking at various points within this square. This changes all three positions at once.

e. To the right of the rainbow square there are scales for RGB and HSV. These change to represent the new values when you perform any of the above operations. You can also make changes in the Color Selector by using these scales. You can either click and drag on the white vertical bar in the RGB and HSV rectangles or enter numbers in the spinners.

f. If you click on the **Close** button at the bottom of the box, the new color that you have created will be transferred to the Diffuse section under Basic Parameters.

g. If you want to escape from the Color Selector box without changing the original color, click on **Reset** and then on **Close**.

h. For now, click on **Reset** and then on **Close**. If you have already clicked on Close and changed the color in Diffuse, reset the values to **R: 255, G: 0,** and **B: 252** by using the spinners in the **Basic Parameters** box.

4. Watch your highlights and shadows: change Shinniness: to **0**. Change Shinniness: to **100**. Change Shin. Strength: to **100**. Change Shin. Strength: to **0**. Restore Shinniness: to **40**. Restore Shin. Strength: to **30**.

5. Change Self-Illumination: to **100**. Restore Self-Illumination: to **0**.

6. Change the background to the checkered background. Change Opacity: to **50**. Change Opacity: to **20**. Restore Opacity: to **100**. Change back to the grey background.

7. Change Shin. Strength: to **100**. Click in the box next to **Soften** so that a check appears. Click again in the box next to **Soften**.

8. In the **Shading** box: Click on the arrow and select **Metal**. Select **Constant**. Restore **Phong**. Restore Shin. Strength: to **30**.

9. Change Self-Illumination: to **100**. Change Opacity: to **50**. Change to the checkered background. Click in the **2-Sided** box so that a check appears. Click in the **2-Sided** box again.

10. Click in the **Wire** box so that a check appears. Click in the **Wire** box again.

11. Clicking in the **Face Map** box will make no visible difference in the sample box. A face map will only appear when the material is transferred to an object in the scene. If you are working with a 3-D object with a number of surfaces or faces that have already been mapped, face map will automatically transfer the material to each surface or face. The next exercise will deal with mapping.

D. Locking the **Basic Parameters** box: If you have spent a long time arriving at a setting in the Basic Parameters box and don't want to chance losing it or someone else playing around with it, you can lock in the settings by clicking on the Lock icon to the left of the RGB boxes. To the left of the **Ambient** and **Diffuse** circles is a sideways U that you can click on to lock the ambient and diffuse settings. To the left of the **Diffuse** and **Specular** circles is a sideways U that you can click on to lock the diffuse and specular settings.

9. Save the changes that you have made to **Exer4.max**. You can compare your work with **Proj4.max** on the CD-ROM.

Using Libraried Materials and Maps

THE MATERIAL/MAP BROWSER

You have been working with the materials that are already in the sample slots to explore how to use the basic parameters of the Material Editor. As you have seen, there are quite a number of different things that you can do this way to create new looks for these materials. 3D Studio MAX also has a large library of materials that are available to you through the Material/Map Browser. Now you will learn how to get at these and apply them to objects in the scene. The Material/Map Browser is accessed through the Material Editor. Open 3D Studio MAX. Click on the **Material Editor** button. In the Material Editor, click on the **Get Materials** button. This opens the **Material/Map Browser**.

Parts of the Material/Map Browser

1. Tool Buttons:

A. The **List** Button: This displays the materials and maps as a list. The blue spheres are materials. The green parallelograms are maps.

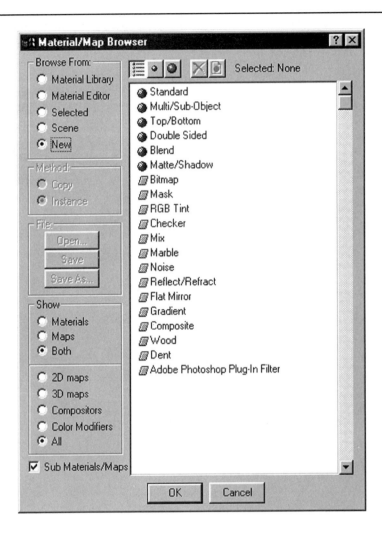

B. The Small Icons Button: This shows the materials and maps as small icons. If you move the cursor over the icon, a label will appear with the name.

C. The Large Icons Button: This shows the materials and maps as large icons.

D. The Delete from Library Button: If you want to remove a material from the library, select the material and then click on this button.

E. The Clear Material Library Button: This removes all materials from the library.

2. The Browse from: section: This selects the source for the materials displayed in the window.

   A. Material Library: This option shows the contents of a material library.

   B. Material Editor: This option shows the contents of the sample boxes.

   C. Selected: This option shows all materials assigned to the selected object in the scene.

   D. Scene: This option shows materials assigned to all the objects in the scene.

   E. New: This option shows the 3D Studio MAX material/map types so that you can create a new material.

3. The Method section: Use this area to place a selected material/map in a submaterial slot.

   A. Copy: This option places a copy in the submaterial slot.

   B. Instance: This option places an instance in the submaterial slot.

4. The File section: This is available when Material Library is selected in the Browse from: section.

   A. Open: This opens a material library.

   B. Save: This saves the opened material library.

   C. Save As: This saves the opened material library under another name.

5. The Show section: These are filters that when selected will only allow those types of materials to be displayed.

   A. Materials/Maps/Both: These filters are always available.

   B. 2D maps/3D maps/Compositors/Color Modifiers/All: These filters are only available when New is selected in Browse from:.

6. Sub Materials/Maps: This box turns the display of submaterials and maps on and off.

Exercise No. 5: Using the Material/Map Library and Creating Your Own Library

Applying Materials from the Material Library to Objects

1. Open Exer3.max from where you saved it earlier or open Proj3.max from the CD-ROM. Save it as Exer5.max to your hard or floppy drive.

2. Open the Material Editor. When you get a material from the browser, it is placed in the active sample slot in the Material Editor. Click on the sample box for Material #6.

3. Click on the Get Material button. The Material/Map Browser appears on the screen.

4. Choose Material Library in the Browse from: section.

5. In the File: section, click on Open.

   A. The Open Material Library box appears.

   B. Click on 3dsmax.mat.

   C. Click on Open.

6. The built-in material/map library opens. Materials have a blue sphere next to them. Maps have a green parallelogram next to them.

7. In the Show section, choose Materials. This applies the filter that will show you just materials, not maps. In the next exercise you will learn about how to apply maps.

8. The display that you are seeing with the list of materials is in that format because the default List button is on.

9. Click on the Small Icons button. Each item is displayed as a small sphere. If you move the cursor over the small icon, the name of the item will be displayed. Click on the small icon to select the item.

10. Click on the Chrome Blue Sky icon. At the top of the browser, it will say: Selected: Chrome Blue Sky.

11. Click on the OK button at the bottom of the browser.

12. The material Chrome Blue Sky will appear in position 6 in the Material Editor.

13. Click on the Get Material button. The Material/Map Browser appears on the screen with the material library already opened.

14. Click on the Large Icons button. Each item is displayed as a large sphere with the name underneath.

    A. To the right of the window where the materials are displayed there is a standard window scroller. You can click on the down arrow to scroll the display down and view more materials. You can click and drag on the button between the two arrows to scroll up and down or you can click on the bar below or above the button to skip to the next group of materials below or above the group currently displayed.

    B. Move the cursor into the white space just to the left of the window scroller, and it will turn into a hand. You can click and drag with the hand in this white space to scroll the display up and down.

    C. The Material/Map Browser is an expandable display. Move the cursor to the very right-hand edge of the browser. The cursor will turn into a double-headed arrow. Click and drag to the right to expand the display.

15. You will notice that when you are using the large icons, you can see a nice picture of the material, but it takes quite a while for the screen display to

catch up with you as you move through the icons. After you become familiar with the materials, it is considerably quicker to work from the default list display than from either the small or large icons.

16. Select **Cherry Red Metal** by clicking on the large icon.

17. Click on the **OK** button to apply this material to position 6 in the Material Editor.

18. At this point you could work in the **Basic Parameters** section to change the color, shinniness, etc. of the material.

19. In the **Perspective** viewport, zoom in to a close-up view of the banister post. You will probably also have to pan to get it into the center of the viewport.

20. Select the banister post.

21. Come back to the Material Editor and click on the **Cherry Red Metal** sample sphere in position 6. There should be a white outline around it to indicate that it is active.

22. Click on the **Assign Material to Selection** button.

23. You have just applied a material to an object that you created and modified.

Creating Your Own Material Library

Whenever you start or reset the program, the material library **3dsmax.mat** is loaded into memory and you can open it as you did above. You can also create your own library from materials in the larger library or ones that you have modified using the parameters section. Anytime that you take a material from the library and modify it, you should give that material a new name. If you don't, you may have trouble trying to duplicate it later from the original material in the library. This could be the basis for a new library that consists of the materials that you are using for a particular scene.

1. In the **Name** window underneath the sample windows, change the name of the material in position 6 to **Post Red**.

2. Click on the material in position 5 and assign it to the beaker by selecting the beaker and using the **Assign Material to Selection** button. Rename the material **Beaker Purple**.

3. Click on the material in position 4 and assign it to the star by selecting the star and using the **Assign Material to Selection** button. Rename the material **Star Blue**.

4. As part of this process you could also have made changes to these materials using the basic parameters or brought in other materials from the material library. Every object in the scene could have a different material assigned to it and each of those materials could have its own name that you gave it.

5. Click on the Get Materials button to open the Material/Map Browser.

6. Click on Scene under Browse from:.

7. Click on the List icon.

8. You will see the names of the materials that you have just created and named.

9. Click on the Save As button. The Save Material Library box opens.

   A. In the File name: area, type in Exer5.mat and then click on Save.

   B. You have just created a new material library for this scene.

10. Click on OK to exit the Material/Map Browser.

11. Now let's add another material to the new library.

12. In the scene, select the ellipse on top of the cone.

13. Assign the material in position 2 to the ellipse and rename that material Ellipse Green.

14. Click on the Put to Library button.

   A. The Put to Library box opens. You can change the name given to the material here if you would like.

   B. Click on OK to assign the material to the library with the name you have already given it.

15. Click on the Get Material button.

   A. The Material/Map Browser opens, displaying the materials in the scene.

   B. The new material—Ellipse Green—has not been added to the materials in the library that you created earlier.

   C. To add it to the Exer5.mat library, you will again have to use the Save As command.

   D. Click on Save As.

      1. The Save Material Library box opens.

      2. Click on Exer5.mat and it will appear in the File name: area.

      3. Click on Save.

      4. A message appears saying A file with the same name already exists. Do you want to replace it?

      5. Click on Yes.

      6. You have now added the material Ellipse Green to this library. Click on OK to close the browser.

16. The Put to Library button will assign a material to whatever library is open at the time, but it will not save it to that library unless you tell it to. In the above exercise you saved the material to the new library Exer5.mat that you had created earlier, but you could also have saved it to the master library 3dsmax.mat or any other library that already exists.

Doing a Quick Render to See the Effect of Materials

You may have found that many materials do not appear quite as you expected when you apply them to objects. Remember that earlier when I was talking about the Material Editor box I mentioned that the materials would appear in the sample boxes as they would look when they were rendered, but that they would not necessarily show up that way in the viewports. This is exactly what I was talking about. The Smooth and Highlight option in the Perspective viewport gives you a better idea of what the scene will look like than the wireframe does, but this is known as a gourand-shaded viewport, and it can show you only general highlights and shadows. It cannot really display specular highlights. In a later section of this book I will be covering rendering in more detail, but in the part of the exercise below you will do a quick render, which will let you see the effects of some materials better and will point out why the next section of the book on mapping is necessary.

I also mentioned earlier that maps can only be applied to objects that have mapping coordinates. This is also true of many materials that have textures, such as wood grains. If you apply a textured material to an object without mapping coordinates all you will get is the general color with no graining effect. As a demonstration of how materials look different when rendered than they do in viewports and of the necessity of mapping coordinates even for some materials, you are going to do a quick render.

If you or anyone else has already done a render with the program, you should also be aware that the Render Scene box retains the settings from the last time that it was used. If this were for an animation, you could be in for a big surprise. The program might try to render the scene frame by frame, and this could take a considerable amount of time. Before you do a quick render for the first time, check the settings in the Render Scene box by clicking on the Render Scene button instead of Quick Render. Check to see that the following settings are present:

- in the Time Output section, Single is selected
- in the Output Size section, 640x480 is selected
- in the Options section, Render Atmospheric Effects is checked and nothing else
- in the Render Output section, Save File is not checked

If the settings in the Render Scene box are those given above, close the Render Scene box and click on Quick Render. If any of those settings are different, correct them and click on the Render button at the bottom of the box. The next time that you want to do a quick render, everything will be set up for it and you can just click on Quick Render instead of having to go through the Render Scene box.

1. In the **Perspective** viewport, zoom in and pan until you have the banister post and beaker taking up almost all of the viewport.
2. Select the beaker in the Perspective viewport.
3. Open the **Material Editor**.
4. Click on slot #5 box that contains the material **Beaker Purple**.
5. Click on the **Get Materials** button.
6. Select the material **Wood Ashen** from the main library.
7. Click on **OK** to assign the material to slot #5.
8. Click on the **Assign Material to Selection** button to assign Wood Ashen to the beaker.
9. Deselect—Edit/Select None—the beaker.
10. Take a good look at both the banister post and the beaker in the **Perspective** viewport. You will notice that the banister post appears considerably duller than the Post Red material in slot #6 that you had previously assigned to it. You will also notice that the beaker to which you just assigned Wood Ashen does not show the wood grains. The banister post just needs to be rendered for you to be able to see the effect of the material. The beaker, however, will not show the wood grains even in the rendering because it has not had mapping coordinates given to it.
11. Close the Material Editor box.
12. Click on the **Quick Render** button, *if* you already know that the **Render Scene** box is properly set up.
    A. The **Render Error** box will open, warning you that the beaker requires texture coordinates and may not render correctly. This is true, but click on **OK** anyway.
    B. When the rendering appears, you will notice that the banister post has rendered considerably differently than it looked in the viewport. It appears much more metallic and like the sample in the Material Editor box. The beaker, however, still appears to have just a general brown color and does not have the texture of wood grain. This is because it does not have mapping coordinates.
13. Save these changes as **Exer5.max**. You can compare this with **Proj5.max** on the CD-ROM.

Applying Mapping Coordinates and Using Maps and Textured Materials

The surfaces of objects either created in 3D Studio MAX or imported from AutoCAD can be treated with a variety of materials and maps. These can come from the library available through 3D Studio MAX or you can import images from other sources such as ones that you scan in yourself. You have already learned how to apply materials that do not have grain or texture to objects. Much more detailed effects can be achieved through applying materials with grain or texture or maps, which have even more detail than materials. Before you can apply materials with grain or maps, however, you have to create mapping coordinates for the object. Mapping coordinates tell the program how to place, orient, and scale the map when it is placed on the object. This is how you would control the direction and size of a wood grain, for example, or the scale and orientation of a wallpaper pattern.

There are times when you do not need to create mapping coordinates. You can save yourself a lot of time and trouble if you understand these exceptions. Reflection and refraction maps don't need mapping coordinates. These maps are based on the rendered view and will change automatically when you change the point of view of the rendering. Three-dimensional procedural maps such as noise or marble don't need coordinates. They are generated by the orientation of the object itself and change automatically if you move or rotate the object. Face-mapped materials also do not need mapping coordinates. They are based on the faces of the object itself and are determined by its geometry.

There are three different ways that you can apply mapping coordinates to objects in 3D Studio MAX. If you are working with an object that is one of the standard primitives in 3D Studio MAX you can simply check the **Generate Mapping Coords.** box in the **Parameters** section when you create the object or come back later to the **Create** command for that object and select this option. If the object was created using the **Shapes** command bar in 3D Studio MAX or was imported from AutoCAD, you will have to use the **UVW Map** modifier to create mapping coordinates. Finally, there are special objects in 3D Studio MAX such as loft objects that have options in their Parameters section that let you apply mapping coordinates to them.

The following exercise will walk you through the process of applying mapping coordinates to standard primitives and imported objects, adjusting those coordinates to achieve the effects that you desire, and bringing in maps from sources other than the 3D Studio MAX library.

Exercise No. 6: Setting Mapping Coordinates, Using Maps, and Importing Maps

MAPPING STANDARD PRIMITIVES:
THE GENERATE MAPPING COORDINATES OPTION

The easiest way to apply mapping coordinates to a standard primitive that has been created in 3D Studio MAX is to check the **Generate Mapping Coordinates** box in the **Parameters** section when you create the object. You can also check this option later if you would like.

Applying Mapping Coordinates

1. Open the file Proj6.max from the CD-ROM. Save this file as Exer6.max to either somewhere on your hard drive or to a 3.5-inch disk. This file contains a sphere, a cylinder, and a box that have all been created using the Standard Primitives option in 3D Studio MAX.

2. Select the sphere. Click on the Modify button. The modifier stack and the parameters for the sphere will open. At the bottom of the Parameters area is a box next to Generate Mapping Coords. Click in the box, and a check will appear. You have just applied mapping coordinates to the sphere.

3. Select the cylinder and apply mapping coordinates to it. Select the box and apply mapping coordinates to it.

4. Select all three objects by choosing Edit/Select All or using the Rectangular Selection tool.

5. Apply a material to all three objects:

   A. Open the Material Editor.

   B. Activate sample slot #4—click on the blue sphere in the lower left-hand sample slot.

   C. Click on the Get Material button. The Material/Map Browser opens. If the material library 3dsmax.mat is not open, open it:

      1. Click in the circle next to Material Library in the Browse from: section.
      2. Click on Open.
      3. In the Open Material Library box, double click on 3dmax.mat.

   D. Select the material for Wood Ashen—the blue sphere—and click on OK. The sphere in sample slot #4 has the map applied to it.

      Note: Do *not* click on the blue parallelogram for the map or you will find that you cannot do the next step. You usually must start with a material and then work your way to one of the layers of bitmaps underneath, unless it is a reflection, refraction, noise, or marble bitmap, which doesn't need mapping coordinates.

   E. Click on the Assign Material to Selection button. All three objects change to the diffuse color for Wood Ashen, but you do not see any grain in the viewport.

   F. Click on the Quick Render button, and you will see the grain displayed in the rendering. Close the Render window.

Displaying Maps in the Viewport

You can also display maps that you apply to objects in the viewports as well as being able to see them when they are rendered. This will slow down the display in the viewports, especially in a complex scene with a number of different objects and maps. Make your own choice about which is the better method for the way that you will be working. It might be a good idea, for example, to use the viewport display until you become more familiar with the system and then once you know what you are doing go to the regular nonviewport display in order to speed up the working process.

1. Click on the Maps bar in the Material Editor underneath the Extended Parameters bar.
   A. Under the Maps column next to the Diffuse row, you will see that the bar is labeled ex #4 (Bitmap) Ashen. . . .
   B. Click on this bar.
      1. The Coordinates and Bitmap Parameters boxes open.
      2. Notice also that the window under the sample boxes now reads: Tex #4.
      3. Click on the arrow next to that window and you will see that there are two levels here now:
         a. Wood Ashen—the level above where you presently are
         b. Tex #4—the level on which you presently are
      To return to the upper level, you would click on Wood Ashen in the window. This is how you would make changes in the basic parameters such as changing the color of the wood. For now, though, stay on the Tex #4 level. If you have returned to the Wood Ashen level you will have to repeat steps A and B above to get back to the Tex #4 level.
   C. Click on the Show Map in Viewport button in the Material Editor.

ADJUSTING MAPPING COORDINATES

When you generate mapping coordinates for a standard primitive, there are some limitations to how much adjustment you can make to the mapping coordinates. The UVW mapping method, which will be explained in the next part of this exercise, offers more options, as you will see. First I'll go through what options are available under this method of mapping. In the Material Editor, the Coordinates box should be open. This is where you will be working.

1. The Texture/Environ circles: Checking one of these two circles will result in the image being treated either as though it were projected onto the surface of the object—Texture—or onto an invisible surface behind the object—Environ. If you select Environ. Mapping, you have a further choice of Spherical, Cylindrical, Shrink Wrap, or Screen. With most texture maps such as the current one, you will not notice any difference between the two. With a highly detailed image such as a photograph that you might import from another source there can be a noticeable difference.

    A. Click on the Environ. circle.

    B. Click on the Texture circle.

2. The UV, VW, WU orientation: In mapping coordinates, UVW coordinates are parallel to the XYZ coordinates of construction. Clicking on the circle next to these options is a quick way to change the orientation of the mapping.

    A. Click on the circle next to VW. This gives you a wider vertical spread in the texture.

    B. Click on the circle next to WU. The horizontal texture goes vertical.

    C. Click on the circle next to UV to restore the original setup.

3. Tiling: Tiling determines how often the map is repeated along each coordinate. Notice that there are two checked boxes under the Tile column. The top one corresponds to the U coordinate, the bottom one corresponds to the V coordinate. These boxes must be checked for tiling to occur along that particular coordinate. To the left of the Mirror boxes, there are two spinner windows under the Tiling column, one for the U coordinate and one for the V coordinate. These spinners determine how many times the map is repeated along each coordinate.

    A. Be sure that there is a check in both of the Tile boxes.

    B. In the U: Tiling window, change the value from 1 to 10 and hit Enter. Change the value back to 1 and hit Enter. Notice that this changes the horizontal repetition.

    C. In the V: Tiling window, change the value from 1 to 10 and hit Enter. Change the value back to 1 and hit Enter. Notice that this changes the vertical repetition.

    D. Change the value to 10 in both the U: and V: Tiling windows and hit Enter. Change the values back to 1 and hit Enter. This changes the repetition in both directions.

4. Offset: Each map has a beginning point where the map will start being displayed on the object. Offset changes this start point for the map. The offset figure can be thought of as a percentage by which the map is shifted left and right (U) or up and down (V). For the U coordinate, entering .25, for example, shifts the map start point 25 percent to the left. Enter -.25 to shift 25 percent to the right. The same figures entered on the V coordinate would result in the same shift, but up and down, respectively.

    A. Change the figure in the U: Offset spinner to .25 and hit Enter.

    B. Change the figure in the V: Offset spinner to .25 and hit Enter.

    C. Change both figures back to 0 and hit Enter.

5. Angle: This spinner rotates the map in degrees counterclockwise around its center.

A. Change the Angle spinner value to 45 and hit Enter.

B. Change the Angle spinner back to 0 and hit Enter.

6. Mirror: This box can be checked to mirror the image either left to right (U) or up and down (V).

A. Check the U: Mirror box.

B. Check the U: Tile box.

C. Check the V: Mirror box.

D. Check the V: Tile box.

THE UVW MAPPING METHOD

The second general mapping method is using the UVW Map option under the Parameters section of the modify panel. A UVW map is applied to individual objects. When you use the generate mapping coordinates method described above, all objects will have the map displayed in the same way. If you want to display the map differently on different objects, you will have to use the UVW map method. If you are using the same wood grain on two different objects, for example, and you want the grain to run one way on one object and a different way on the other, then you would have to map each object using the UVW method. UVW mapping also must be used on any object that is imported from AutoCAD or any object that is created by using the Shapes option. UVW mapping also lets you apply different maps to different faces of the same object. Now let's apply UVW maps to the objects in the exercise.

1. Clear the generate mapping coordinates option from each object:

A. Select the sphere in the Perspective viewport.

B. Click on the Modify button in the command panel.

C. Clear the check from the Generate Mapping Coords. box.

D. The map will disappear from the sphere.

E. Do the same for the cylinder and then for the box.

F. Leave the box selected with the Modify button active.

Using Planar Mapping on the Box

1. Be sure that the box is selected. Under Modifiers, click on UVW Map.

2. Under Parameters, you will notice that the default is Planar, so you don't have to select it.

3. Now it is time to learn about the gizmo.

A. Notice that there is an orange line around the center of the box. This is the gizmo.

B. Click on the Sub-Object button in the Modifier Stack area. The gizmo turns yellow.

    C. Click on the **Select and Move** button on the toolbar.

    D. Click and drag the gizmo above the box.

4. Now you can see the gizmo better, since it is not partly hidden by the box. In planar mapping, think of the gizmo as the screen onto which the map is projected. The Z coordinate that you see near the gizmo is the direction from which the projection is coming and going to both sides of the gizmo. The yellow lines and the green line show the extent of the gizmo, or the size of the image. The green line represents the right side of the image. By manipulating the gizmo, you can manipulate the image.

    A. Move the gizmo: You still should have the **Select and Move** button activated. Click and drag on the gizmo to move it around. Watch the image change as you put different parts of the image over the box.

    B. Rotate the gizmo: Click on the **Rotate** button on the toolbar. Watch the image change as you rotate the gizmo.

    C. Scale the gizmo: Choose the **Select and Uniform Scale** option on the toolbar. Watch the image change as you scale the gizmo.

    D. In the **Modifiers Command** box, find the **Alignment** part of the **Parameters** section. Click on **Fit**. This will restore the gizmo to its original position.

5. When you are working in UVW mapping, you can still make the same changes to the image in the **Coordinates** section of the Material Editor.

    A. You can tile using the **Tile** box and **Tiling** spinners. Make some changes in these areas to see how they affect the image.

    B. You can mirror using the **Mirror** box and the **Tiling** spinners. Make some changes in these areas to see how they affect the image.

    C. You can use the **Offset** spinners. Make some changes here to see the effects.

    D. You can change the angle. Make some changes here to see the effects.

    E. You can change the UV/VW/WU orientation. Click on these to see how they affect the image.

    F. Return these values to what they were originally: **UV** checked, **Angle:** 0, **Tile** boxes checked, **Tiling** spinners: 1, **Offset** spinners: 0, **Mirror** boxes unchecked.

Using Cylindrical Mapping on the Cylinder

When you are using UVW mapping, objects of different shapes need to be mapped using the appropriate option for each shape. There are a number of options available in the **Mapping** area of the modifiers' parameters that you can use. Let's take a look at the **Cylindrical** option.

1. Turn off the Sub-Object button in the modifier stack.

   Note: If you do not turn off the Sub-Object button, you will not be able to deselect the box or select anything else.

2. Deselect the box—Edit/Select None.
3. Select the cylinder in the Perspective viewport.
4. The Modify button on the command panel should still be on.
5. Click on UVW Map.
6. In the Parameters area, click on Cylindrical.
7. Watch the top of the cylinder and click on Cap.
8. Turn on the Sub-Object button in the modifier stack to select the gizmo.
9. Click on the Select and Move button on the toolbar. Move the gizmo around to see how it affects the image.
10. Click on the Rotate button on the toolbar. Rotate the gizmo to see how the image is affected.
11. Choose the Select and Uniform Scale option on the toolbar. Scale the gizmo.
12. Make some changes in the Coordinates section of the Material Editor to see how they work with the cylinder.
13. Restore the values in the Coordinates section to what they were at the beginning.
14. In the Alignment section of the Parameters section, click on Fit.

Using Spherical Mapping on the Sphere

1. Turn off the Sub-Object button in the modifier stack.
2. Deselect the cylinder—Edit/Select None.
3. Select the sphere in the Perspective viewport.
4. The Modify button on the command panel should still be on.
5. Click on UVW Map.
6. In the Parameters area, click on Spherical.
7. Turn on the Sub-Object button in the modifier stack to select the gizmo.
8. Click on the Select and Move button on the toolbar. Move the gizmo around to see how it affects the image.
9. Click on the Rotate button on the toolbar. Rotate the gizmo to see how the image is affected.
10. Choose the Select and Uniform Scale option on the toolbar. Scale the gizmo.
11. Make some changes in the Coordinates section of the Material Editor to see how they work with the sphere.

12. Restore the values in the Coordinates section to what they were at the beginning.

13. In the Alignment section of the Parameters area, click on Fit.

14. Turn off the Sub-Object button in the modifier stack.

15. Deselect the sphere—Edit/Select None.

IMPORTING MAPS FROM OUTSIDE 3D STUDIO MAX

You are not limited to the textures and bitmaps that are available in the materials library that accompanies 3D Studio MAX. You can also import bitmaps from outside sources or ones that you scan into a file yourself. 3D Studio MAX will support the following file formats: .flc, .gif, .ifl, .jpeg, .rla, .tga, and .tif. There are several files such as this already available for you to try on the CD-ROM accompanying this book in the textures section. These files are from the CD-ROM that comes with Judy Juracek's marvelous book *Surfaces* and are used here with her permission. They are just a sample of the hundreds of texture files that come with her book. The following part of this exercise will take you through the steps of importing a .dxf file and then applying an outside map to it. You could also, of course, apply such files to objects that you had created in 3D Studio MAX just as easily.

Import a .dxf File

1. Click on File/Import.

2. The Select File to Import box opens.

   A. In the Files of type: section, select AutoCAD (*.DXF).
   B. In the Look in: section, select the drive for your CD-ROM.
      1. Select the 3dstudio folder.
      2. Click on Teapot1.dxf.
      3. Click on Open.

3. The Import DXF File box opens.

4. Click on OK. The teapot is imported into the scene.

5. Click on the Select and Move button and move it in front of the sphere, cylinder, and box in the Perspective window.

6. Choose the Select and Uniform Scale option and scale it up to about the same size as the other objects.

7. After it is scaled, move it again so that you have a good view and it is on the Perspective plane with the other objects.

8. You should now have a good view of the teapot with it selected in the Perspective viewport.

9. Click on the Modify button in the command panel.

10. Just underneath the Modify button in the Name window, rename the object Teapot.
11. In the Modifiers section, click on UVW Map.
12. In the Parameters section, click on Cylindrical and Cap.
13. You have just imported the .dxf file Teapot1.dxf, resized it, renamed it to Teapot, and given it UVW mapping coordinates.

Import a Texture (Bitmap) File from an Outside Source

1. In the Material Editor, click on the sphere in sample slot #6. The white outline around the box will appear.
2. If there is a + on the Maps bar in the Material Editor, click on it to open the rollout menu underneath. If there is a – on the Maps bar, move the display upward using the hand function of the cursor so you can see the rollout menu underneath.
3. In the area that opens underneath the Maps bar, click on the bar labeled None in the Maps column to the right of the Diffuse spinner.
4. The Material/Map Browser opens.
    A. In the Browse from: section, if New is not selected, click on it.
    B. Select Bitmap from the list in the large window.
    C. Click on OK.
5. The window underneath the sample boxes will now say Tex #7 and the Type: bar next to it will say Bitmap.
6. In the Bitmap Parameters section, there is a blank bar next to Bitmap:.
7. Click on this bar.
8. The Select Bitmap Image File box will open.
    A. In the Drives: window, select your CD-ROM drive.
    B. In the Folders: section, open the folder Texture on the CD-ROM.
    C. In the large box under File name:, click on ma019.tif. This is a marble texture file.
    D. Click on OK.
9. The marble texture on the file ma019.tif will appear on the sphere in sample slot #6.
10. Click on the Assign Material to Selection button. The teapot turns green, but you cannot see the texture. This is because you have not told the program to show this map in the viewport yet. Each time that you bring in a new bitmap from the material library or outside you have to tell the program to show that particular map in the viewport if you want it displayed there. Otherwise the details will only show up when you render the scene.
11. Click on the Show Map in Viewport button.

12. The marble texture appears on the teapot.

13. At this point you could manipulate the gizmo or change the settings in the **Coordinates** section of the Material Editor to alter the appearance of the map to whatever you desire.

14. Deselect the teapot.

15. Save the file as Exer6.max in whatever location you desire. Compare it with Proj6a.max on the CD-ROM.

LIGHTS, CAMERA, ACTION: ADDING LIGHTS, CAMERAS, AND ANIMATION TO YOUR SCENE

For the lighting designer as well as the other designers, one of the aspects of 3D Studio MAX that makes it so intriguing is the ability to add lighting instruments to a scene, color those lighting instruments, view the effects created by the lighting from different angles by using cameras, and animate the scene and create lighting cues. This section will cover the processes that allow you to create your lighting, view it from different camera angles, and then animate a light cue or create any other simple animation.

LIGHTS

 Lights are created much like other objects are created in 3D Studio MAX and can be moved, rotated, etc. in exactly the same way. You begin in the command panel with the Create button and then click on the **Lights** button. Below the **Object Type** bar you will see four buttons: **Omni**, **Directional**, **Target Spot**, and **Free Spot**. These are the four types of lights that you can create. Each type has its own characteristics and uses.

The Omni Light

An omni light is a point source of illumination. The light projects equally in all directions from an omni source. The omni light does not cast shadows and does shine right through objects. You can, however, instruct omni lights to not illuminate an object and set attenuation for them—choose an end to the beam beyond which no light will go. When you begin working on a scene in 3D Studio MAX, two invisible omni lights are provided so that you can see what you are doing. As soon as you add a light to the scene, these two sources of light are automatically turned off.

The Directional Light

Directional lights cast parallel rays of light much like a beam projector in the theatre. These are often used to simulate sunlight, moonlight, etc.

The Target Spot

The target spot can be thought of much as you would a stage lighting instrument. You can change its beam spread, soften or harden its edge, increase or decrease its range, etc. It casts shadows and lets you create other special effects.

The Free Spot

Free spots are the follow spots of 3D Studio MAX. They can be set up to follow an animated path or can be linked to another object so that when it moves the free spot moves with it.

I have been writing about these lights almost as though they were equivalent to stage lighting instruments. You should not think of them as a one-for-one substitution, however. In general you are trying to create a look to a scene in 3D Studio MAX that will require a lot more stage lighting instruments to create on stage. A good rule of thumb is the fewer the lights that you use to light a scene in the program, the better—not a bad rule of thumb for theatre either. One directional light, for example, will end up being translated onto a theatrical lighting plot as a dozen or so beam projectors or PARcans. The following exercise will take you through how to create the different kinds of lights, set their parameters, color them, etc.

Exercise No. 7: Creating and Using Lights

Open Proj7.max from the CD-ROM. Save the file as Exer7.max on a floppy disk or to your hard drive. This contains a simple scene that will be used to show you the effects of the lights and their parameters. Make sure that the **Degradation Override** button on the status bar is depressed. You don't want the highlighted and shaded viewport—Perspective—to turn to wireframe on you when you are trying to set up lights.

Omni Light

1. Click on the **Create** button in the command panel.
2. Click on the **Lights** button in the button line below it.
3. Click on the **Omni** button in the **Object Type** section.
4. In the **Top** viewport, click and drag to create the omni light.
5. Typically, as with most lights, as soon as these lights are created, the next step is to move them into position.
   A. Working in the **Top** and **Front** viewports, select and move the light up and into the suspended lampshade over the center of the table. As you are moving it about, watch your **Perspective** viewport to get a feeling for what is happening with the light coming from this source.
   B. Think of this light as your practical for the scene.

6. Name the light **Practical** in the **Name and Color** box.

7. Click on the **Modify** button in the command panel. The modifiers, modifier stack, and general parameters for the light open.

A. Set the color:

   1. Click on the grey button between the On box and the Exclude button in the **Color** section.

   2. This opens the **Color Selector** box. You can use this box to choose the color for the light much like you used it in the Material Editor earlier or you can just use the RGB and/or HSV spinners in the Color area.

   3. For the time being, just set **RGB** values of R: 211, G: 211, and B: 180 and HSV values of H: 43, S: 37, and V: 211 to give us an unsaturated, warm light from the practical. You can always come back and change this later. After you have set the color you will notice that the grey button now takes on the color that you have set.

B. The **Multiplier** spinner: The **Multiplier** spinner at the bottom of the color section can be thought of as somewhat equivalent to your dimmer. It initially comes on at a low level—1. Each time you change the number in the multiplier, you multiply the intensity of the light source by that amount. Set it to 2, for example, and you will have twice as much light coming from the omni. Set it to .5 and you will have half as much light coming from the omni. Scroll the multiplier up and down to see the effect, but return it to 1 for the time being.

C. The **On** box: The **On** box lets you turn the light on and off to see its effect. Click in the box to turn it off. Click again to turn it on.

D. The **Exclude** button: The **Exclude** button lets you pick objects that you don't want to be hit by the light. Click on it, and the **Exclude/Include** box opens. On the left is a list of all of the objects in the scene. Click on an object to select it and then click on the arrow that points to the box on the right to move it into the **Exclude** category. You can move it back by clicking on it in the box on the right and then clicking on the arrow pointing to the box on the left.

   1. Select **Table Base** and move it to the **Exclude** box on the right.

   2. Select **Cyc** and move it to the **Exclude** box on the right.

   3. Click on **OK**.

E. **Attenuation:** The attenuation settings control where the light coming from the omni begins and ends. Right now, both of these are set pretty high. Click on the **Show** box. Two spheres will appear in the viewports. Actually, you will probably only see one—the one representing the **Start Range**. The one for the **End Range** is probably completely outside the viewports.

1. Set the start range to 3' so that the light will hit the tabletop.
2. Since you have excluded the cyc, you won't need to reset the end range to keep the omni light off of it.
3. Click on the Use box to turn the attenuation on.
4. Be sure that the Perspective viewport is active.
5. Do a quick render to see the effect of what you have done with the omni light. Occasionally the rendering function will not display its result. If this should happen—if no picture appears even though it seems to be trying to render—click on the name of another viewport and then click on the name of the Perspective viewport again to reselect it. Try the quick render again.
6. Notice in the rendering that the shade above the table seems to be illuminated even though it is outside of the start range of the omni light. This is because when I created the shade I made the material that is assigned to it both translucent, with an opacity setting of 50, and self-illuminating with a setting of 75. It is providing its own illumination. I did this for the same reason that we normally use low-wattage lamps in practicals on the stage. If I had tried to use the omni to illuminate it by setting the start range at 1 inch, it would have appeared intensely bright in the scene because the omni is so close. By setting the start range of the omni beyond the shade and making the shade self-illuminating, I was able to control the intensity of both separately.
   F. Deselect the omni light—Edit/Select None.

Ambient Light

Remember that I earlier said that when you create a light source in 3D Studio MAX the two initial omnis are automatically turned off. This is true, but there still may be some ambient light that the program places in the scene. This light can also be controlled as to color and intensity. The lower the level of ambient light the higher the contrast in the scene. The higher the level of ambient light the more washed-out the scene looks. You can also use colored ambient light to tint the entire scene. The best practice is often to set your ambient light to black and then add it and color it as desired after you have applied all the other lights. This lets you see the individual effect of the other lights before making the decision about whether to use ambient light. The control for the ambient light is under the pull down menu Rendering in the Environment section.

1. Click on Rendering/Environment.
2. The Environment box opens.
   A. Click on the box underneath the words Ambient Light:.
   B. The Color Selector box opens.

1. You can use the **Hue** box on the left or the **RGB** spinners to control the color.
2. The value (V:) spinner controls the intensity.

C. For now, set the ambient light to black and exit the box by clicking on **Close** on the Color Selector box and then on the X in the upper right-hand corner of the Environment box.

Target Spot

The target spot is the most versatile light that is available in 3D Studio MAX. You can control the size of the beam, the shape of the beam—circular and rectangular—and the color of the beam and you can project images through it. You could even scan in a gobo and project that through it if you wanted. You are going to create a target spot to light the cyc behind the table and chairs in the scene.

1. Click on the **Create** button on the command panel.
2. Click on the **Lights** button in the row underneath.
3. Click on the **Target Spot** button in the **Object Type** section.
4. To create and aim the target spot, you click and drag:
   A. Click to the right side of the floor circle in the **Top** viewport and then drag the cursor in the direction of and all the way to the cyc. Release the mouse button and you will have created and aimed the target spot.
   B. At the point where you clicked, there will be a white triangle that designates the position of the light. There is also a set of XYZ axes located there. In the direction that you dragged the cursor, there will be a blue cone formed with a yellow box at the center of its base. This is the target that gives the spot its name.
5. Reposition the spot and refine its aim. I had you position the spot where you did and drag as much as you did so that you could more easily sort out one end of the spot from the other. If you only do a click and a short drag, it can be quite difficult to see the whole spotlight and its target point. I also wanted you to get off to the side of and away from other objects so that when you tried to move the light later you didn't start accidentally selecting other objects instead.
   A. Click on the **Select and Move** button on the toolbar.
   B. Select the white triangle that is the light itself in the **Front** viewport and move the light directly above the table and the lampshade and about on line with the center top of the cyc.
   C. Refine this position in the **Left** viewport so that it is directly above the lampshade and on line with the top of the cyc.
   D. In the **Front** viewport, select the yellow box that is the target point for the spot. It will turn white. Move it so that it is aimed at the center of the cyc.

E. Refine this position in the Left viewport so that it is directly behind the center of the cyc. Don't worry that the cone, which represents the spread of the spot, doesn't cover the entire cyc. You will change this later.

6. Select the target spot itself rather than its "target." The spot itself is indicated on the screen by the white triangle that shows its position. The target is indicated by the yellow box. You can also select the target spot by using the Select by Name button.

7. Name the spotlight: In the Name and Color box of the command panel, rename the spotlight Cyc Light.

8. Click on the Modify button in the command panel and the modifiers, modifier stack, and general parameters for the cyc light will open. As you are about to see, there are considerably more parameters for a target spot than there were for the omni. Move the cursor over to the command panel below the General Parameters bar to a space where it turns into a hand. Click and drag the General Parameters section upward so that you can see all of the options, or for now at least the top part. Let's start with the General Parameters section. This should look fairly familiar, as it is similar to the one you worked with on the omni.

General Parameters

1. Color: Click on the Color button between the Exclude button and the On box. When the Color Selector box opens, make the color a light blue. Set the following values: R: 180, G: 231, B: 236; H: 131, S: 61, V: 236. Click on OK.

2. Exclude the Table Top, Floor, Bowl, and Shade so that you do not hit them when you expand the size of the spot.

3. Attenuation: Show the attenuation. Change the Start Range: to 6' and the End Range: to 35'. This should put its end range behind the cyc. Click on Use to activate attenuation.

Spotlight Parameters

1. Hotspot and Falloff spinners: You can think of these as similar to the beam angle and field angle of a lighting instrument with a couple of differences. First of all, they are calculated in degrees. The hotspot is the bright center of the light; the falloff defines where the edge of the light is located. They also control the sharpness of the light, however, unlike beam angle and field angle. If the hotspot and the falloff are the same, you will have the hardest edge. As the hotspot and falloff get farther apart, the edge gets softer. Let's give this spot a fairly sharp edge.

A. Set the Hotspot to 80 degrees.

B. Set the Falloff to 85 degrees.

2. **Circle** and **Rectangle** Options: Clicking in either the circle next to **Circle** or the one next to **Rectangle** lets you choose a circular or rectangular beam of light. Since you are trying to light just the cyc with this instrument, click on **Rectangle**. If you look carefully at the beam of light coming out of the instrument, as shown by the lighter blue and darker blue lines, you will notice that this isn't really a rectangle. Actually, it's a square. That is because you haven't adjusted the aspect ratio yet.

3. The **aspect ratio** is controlled in the spinner next to **Asp:**. The aspect ratio is a number that is produced by taking the width of a rectangle and dividing by the height. A square has an aspect ratio of 1. A rectangle twice as high as it is wide has an aspect ration of .5. A rectangle twice as wide as it is high has an aspect ratio of 2. For this scene, enter an aspect ratio of **1.7**. This should give you a rectangle that fits the size of the cyc nicely with some to spare. Now might also be a good time to take a look at just how well your instrument is aimed. Do you need to readjust the position of the target point so that the entire cyc is covered by the light coming from this instrument?

4. **Overshoot:** When this option is checked, the instrument casts light in all directions, but only casts shadows within its falloff arc. Do *not* check this box as part of this exercise.

5. **Show Cone:** When this box is checked, the blue cones that show the hotspot and falloff will also be seen when the instrument is not selected. With the box unchecked, you will only see the cones when the instrument is selected. Leave this unchecked for now.

6. **Projector:** Check this box to use the target spot as a projector to project an image that you have selected from the material/map library or one that you have scanned into a file such as your own gobo, photograph, etc. The **Assign** button and the button to the right of **Map:** are used in assigning a material or map to the target spot when it is used as a projector. Click on the **Projector** box so that a check appears.

   A. Assigning a material/bitmap from the material library as an image:
      1. Click on the **Assign** button. The **Map/Material Browser** opens.
      2. Click on **Browse from: Material Library**. If the library does not open, you will have to open it in the **File:** section of the browser.
      3. Click on **Tex #3 (Bitmap) FOLIAGE.tga**.
      4. Click on **OK**. That name appears on the blank button next to **Map:**.
      5. Click on the button next to **Map:**.
      6. The **Put to Material Editor** box opens. Here you can select which sample slot that you would like to use in the Material Editor. If slot #1 is not selected, select slot #1 by clicking on it. Click on **OK** to assign the map to slot #1.

7. Open the Material Editor. Here you can do any editing that you would like on the map such as changing the tiling, angle, etc. For now, let's leave this area alone. Be sure that slot #1 does have the white outline around it, however.

8. Close the Material Editor.

9. Now let's go back to the general parameters Color section and change the color and intensity so we can get a brighter image out of the bitmap.

    a. Click on the blue-colored button to open the Color Selector.

    b. Change the color to white and set these values: R: 255, G: 255, B: 255, H: 0, S: 0, V: 255.

    c. If after you look at the rendered image you still think that you need more intensity, you could also run up the multiplier. Increase the multiplier to 2.

10. Make sure that the Perspective viewport is active and do a quick render to see what the scene looks like. Close the rendering that opens by clicking on the X in the upper right-hand corner. Now let's change the bitmap to one that is imported from outside the material library such as one that you have scanned in yourself into a file.

B. Assigning a material/bitmap from outside the program as an image:

1. Return to the Spotlight Parameters section and click on Assign.

2. The Material/Map Browser opens.

3. Click on New in the Browse from: section. Click on Bitmap in the large box on the right. Click on OK.

4. Click on the button next to Map: The Put To Material Editor box opens. Make sure that slot #1 is selected and click on OK.

5. Open the Material Editor. Notice that in slot #1, there is a big black sphere. You have not actually selected a bitmap to place in the slot yet.

6. In the Bitmap Parameters section of the Material Editor, click on the large blank button next to Bitmap:.

7. The Select Bitmap Image File box opens.

    a. Here is where you would locate the file that you had scanned in or had available from another source on a 3.5-inch disk, CD-ROM, etc. For now, though, you'll use a file in the texture folder on the CD-ROM that came with the book.

    b. Under Drives:, select the CD-ROM drive.

    c. Under Folder:, select the texture folder.

    d. In the large box under File name: click on the file s152.tif.

    e. Click on OK.

8. The file s152.tif appears on the sphere in slot #1. This is another of the files from Judy Juracek's *Surfaces* book. There are hundreds more on the CD-ROM that accompanies the book.

9. Now would be the time to make changes in the Coordinates section of the Material Editor such as tiling, angle, etc. For the time being, though, do not make any changes.

10. Close the Material Editor and do a quick render to see the result.

11. Close the rendering.

C. Further notes on using the target spot as a projector: In addition to using files from outside sources such as *Surfaces*, the number of sources available are limited only by your ability as a researcher and the availability of a scanner. Find a photograph, drawing, gobo, etc. and scan it onto a 3.5-inch disk using your scanner. Save it on the disk as a .gif, .jpeg, .tga, .tif, .rla, .ifl, or .flc file. Then follow the process outlined above to assign it to the projector from your a: drive instead of the CD-ROM drive in the Select Bitmap Image File box.

You may have also noticed the keystoning that occurred in the images because the projector is located above the lampshade. While this is a real problem with projecting images in the theatre, in 3D Studio MAX you can easily overcome the problem by dropping the projector down to a position straight out from the front of the cyc, screen, or backdrop. Then use the Exclude button to exclude every-thing in the scene except the cyc, screen, or backdrop. You now have one of those wonderful instruments that we all wish we really had that can project right through a piece of furniture without leaving an image on the furniture or casting shadows.

7. The projector was fun, but let's get back to the lit cyc so you can do some other effects on it using just lighting instruments.

A. Click on the Projector box to remove the check and turn it off.

B. Restore the color readings of R: 180, G: 231, B: 236, H: 131, S: 61, V: 236.

C. Change the multiplier to .5.

Shadow Parameters

The Shadow Parameters area lets you make choices about what kind of shad-ows you would like the program to create from the target spot. The options available are not necessarily the ideal ones. If you want soft-edged shadows, for example, you must use shadow maps, but this method of producing shad-ows is not as accurate as ray tracing. Consider starting with one method and then after the lighting is completed and you have looked at the rendering try-ing the other method so you can see the difference.

1. The **Cast Shadows** box: If this box is checked, the instrument will cast shadows, if unchecked it will not. If you are using the target spot as a projector, this box must be checked.

2. The **Use Global Settings** box: If you have chosen to cast shadows, then you must decide what kind.

    A. Check this box if you want the settings below to apply to all target spots.

    B. Leave this box unchecked if you want these settings to apply to just the selected target spot. Once this choice is made for one target spot you will have to make the choices below for all of them.

3. The **Use Shadow Maps/Ray Traced Shadows** circles: You can click on one or the other of these circles.

    A. **Shadow maps** are generated during the rendering process. Shadow maps can have soft-edged shadows. Ray traced shadows cannot. Ray traced shadows are more accurate than shadow maps but take more calculation time.

    B. **Ray traced shadows** always produce a hard edge. Ray tracing is the only method that will produce shadows from wireframe objects and cast accurate shadows from translucent and transparent objects.

4. Settings for shadow maps and ray traced shadows: The boxes and spinners below the Use Shadow Maps/Ray Traced Shadows circles are settings that you adjust depending upon which of the choices you have made.

    A. **Map Bias:** This is used only for shadow maps. Decreasing or increasing the setting moves the shadow closer to or further away from the object casting the shadow.

    B. **Size:** This sets the size of the shadow. Higher settings will give you more detailed shadows and thus a harder edge. This is used only for shadow maps.

    C. **Smp Range:** The sample range is a shadow map setting. It also affects the edge of the shadow. Smaller settings produce harder-edged shadows. Larger settings produce softer-edged shadows.

    D. **Absolute Map Bias:** This is another shadow map setting. When checked, shadows are calculated for each individual object. When unchecked, shadows are calculated for the scene as a whole.

    E. **Ray Trace Bias:** This is the only ray traced setting. Decreasing and increasing the setting moves the shadow toward or away from the object.

    For the target spot used on the cyc, do not check either the **Cast Shadows** or the **Global Settings** box. If you were using the instrument as a projector, though, you would need to check the Cast Shadows box.

5. Deselect the cyc light.

The Directional Light

The directional light casts parallel rays of light that imitate sunlight or moonlight. One thing to keep in mind is that it casts light in both directions—in front of and behind the symbol in the scene. Setting the parameters for the directional light is very similar to setting those for the target spot, and many of the same options such as the ability to be used as a projector are available.

1. Click on the Create button in the command panel.
2. Click on the Lights button in the row underneath.
3. Click on the Directional button under Object Type.
4. You create the spot in the scene by clicking. A white box will appear in the viewport where you clicked with either a light blue and dark blue rectangle or circle outside of it depending upon whether the circle or rectangle option was last checked. If you look at the directional light box in another viewport, it will be an arrow indicating the direction of the light. The directional arrow will point down the Z axis of the box in which the spot was created. You will need to use the Rotate command to point the arrow in the direction that you would like.
5. Activate the Top viewport and zoom extents in that viewport.
6. Working in the Top viewport, click to create the directional light at a point on line with the center of the table and as far to the right in the viewport as you can. In the Top viewport, the light will look like a white box surrounded by two large, blue circles or rectangles. In the Front viewport, it will look like a white arrow perpendicular to a blue line. The arrow represents the direction in which the light is pointed. Think of the circle or rectangle as representing the size of the beam of light coming from the instrument. Remember that this light creates parallel rays, so the bigger the circle or rectangle, the bigger the beam of light.
7. Go to the Front viewport and move the light upward so that it is on line with about the middle of the cyc vertically.
8. Rotate the light so that the arrow is pointing at the table.
9. Go to the Name and Color box in the command panel and rename the light Sunlight.
10. Click on the Modify button in the command panel to change the parameters for the light.
   A. General Parameters:
      1. Change the color to a warm bastard amber: R: 226, G: 146, B: 92, H: 17, S: 151, V: 226.
      2. Change the multiplier to 1.3.
      3. Exclude the cyc.

B. Directional Parameters:
   1. Change the hotspot to 8'.
   2. Change the falloff to 8'6".
   3. If Rectangle is selected, select Circle.
C. Shadow Parameters:
   1. Put a check mark by Cast Shadows.
   2. Do *not* check Use Global Settings.
   3. Select Use Shadow Maps. Start with the settings as they are for the shadow map.
D. Activate the Perspective viewport and do a quick render. Take a close look at the shadows.
E. Change to Use Ray Traced Shadows. Do another quick render. Notice the difference in the shadows. Notice also that rendering the ray traced shadows takes considerably longer. After you have closed the Render window, change the shadow parameters back to Cast Shadows.
F. Now let's use the directional light to project a bitmap. The way that you apply a material/map for a directional light is exactly like the way you do it for the target spot.
   1. Reset the color to white: R: 255, G: 255, B: 255, H: 0, S: 0, V: 255.
   2. Click on Projector and then on the Assign button.
   3. In the Material/Map Browser that opens, select the Material Library and open the library 3dsmax.mat if it isn't already open.
   4. Select Tex #15 (Bitmap) INFERNO.tga and click on OK.
   5. Click on the Map: button that has the name of the bitmap in it.
   6. The Put To Material Editor box opens. Select slot #1 and click on OK.
   7. Open the Material Editor. You should see the Inferno bitmap in slot #1. At this point, you could make changes in the coordinates such as tiling, angle, etc. if you wanted. For now, don't change anything.
   8. Close the Material Editor.
   9. Do a quick render.
   10. Deselect the directional light.
11. Save the scene as Exer7.max in the location of your choosing. Compare it with Proj7a.max on the CD-ROM.

CAMERAS

Now that you have created a scene and lit it in 3D Studio MAX, you are ready to try out a camera. As you have seen, you can render in any viewport, though usually you would want to use the Perspective viewport. Using cameras, however, gives you even more flexibility than using the Perspective viewport. The other advantage of using a camera is that you can animate the view. Cameras are created in 3D Studio MAX much like any other object, and they will appear in a viewport like an object. To create a camera, you click on the **Create** button in the command panel and then on the Camera button.

Exercise No. 8: Creating, Assigning, and Adjusting a Camera

1. Open your Exer7.max or Proj8.max from the CD-ROM.
2. Save the scene as Exer8.max on your hard drive or to a 3.5-inch disk.
3. Activate the **Top** viewport and zoom back so that there is about one and a half times as much space from the table to the bottom of the viewport as there is from the table to the cyc. You need to get back to a wider view so that you will have room to set up the camera.
4. Click on the **Create** button and then on the **Camera** button.
5. In the **Object Type** area, you have a choice of **Target** or **Free**.
   A. A **target camera** is aimed at a specific target or area that you create when you create the camera. This type is the best kind to use if the camera itself is not going to move along a path or trajectory.
   B. A **free camera** is the best kind of camera for when you want the camera to move along a path or trajectory.

   Click on **Target**.
6. You can create target cameras in the viewport by clicking on the camera position and then dragging to the target area.
   A. Click a little to the right of the bottom center of the **Top** viewport and then drag the cursor to just short of the center of the table. Release the mouse button, and you will have created a camera.
   B. Click on the **Select and Move** button. In the **Left** viewport, click on the camera—the white object with the XYZ axes by it—and move it upward so that it is about on line with the center of the cyc.
   C. Click on the camera's target—the dark blue box at the end of the blue line coming from the camera—and move it upward so that it is slightly above the table. This can be tricky. There are a lot of objects right there that you could accidentally select, such as the floor, table base, one of the chairs, etc. You may need to go to the **Select by Name** button, click on it, and after the **Select Objects** box opens, click on Camera01.Target, and hit the **Select** button. This is one of the reasons that I've been having you name objects, lights, etc.

If you assign a name to everything, it can be easier to use the Select by Name box when it becomes necessary in a crowded scene. You have now created a camera and aimed it in a general direction. Let's assign it to a viewport so that you can see the camera's view and adjust it.

7. Activate the **Perspective** viewport and then right click on its name in the upper left-hand corner of the viewport.

   A. Click on **Views** and then on **Camera01**.

   B. The viewport changes to **Camera01**. You are now looking at the view through the lens of the camera.

   C. Go to the **Select by Name** box and select **Camera01**.

   D. Working in the **Top** and **Left** viewports, move the camera around until the view in the **Camera01** viewport is looking slightly down onto the table and includes most of the floor. The view should let you see the cyc, but not its top or side edges. The view should also let you see the hanging lamp above the table. It is usually much easier to achieve this kind of view with the camera than it is working in the Perspective viewport using the Arc Rotate, Zoom, and Pan buttons. After working with both the Perspective viewport and camera viewports, most designers usually end up using camera viewports. You will also notice that some of the navigation controls down on the lower right-hand corner of the screen have changed. You now have some controls specific to the camera.

Camera Navigation Controls

 The **Dolly Camera** Button: For a target camera, this moves the camera in and out of the scene along a line with its target. Click and drag the mouse in the **Camera** viewport to dolly. If you go past the target, the camera flips around and points back at the target. This is sort of like the **Zoom** control in the Perspective viewport.

 The **Perspective** Button: This acts sort of like a cross between field of view and dolly. It maintains the composition of the scene, but changes the perspective flare. Click and drag in the **Camera** viewport after the button is activated.

 The **Roll Camera** Button: This rotates the camera around a horizontal plane, that is, it tilts it from side to side. Click and drag horizontally in the viewport after the button is activated.

The **Truck Camera** Button: This is the same button that was used for pan in the Perspective viewport. It moves the camera and its target parallel to the viewing plane.

The **Orbit/Pan Camera** Button: The detent on the corner of the button indicates that there is a pop-up button underneath. The **Orbit** button rotates the camera around its target. The **Pan** button rotates the target around the camera.

Take a little time to work with each of the above buttons so you can get an idea of its operation. When you are finished, return to a view close to the one that you had at the beginning.

8. Make sure that **Camera01** is still selected. Click on the **Modify** button in the command panel. The **Camera Parameters** area opens underneath. Make a note of the **Lens:** and **FOV:** settings. You will want to return to these later. These are the basic parameters that you might want to consider changing:

   A. **Lens:** This spinner lets you set any lens for the camera that you would like, in millimeters (mm).

   B. **FOV:** The field of view for the camera can be set here, in degrees.

   C. **Stock Lenses:** Clicking on any of these buttons lets you pick a standard camera lens. Click on several to see what the standard lenses look like, but reset your **Lens:** and **FOV:** spinners to the settings you made a note of earlier when you are finished.

   D. **Show Cone:** When checked, the camera's field of view will be displayed in the noncamera viewports if the camera is not selected. If the camera is selected, the FOV will be displayed regardless of whether the box is checked.

   E. **Show Horizon:** When checked, the camera's horizon line will appear in the viewports as a dark grey line.

9. Get back into the view of the scene with the camera described earlier and do a quick render.

10. Deselect the camera.

11. Save the scene as **Exer8.max** in a location on your hard drive or to a 3.5-inch disk.

12. Compare what you have done in **Exer8.max** with **Proj8a.max** on the CD-ROM.

BASIC ANIMATION

This section will take you through a simple animation such as you might use to demonstrate a lighting cue. Since this book is intended primarily for the theatrical designer, it will not cover the extensive animation capabilities that are possible with 3D Studio MAX. If you are seriously interested in animation, I recommend that you spend some time with the *Tutorial* book that accompanies the program. In particular, *Tutorial 9* deals with using the Track List function of 3D Studio MAX and how to use it to create more complex animations. It covers animation in depth and gives clear and relatively easy-to-follow directions and examples.

For a simple animation such as a light cue or a scenery shift, the first element that you need to consider is time. How long is the light cue going to take, for example? The next element to consider is the number of frames per second that you want to use to show the animation. The standard animation format is around thirty frames/sec. If you are going to show objects moving and want them to move smoothly, you are probably going to have to use twenty to thirty frames/sec. For a light cue, however, you may be able to use a lower frame per second rate of ten to twenty frames/sec. After creating a few animations you will learn what rate you can use to show the effects that you want to demonstrate. Why is this important? Why not just use the standard 30 frames/sec. rate for everything? The answer lies in the size of the file that is created in animation. Animation files are very large. The time of the animation multiplied by the number of frames per second gives you the number of frames that you are going to have to use to do the animation. So for a ten-second animation at a rate of 30 frames/sec, you would have to set up a three hundred-frame animation. When you render an animation, each frame is rendered separately and then played back at the 30 frames/sec. rate. Each separately rendered frame takes about 10 Kb of file size using the smallest screen size available in 3D Studio MAX—320 × 240 pixels. So even using the smallest screen size, a ten-second animation at 30 frames/sec. will produce a file of 3 MB in size. A standard 3.5-inch disk will only hold 1.4 MB. Unless you have a Zip drive or a tape drive you will have to keep these animation files on your hard drive. If you are short of hard drive space, animation files will eat up that space very quickly. It is very important that you understand how to place files on your hard drive in folders and how to locate those files later so that you can delete them when they are no longer needed. Otherwise it won't take long before you have run out of space on the hard drive. If you don't already understand how to place, locate, and delete files from your hard drive, you will need to learn how before you start creating animation files.

Once you have decided on the length of the animation and the frames/sec. rate that you want to use, multiply the two together to give you the number of frames that you will need to create. In the exercise below you will be creating a twenty-second light cue at a rate of 20 frames/sec. You will need four hundred frames to create this cue. It is also important to understand the frame rate so that you can place changes in the animation accurately. If you are creating a multiple-part light cue, you may have different changes occurring at different points in time. Say, for example, that you have a change that is to start at the beginning of the cue and then finish seven seconds into the cue. That change would have to be placed in frame 140—20 frames/sec. × 7 sec. Any frame where a change is located in an animation sequence is known as a *key frame*. Key frames mark the end of one change and the beginning of another. In multiple-part animations, that means that you will have to create overlapping changes in parts. Say, for example, that you had two lights changing in the cue, or animation sequence, and you wanted one light to fade up in a 10 count and the second one to fade out in a 20 count, with both of them starting their fades at the same point in time. At the beginning of the animation sequence, you would have the first light out and the second light up. Let's assume a 20 frame/sec. rate. At frame 200, you would turn the first light up and the second light halfway out. Then at frame 400, you would turn the second light all the way out. When you ran the animation sequence, the animator would take the first ten seconds to take the first light completely up and the second light halfway out and then the second ten seconds to take the second light the rest of the way out. If, on the other hand, you had placed the complete change for the first light in frame 200 with no change in the second light occurring in that frame and placed the complete change for the second light in frame 400, the following would happen: The first light would take ten seconds to come up, but the change in the second light would not begin until frame 200, or ten seconds into the animation. The second light would then take the last ten seconds of the animation to go out.

If you were using animation to demonstrate the sequence of a scene shift, understanding this principle also becomes very important. The timing of moving wagons about on stage so that they clear one another could be worked out and demonstrated using an animation sequence.

 You use the **Time Configuration** button to open the **Time Configuration** box. In the Time Configuration box, you can set the number of frames in the animation and the frame rate.

After you have the number of frames in the animation and the frame rate set, you can begin creating the animation sequence. Start with the scene set up for the beginning of the cue or change. Save that scene. Use the **time slider** to go to the frame number where the first change will finish. This is a key frame.

Turn on the Animation button. Make the changes in the scene that are to happen between the beginning and that frame number. Move the time slider to the frame number where the next set of changes will finish. Make the changes in the scene that will happen between the last key frame and this one. Continue making changes in each key frame until you reach the end of the animation sequence. After changes have been made in the last frame, turn off the Animation button and save the scene. Next the scene will have to be rendered. Then you will be able to play it back.

Exercise No. 9: Animating a Lighting Cue

To set up a simple animation you begin by saving a scene with the starting setup in an animation frame. You go to a new animation frame and make changes in the scene. The scene is then rendered to an animation format (.avi). This exercise will take you through some changes in the scene for which you have just set up lights and a camera in the last two exercises. You will be creating a multiple-part light cue for the scene and then watching the cue happen.

1. Open Exer8.max from your location or Proj9.max from the CD-ROM.
2. Save it as Exer9.max to a location on your hard drive or to a 3.5-inch disk.
3. Click on the Time Configuration button to open the Time Configuration box.
    A. In the Frame Rate area, click on the circle next to Custom.
    B. In the FPS: window, reset the spinner to 20.
    C. In the Animation: area, reset the length to 400 and the end time to 400.
    D. In the Time Display area, there should be a dot in the circle next to Frames.
    E. Click on OK. The time slider should be located at the far left side of the screen just under the Left viewport and should read 0/400.
4. Next let's set up a beginning light cue for the scene. You are going to set up a sunset cue that will be changed to a night cue with the practical coming on at the end of the cue.
    A. Click on the Select by Name button and select the Cyc Light. Click on the Modify button.
    B. In the General Parameters section of the command panel, make the following changes to the Cyc Light.
        1. Change the color to more of a sunset color: R: 236, G: 116, B: 56, H: 14, S: 194, V: 236.
        2. Change the multiplier to 1.5.

C. Next let's kick up the intensity of the side light a little bit:
   1. Select the Sunlight directional light. The Modify button should already be active and its parameters will appear in the command panel.
   2. Change the multiplier to 1.4.
   3. Under Shadow Parameters, select Use Shadow Maps. This will speed up the rendering.
D. Let's also add a light like the Sunlight light, but from the other side of the stage in a different color for moonlight later in the scene. The easy way to do this is to make a copy of the Sunlight directional light, move it into its new position, and then change its parameters. You will then run it down on the multiplier until it is needed.
   1. Activate the Top viewport.
   2. Click on the Select and Move button. Select the Sunlight instrument.
   3. Hold the cursor over the Sunlight instrument. The single cursor arrow should change to four small black ones that form crosshairs.
   4. Depress the Shift key.
   5. Click and drag the mouse to the left side of the viewport. When you get to a position about the same distance away from the table on the left side of the viewport, release the mouse button and Shift key.

   Note: The clone of the instrument that you created by this method will lag well behind the cursor while you're dragging it. It will catch up with the position where you released the mouse button. Give it a little while before you do anything else.

   6. The Clone Options box will open.
      a. Make sure that there is a dot in the circle next to Copy.
      b. Rename the instrument Moonlight.
      c. Click on OK.
   7. Re-aim the instrument:
      a. Use the Rotate command to turn it around 180 degrees so that it is pointed back at the table.
      b. In the Front viewport, move it up so that it is about on line with the top of the cyc.
      c. Then use the Rotate command to point it down at the table.
      d. When you are done, the instrument should be on the opposite side of the scene from the Sunlight instrument, but higher vertically and still pointing at the table.

8. The Modify box should still be open, but with the copy Moonlight in it now.
 a. At this point you might want to do a quick render to check the focus and then readjust the way the instrument is aimed. Be sure that you activate the Camera01 viewport before you do the quick render.
 b. Under Directional Parameters, remove the check from the Projector box.
 c. Change the color to a pale slightly grey-blue: R: 163, G: 195, B: 207, H: 139, S: 54, V: 207.
 d. Change the multiplier to .7.
 e. Check under Shadow Parameters: to see that Cast Shadows and Use Shadow Maps are checked.
9. Change the multiplier to 0 under General Parameters. It will be run back up at a later frame in the animation. Do not use the On/Off box to turn the instrument off. The On/Off box seems to confuse the animation, and the wrong instrument might come up.

E. Turn the Practical light way down:
 1. Select the Practical omni light.
 2. Change the multiplier to .5.

F. Remember though that the shade is self-illuminating and has to be changed as well.
 1. Select the shade. The Modify button is still selected.
 2. Open the Material Editor. Activate sample slot #2. This should be the green Material #2, which is what was used on the shade. The white outline should appear around the sample slot and triangles should be in the corners to indicate that it is hot. You probably didn't remember that you used Material #2 for the shade, did you? If you had renamed this material before you applied it to the shade then it would have been easier to find now. You could have just gone to the material library for the scene and selected Shade Material or a name like that. I just wanted to give you an example of the importance of renaming materials before you apply them so that they can be found later.
 3. Under Basic Parameters in the Material Editor:
  a. Change self-illumination to 25.
  b. Change opacity to 75.
 4. In the Name window under the sample slots, rename Material #2 as Shade Material.
 5. Click on the Assign Material to Selection button.

6. Close the Material Editor.

7. Deselect the shade—Edit/Select None.

5. Make sure that the Camera01 viewport is active and do a quick render, just so you can see what the scene looks like.

6. Make sure that the time slider underneath the Left viewport reads 0/400, meaning frame 0 of 400.

7. Save the scene—File/Save.

8. Go to frame 380: Move the time slider to the right so that it reads 380/400.

9. Turn on the Animate button. Notice that there is a red frame around the Camera01 viewport.

10. Now let's change to the night scene without turning on the Practical instrument.

   A. Select the Cyc Light instrument. The Modify button should still be active.
      1. Change the Cyc Light color to a deep blue: R: 56, G: 56, B: 120, H: 170, S: 136, V: 120.
      2. Change the multiplier to 1.0.

   B. Select the Sunlight instrument. The Modify button should still be active. You are going to run it down. In the command panel:
      1. Under General Parameters, change the multiplier to 0.

   C. Select the Moonlight instrument. The Modify button should still be active. You are going to run it up. In the command panel:
      1. Under General Parameters, change the multiplier to .7.

11. Go to frame 390: Move the time slider to the right so that it reads 390/400. This is a half-second after the sun has finished setting.

12. Now let's turn on the overhead lamp, but in two parts with the shade coming up first and then the omni light coming up a half-second later. The slight delay will give the overhead lamp coming on just a little bit more realistic appearance.

   A. Select the shade.
      1. Open the Material Editor.
      2. Click on sample slot #2. The Name window should read Shade Material and there should be a red outline around sample slot #2.
      3. Under Basic Parameters in the Material Editor:
         a. Change the self-illumination to 75.
         b. Change the opacity to 50.
      4. Click on the Assign Material to Selection button.

13. Go to frame 400: Move the time slider to the right so that it reads 400/400.

   A. Select the **Practical** instrument. This is the omni light inside the shade.

      1. The **Modify** button should still be on and the parameters for the practical should appear in the command panel.

      2. Change the multiplier to .7.

      3. Deselect the practical instrument.

14. Turn off the **Animate** button.

15. Save the scene—Ctrl + S or File/Save.

16. Next the scene has to be rendered, but not using quick render as you have so far.

   A. Click on the **Render Scene** button. The **Render Scene** box opens.

   B. Select **Active Time Segment** in the **Time Output** area.

   C. Select 320×240 in the **Output Size** area.

   D. Click on the **Files** button in the **Render Output** area. The **Render Output File** box opens.

      1. Under **List types of files:**, click on the arrow to the right of the window.

      2. Click on **AVI File (*.avi)** in the pullout that opens.

      3. In the small window under **File name:**, double click to the right of *.avi.

      4. *.avi should be highlighted.

      5. Type in **Exer9.avi**.

      6. Directly under **Folders:** it should read C:\3DSMAX\Images. This would save the file to the **Images** subfolder under the **3DSMAX** folder on your hard drive. If you know how to get there so that you can delete this file later, don't change anything. If you want to change the folder or subfolder on your hard drive that the file will be saved in, now is the time to do it. If you want to change the location the file is saved in, double click on the **C:** folder in the large window underneath **Folders:**. Scroll the window up and down to locate the folder in which you would like to place the file. Double click on that folder. If it is to go into a subfolder under that folder then double click on the subfolder you want. When you have got the save path for your hard drive set up properly you are ready to proceed. Remember where you put this file so that you can delete it later. This will be a large file and it cannot be saved to a 3.5-inch disk.

      7. Click on **OK**.

    E. The Video Compression box opens. Click on OK.

    F. Make sure that the Save File box is checked in the Render Output area.

    G. Click on the Render button.

    H. The scene is rendered frame by frame, one frame at a time. This will take a while—go get a cup of coffee or a soft drink.

17. When the rendering is complete, close the window in which the rendering was done.

18. Click on File on the pull down menu bar, then on View File.

19. The View File box opens. Under List files of type:, select AVI File (*.avi).

20. Under Folders: you will need to select the folder and possibly the subfolder to which you saved the file Exer9.avi.

21. When you have the correct folder, the file name Exer9.avi will appear in the large box under File name:.

22. In the large box under File name:, click on Exer9.avi.

23. Exer9.avi should move up to the small box under File name:.

24. Click on OK.

25. The Media Player should open with a window underneath showing the opening frame of the scene.

26. Click on the Play button, usually a single arrow that faces to the right, to play the scene.

27. You have just animated your first scene in 3D Studio MAX and played back the animation. You can compare your work with Proj9.avi on the CD-ROM.

RENDERING AND EXPORTING RENDERINGS TO OTHER PROGRAMS

You have already learned how to do a quick render and how to render an animation in 3D Studio MAX. This section will explain about the other options available in the Render box. Rendering in 3D Studio MAX serves several purposes. First of all, it lets you see the highest resolution of all of the materials and effects in the program. Many materials, bitmaps, etc. are not fully displayed in the viewports and have to be rendered for you to be able to see their effects. The second function of rendering is letting you convert the rendering into another format that can be viewed and/or printed with another program. 3D Studio MAX does not have its own printing function. If you want to print out a copy of a rendering, you will have to save it as a file that is compatible with another program, open that file in the other program, and then print it from the other program. Files from 3D Studio MAX can be printed in a program such as Painter and can also be used as the basis for a more stylized rendering. The details of that procedure will be explained later in this book.

 The Render Scene button opens the Render Scene box. Here is where you set up the specifications for your rendering and make decisions about size, style, etc. This is also where you instruct the program to render for an animation. The major features of the Render Scene box are described below.

The Common Parameters Section

The Time Output Section

Single: Select this option if you just want to do a single rendering of the scene in the currently active viewport. Use this option unless you are doing an animation.

Active Time Segment: This is the most common option used for animation. It renders each frame of the animation one at a time.

Range: This lets you select a range of frames from an animation sequence to render.

Frames: This lets you select whatever specific frames from an animation sequence to render. Separate the frame numbers with a comma when entering the ones you want to render.

The Output Size Section

This is where you determine the size of the rendering. The buttons let you pick standard formats that correspond in aspect ratio—width/height—to the sizes available in the viewports. The numbers are in pixels. These relate to the following dimensions in inches: 320×240 = 4.444 inches × 3.333 inches, 256×243 = 3.556 inches × 3.375 inches, 512×486 = 7.111 inches × 6.75 inches, 640×480 = 8.889 inches × 6.667 inches, 720×486 = 10 inches × 6.75 inches, 800×600 = 11.111 inches × 8.333 inches. You can also enter your own format in pixels by using the Height: and Width: spinners. For the most part you are usually better off picking one of the standard formats. Trying to set up an unusual format can result in unwanted cropping and occasionally distortion.

The Options Section

Video Color Check: Use this to check video color compatibility.

Force 2-Sided: This will render both the outside and inside of objects. This drastically increases rendering time.

Render Hidden Objects: This will render all objects in a scene, even those that are normally hidden such as cameras, lighting instruments, etc.

Render Atmospheric Effects: This will render special effects such as fog.

Super Black: This is used for video compositing. If you don't know what that means, leave it off for now.

Render to Fields: This is used for rendering for television monitors.

The Render Output Section

This is the section that controls the saving of a rendering to a file or some kind of attached device such as a video device. You have already used this section of the Render Scene box when you saved an animation. The catch to using this section is that you have to know that you want to save the rendering before you see it. If you decide that you want to save a rendering using this section and then after it is displayed you decide that you don't want the file, it has already been recorded in whatever location you determined. You will then have to locate that file using Windows Explorer or My Computer in Window95 or NT and delete the file—just another reason why you need to know your way around your hard drive and understand how to place files in locations that you can later find them and delete or move them.

The Files: button opens the Render Output File box. In this box you assign a name to a file, select a file type, and choose a location for the file that you are saving. Elements of the Render Output File box are:

The Drives: Section: If you click on the arrow next to the window under Drives:, a pullout will open where you can select the drive that you want to save the file on. The a: drive is usually the "floppy disk" drive on your computer. If you want to save the file to a 3.5-inch disk, you would click on this drive. The c: drive is usually your hard drive. It is possible for a computer to have more than one hard drive or for it to be given another name. You have to understand the drive system on your own computer in order to save files properly. If you are saving to your hard drive then the Folders: window above the Drives: window is also important. There will be more on this later. Although the a: drive is normally the 3.5-inch disk drive and the c: drive is usually the hard drive, there is often more variation in drive assignment from computer to computer. Most computers today have a CD-ROM drive, which is often called d: or e:, though not always. Remember that ROM stands for read only memory. You cannot save a file to a CD-ROM. Increasingly, many computers are coming with tape drives or Zip drives. These are devices that let you store files outside the computer and have much larger capacity than the 3.5-inch disk. A 3.5-inch disk will only let your store about 1.4 MB of information. A Zip drive will usually let you store around 100 MB of information and a tape drive from 4 to 8 GB of information. Given the size of many graphics files, these larger-capacity external storage systems are often a worthwhile investment. The letter assigned to them in the Files: area will vary from one computer to another and depend upon who was responsible for the installation of the system. You will need to find out how these drives are designated on your computer in order to use them.

The Folders: Section: The Folders: section of the box is your next stop after you have chosen a drive. All hard drives are divided up into sections or folders to help you locate files more easily. Think of your folders as a filing system. Whenever you install a program, most of the files associated with the operation of the program are placed in a folder that is created as part of the installation process. If you know the name of the folder then you can locate the parts of the program more easily. You can also create folders yourself to establish your own filing system and help you place and locate files more easily. Most CD-ROMs come with folders to divide up the information that is on them. It is also possible to create folders on a 3.5-inch disk, Zip drive, or tape drive. By making choices here, you decide where to place the file on your hard drive, Zip drive, etc.

The List files of type: Section: Clicking on the arrow next to the window under List files of type: allows you to select the type or format of file that you will be creating. Different programs use different types of files. If you want to use this file in Painter, for example, you will need to know what kind of files can be used in Painter. If you are creating an animation file you will need to know the kind of files your animation viewer uses. File type is designated by an extension—the three or four letters after the period. When you are giving a file a name you do not have to include an extension, but leaving it off will create a lot of problems for you further down the road. Always include extensions when naming a file. The following is a list of the file types you can create for a rendering and where those files can be used:

AutoDesk Flic Image File (*.flc, *.fli, *.cel): This is a file type used by AutoDesk for several of its animator programs. Unless you have one of these programs you will probably not want to use this file type.

AVI File (*. avi): This is one of the most common file types used in animation viewers. If you are creating an animation, this is the file type you will most likely use. Single AVI files can also be opened in Painter, but not in Adobe Photoshop.

BMP Image File (*.bmp): This is often referred to as a "bitmap" file. Do not confuse this use of the term with the way that 3D Studio MAX uses the term *bitmap* to refer to any file type that can be applied to an object as a texture. A BMP file is a type of graphic file used for display on computer monitors. Most of the icons that you see on your computer screen are BMP files. The BMP file is large in size. It can be opened in Painter, but not in Adobe Photoshop.

Encapsulated Postscript File (*.eps, *.ps): Used by many commercial printers, this type cannot be opened in Painter, but it can be opened in Adobe Photoshop.

JPEG File (*.jpg): A widely used compact graphic format, this file type can be opened in Painter, Adobe Photoshop, and many other graphic programs. It is a good choice for exporting a file to Painter or other graphics program.

PNG Image File (*png): This is a compact graphics file type that is intended to supplant the GIF file type. So far it has not found widespread use in spite of its advantages. It cannot be opened on Painter, Adobe Photoshop, or many other graphics programs.

RLA Image File (*.rla): This format lets you include separate channels for different elements of the graphics. It cannot be opened in Painter or Adobe Photoshop.

Targa Image File (*.tga): Originally developed for video, this is a widely used commercial graphics file type. These are relatively large files, but they have good detail. They can be opened in Painter, but not in Adobe Photoshop.

TIF Image File (*.tif): This is a popular graphics file format with commercial printers. It has a large file size, but excellent detail. It can be opened in Adobe Photoshop and in Painter.

The File name: Section: The File name: area has two parts. The small window under File name: is where you enter the name and extension of the file you want to create. If you want to save a rendering file as a .jpg type, for example, you would select .jpg as the file type and then enter the name that you are giving the file followed by .jpg here. The large box under File name: will show you the other file names of that type that are already included in the drive and folder that you have selected.

The OK Button: When you have got all of the above set up to your satisfaction, click on OK to save the file at the same time that it is being rendered.

The Cancel Button: If you want to get out of the Render File Output box without telling the Render Scene box to save a file, click on Cancel.

The Save File Box: If you want to save the rendering as a file, be sure that there is a check in this box.

The Bottom of the Render Scene Box

The Render Viewport: Box: The box to the right of Render Viewport: shows you the name of the currently active viewport that is about to be rendered.

The Render Button: When everything is set up and you want to create the rendering and save it to a file, if selected, click on this button.

The **Close** Button: If you want to leave the box without creating a rendering, but you want to save the settings that you have made, click on this button.

The **Cancel** Button: If you want to leave the box without creating a rendering and you want to cancel the settings that you have made, click on this button.

 The **Quick Render** Button: This lets you render the scene according to whatever settings are currently in the Render Scene box without opening the box.

The **Render Last** Button: This repeats the last rendering that you did.

SAVING A RENDERING TO A FILE AFTER THE RENDERING IS FINISHED

As I pointed out earlier, in order to save a rendering to a file using the **Render Scene** box, you must already know that you want to do so before you render the scene. This is certainly not always the case. There will be many times that you won't decide to save a rendering until after you have seen it. You can also do this in 3D Studio MAX. When a rendering is finished it will be displayed on the screen in a box that contains the rendering. In the upper left-hand corner on the blue bar, the name of the viewport being rendered is displayed. Just below that is a red button, a green button, a blue button, a black/white circle button, a button with an X on it and a button that looks like a 3.5-inch disk. By clicking on the red, green, and blue buttons you can disable the red, green, and/or blue channels of the image. Clicking on the black/white circle displays the alpha channel of the image. The X button clears the image from the screen but leaves the box open.

The button that looks like a 3.5-inch disk will allow you to save the image. Click on this button, and the **Browser Images for Output** box opens. This box is almost identical to the **Render Output File** box that I discussed earlier. Set it up by selecting the drive, picking the folder and subfolder if desired, picking the file type, and giving the file name in exactly the way that you would set up the Render Output File box. Then when you are ready to save the file, click on **OK**.

SAVING A RENDERING FOR USE IN PAINTER

If you want to use one of your renderings as the basis for a treatment in Painter, you will need to save it as a file that can be opened in Painter. The information given previously about the **Render Scene** box, **Render Output File** box, and the **Browser Images for Output** box tells you about the different ways that you can save the rendering to a file. There are decisions that you will have to make about the size of the rendering and the file type on which you may need some more information. Below I give some comparisons of file type sizes for typical renderings to help you decide how to choose the file type. The file types given in the chart below are the only types that you will be able to open in Painter. I also give some comparisons of different rendering sizes in the .jpg file type to help you decide how to choose the size of the rendering. These are typical file sizes. The exact size will vary some depending upon the content of the rendering.

Rendering Size	=	File Size in .jpg Format	Format	=	File Size for 320 × 240 Rendering
320 × 240	=	6 KB	.jpg	=	6 KB
640 × 480	=	16 KB	.tga	=	206 KB
720 × 486	=	17 KB	.bmp	=	226 KB
800 × 600	=	21 KB	.avi	=	18 KB

As you can see, the .jpg format produces the most compact file size. For small files such as a 320 × 240 rendering, this probably won't make a lot of difference, but after you get up into some of the larger rendering sizes it can mean a rather large file size. For example, an 800 × 600 rendering size in the .bmp format produces a file size of 1,407 KB or 1.4 MB, which is too large to fit on a 3.5-inch disk. For the purposes that you will be using these files in Painter, I would recommend that you use the .jpg format in a 640 × 480 rendering size. This should be adequate for most needs. You can always increase the size of the image once it is in Painter if you need to. Follow these steps to render and save a file using the **Render Scene** button:

1. Activate the viewport from which you want to render.
2. Click on the **Render Scene** button. The **Render Scene** box opens.
    A. Under **Time Output**, click on **Single**.
    B. Under **Output Size**, click on the **640×480** button.
    C. Under **Render Output**, click on the **File** button. The **Render Output File** box opens.
        1. Under **Drives:**, select the drive to which you want to save the file.
        2. Under **Folders:**, select the folder to which you want to save the file. This is usually unnecessary with the a: or 3.5-inch drive selected.
        3. Under **List files of type:**, select **JPEG File (*.jpg)**.
        4. In the small **File name:** box, clear the entry and type in your file name followed by .jpg.
        5. Click on **OK**. You are returned to the Render Scene box.
    D. Make sure that there is a check in the **Save file** box under **Render Output**.
    E. Click on the **Render** button. The scene will be rendered and saved to the file at the same time.

Note: If you want to save the rendering as a file after the rendering has already been done, click on the icon that looks like a 3.5-inch disk above the rendering. The Browse Images for Output box opens. Follow steps C1–C5 above.

PRINTING A RENDERING

You cannot print a rendering directly from 3D Studio MAX. You will have to save the rendering as a file using one of the methods outlined above. You can then open the file in another graphics program that handles that file type and print from that program. Painter will let you open file types of .jpg, .tga, .bmp, .tif, and .avi. Adobe Photoshop will let you open file types of .jpg, .eps, and .tif. If you are planning on using a program other than these two to print your renderings from 3D Studio MAX, check on what file types that program will let you open before you save the rendering to a file.

Exercise No. 10: Putting It All Together

The purpose of the following exercise is to give you practice working on a real set in 3D Studio MAX. This exercise uses the set for a production of *The Seagull* by Anton Chekhov, which was designed by Marianne Custer and performed at The University of Tennessee. You'll be dealing with Act I, but there are also renderings and ground plans included on the CD-ROM for Acts II–IV as well if you'd like to continue the exercise on your own. This set was designed for a thrust theatre in which the audience surrounds the stage on three sides. As you work through the exercise, various features of the set will be described to help you understand what is going on. This exercise is also designed to give you practice in working with units imported from AutoCAD. All of the elements of the set have already been constructed in AutoCAD and exported from it as .dxf files. You will be bringing in the various elements of the set, assembling them, giving them textures, and lighting them to create the set that you are about to see. This was a relatively simple set that will be easy to work with in 3D Studio MAX.

To give you an idea of what you are about to assemble, first take a look at the file seagull1.jpg that you will find in the 3dstudio folder on the CD-ROM. This is a rendering created in 3D Studio MAX for Act I. You should be able to open this file in Painter, Adobe Photoshop, and any number of other programs that can handle .jpg files. You could even look at it in Netscape or any Web browser. You can also look at renderings for Act II (seagull2.jpg), Act III (seagull3.jpg), and Act IV (seagull4.jpg). In AutoCAD, you can also bring up the file seglplan.dwg from the 3dstudio folder on the CD-ROM. This is a ground plan for all four acts in the actual theatre where the play was performed. Notice that each act is on separate layers. When the file initially opens, you will be in Act I. By turning layers on and off, however, you can also bring up Acts II–IV.

As I indicated earlier, all of the pieces for the set have already been created in AutoCAD and exported as .dxf files, so that is how you will be bringing them in. Let's start with the basic platforming.

1. Open 3D Studio MAX.
2. Import the file platform.dxf from the 3dstudio folder of the CD-ROM.
   A. This is the lower platform area for the set. There are three small projections sticking out of the sides of the platform area. These represent the ends of aisles through the audience area and are entrances used by the actors.
   B. Click on the Modify button.
      1. Click on UVW Map.
      2. Scroll down to the Parameters area and select Cylindrical mapping with a Cap.
      3. In the Alignment section, click on Fit.
3. Import the file step.dxf.
   A. This is the step unit between the lower area of platforming that you just brought in and the upper area of platforming. You will note that it came in perfectly in position with the lower platform. It does not have to be moved around. This is because both of these set units were originally created in the same drawing space and thus they share the same origin. After they were created, they were then extracted from the drawing as separate blocks, but those blocks still share the same original origin. So when you import them into 3D Studio MAX, they are already perfectly aligned with one another.
   B. Click on the Modify button.
      1. Click on UVW Map.
      2. Scroll down to the Parameters area and select Cylindrical mapping with a Cap.
      3. In the Alignment section, click on Fit.
4. Import the file upplat.dxf.
   A. This is the upper platform unit. The long end of this platform heading away from the central acting area also represents entrances for the actors to the acting area. As you can see, this was pretty close to a full arena setting. You will notice once again that this section of platforming came into the program perfectly aligned with the other two because all three files share the same origin.
   B. Click on the Modify button.
      1. Click on UVW Map.
      2. Scroll down to the Parameters area and select Cylindrical mapping with a Cap.
      3. In the Alignment section, click on Fit.

5. Now is the time to apply some texture. All three sections of the set that you have brought in will be sharing the same texture.

   A. Select all three platform pieces: the upper platform, the step, and the lower platform.

   B. Open the Material Editor.
      1. Click on the Get Material button.
      2. In the Material/Map Browser that opens, browse from the material library.
      3. Select Wood Ashen and click on OK.

   C. You are returned to the Material Editor with Wood Ashen in sample slot #1.

   D. Click on Assign Material to Selection button. This applies the material to the set pieces.

   E. Close the Material Editor.

6. Do a quick render to see what it looks like. You will notice that the grain scale is not what you might want for a set. It looks sort of like one big piece of wood. Close the Render window. Now you are going to change the tiling scale of the UVW mapping to make the material that you applied look more like many separate planks rather than just one piece of wood.

7. Select just the lower platform.

   A. If it is not already selected, click on the Modify button on the create panel.

   B. In the Parameters area, go to the V Tile spinner and change the value to 20.0.

   C. Do a quick render to see the result. Close the Render window.

   D. Try changing the values for the U and W Tile spinners and then do a quick render after each so that you can see the effect of these spinners on this material. When you are finished experimenting, set the U Tile to 1.0, V Tile to 20.0, and W Tile to 1.0.

8. Select just the step unit. Change the V Tile spinner for it to 20.0.

9. Select just the upper platform. Change the V Tile spinner for it to 20.0.

10. Save the work that you have done so far as the file name seagl1.max in whatever location you would like either on your hard drive or to a floppy disk. If you have not printed out the Act I ground plan from AutoCAD you should do so now so that you will have it as a reference for locating the rest of the set items that you will be importing. Bring up the file seglplan.dwg in AutoCAD and print it out on a piece of 8.5- × 11-inch paper, using the "scaled to fit" option.

11. Import the file bush1.dxf.
    A. This is a basic foliage plant that was created in AutoCAD and exported as a .dxf file. You are going to use it to make all of the plants for Act I. You'll notice that it was created separately from the ground plan and comes in at the drawing origin point.
    B. Click on the Modify button. You will notice that the bush comes in with the name topiary01.
       1. Click on UVW Map.
       2. Scroll down to the Parameters area and select Spherical mapping.
       3. In the Alignment section, click on Fit.

12. Next you'll apply some texture to the bush.
    A. Open the Material Editor.
       1. Click on sample slot #2.
       2. Click on the Get Material button.
       3. In the Material/Map Browser that opens, browse from the material library.
       4. Select Foliage Opacity (std.) and click on OK.
    B. You are returned to the Material Editor with Foliage Opacity (std) in sample slot #2.
    C. Click on the Assign Material to Selection button. This applies the material to the bush.
    D. Close the Material Editor.

13. Now you are going to create clones of the bush and scale it to a variety of sizes.
    A. Choose the Select and Uniform Scale option of the Select and Scale button.
    B. Scale the bush topiary01 up to about the size of the largest bush on the ground plan.

14. Clone the bush—Edit/Clone.
    A. Use the Select and Move command to move the clone off of the top of the old bush. You'll notice that the new bush has a name of topiary02.
    B. Keep cloning and moving until you have all of the bushes that you need in their approximate locations.
    C. Use the Select and Uniform Scale command to change the size of the bushes so that there is some variation.
    D. Use the Select and Move command to move the bushes into final position.
    E. Use the Select and Rotate command to rotate them as well to create more variation.

F. Take a look at the whole thing by doing a quick render. Make any changes to the bushes that you want.

15. Next let's bring in the bench. This bench was designed in two parts because it consists of two different materials. There is a set of legs for the bench that will be made of brass. The slats that form the seat of the bench are made of wood. The bench will therefore be brought in as two separate files so that each part can have a different material applied to it.

A. Import the file benchbot.dxf.

B. Click on the Modify button.
   1. Click on UVW Map.
   2. Scroll down to the Parameters area and select Box mapping.
   3. In the Alignment section, click on Fit.

C. Open the Material Editor.
   1. Click on sample slot #3.
   2. Click on the Get Material button.
   3. In the Material/Map Browser that opens, browse from the material library.
   4. Select Brass (std) and click on OK.

D. You are returned to the Material Editor with Brass (std) in sample slot #3.

E. Click on the Assign Material to Selection button. This applies the material to the bench bottom.

F. Close the Material Editor.

G. Import the file benchtop.dxf.

H. Click on the Modify button.
   1. Click on UVW Map.
   2. Scroll down to the Parameters area and select Planar mapping.
   3. In the Alignment section, click on Fit.

I. Open the Material Editor.
   1. Click on sample slot #4.
   2. Click on the Get Material button.
   3. In the Material/Map Browser that opens, browse from the material library.
   4. Select Wood Cedar Boards and click on OK.

J. You are returned to the Material Editor with Wood Cedar Boards in sample slot #4.

K. Click on the Assign Material to Selection button. This applies the material to the bench top.

L. Close the Material Editor.

16. The top and the bottom of the bench were created together, so they came in aligned with one another even though they are not in position on the set. Let's use the Group command to lock them together as a unit so that they can be moved around as one piece.

    A. Select both the bench top and bench bottom.
       1. You can use the Select Object button with the window option and click and drag to form a window that includes both.
       2. Or, you can use the Select by Name button to open the Select Objects box and pick the names benchbot01 and benchtop01.

    B. Click on the pull down menu Group/Group.
       1. The Group name box opens.
       2. Name this group Bench.

    C. Now that the top and bottom are grouped together, move the bench into position on the set. Note that you will need to move the group both horizontally and vertically to get it into position. You will also need to rotate it. This operation will take the use of more than one window and probably several Zoom commands.

    D. Do a quick render to check the position of the bench.

17. Next, there is a set of columns that are going to be a part of the scenery for the "play within the play" in Act I.

    A. Import the file columns.dxf.

    B. Click on the Modify button.
       1. Click on UVW Map.
       2. Scroll down to the Parameters area and select Cylindrical mapping with a Cap.
       3. In the Alignment section, click on Fit.

    C. Open the Material Editor.
       1. Click on sample slot #5.
       2. Click on the Get Material button.
       3. In the Material/Map Browser that opens, browse from the material library.
       4. Select Marble Travertine and click on OK.

    D. You are returned to the Material Editor with Marble Travertine in sample slot #5.

    E. Click on the Assign Material to Selection button. This applies the material to the columns.

    F. Close the Material Editor.

18. Move the columns vertically to place them in position on the set.

19. Because the play is being performed in an almost complete arena situation, the "curtain" for the "play within the play" in Act I is circular. Bring it in next.

   A. Import the file curtain.dxf.

   B. Click on the Modify button.

      1. Click on UVW Map.

      2. Scroll down to the Parameters area and select Cylindrical mapping with no cap.

      3. In the Alignment section, click on Fit.

   C. Open the Material Editor.

      1. Click on sample slot #6.

      2. Click on the Get Material button.

      3. In the Material/Map Browser that opens, browse from the material library.

      4. Select White Plastic and click on OK.

   D. You are returned to the Material Editor with White Plastic in sample slot #6. Now you are going to modify the White Plastic object using the Material Editor to make it look like scrim.

      1. In the Basic Parameters area:

         a. Change shinniness and shinniness strength to 0.

         b. Change opacity to 60.

         c. Leave self-illumination at 0.

      2. In the Name box just above the Basic Parameters area, change the name of the material from White Plastic to White Scrim. Whenever you modify a material, you should rename it so that you can locate it later.

   E. Click on the Assign Material to Selection button. This applies the material to the curtain.

   F. Close the Material Editor.

20. Move the curtain into position vertically so that its bottom just rests on top of the upper platform.

21. The next set piece to bring in is going to be the "sky." The set designer wants a small sky over the top of the acting area. Because of the nature of the theatre, this cannot be a very large piece and will only be used in Acts I and II, which take place outdoors. It will be struck before Act III.

   A. Import the file sky.dxf.

   B. Click on the Modify button.

      1. Click on UVW Map.

    2. Scroll down to the Parameters area and select Cylindrical mapping with a Cap.

    3. In the Alignment section, click on Fit.

C. Open the Material Editor.

    1. Click on sample slot #1. You are now starting to reuse the sample boxes. It could be important later on to remember which materials you used. This sample box was first used for Wood Ashen, which was applied to the platforms.

    2. Click on the Get Material button.

    3. In the Material/Map Browser that opens, browse from the material library.

    4. Select Blue Plastic and click on OK.

D. You are returned to the Material Editor with Blue Plastic in sample slot #1. Now you are going to turn it into pale blue scrim.

    1. Working in the Basic Parameters section:

        a. Change shinniness and shinniness strength to 0.

        b. Change opacity to 60.

        c. Change self-illumination to 20.

        d. Click on the color block next to Ambient.

            1. The Color Selector opens.

            2. Move the Whiteness slider or change the R, G, and B spinners to read: R: 165, G: 168, B: 198.

            3. Click on the Close button.

        e. Click on the color block next to Diffuse.

            1. The Color Selector opens.

            2. Move the Whiteness slider or change the R, G, and B spinners to read: R: 196, G: 196, B: 255.

            3. Click on the Close button.

    2. In the Name box just above the Basic Parameters area, change the name of the material from Blue Plastic to Blue Scrim.

E. Click on the Assign Material to Selection button. This applies the material to the sky.

F. Close the Material Editor.

22. Move the sky horizontally to place it in position on the set. Move it vertically so that it is about half the height of the curtain above the top of the curtain.

23. The last set pieces that you are going to bring into the scene are the Japanese lanterns that will decorate the area outside of the curtain and provide illumination for the play within the play.

A. Import the file lantern.dxf.

B. Click on the Modify button.
  1. Click on UVW Map.
  2. Scroll down to the Parameters area and select Cylindrical mapping with a Cap.
  3. In the Alignment section, click on Fit.

C. Open the Material Editor.
  1. Click on sample slot #2. Remember that the Foliage Opacity material is now going to be replaced by a new one.
  2. Click on the Get Material button.
  3. In the Material/Map Browser that opens, browse from the material library.
  4. Select Paper Standard and click on OK.

D. You are returned to the Material Editor with Paper in sample slot #2. Now you are going to turn it into parchment around a Japanese lantern.
  1. Working in the Basic Parameters section:
    a. Change self-illumination to 80.
    b. Change opacity to 90.
    c. Click on the color block next to Ambient.
      1. The Color Selector opens.
      2. Move the Whiteness slider or change the R, G, and B spinners to read: R: 162, G: 132, B: 79.
      3. Click on the Close button.
    d. Click on the color block next to Diffuse.
      1. The Color Selector opens.
      2. Move the Whiteness slider or change the R, G, and B spinners to read: R: 132, G: 115, B: 87.
      3. Click on the Close button.
    e. Click on the color block next to Specular.
      1. The Color Selector opens.
      2. Move the Whiteness slider or change the R, G, and B spinners to read: R: 210, G: 210, B: 210.
      3. Click on the Close button.
  2. In the Name box just above the Basic Parameters area, change the name of the material from Paper to Japanese Lantern.

E. Click on the Assign Material to Selection button. This applies the material to the lantern.

F. Close the Material Editor.

24. Move the lantern into position as one of the six lanterns. Clone it to form the other five and position them. Vertically, the two lanterns closest to the curtain should have their tops just slightly below the top of the curtain.

The two lanterns next furthest away from the curtain should have their tops just slightly below the bottom of the previous two lanterns. The two lanterns furthest away from the curtain should have their tops slightly below the middle of the two lanterns closer to the curtain. Do another quick render to see how everything looks.

25. The next step is to apply some lighting to the scene. Click on the **Create** button and then on the **Lights** button underneath it.

   A. Start with an omni light inside the curtain between the two columns to give us some light for the part of the scene that must be played there.
      1. Click on **Omni** under the **Create** and **Light** buttons.
      2. Click and drag in one of the windows to create the omni light close to the center of the curtain between the two columns.
      3. Move the light vertically or horizontally into position between and just above the tops of the two columns.
      4. Click on the **Modify** button to make changes in the light after it is positioned.
         a. Click on the **Color** box next to the **On** window to set its color or use the **R, G**, and **B** spinners to set readings of R: 241, G: 197, B: 168.
         b. Set the multiplier to 3.0.
         c. In the **Attenuation** area, set the start range to 0 and the end range to 65.
         d. Be sure that there is a check in the **On, Use**, and **Show** windows.
         e. Rename the omni light **Curtain Light**.

   B. Now you make a clone of the omni you just created to use as an instrument to represent the three S.L. lanterns.
      1. Clone the Curtain Light omni and name the new one **sl lantern**.
      2. Move it to just D.S. of the center of the three S.L. lanterns.
      3. Click on the **Modify** button and reset the general parameters for the light:
         a. Set the multiplier to 2.0.
         b. Set the attenuation end range to 100.

   C. Clone the **sl lantern** to create an **sr lantern light**. Move it to just D.S. of the center of the three S.R. lanterns.

   D. The next series of steps in this exercise will take you through the entire process of bringing an outside material or pattern into 3D Studio MAX and using it as a gobo or projection in a lighting instrument. It is simpler to just use the materials that are already available in the program, but they may not satisfy all of your needs. The same process that you are about to follow, for example, could be used to bring in a standard pattern or gobo that you have scanned off of the real thing or a drawing or photo and then saved as a file. You will need to first get out of 3D Studio MAX and into the file management program that you prefer such as Windows Explorer.

1. Locate the file seafol.tga in the 3dstudio folder on the CD-ROM. This file is actually a modified version of the foliage.tga file that is available in the standard 3D Studio MAX library. In order to create this file I copied the foliage.tga file into Painter, saved it under the new name, and then changed the dark green background color in the file to a blue that I wanted for this exercise. If you had scanned in a pattern, gobo, photo, or drawing that you wanted to use, you could then follow the rest of these procedures to use it as a pattern with a lighting instrument.

2. Copy this file to the maps folder of the main 3D Studio MAX folder—usually 3dsmax—on your hard drive.

3. Get back into 3D Studio MAX.

4. Open the Material Editor. Now you are going to place the file seafol.tga into the material library so that it is available for use.

   a. Click on sample slot #1 to activate it.

   b. Click on the Get Material button. The Material/Map Browser opens.

   c. Browse from the material library.

   d. Select any bitmap (green parallelogram) such as Sky.jpg and click on OK.

   e. You are returned to the Material Editor.

   f. Go to the Bitmap Parameters area of the Material Editor.

   g. Click on the bar next to Bitmap: with the name of the bitmap that you selected, such as Sky.jpg.

   h. The Select Bitmap Image File box opens.

      1. If you are not already in the folder maps under the main 3D Studio MAX folder—usually 3dsmax—go there now.

      2. Locate the file seafol.tga in this folder and click on it to select it.

      3. With the name seafol.tga in the File name: area, click on OK.

      4. You are returned to the Material Editor.

   i. Go to the Name window just underneath the sample slots and give it the name seagull foliage.

   j. Click on the Put to Library button. When the Put to Library box opens, the name seagull foliage should already be in the box. If it is not, place it there and click on OK.

   k. Close the Material Editor. You have just moved the file

seafol.tga into the material library as a bitmap and saved it under the name **seagull foliage**. This will now be available to you to use as a material.

5. Create a target spot that is located approximately 38 feet D.S. of the steps just below the curtain. Its target should be the steps just D.S. of the curtain. Move it to a height approximately 18 feet above stage level.

Note: If you aren't sure about distances, the first thing to check is that you are in the proper units. Click on **Views/Units Setup** and select **US Standard** and **Feet w/fractional inches**. Then you can use the **Tape** in the **Helpers Menu** under the create panel to measure off distances.

6. Rename the target spot that you just created **gobo1** and its target **gobo1 target**.
7. Select the target spot **gobo1** and click on the **Modify** button.
   a. Set the multiplier to **3.0**.
   b. In the attenuation area, there should be no check by **Use** or **Show**.
   c. Under **Shadow Parameters**, there should be no check by **Cast Shadows**.
   d. Under **Spotlight Parameters**, set a hotspot of **50.0** and a falloff of **55.0**.
      1. Place a dot by **Circle** and a check by **Show Cone**.
      2. Place a check by **Projector**.
      3. Click on the **Assign** button.
         a. The **Material/Map Browser** opens.
         b. If you are not already browsing from the material library, select that option.
         c. Click on **seagull foliage**; it's all the way down at the bottom of the list.
         d. Click on **OK**.
   E. Do a quick render to see how all of this looks.
   F. One more target spot on the bench should finish up the lighting for this scene. You'll create one pointing straight down with a soft edge and a pale blue color.
      1. Click on the **Create** button, then on the **Light** button and then on the **Target Spot** button.
      2. Click and drag in the **Left** or **Front** viewport to create a target spot pointing straight down at the bench. The target should be on the stage floor directly below the bench.
      3. Move the target spot and its target in the **Top** viewport so that it is directly over the bench and pointing down at it.

4. Move the target spot in the Left or Front viewport so that it is about 12 feet above the bench.

5. Rename the target spot as Bench Special and its target as Bench Target.

6. Select the Bench Special instrument and click on the Modify button.

   a. In the General Parameters area:

      1. Click on the Color box between the On box and the Exclude button to open the Color Selector, or set the RGB spinners to: R: 91, G: 153, B: 229.

      2. Set the multiplier to 0.5.

   b. In the Attenuation area, make sure that neither Use nor Show are selected.

   c. In the Spotlight Parameters area:

      1. Set the hotspot to 20.0 and the falloff to 50.0.

      2. Be sure that Circle is selected.

   d. In the Shadow Parameters area, select Cast Shadows and Use Shadow Maps.

   G. Do a quick render to see how all of this looks.

26. Next you are going to create a target camera and set it up to view the scene.

   A. Click on the Create button, then on the Camera button, and then on the Target button.

   B. In the Top viewport, click beyond the gobo spot away from the stage and drag toward the stage to create the camera and its target. Don't worry about getting too precise with this, as you will be using the camera controls to move it around. This camera will be created as Camera 01.

   C. You may want to move the target of the camera, however, so that it is on the steps right at the base of the curtain.

   D. Right click on the name of the Perspective viewport. In the box that opens, click on Views/Camera 01.

   E. Now go to the camera controls at the lower right-hand corner of the screen and reposition the camera to give you a view of the whole stage from slightly above. Refer to the rendering seagull1.jpg as a reference.

   F. Do a quick render to see how it looks through the camera.

   G. Move the camera around to several other views and do a quick render from each to get an idea of how the scene will look from different points of view.

27. Finish it all off by doing a full rendering from a view that you like and save it to a file.
    A. Get into the camera view that you prefer.
    B. Click on the Render Scene button. The Render Scene box opens.
        1. Under Time Output, select Single.
        2. Under Output Size, select a width of 640 and a height of 480.
        3. Under Render Output, click on the Files button. The Render Output Files box opens:
            a. Under List files of type:, select the file type that you want to create. I would suggest JPEG File *(.jpg), but there are a number of other choices.
            b. In the File name: window, give it a name followed by the extension .jpg or whatever extension is appropriate to the file type that you selected.
            c. In the Drives: and Folders: areas, select the location to which you want to save the file that you will be creating.
            d. Click on OK. You are returned to the Render Scene box.
        4. Click on the Render button. You have just finished creating and lighting a scene and saving it as a rendered file.
28. Click on File/Save. You have just saved the 3D Studio MAX file and can come back to rework it at any time.
29. The rendering file that you just created could now be printed out from another program such as Painter, could be imported into Painter to be used as the basis of a more stylized rendering, or could be used as a background for a figure in Poser.
30. Also available on the CD-ROM in the 3dstudio folder are the files seagull2.jpg, seagull3.jpg, and seagull4.jpg. These are all renderings of Acts II–IV of this production of *The Seagull*. Available as well are the files seagul2.max, seagul3.max, and seagul4.max, which are the 3D Studio MAX files for those acts. You can make copies of all of the files on your hard drive for further experimentation and work on the play.

USING ADVANCED TECHNIQUES

This book has been written as an introduction to the programs it covers for theatrical designers and technicians and to help you integrate the use of the programs with one another—something that is not covered in any of the program manuals. It was never intended to be a comprehensive work covering everything that is possible with the programs. This is especially true of 3D Studio MAX. However, now that you understand the basics of working in 3D Studio MAX, you may want to explore the numerous other techniques that are possible with the program. The best advice that I can give you in that regard is to pull out the *Tutorial* manual that accompanies 3D Studio MAX. Unlike the onscreen help and the other manuals that you will find packaged with the program, this book is written in a format that is relatively easy to follow and understand. It walks you through the steps of each technique with examples that you actually create in the program. If you have completed all of the exercises in this book, the *Tutorial* manual will be easy for you to follow and use.

Some of the techniques that I would especially recommend as worth exploring are:

Environment: By using the camera in combination with the Rendering/Environment settings, you can create fog, fire, and lighting effects in your scene.

Space Warps: Space warps act as "force fields" on other objects. By using them, you can create ripples, waves, explosions, wind, rain, and snow effects.

Shapes: Learn more about the advanced work that you can do with shapes involving loft objects, morphs, and booleans. Loft objects let you combine two or more shapes into extremely complex 3-D objects. Deforming loft objects gives you yet more ability to create unusual shapes. Morph commands, as the name implies, metamorphosize one object into another. Booleans are objects that you create by adding or subtracting the geometry of two or more other objects.

Transforms: These are the 3D Studio MAX tools that utilize the multiple coordinate systems of the program. If precision in positioning, scaling, rotating, moving, etc. is important to you, you should explore the use of these tools.

Track View: If you are serious about animation, then you should learn to use the track view method of creating animations. It is a tool that will greatly aid your efforts to create complex animations.

Hierarchy: The process involving different types of hierarchies is another important animation tool that allows you to link and unlink objects in ways that create yet more complex animations.

Commercial Gel Colors for your Instruments: It is relatively easy to use the equivalent of commercially available color filters for your instruments in 3D Studio MAX. Use a scanner to scan in the colors from your favorite swatch book. Then using either Painter, PhotoShop, or some similar program, "sample" these colors and read their RGB values. These RGB values can then be plugged into the color section of the various lighting instruments in the program to give you the equivalent of these "gels" in your renderings. In the 3DStudio folder of the CD-ROM accompanying this book you will find three databases titled rgbcolor.dbf (dbase III), rgbcolor.csv (text and commas), and rgbcolor.wdb (MSWorks). These contain the RGB values for all Roscolux colors that have been obtained by using the above method.

In addition to the above techniques that are available in the program itself, depending upon the version that you have purchased, there may be a variety of other programs that came packaged with it. Each of these separate programs can be extremely useful depending upon your particular situation. Character Studio, for example, allows you to create your own 3-D figures. Animator Studio provides the basics for 2-D animation and digital moviemaking and Animator Pro deals more heavily in 3-D animation. The World Creating Tool Kit is an accompanying disk that theatre practitioners should especially examine. It contains a wide variety of already created 3-D objects that you can import into your work such as trees, bushes, chairs, tables, etc.

POSER

INTRODUCTION

Poser is the easiest of these four programs to learn, but it is still extremely versatile. The basic use of Poser is to create human figures that can be used in any of the other three programs. There are a large number of figure types and poses that are available in the program ready for your use. If you find that none of these suits your needs, however, you can also change the dimensions of any of the stock figures and pose the figures in any position that you would like—including some anatomical impossibilities. You could, for example, take the basic female figure and by changing the appropriate body parts make it pregnant or give the basic male figure a potbelly of whatever size you want. Each of the body parts can also be moved separately to create the particular pose that you desire. The figures can be displayed on the screen in a variety of styles such as skeleton, wireframe, outline, flat shaded, etc. Props and backgrounds can be added to the figure, and it can be animated. Another interesting feature of Poser is that props can be substituted for parts of the figure to create other kinds of figures. You can take a bull's head and place it on a man's body to create a Minotaur, for example. There are some stock props available in Poser, but you can also import props from AutoCAD or 3D Studio MAX.

This section covers Poser 3. Poser 4 is identical in layout and operation to Poser 3, but has much larger libraries with more figure types, poses, hairstyles, props, etc. available. You will easily be able to learn Poser 4 from these instructions. If you have Poser 2, go to the CD-ROM and print out one of the Poser 2 files. These are identical in coverage to this section of the book, but cover Poser 2 rather than Poser 3. The different versions work very similarly. Poser 3 does offer some substantial differences from Poser 2, however, as well as a lot of cosmetic ones. Poser 3 gives you more hand and facial detail with which you can work, includes some nonhuman figures, and offers a number of different options not available on Poser 2 such as background textures. The immediately apparent difference between the two versions is a completely changed appearance and screen layout.

Once you have created the figure in Poser it can then be exported for use in Painter, AutoCAD, or 3D Studio MAX. In Painter, a figure can become the basis for a costume rendering or can be added to a scenic rendering. In AutoCAD or 3D Studio MAX, it can be added to a model or drawing to give the feeling of human scale and action. Poser gives the designer a quick, extremely versatile method of creating human figures in a wide variety of types, shapes, and poses for use in their drawings, models, and renderings. A simple, but very useful program.

Becoming Familiar with the Opening Space

The first time that you open Poser, you will see something similar to the figure labeled The Poser Opening Screen. This is a typical opening screen for Poser. The following text will take you through the parts of the Poser screen.

The Pull Down Menu Bar

Running across the top of the screen is the pull down menu bar with the words File, Edit, Figure, Display, etc. on it. This is used to access the various tools and features of Poser. Here you can also make choices about exactly what is displayed on the rest of the screen. Click on any of the words on the bar to open the pull down menu underneath. Familiarize yourself with which

THE POSER OPENING SCREEN

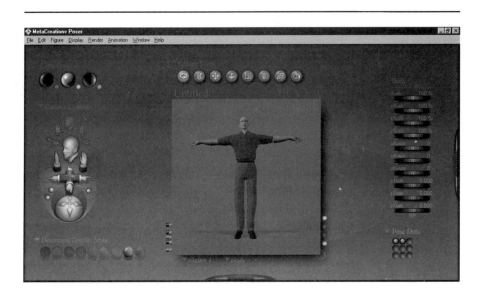

tools and features are located where on the bar. For Poser 3 on Mac platforms, the pull down menu bar is displayed if you move the cursor to the top area of the work space.

File

New: This lets you start a new figure. It returns the main screen to exactly what you see when you first open the program.

Open: This lets you open a previously saved figure.

Close: This closes the figure that is currently on the screen.

Save: This saves changes to an already named figure file.

Save As: This lets you name the currently active figure and create a file.

Revert: This restores the last saved version of the current file. It undoes any unsaved changes.

Import: This opens another pull down menu that allows you to import other kinds of files such as backgrounds, props, etc.

Export: This opens another pull down menu that allows you to export the file in formats for use in Painter, AutoCAD, 3D Studio MAX, and other programs.

Print Setup: This opens the setup box for your printer so you can make changes.

Print: This prints the current figure.

Exit: This closes the program.

Edit

Undo/Undo Change/Redo Change: This undoes or redoes the last change. It will not go back more than one step.

Cut: This is available only with certain tools like the Animation palette.

Copy: This copies the current display to the clipboard as a .bmp file.

Paste: This is available only with certain tools like the Animation palette.

Delete Prop: This is used as a shortcut method to delete props from a scene. Select the prop and then use this command.

Restore: This opens a pull down menu that lets you selectively restore parts of the scene to their default values. You can restore an element (body part), the figure, lights, camera, or all to what they were when you first started working. This allows you to retain, for example, the settings that you have created for the camera and lights, but go back to the beginning on the figure. **Note:** This is not the same as the Revert function, which restores you to the last saved set of all values in the file.

Memorize: This lets you change the default values for the file. If you get to a setting for an element, figure, lights, camera, or all that you would like to use as the fallback value in Restore, you can do so by clicking on Memorize and then on element, figure, lights, camera, or all.

Properties: This opens the Properties dialogue box for an element, prop, light, or camera that has already been selected. A faster way to open this box is to double click on the element, prop, light, or camera. The dialogue box lets you change certain properties. For example, if you double click on a hand, you can make the hand invisible or change its ability to bend. Exactly which properties can be changed depends upon the particular item selected.

General Preferences: This opens the General Preferences box. Here you can change the background and foreground colors, and turn on or off certain settings such as whether body parts can be bent and whether the currently selected element is highlighted. Click on the button labeled Background Color or the one named Foreground Color to select a new color.

Figure

This is usually the first place that you go to when you begin working in Poser. This is where you select the general figure type and height and can change other aspects of the figure.

Figure Height: This lets you select a height for your figure. Your choices range from Baby all the way up to Heroic Model. Try several of these and see the differences in the figures on the screen.

Replace Body Part with Prop: This command lets you change a body part to a prop such as a bull's head to create a Minotaur or some other constructed creature. It is not available until certain other steps have already been completed. I will cover how to do this in a later part of the book.

Set Figure Parent: This allows you to link two figures in a parent-child relationship so that when any operation is performed on a parent figure, the same operation is applied to the child figure.

Use Inverse Kinematics: This lets you turn on and off inverse kinematics for legs and arms. Inverse kinematics help you create natural-looking poses and animations. With IK on, when you move one body part, the other parts of the body that would naturally be affected by such a movement change as well. With IK for the legs on, for example, when you move the hips, the legs change position without affecting the position of the feet. With IK off, each body part moves completely independently of the others. Most of the time, you will probably want to leave IK turned on unless you are deliberately trying to contort the body into anatomically impossible positions. **Note:** When you change the settings on inverse kinematics, a dialogue box will open asking you about key frames in animation. Unless you are dealing with animation, click on the Don't Make Key Frames button.

Use Limits: Click on this to toggle the limits on or off. Limits are restrictions that Poser places on the range of motion of body parts according to what it considers "natural." These can be useful until you have more experience posing your figure. It can keep you from getting into extremely contorted positions.

Genitalia: This lets you make the Male Nude and Male Nude Detailed figures anatomically correct, or not.

Drop to Floor: This drops a figure from an elevated position so that its lowest point is on the floor.

Symmetry: The options under this menu item copy the shape and pose of one limb to another. This can be a time-saver.

Delete Figure: This deletes the selected figure from the scene.

Hide Figure: This temporarily removes a selected figure from view. This can sometimes help in selecting parts of a second figure.

Show All Figures: This returns all hidden figures to view.

Create Walk Path: This is used in animation.

Display

Camera View: You can select the view of the figure that you would like here—Left, Right, Top, Front—or you can choose the Main, Dolly, or Posing camera. See the section on cameras (see page 174) for more details.

Document Style: Lets you choose how the figure in the document window will be displayed. Your choices are: Silhouette, Outline, Wireframe, Hidden Line, Lit Wireframe, Flat Shaded, Sketch, Smooth Shaded (the default in Poser 3) or Texture Shaded.

Figure Style: This lets you set the style of the figure as the same as the rest of the document or choose a different style. The same options are available as in Document Style.

Element Style: This lets you set the style of an element to the same as the rest of the document or choose a different style. The same options are available as in Document and Figure Style.

Tracking:

Bounding Boxes Only: This displays body parts as boxes. This produces the quickest tracking of moving figures for animation.

Fast Tracking: This is an improved, faster-reacting display in Poser 3. It is the recommended choice.

Full Tracking: This selects a slower-reacting, but more detailed display of changes.

Depth Cued: This lights the figure so that the parts closest to you are brighter than the parts further away.

Ground Shadows: This displays shadows from lights on a ground plane of display.

Figure Circle: This is also referred to in the text and help commands as the Figure Ring. It displays as a large circle or ring that encloses the entire body. When this is displayed, you can move, rotate, etc. the entire body or figure by clicking and dragging on it.

Bend Body Parts: When this is checked, body parts will bend naturally. When unchecked, you can disable the bending of a specific body part.

Foreground Color: This opens the Color box to let you choose a different foreground color.

Background Color: This opens the Color box to let you choose a different background color.

Paper Texture: This lets you choose a texture for the background behind the figure. Your choices are Paper Grain, Noise, Noise Embossed, Weave, Weave Embossed, Grid, Graph, Legal, or None.

Paste onto Background: This lets you copy a picture of the current figure onto the background. If you change to a different view after doing this, you will see the pasted image behind the current figure.

Show Background Picture: This displays the current background.

Clear Background Picture: This clears pasted images from the background.

Guides: This displays a variety of guides to help you achieve a perspective view. Select each of these one at a time so that you can see how they appear.

Ground Plane: This is the "floor." It will take on different appearances in different display types. Try changing from Outline to Wireframe to Flat Shaded with this turned on.

Head Lengths: This shows you the height of the figure in "heads," a traditional method of proportioning figure height. The Ideal Adult figure is eight heads tall. The Fashion Model figure is nine heads tall.

Hip-Shoulder Relationship: This creates a hip line and a shoulder line so that you can more easily see the angle you have established between the two.

Horizon Line: This gives you a horizontal reference. When you start moving cameras around, this can help keep you oriented to how much you have tilted a view.

Vanishing Lines: This gives you a guide to the perspective. By matching vanishing lines for the figure with vanishing lines for the background, you can keep them both in the same perspective.

Render

The Render pull down menu lets you render a final view of a scene and control the appearance of that rendering.

Render: This creates a rendering of the scene that uses all of the choices you have made under Render Options and Surface Material below. Go ahead and click here to see a rendering with the default options for the program.

Antialias Document: This creates smoother, softer edges in the document.

Preset Render: This gives you a choice of a Fast or a Clean rendering. Both of these are "preset" and do not use the rendering options. The fast rendering tends to create jagged edges but is quick. The clean rendering eliminates the jagged edges but is slower. Try them both out to see the difference.

Smooth Render: This is another render method with choices made by the program. You also have a Fast or Clean option much like the preset render options. This method is faster than a preset render because it does not apply bump or texture maps to the figure. Try out both options.

Render Options: Click here to open the Render Options box, where you can specify the size and details of your rendering.

Render to: This lets you specify the window in which the rendering will occur.

Main Window: This is faster and keeps the desktop from becoming cluttered with extra windows. There is only one size that can be rendered with this option: 640×480.

New Window: This creates the rendering in a different window from the main window. It allows you to choose different window sizes and specify the dimensions in pixels, inches, or centimeters. It also lets you specify the resolution. Click on the down arrow in the appropriate box to select the scale. Click to the right of the number in the Width, Height, or Resolution box and then drag to the left to change the size or resolution. After the number is highlighted, type in the new number. You can also just click to the right and then use the Backspace key before entering a new number. When you change the width or height, the size of the other will automatically change to maintain the standard aspect ratio used by Poser—width/height = 1.333. Select New Window and set a width of **720** pixels for your next rendering.

Surface Detail: This gives you choices about how the surface of the figure is rendered.

Anti-Alias: Select this for softer, smoother edges.

Use bump maps/Use texture maps: If you have applied bump or texture maps to the surface of the figure, selecting these options will let you see them in the rendering. There will be more on how to apply these later. In general though, it's a good idea to keep these selected. If you aren't using the maps, it won't make any difference in the rendering.

Cast shadows: If this is selected, the program will show shadows in the rendering. Shadows take longer to render. If you are in a hurry, you might want to deselect this option.

Render Over: This lets you choose the background for your rendering.

Background Color: This renders over the background color selected in General Preferences (Edit/General Preferences). The default is black unless you change it.

Black: This creates a rendering with a black background even if you have a different background color or have imported a background picture.

Background Picture: If you have imported a background image, this option will render over that image.

Surface Material: This opens the Surface Material box for loading bump and texture maps. More will be discussed on this option later.

MINIEXERCISE

Take the time now to try a rendering so that you will be basically familiar with the procedure. Before rendering though, go to the Foreground Color and Background Color selections under Display and select a new foreground color and background color. Then return to the Render Options box and try out these settings: Select New Window. Set the width to 350 pixels; the height will automatically go to 350 pixels. Check Anti-aliasing, Use bump maps, Use texture maps, and Cast shadows. Select Background Color. Click on the Render Now button. The Render window will open with the new rendering in it, after a little while; however, it may not be full-size. The Render window can be moved around by clicking and dragging on the blue bar at the top of the window. If you move the cursor over the lower right-hand corner of the window, the cursor will change to a two-sided arrow. Click and drag to increase or decrease the size of the window. The window will expand or decrease in size after you have released the mouse button. Close the Render window by clicking on the X in the upper right-hand corner. Select Don't Save in the dialogue box that opens when you try to close the window. If you wanted to save this particular rendering as a separate file, you would have clicked on the Save option in this dialogue box. The options you selected earlier in the Render Option box are now selected, and this is how the program will render the next time that you click on Render.

Animation

The Animation pull down menu contains the commands that you will need to create an animation using Poser.

Animation Setup: Clicking here will open the Animation Setup dialogue box. Here you can set the Frame Width and Height just like you did back in the Render Options box. You can also set the Frame Rate and Frame Count. Duration will reflect changes made in the Frame Rate and Frame Count areas.

Make Movie: This opens the Make Movie box. Here you can give the movie a file name, select the Sequence Type (file type), select the Resolution (frame size), select the Quality (Display or Render settings), and set the Frame Rate and the Time Span.

Retime Animation: This opens the Retime Keys box. This box lets you expand or compress the number of frames between two key frames so that you can change the time that it takes for a motion to happen.

Resample Keyframes: This opens the Resample Keyframes box that lets you control the method by which key frames are created.

Play Movie File: This accesses the Open box to let you locate and play a movie file.

Window

The Window pull down menu lets you control what tools and control boxes appear on the screen, show a background image that you have imported, and control the size of the document window. If you look carefully at the screen, you will notice that many of the elements available under this pull down menu are also named at various locations about the screen in a faint grey text. If you double click on that text in many cases it will open the options that are also available by using the pull down menu under Window. In the case of the libraries and the animation controls, there are two "handles" that appear on the far right-hand edge of the screen and the far bottom edge of the screen. Clicking on each of these "handles" will open and close either the libraries or the animation controls.

Libraries: The Libraries menu can be opened by clicking here or on the pull-out handle on the far right-hand side of the screen. The Libraries area for Poser contains sections on Figures, Poses, Faces, Hair, Hands, Props, Lights, and Camera that are available. If you open the Libraries menu, you can close it by clicking here or on the pullout handle that will be just to the left of the Libraries pullout.

Animation Palette: Clicking here opens the Animation palette for controlling animations. Click here again or click in the small box in the upper left-hand corner of the display to close it.

Graph: Click here to open the Graphic Animation display. To close the display, you must click in the small box in the upper left-hand corner of the display.

Walk Designer: Click here to open the Walk Designer box for animating walking movement. To close the box, click here again or on the X in the upper right-hand corner of the box.

Joint Parameters: Click here to open the Joint Parameters box. This box allows you to change the motion action of joints. Click here again or on the X in the upper right-hand corner of the box to close it.

Camera Controls: Click here or double click on the text Camera Controls on the left-hand side of the screen to open and close the camera controls. Click on the down-facing arrow next to the text Camera Controls to choose whether to select a view from a particular camera.

Document Tools: Click here to display the document tools on the edges around the document window or the area in which the figure is displayed. The specific document tools will be covered in a later section.

Preview Styles: Click here to reveal the Document Display Style buttons at the lower left-hand corner of the screen. You can also turn these buttons on and off by double clicking on the text Document Display Style in that area. Hold the cursor over each of the circles in this area to see the name of the preview style or document display style associated with that circle. Click on the circle to change the display style, e.g. Silhouette, Outline, Wireframe, Hidden Line, Lit Wireframe, Flat Shaded, Sketch, Smooth Shaded, or Texture Shaded. Click on the downward-facing arrow to select whether you want to change Document, Figure, or Element display styles.

Editing Tools: Click here to reveal the eight Editing Tool buttons above the Figure area. You can also reveal them or turn them off by double clicking on the text Editing Tools in that area. These are the tools that you will use to move, rotate, etc. body parts, cameras, lights, etc. The name of each will appear as you move the cursor over the button associated with the tool.

Light Controls: Click here to reveal the controls for each of the three lights that are available to you in Poser. Double click on the text Light Controls as well to turn the controls on or off.

Memory Dots: The Memory Dots area lets you record setups for poses, the work space (UI), or cameras. You can store or restore nine different setups in each of these areas by clicking on the appropriate dot in this area when it is displayed. Click on the down arrow to choose between Poses, Workspaces (UI), or Cameras. Double click on the dot's name to turn the memory dots on or off.

Parameter Dials: The parameters for each element or body part are turned on or off here. Click on the pull down menu or on the name of the selected element or body part that appears on the screen away from the Element pop-up. In the opening screen, these parameter dials will appear in the area underneath the Library pullout when it is open and will not be visible unless the Library pullout is closed. When the parameter dials appear on the screen, there is also a small tab that appears just below them. You can click and drag on this tab to hide or reveal more dials.

Animation Controls: The animation controls can be opened by clicking here on the pull down menu or by clicking on the "handle" on the lower edge of the screen.

Show All Tools: This turns on all of the tool and control displays.

Hide All Tools: This turns off all of the tool and control displays.

Tool Titles: This turns on or off the light grey titles of the tool and control displays that appear on the screen. With these turned off, you cannot double click on them to activate the particular tool or control display.

Note on Opening and Closing Tools and Controls in Poser

The various tools and controls in Poser 3 that can be opened and closed via the Window pull down menu can also be opened and closed from the screen itself if there is a check mark next to the Tool Titles command in the Window pull down menu. This will cause the name of the various tools and commands to appear on the screen in a pale grey. When you move the cursor over the top of one of these titles, the color will change to white. You can then close or open the various items by double clicking on the title. The location of all of these elements on the screen can also be controlled from the title of the element. You can click and drag on the title to move the entire element about the screen.

THE DOCUMENT WINDOW

The area where the figure appears in Poser 3 is named the document window. The figure plus its foreground, background, etc. is referred to as the document. The controls around the edges of this window allow you to change many aspects of the appearance of the figure, its background, and its foreground.

Starting at the upper left-hand corner just outside the figure space is the file name of the document. When you first open Poser 3 this will read Untitled until you have saved the figure and given it a name; then the name of the file will appear in this space. The entire document can be made to appear and disappear by double clicking on the file name. Located around the outside of the document window are the document tools. These can be turned on and off by clicking on Display/Document Tools on the pull down menu.

Just above the upper right-hand corner of the document appears the window size in pixels. When you first open Poser 3, this will be 350×350. Double click on the window size to open the Set Window Size box, where you can change the height and width of the window and lock its size. Along the lower right-hand side of the document window you will see four circles or dots.

**THE DOCUMENT
WINDOW**

These dots allow you to change the colors of various elements of the document. Click and hold on the top of the four dots to open the Foreground Color box. Still holding down the mouse button, move the cursor around in the box to choose the color that you would like. When you have that color selected, release the mouse button to select it. You can also choose a foreground color via a much more detailed and less annoying display by clicking on Display/ Foreground Color on the pull down menu. The second dot from the top opens the Background Color box, where you can choose a color. You can also choose a background color by using the more detailed box available by clicking on Display/Background Color on the pull down menu. The third dot from the top opens the Shadow Color box, where you can control the color of the shadow that appears by the figure. The fourth dot from the top opens the Ground Color box, where you can control the color of the ground underneath the figure.

At the lower right-hand corner of the document window appears a three-quarter circle that activates the Resize Window command. Move the cursor over the three-quarter circle and a double-ended arrow will appear. Click and drag to change the size of the document window. Just underneath the left-hand side of the document window appears the Figure pop-up and the Element pop-up. If there is more than one figure in the document, you can click on the down arrow of the Figure pop-up to select the particular figure on which you would like to work. Click on the down arrow of the Element pop-up to select the element, body part, camera, etc. on which you would like to work. On the lower left side of the document window you will see five buttons. They will be either black or red in color. These are on/off switches, with red indicating that the switch is on and black indicating that the switch is off. The top button controls **depth cuing**. With depth cuing activated, the figure or parts of the figure further away from the viewer will be darker to give more of a feeling of depth. The second, third, and fourth buttons activate one of the tracking options. Only one of these may be selected at a time. The second button activates **box tracking**. Box tracking turns each body part into a box. This tracking method offers the fastest response time when rearranging the position of body parts. The third button actives **fast tracking,** which changes the body part selected to a box as it is moved, but then automatically restores it to the display style that you have selected when you stop moving it. This is usually the most useful tracking method. The fourth button activates **full tracking**. This method maintains the display style as body parts are moved. This method can be extremely slow in responding depending upon the processor speed and RAM of your particular computer.

THE LIBRARIES

The **Libraries** area of Poser contains many of the choices about figures, poses, etc. for the program. The libraries can be opened in two ways. You can click on the **Window** pull down menu and then on **Libraries,** or if you look carefully at the right-hand edge of the screen, you will see a "handle." Move the cursor over the handle and it will highlight. Click on the handle and the libraries will open.

When the libraries area opens, the following sublibraries are available: **Figures, Poses, Faces, Hair, Hands, Props, Lights,** and **Camera.** Click on each of these to display the options available in each area. After you have selected one of the options you can return to the main library menu by clicking on whatever sublibrary title is at the top of the Libraries area.

Figures

The **Figures** sublibrary allows you to select the figure type with which you would like to work. Immediately below the Figures title at the top of the library is a bar with a down arrow on it. Click on the down arrow to display the pop-up menu for the various figure types available. The list that appears will include: **Additional Figures, Animals, People, Poser2 Hi, Poser2 Lo, Tutorial,** and **Add New Category.** Each of these options offers you different choices concerning the figure. For the time being, click on **People.** The choices available under People appear on the left side of the library under the pop-up menu. On the right side there is a scroll bar. Click and drag on the scroll bar to display the figure types that are available in this sublibrary: **Business Man,**

Business Woman, Casual Child, Casual Man, Casual Woman, Nude Child, Nude Man, Nude Woman. Click on the figure that you would like to see in the document window and it will be highlighted. Below the figure type displays in the library you will see a check, a double check, a plus, and a minus. These are controls for what will happen with the figure that you have selected. If you click on the check, the figure type that you have highlighted will be substituted for the figure that is currently in the document window. The double check adds the highlighted figure to the figure already in the document window. The plus is used to add a modified figure to the currently open library. If you have changed a figure in some way and would like to save it to the library, use the plus to do so. The minus is used to delete a figure from the currently open library. The other options available under the figures pop-up menu include:

Animals: Figure types of a cat, dog, dolphin, horse, and raptor are available here.

Poser2 Hi: These are high-resolution figure types that are compatible with Poser 2.

Poser2 Lo: These are low-resolution figure types that are compatible with Poser 2.

Additional Figures: These are options that let you work with just a right or left hand without the rest of the figure, just a man or a woman's head without the rest of the figure, a mannequin, a skeleton, or a stick figure.

Add New Category: This lets you create a new sublibrary of your own.

Poses

The Poses sublibrary lets you choose from a wide variety of preset poses for your figure. Click on the down arrow bar to display the pop-up menu with the list of pose categories: Action Sets, Animation Sets, Classic Sets, etc. Once you have chosen one of these sets, the poses available in the set will be displayed on the left side of the Library area. The scroll bar on the right side will let you view the options. Click on the pose that you would like to highlight it. Click on the check mark at the bottom of the library to apply that pose to the figure in the document window.

Faces

The Faces sublibrary lets you choose facial expressions for the figure in the document window. The pop-up menu offers the categories of Basic Expressions and Phonemes. Select the expression that you would like by clicking on it to highlight it and then click on the check mark at the bottom to apply that expression to the figure in the document window.

Hair

The Hair sublibrary lets you choose a hair style for the figure in the document window. The pop-up menu offers the categories of Hair Types and Hair Types for Poser2 Figures. Select the hair type that you would like by clicking on it to highlight it and then click on the check mark at the bottom to apply that hair type to the figure.

Hands

The Hands sublibrary lets you choose a pose for the hands of the figure in the document window. The pop-up menu offers the categories of Basic Hands,

Counting, Hand Puppets, Poser2 Figure Hands, and Sign Language. Once you have selected the category that you would like, you can select the hand pose from the display in the library. Click on the pose desired to highlight it. Click on the check mark at the bottom to apply that hand pose to the figure in the document window. After you click on the check mark, you will be prompted as to whether you want the hand pose to be applied to the right hand or the left hand of the figure.

Props

The Props sublibrary lets you choose a prop to be added to the figure in the document window. Prop types available are Ball, Box, Cane, Cone, Cylinder, Square, Stairs, and Torus. Click on the prop desired to highlight it and then click on the check mark at the bottom of the library to add it to the document window.

Lights

The Lights sublibrary lets you choose from a variety of preset lighting arrangements for the figure in the document window. Click on the option displayed to highlight it and then click on the check mark at the bottom of the library to apply it to the document window.

Camera

The Camera sublibrary lets you pick a preset camera angle from which the figure can be viewed. Click on the option displayed to highlight it and then click on the check mark at the bottom of the library to apply that view to the document window.

THE EDITING TOOLS

The editing tools affect what happens to the figure when you click or click and drag with the cursor or mouse. These are the tools that let you change the position of body parts, lights, cameras, etc. The Editing Tools bar can be opened and closed by clicking on the pull down menu Window/Editing Tools or by double clicking on the title Editing Tools that appears in grey on the screen. The function of each tool will sometimes change depending upon whether you are working with a body part, a light, or a camera. These are the tools and their basic functions:

 The **Rotate** Tool: This rotates a body part, the entire body, or a camera.

 The **Twist** Tool: This twists a body part, the entire body, or a camera from side to side.

The **Translate** Tool: This moves a body part, the entire body, or a camera vertically or horizontally.

 The **Translate In/Out** Tool (Z): This moves the body part, the entire body, or a camera along the Z axis, toward you or away from you.

 The **Scale** Tool: This changes the proportions of a body part, the entire body, or the view from a camera.

 The **Taper** Tool: This is only available for body parts. It tapers one end of an element.

 The **Chain Break** Tool: This is only available for use on body parts. When placed on a body part, this tool breaks the chain of parts connected to it. For example, if you put the **Chain Break** tool on the chest, that means that the chest will remain stationary when you move (translate) other body parts.

 The **Color** Tool: This lets you change the color of objects, the foreground, the background, the shadow, etc. in the document Window.

THE PARAMETER DIALS

When the screen initially opens for Poser, the parameter dials are located on the right-hand side of the screen. If they are in this initial position and the libraries are open, you will not be able to see them—they will be hidden by the libraries. The parameter dials can be opened or closed by clicking on the pull down menu **Window/Parameter Dial** or double clicking on their title. The title for the parameter dials is the name of the element that has been selected using the **Element** pop-up that is below the middle of the document window. For example, if you click on the Element pop-up below the middle of the document window and select **Chest**, then the title above the parameter dials will read **Chest**. These dials allow you to make changes in the sizes and proportions of body parts, relative proportions of the overall body, and the scale and dolly of the camera and control the shadow, size, position, color, and intensity of the lights. The exact parameter dials that will appear will change with each element that is selected. Below the parameter dials you will also see a "tab"— a line with a half circle below it. You can increase or decrease the number of parameter dials displayed by clicking and dragging on this tab. There are two ways to change the settings on a parameter dial. First, position the cursor over the dial. You will notice that it changes to a double-ended arrow. Click and drag to the right or left to increase or decrease the dial setting. Second, double click on the dial for which you would like to change the setting. This opens the

Edit Parameter Dial box for that value. You can now change the value numerically in this box and then click on OK to establish that value.

DISPLAY STYLE

The display style controls are a group of nine spheres that appear in the lower right-hand corner of the screen when Poser is initially opened. They can be turned on or off either by the pull down menu Window/Preview Styles or by double clicking on the title Display Style on the screen. These control the display style of the document window, the figure, or a particular element. To the left of the title on the screen is a down arrow. Click on the down arrow to display a pop-up menu. In this pop-up menu you can choose whether you want

to control the display style of the entire document, a figure, or just an element of a figure. Click on the appropriate sphere to establish the display style that you desire. As you move the cursor over the top of each sphere, the name of that display style will appear above the controls. Click on the sphere to change the display style of the document, figure, or element. The display styles available are:

Silhouette: When you choose this, all you can see is the outline of the figure with the figure displayed in white.

Outline: With this option, the elements of the figure are shown outlined in white against the background.

Wireframe: If you choose this, each element of the figure will be shown as a transparent 3-D wireframe outline.

Hidden Line: This option is like the **Wireframe** control, except that each element is not transparent.

Lit Wireframe: This is like the **Hidden Line** control except that the wireframe outline will accept lighting.

Flat Shaded: With this option, 3-D surfaces are displayed as a series of planes.

Sketch Shaded: When you choose this style, the display appears like an outlined sketch with rough shadows.

Smooth Shaded: This is a good display style that appears realistic and can be worked in quickly. This is recommended for most work.

Texture Shaded: This style is the most realistic-looking of all of the display styles. It can be slow responding to changes, especially with computers that have slow processors or minimum RAM.

LIGHT CONTROLS

The Light Controls area can be turned on or off either by clicking on the pull down menu Window/Light Controls or double clicking on the title Light Controls on the screen. The light controls appear as three spheres with a dot beside each one. Each sphere represents one of the three lights that are available to you in Poser. Click on the sphere to display the location of the light in the document window and bring up the parameter dials for that light. You can also change

**LIGHT
CONTROLS**

the color of the light by clicking and holding on the small dot next to the sphere. Then still holding down the mouse button, you can move the cursor around in the window that opens to select a new color. Using the parameter dials to change colors is much more precise and controlled than using the color dot.

Camera Controls

The Camera Controls area can be opened or closed by either clicking on the pull down menu Window/Camera Controls or by double clicking on the title Camera Controls on the screen. This group of controls allows you to modify the view of the figure in the document window by controlling the camera through which the window is seen. Next to the title is also a down arrow that when clicked on opens a pop-up menu that lets you choose from preset camera views. These preset views include:

Main Camera: This gives a front view of the whole figure.

From Left: This gives a view from left side of the whole figure.

From Right: This gives a view from right side of the whole figure.

From Top: This gives a view from top side of the whole figure.

CAMERA CONTROLS

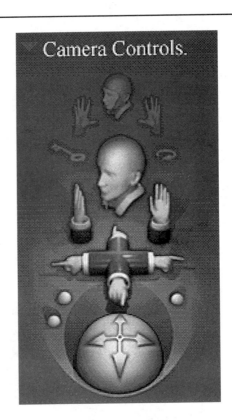

From Front: This gives a view from front side of the whole figure, which is the same as Main.

Face Camera: This gives a front view of just the face of the figure.

Posing Camera: This camera uses the figure as its center of rotation.

Right Hand Camera: This gives a front view of just the right hand of the figure.

Left Hand Camera: This gives a front view of just the left hand of the figure.

Dolly Camera: This camera rotates around itself and can move between figures.

Flyaround Camera: This camera automatically rotates the figure and keeps rotating it until you click with the mouse button to stop the rotation.

The other parts of the camera controls will be discussed in more detail in an exercise later in this section of the book.

POSE/CAMERA/UI DOTS

The Memory Dots area can be revealed or hidden by either clicking on Window/Memory Dots on the pull down menu or double clicking on the title on the screen. The particular title displayed may be either pose, camera, or UI (workspace layout) depending upon which is selected by using the pop-up menu that appears when you click on the down arrow by the title. The Memory Dots area is a quick way to record and recall a setup for a pose, a camera, or a work space layout. Select which of the three that you want to record or recall by clicking on the down arrow next to the title and choosing from the pop-up menu. The UI dots are used for recording work space layouts, for example. Move the work space elements around by clicking and dragging on the title of each. When they are in a position that you like, click on a UI memory dot to record the layout. When you want to restore that work space layout, simply click on the same UI memory dot. The same basic procedure is used for recording pose or camera setups into the memory dots, except that you would use a Pose or Camera memory dot, respectively.

MEMORY DOTS

Exercise No. 1: Selecting and Modifying a Pose

When Poser opens, you already have a **Male Casual** figure in the document window ready for work. Before I walk you through the operation of the various body and pose commands, however, let's take some time to examine the wide variety of already posed figures that come with the program. Familiarity with the figure types, heights, hand positions, and the poses already in the libraries will greatly speed up your work. If there is a pose in the library that you can modify slightly to fit your needs, that is always quicker than starting from scratch.

SELECTING A POSE

Before starting this exercise, be sure that there is a check next to **Tool Titles** under the **Window** pull down menu. This will assure that all of the various tools available can be accessed from the screen.

1. Figure height: Click on **Figure/Figure Height** to reveal the selection of ages and heights.
   A. Try out several of the different ages and heights to see the effect on the figure.
   B. Select a figure height of **Ideal Adult**.
2. Libraries: Open the **Libraries** area by clicking on **Window/Libraries** or by clicking on the tab on the right-hand side of the screen. The following options are now available: **Figures, Poses, Faces, Hair, Hands, Props, Lights,** and **Camera**. In this exercise, you will work with all of these except props, lights, and camera. There are separate exercises for each of those.
   A. Figures: Click in the **Figures** section of the libraries and the **Figures** library will open. At the top of the library is a block labeled **Figures**. To the left side of that block you will notice a group of seven dots. Move the cursor over each of these dots in turn. The name of the library associated with the dot such as **Poses, Faces,** etc. will appear. You can switch to that library by clicking on the dot. To the right in that block you will notice a double-ended arrow bent 90 degrees. If you click on the bent arrow you will return to the main libraries. If you have gotten out of the Figures library, return to it now.

   Just beneath the block labeled Figures you will see a small block with a down arrow in it. This is the pop-up menu. Click on this and the following sublibraries or options will appear. Click on each of these in turn and the options available under these categories will appear.
      1. Additional Figures: This sublibrary includes some substitutions for the standard figures that may occasionally prove useful. Notice that to the right side of the small pictures of the figures in the library is a

scroll bar. Click and drag on this scroll bar to see all of the options available.

a. **Hand Left:** This option substitutes a left hand for the full figure. Go ahead and click on this option. Notice that it is highlighted and in the block at the bottom of the library a check, double check, plus, and minus appear. Click on the check to substitute the highlighted figure for the one in the document window. You will be prompted for whether you want to keep the current proportions through the figure change. Click on **OK.**

Note: If you wanted to add the highlighted figure to the one already in the document window, you would click on the double check. If you had made a change in the figure and wanted to add it to the current library, you would click on the plus. If you wanted to delete the current figure from the current library, you would click on the minus.

b. **Hand Right:** This option substitutes a right hand for the current figure.
c. **Head Man:** This option substitutes just the head of a male for the current figure. Go ahead and click on the Head Man option to highlight it. Then click on the check to replace the hand left option with the Head Man option.
d. **Head Woman:** This option substitutes the head of a female for the current figure.
e. **Mannequin:** This option replaces the current figure with a simulated wooden mannequin figure such as you may have used in figure-drawing class. Click on this option to highlight it and then click on the check to substitute it for the current figure.

Other options available are **Skeleton Man, Skeleton Woman, Stick Child, Stick Man,** and **Stick Woman.** They can each be substituted for the current figure in the same manner.

2. **Animals:** In Poser 3 you also have some animal figures available in addition to people figures. Go back to the pop-up menu under the Figures block and click on the **Animals** option. Move the scroll bar up and down and you will see that your options are **Cat, Dog, Dolphin, Horse,** and **Raptor.** Click on one of these to highlight it. Then click on the check to substitute it for the current figure.
3. **People:** This is the sublibrary that you will probably be working with most often. Select this option from the pop-up menu. It contains the various choices for human figures. The options available are: **Business Man, Business Woman, Casual Child, Casual Man,**

Casual Woman, Nude Child, Nude Man, and Nude Woman. Click on the one of these with which you would like to work to highlight it. Click on the check to replace the current figure with this one. Note that for the nude man to have genitalia, you must have a check mark next to *Figure/Genitalia* on the main pull down menu.

4. Poser2 Hi: This option lets you work with high-resolution figures that can also be used in Poser 2. If you are sending a file to a shop, colleague, etc. who has Poser 2 instead of Poser 3 he or she will be able to read a file that uses one of these figures.

5. Poser2 Lo: This option lets you work with low-resolution figures that can also be used in Poser 2.

6. Tutorial: The Tutorial sublibrary contains a man and a dog that are specifically designed for use with the Tutorial that accompanies Poser 3.

7. Add New Category: If you would like to create a new figure library of your own, this is where to do it. You could, for example, have a library of figures and poses that you created for a specific show or production. If you click here you will be prompted for a name for the new sublibrary. **Warning:** If you create a new category, you may not be able to delete it later. Exercise caution in creating new categories.

Select one of the man or woman figures from the People sublibrary before moving on to the next section of the exercise.

B. Poses: Click on the double-ended bent arrow in the Figures block to return to the main libraries. Then click on the Poses block. The Poses library will open. This is where you can select a variety of preset poses for your figures. Click on the pop-up to see the subcategories that are available: Action Sets, Animation Sets, Classic Sets, Comic Sets, Creative Pose Sets, Dance Sets, Fighting Sets, Pose Sets, Running Sets, Sports Sets, Standing Sets, Tutorial, Walk Designer, and Add New Category. All of these except the last three have a variety of poses in them that you can use on the figure in the document window. Tutorial is used with the tutorial that accompanies the program. Walk Designer is used with animation. Add New Category is used to create your own new sublibrary for saving poses that you have created or modified.

1. Open one of the subcategories such as Action Sets by clicking on it in the pop-up menu.

2. Scroll up and down in the subcategory to view the poses available in that set.

3. Click on a pose to highlight it.

4. Click on the check to apply the pose to the figure in the document window.
5. Try out several different poses in several different subcategories.
6. Note that you can also apply the poses to the document window by double clicking on the icon that illustrates the pose instead of clicking once to highlight it and then clicking on the check.
7. When you are ready to move on, restore to the opening pose by going to the Default pose in the Pose Set.

C. Faces: This time, select another library by going up to the Poses title block at the top and moving the cursor over the small dots on the left side of the block. When the cursor is over the Faces dot, click the mouse button. The Faces library will open. The two subcategories available on the pop-up menu are Basic Expressions and Phonemes.
1. Select the Basic Expressions subcategory by clicking on it in the pop-up menu.
2. Scroll up and down to examine the options available.
3. Double click on one of the options to apply it to the figure in the document window.
4. Apply several of the other options available to see how they look.

D. Hair: Go to the Hair library either by clicking on the double-ended arrow or the appropriate small dot in the title block at the top of the library section. The options available in the pop-up menu are Hair Types, for use on Poser 3 figures, and Poser2 Fig Hair, for use on Poser 2 figures.
1. Select the Hair Types subcategory by clicking on it in the pop-up menu.
2. Scroll up and down to examine the options available.
3. Double click on one of the options to apply it to the figure in the document window.
4. Apply several of the other options available to see how they look.

E. Hands: Go to the Hands library either by clicking on the double-ended arrow or the appropriate small dot in the title block at the top of the library section. The options available in the pop-up menu are Basic Hands, Counting, Hand Puppets, Poser2 Fig Hands, Sign Language, and Add New Category.
1. Select the Basic Hands subcategory by clicking on it in the pop-up menu.
2. Scroll up and down to examine the options available.
3. Double click on one of the options to apply it to the figure in the document window.
4. You will be offered the option of applying the hand type to the left hand or the right hand of the figure. Click on the one that you want.

    5. Apply several of the other options available to see how they look.

   F. Close the libraries by either clicking on the tab on the left side of the Libraries area or by clicking on Window/Libraries in the main pull down menu.

3. Preview, or Display, Style: The preview, or display, style controls how the figure, document, and elements appear in the document window. There are a variety of display styles available. Be sure that there is a check mark next to Preview Styles in the Window pull down menu. If there is, there will be a series of nine spheres displayed on the screen below the Display Style title. The Display Style title on the screen may read Document Display Style, Figure Display Style, or Element Display Style depending upon which of these has been selected from the pop-up menu. Click on the down arrow next to the Display Style title on the screen above the nine spheres and the pop-up menu will appear. The display style will determine how the figure appears in the document window. Different display styles have different purposes. Some make adjusting the body parts easier. Others save on memory and speed up the adjustment process. You can apply a display style to the entire document, just the figure in the document, or just an element of the figure by clicking on the appropriate choice in the pop-up menu. Click on Document Display Style.

    Move the cursor over the top of the spheres under the Document Display Style title on the screen. The name of each display style available will appear as you move the cursor over the sphere associated with it. Click on each in turn to see how that display style appears.

   A. Silhouette (also available by hitting Ctrl + 1): The entire figure appears only in outline with this style. There is no detail.

   B. Outline (Ctrl + 2): Each element of the figure appears in an outline with this style.

   C. Wireframe (Ctrl + 3): With this style, the figure is covered with a mesh. This mesh will not react to light.

   D. Hidden Line (Ctrl + 4): With this option the figure is covered with a mesh as in wireframe, but you only see the mesh surfaces facing toward the camera. Back surfaces and hidden surfaces are not displayed. This mesh also does not react to light.

   E. Lit Wireframe (Ctrl + 5): This display is like the Hidden Line option, but the mesh does react to light.

   F. Flat Shaded (Ctrl + 6): The figure is displayed as though each surface of the mesh is a flat surface and is colored with this style.

   G. Sketch Shaded (Ctrl + 7): The figure is displayed in a hand-drawn style in this display.

H. Smooth Shaded (Ctrl + 8): The figure is displayed as a smooth surface that reacts to light in this style. This is usually the most useful of the display styles.

I. Texture Shaded (Ctrl + 9): If you have applied texture mapping to the figure, this style is used to display it.

Select the Smooth Shaded display style.

4. Document Tools: Make sure that there is a check mark by Document Tools in the Window pull down menu. This activates a variety of controls around the edges of the document window. This part of the exercise will work you through the use of each of them in turn.

A. File Name: The file name for the document is just outside the upper left-hand corner of the document window. When you first start up Poser it is Untitled. When you save the document and give it a file name, that name will appear in place of Untitled. Double click on the file name to close the document window. Double click again to make it reappear.

B. Document Size: The size of the document in pixels appears just outside the upper-right hand corner of the document window. When Poser opens, this is typically 350x350. Double click on the document size and the Set Window Size box opens. Here you can change the width and the height of the document window, lock the size of the window, and constrain the aspect ratio. Click on OK to close the Set Window Size box.

C. Color Dots: Along the lower right-hand side of the document window are the color dots. These are four dots just outside of the window. Incidentally, you might want to note that the User Guide for Poser has the order of these color dots incorrect. Working from top to bottom, these dots let you control:

1. Foreground Color: Click on the top dot with the mouse and hold the mouse button down to make the Foreground Color box appear. Still holding down the mouse button, move the cursor around this box to select a foreground color. When you have the color that you want, release the mouse button. Quite frankly, I find this method of color selection a pain in the neck and extremely inaccurate. Go to the pull down menu Display/Foreground Color to open a color box for selecting the foreground color that is much easier to use and offers a lot more options.

2. Background Color: Click on the second dot with the mouse and hold the mouse button down to make the Background Color box appear. This box requires working in the same manner as the

Foreground Color box. A much easier box to use as well as one that is much more accurate can be opened by clicking on Display/ Background Color. Select a background color using this box.

3. Shadow Color: Click on the third dot with the mouse and hold the mouse button down to make the Shadow Color box appear. This box also requires holding down the mouse button while you move the cursor around the box to pick the color. When you have the color that you want, release the mouse button to make the selection. Unfortunately, there is no alternative method for picking shadow color like there is for foreground and background color.

   a. Make sure that there is a check mark next to Display/Ground Shadows on the pull down menu, or shadows will not be displayed.

   b. Select a shadow color using the Shadow Color dot.

4. Ground Color: Click on the fourth dot with the mouse and hold the mouse button down to make the Ground Color box appear. Keep holding down the mouse and move the cursor around the box to find the ground color that you want. When you have it chosen, release the mouse button to select it. Ground color will only appear if you place a check mark by Ground Plane under the pull down menu Display/Guides/Ground Plane. There is no alternate method for selecting a ground color.

D. **Resize Window** Dot: At the lower right-hand corner of the document window there is a three-quarter circle. If you place the cursor over that circle it will change to a double-ended arrow. You can click and drag with the cursor to change the size of the window. This is a visual change and is not a very accurate way to resize the window.

E. **On/Off** Buttons: Just above the lower left-hand corner of the document window are a set of five **On/Off** buttons. When these are red in color they are on. Black indicates that a button is off. Click on the red or black button to turn it on or off. Working from top to bottom:

1. The **Depth Cuing** Button: This gives the view in the document window a sense of depth. As parts of the figure move further away, they fade out. Try turning this button on and off.

2. The next three buttons all control the tracking of the figure through changes. Only one of these three buttons can be on at any given time.

   a. The **Box Tracking** Button: With this option, each element of the figure is represented as a box. This can save time when setting up and working through an animation.

      b. The Fast Tracking Button: With this option, each element of the figure is represented as a box only when the figure is moving.

      c. The Full Tracking Button: This shows the figure using the display style that you have chosen. For most theatrical uses, this is the tracking method that should be selected.

  F. Figure Pop-Up: Just to the right and below the lower left-hand corner of the document window are the words Figure 1 and a down arrow to the left of those words. The down arrow is the Figure pop-up menu. If you have more than one figure in the document window, click on this arrow to select which figure you would like to work on.

  G. Element/Body Part Pop-Up: Just to the right of the Figure pop-up is the Element/Body Part pop-up arrow. Click on this arrow and a large pop-up menu appears from which you can select a body part or element for working. In the next step you will learn how to use the parameter dials to modify body parts or elements after they have been selected.

5. Modifying a part of a figure: In addition to being able to choose different figure types from the libraries and heights from the pull down menu, you can also modify each element or body part in any figure that you select. This is done by selecting the particular body part or element that you want to modify and then using the parameter dials to make the modification. Under the pull down menu Window, be sure that there is a check mark next to Parameter Dials so that they will be displayed. When you first open Poser, the parameter dials are displayed in the same areas as the libraries, so you will also need to have the libraries closed in order to see them.

  A. Open the libraries and select either the Female Nude or Male Nude figure so that you can see the effect of modifying elements of a figure more easily. Close the libraries.

  B. Click on the Element pop-up—the down arrow under the bottom center of the document window.

  C. Click on Abdomen on the pop-up. Look at the right-hand side of the screen. You should see the following parameter dials displayed under the title Abdomen: Taper, Scale, X-Scale, Y-Scale, Z-Scale, Twist, Side-Side, and Bend. The particular dials that will appear will vary with the element or body part that has been selected. Each of these dials can be increased or decreased in value to change that particular aspect of the element or body part.

    1. Move the cursor over the Scale dial. Notice that it changes to a double-ended arrow. Click and drag to the right to increase the

size of the abdomen. Click and drag to the left to decrease the size of the abdomen. Return the Scale dial to a value of 100%.

2. Move the cursor over the Scale dial so that it changes to a double-ended arrow. Double click. This opens the Edit Parameter Dial box. Using the keyboard, enter a new value for the parameter. Click on OK.

D. Enter new values for each of the parameter dials to see the result and then return those values to their default values.

E. Select a new body part or element by moving the cursor over the body part in the document window and then clicking. You should notice that the name of the selected body part or element will appear at the Element pop-up location below the document window as well as in the title over the top of the parameter dials as it is selected.

F. Modify some of the parameter dials for the newly selected body part or element and observe the results. Restore the value of any parameter that you have modified to its default value.

MODIFYING A POSE

Select a basic body type and pose with which you would like to work, and then you can begin changing that pose to something that is more specific. This involves using the editing tools that I covered in a basic way earlier.

1. Selecting an element or the entire body: There are a number of different ways that you can select the entire figure, or body, or just parts of that figure, or elements. Once either the body or one of its elements has been selected, the various editing tools can be used to modify the body or element.

A. Using the Figure pop-up:
   1. Click on the down arrow of the Figure pop-up under the lower left-hand corner of the document window. If there is more than one figure that is a part of the document, this pop-up will let you choose which figure will be selected.
   2. If there is only one figure in the document, you will only see the words Figure 1 in the pop-up.

B. Using the Element pop-up:
   1. Click on the down arrow of the Element pop-up to the right of the Figure pop-up below the document window. Move the cursor to the element—Abdomen, Thigh, etc.—to select a part of the figure, or to Body to select the entire figure. Click on the element that you would like to select. Notice that the name of the element appears next to the down arrow that activates the Element pop-up.

You will also notice that you can select lights and camera positions using this pop-up. There will be more on using the lights and cameras in a later exercise.

2. Select **Body** from the Element pop-up. This selects the entire figure.

C. Activating the **Figure Circle**: You can also select the entire figure or body by just clicking on the **Figure Circle** in the document window. In order to use this method, however, the Figure Circle must be activated. Click on the **Display** pull down menu. If there is no check next to **Figure Circle** then click on **Figure Circle**. A check mark next to Figure Circle in the pull down menu indicates that the Figure Circle is turned on.

1. Move the cursor into the document window. You will notice that a circle that encloses the entire figure is turned on anytime that the cursor is within the document window. This circle is the **Figure Circle**.

2. Select **Abdomen** using the Element pop-up. Notice that the abdomen part of the figure is outlined in red in the document window to indicate that it has been selected.

3. Move the cursor into the document window. Notice that the Figure Circle appears in Grey. Move the cursor over the top of the Figure Circle. Click once on the **Figure Circle**. You have just used the Figure Circle to select the entire figure or body. Move the cursor away from the Figure Circle. Notice that the Figure Circle is now red instead of grey, when you move the cursor off it, and the Element pop-up below the document window now reads body.

D. Selecting an element using the mouse: Just as you used the mouse to select the entire figure or body using the Figure Circle, you can also use the mouse to select a body part or element.

1. Move the cursor over a body part in the document window. Notice that the body part or element will be outlined in grey.

2. Click on the element. You have now selected that element. Notice that it is now outlined in red, when you move the cursor off it, and its name has now appeared next to the down arrow of the Element pop-up.

E. Select the abdomen of the figure using one of the methods outlined above.

2. Using the editing tools: If you move the cursor over the top of the editing tools, the name of each tool will appear. Click on that tool to select it and it will highlight. A caution about using the tools with elements: You click on a body part to select a body part. You click and drag to use a tool. It is very easy to accidentally select a new body part while you are trying

to use a tool on another body part. After you have selected a body part and a tool, you can use the tool by clicking and dragging anywhere in the main window. You do not have to click and drag close to or on top of the body part. By clicking and dragging away from the entire figure, you can use the tool without accidentally selecting another body part.

A. The Rotate Tool: The Rotate tool bends a body part at its joint. It works in three dimensions so it can also get you into contorted positions quickly. Work carefully with the Rotate tool. Click on the Rotate button. Until you develop skill with this tool it can be a good idea to just move it perpendicular to the body part or parallel to the body part. Click and drag perpendicular to the body part to move it in that direction. Click and drag parallel to the body part to move it toward or away from you. Remember that the Edit/Restore/Element command will get you back to where you started before you began rotating the body part.

1. Rotate the abdomen in several different directions.
2. Rotate it to a position that you like or use the Edit/Restore/Element command to restore it to where you began.

B. The Twist Tool: The Twist tool rotates a body part around its own axis. Click on the Twist button. Click and drag from side to side on the screen to twist the abdomen.

   Twist the abdomen to a position that you like.

C. The Translate/Pull Tool: The Translate tool moves the body part vertically and horizontally. For the abdomen you will only be able to move it from side to side at its juncture with the hips. Click on the Translate button. Click and drag from side to side to move the abdomen.

1. Select another body part such as an upper arm.
2. Use the Translate tool to move it.

D. The Translate In/Out (Z) Tool: The ZTranslate tool moves the body part toward and away from you. Click on the ZTranslate button. Click and drag up to move the part away from you. Click and drag down to move the part toward you.

E. The Scale Tool: The Scale button lets you change the size of the body part or element selected. Reselect the abdomen. Click and drag vertically to change the vertical size. Click and drag horizontally to change the horizontal size. You can control scale much more precisely by using the parameter dials.

F. The Taper Tool: The Taper button lets you change the relationship between the size of the two ends of a body part. Move the cursor horizontally to affect the taper. Different body parts will taper in different ways depending upon their relationship to their connected parts. Try tapering the abdomen using the cursor and mouse. You can also control taper more precisely by using the parameter dials.

G. The **Chain Break** Tool: The **Chain Break** tool removes a link between two body parts. Click on the **Chain Break** tool, then click on the body part you want to isolate so that it will not move if you move other body parts. A Chain Break symbol will appear. If you use the Translate tool to move the hand up and down, for example, the lower and upper arm will follow. Place a chain break on the forearm, and when you move the hand, the forearm will not move.

1. Move a hand up and down with the **Translate** tool. The forearm and shoulder will follow.
2. Place a chain break on the forearm.
3. Move the hand up and down with the **Translate** tool. The forearm and shoulder will not follow.
4. Remove the chain break from the forearm by clicking on the **Chain Break** tool and then clicking on the forearm. When you click on the **Chain Break** tool, the figure will show you where chain breaks are located. You cannot remove the chain break on the hips.

H. The **Color** Tool: The **Color** tool lets you quickly change the color of parts of the figure. Select either the **Male** or **Female Casual** figure from the library so that you can get a better idea of how the Color tool works.

1. Click on the **Color** tool to select it. It doesn't matter if you have an element or the body selected on the figure. The Color tool only works on the color of diffuse materials such as skin, clothing, etc.
2. Move the Color tool over the top of a part of the figure such as its skin, the shirt, pants, shoes, etc.
3. Click and hold on the mouse. The **Diffuse Material Color** box opens.
4. Still holding down the mouse button, move the cursor around the Diffuse Material Color box. When you have selected the color that you would like, release the mouse button. That color will be applied to the part of the figure where you had originally clicked.
5. Try out the Color tool on other parts of the figure such as the shirt, pants, shoes, etc.

I. The **Drop to Floor** Tool: The **Figure/Drop to Floor** command lets you drop the figure to the floor from any position that you have moved it to using the tools in the toolbox.

Drop the figure to the floor.

3. Arrgh . . . I can't get out of this mess!: Escape mechanisms: It is very easy to get yourself into something that you seriously dislike by using

the various tools. Scale can do it to you very quickly, for example. So let's review some of the escape mechanisms built into Poser before you go any further. You have got to be thinking about using these commands for them to do you any good, however. If you just start clicking around haphazardly, you will rapidly get into a place from which your only choice will be starting all over again.

A. Undo: Edit/Undo/Undo Change/Redo Change will reverse the last action that you did. It will only go back *one step*, however. You cannot back up multiple steps as in AutoCAD, 3D Studio MAX, and other programs.

B. Memorize: Edit/Memorize lets you memorize the position of an element, figure, light, or camera. If you have a figure in a position that you know you like, use this command to memorize it before you try out something new. Then you will be able to return to it if you get in trouble.

C. Restore: Edit/Restore lets you return to the position of an element, figure, light, or camera. Use this command to get back to a position that you have memorized.

4. The Inverse Kinematics Function: Inverse kinematics, or IK, is a function of Poser that helps you to maintain a natural pose as you move body parts. The "chain" that you are breaking when using the Chain Break command is the one that IK establishes. In natural motion, when one body part moves, the other body parts attached to it move as well. The following part of the exercise will help demonstrate the effects of IK.

A. Remove any chain breaks except for the one on the hips.

B. Turn off IK: Click on Figure/Inverse Kinematics/ and then on any of the four options—Left Leg, Right Leg, Left Arm, or Right Arm—that have a check mark by them. You will need to follow the whole series of steps for each option that has a check mark by it.

C. Select the Translate tool in the toolbox.

D. Select the hips of the figure.

E. Move the hips up and down—the entire figure follows the movement of the hips, but the relationship between the parts doesn't change.

F. Turn on IK for the legs. Follow the same procedure as above to place a check mark by both legs.

G. Select the hips of the figure.

H. Move the hips up and down—it looks like the feet are planted on the ground, and when you move the hips, the legs bend.

5. The Use Limits Function: Use Limits is a function of Poser that keeps the range of motion of body parts within natural limits. Selecting this option

will help you to avoid too many impossibly contorted positions. It does not apply to the parts involved in IK. Unless you are deliberately trying to create a contorted position, it is usually a good idea to have Use Limits checked.

A. Turn Use Limits on: Click on Figure on the pull down menu. If there is a check by Use Limits, it is on. If there is no check by Use Limits, it is off; click on it to turn it on.

B. Select the Translate tool in the toolbox.

C. Select the abdomen of the figure.

D. Move the abdomen from side to side. Notice that you can only go so far with this motion. The abdomen will stop moving when you reach a certain point.

E. Turn Use Limits off.

F. Move the abdomen from side to side. Notice that now you can do some physically impossible things with the abdomen.

G. Restore the position of the abdomen to a natural position.

6. The Symmetry Function: The Symmetry command under the Figure pull down menu can help you quickly balance a figure with modifications. If you change an aspect of an arm, for example, such as its length, the Symmetry command will let you apply exactly the same change to the other arm.

A. Select the left forearm and lengthen it using the Scale command.

B. Click on Figure/Symmetry/Left to Right. The right forearm will be lengthened by the same amount.

C. Take a careful look at the other options available under the Symmetry command. Many of them can be extremely useful when you are modifying the proportions of figures.

7. Adding another figure to your scene: You can easily add one or more figures to the scene in Poser. These additional figures can be manipulated in precisely the same way as the first figure, with all of the same choices of body type, etc.

A. Open the libraries.

B. Select the Figures library.

C. Click on the figure type that you would like to add to the document window.

D. Click on the double check at the bottom of the library.

E. When the second figure appears it may be superimposed on top of the first figure. Click on the Body button on the toolbox and then move it out of the way.

F. After the second figure has been added, notice that the Figure pop-up at the bottom of the document window says Figure 2 to indicate that the second figure is selected. If you want to select the first figure instead, just click on the Figure pop-up and then on Figure 1.

G. Deleting a figure: You can delete any figure from the scene. First select the figure that you want to delete using the Figure pop-up menu, then click on Figure/Delete Figure. *Do not* delete the second figure at this point.

8. Hiding a figure: If you are working with more than one figure, it can often be useful to make one of the figures temporarily disappear so that it is easier to work with the other one. You can do this by using the Hide Figure command.

A. Select the figure that you would like to hide using the Figure pop-up.

B. Click on Figure/Hide Figure on the pull down menu. The figure will disappear.

C. To make it reappear, click on the Figure/Show All Figures command on the pull down menu.

D. Now use the Figure/Delete Figure command to eliminate the second figure.

9. Using the memory dots: In addition to using the Edit/Memory commands available on the pull down menu you can also use the Pose dots to remember poses that you have created for a figure. Anytime that you have created a pose and want to temporarily save it for this working session, you can use one of the pose dots to do so. Be sure that the memory dots are turned on and there's a check mark next to the words Memory Dots under the Window pull down menu.

A. Move the figure into the position that you would like to save using the editing tools, parameter dials, etc.

B. Click on the down arrow next to the memory dots on the screen.

C. Select Pose Dots from the pop-up menu that appears.

D. Click on one of the dots. This saves the pose to that dot. You must remember which dot you used to save different poses. Notice that the color of the dot changes.

E. Move the figure or part of the figure to a new position.

F. Click on another of the dots. This saves the new pose to that dot.

G. Click on the dot that you clicked on earlier to restore to the first pose.

H. Click on the dot that you clicked on second to restore to the second pose.

    I. The Camera dots can be used in a similar way to save camera positions and the UI dots will save screen setups.

10. Saving your work: After creating your figure you will want to save it to a file so that you will have a permanent record that can be used again at a later date. Saving it as a file also lets you stop at any point in your work and then come back and pick up where you left off. If you have not previously saved the figure as a file, you will have to use the Save As command to give it a file name and assign it to a drive and folder:

    A. Click on File/Save As. The Save Pose As box opens.

    B. In the File name: window, enter a name for the file, such as fig1, followed by the extension .pz3. For example, fig1.pz3.

    C. Your only choice in the Save as type: window will be Poser 3.0 File (*.PZ3).

    D. In the Save in: window, select the drive and folder, if you want to place it in a folder and/or subfolder, where you would like the file to be saved. This is where you must decide if you want to save the file to your hard drive, to a floppy drive, or to a Zip drive.

    E. Click on the Save button.

    F. You have just saved the file with the name you have chosen to the location you selected. You will need to remember both of these to retrieve the file later. The next time that you open the file you can save any changes that you make to the same name and location by just clicking on File/Save rather than using the Save As command. If you would like to save the changes to a new file name or location you will have to use the Save As command again. Compare the file that you have saved to the file Exer1.pz3 on the CD-ROM.

USING PROPS

Poser comes with a selection of props that you can add to the figures to give them more realism or a feeling of style. These props can be attached to a body part such as a hand so that your figure can be holding a sword or carrying a briefcase. You can also import props that you have created in AutoCAD, 3D Studio MAX, and other sources as well. Yet another unique feature of Poser is its ability to combine a prop with a figure to create a hybrid creature from your imagination. Exercise No. 2 will take you through the process of adding, using, and importing props.

Exercise No. 2: Adding, Using, and Importing Props

ADDING A PROP FROM THE POSER LIBRARY

1. Open Poser. Working in the opening screen, open the libraries. Under Figures, select Casual Man and apply it to the figure in the document window. Under Poses, select Conversation from the Standing Set and apply it to the figure.

2. Now you'll add a cane to the figure.

   A. Open the Prop library.

   B. Click on Cane.

   C. Click on the check mark at the bottom of the library.

   D. The cane will appear in the document window with the figure.

3. Next, let's work with the cane and the figure.

   A. Click on the Translate tool and move the cane to the side. The cane is already selected so you don't have to click on it to select it. If you accidentally select a body part of the figure, you can reselect the cane by using the Element pop-up button on the bottom of the main window or clicking on the cane.

   B. Scale the cane to the right size for your figure.

   C. The prop origin: When the prop appears you may notice that there are X,Y,Z crosshairs near it. This is the prop origin. If you do not see the prop origin crosshairs you can turn them on by using Properties on the pull down menu. Select the cane if it isn't selected. Then click on Edit/Properties. The Prop Properties box will open. Place a check in the Display Origin box and click on OK. You can move the position of the prop origin by using the Origin X, Origin Y, and Origin Z parameter dials. If you wish to rotate the prop, it will rotate around this origin point. By moving the prop origin, you can change how the prop rotates.

   D. Position the prop so that it looks like it is being held in the right hand of the figure. You will probably have to use several tools to do this: Translate and Twist will certainly be necessary. The Translate In/Out button will probably also be useful to move it closer to you and further away. You will probably also need to get into the view from the From Top camera and the Right Hand camera.

   E. Color the prop: With the cane selected, click on Render/Surface Material.

      1. The Surface Material box will open.

      2. Click on Object Color and select a basic color for the cane.

      3. Click on Highlight Color and select a highlight color for the cane.

4. Click on **Ambient Color** and select a black or grey.

5. Click on **OK**.

Note: You can also color the cane by using the **Color** tool in the editing tools.

F. Attach the prop to a body part: If you want the prop to move naturally with a part of the body such as the right hand, you must attach it to that body part.

   1. Move the prop into the exact position that you want. It may be useful to try out several different camera views to help you see its position better. Click on **Display/Camera View** and then on **Left, Right, Front,** or **Top** camera to select different camera views. If you change the camera view, you may have to reselect the cane before it can be moved, twisted, etc.

   2. When the prop is in position: Check to be sure the cane is selected. Click on **Edit/Properties**. The **Prop Properties** dialogue box opens. Click on the **Set Prop Parent** button.

   3. The **Choose Parent** box opens. Click on the button next to **Parent:** and select **Right Hand**.

   4. Click on **OK**. You return to the **Prop Properties** box. Click on **OK**.

   5. Select the right hand of the figure and move it around. The cane will move with it.

4. Save this figure and prop together as fig2a.pz3. Click on **File/Save As** and give it the name and a location. You can compare your work with the file Exer2a.pz3 on the CD-ROM.

IMPORTING A PROP FROM AUTOCAD OR 3D STUDIO MAX

If you have created a prop in AutoCAD or 3D Studio MAX, you can use it in Poser. If you have exported it directly from AutoCAD as a .dxf file, however, you will not be able to use it in Poser. Files exported directly from AutoCAD do not have any facet entry data, and you will get a warning telling you so if you try to bring in a .dxf file directly from AutoCAD. To import a prop from AutoCAD, you must first export it from AutoCAD as a .dxf file. Then you will have to import that file into 3D Studio MAX. In 3D Studio MAX, you will have to give it **UVW mapping** and exported it as a .3DS file. While it is in 3D Studio MAX you can also add a texture to it if you would like using the **Material Editor**. In the Poser Folder on the CD-ROM, there is a file named sword.3ds. This file was drawn in AutoCAD, exported as a .dxf file, imported into 3D Studio MAX, given UVW mapping and had a brass texture added. It was then exported from 3D Studio MAX as sword.3ds.

Any file that you created in 3D Studio MAX would just have to be exported as a **.3DS** file to be usable in Poser.

1. Open Poser or click on File/New to start a new scene. If you haven't saved the old one, you will be given an opportunity to do so.

2. Open the libraries, if they aren't already, and select Figures and then the Male Casual figure. Apply this figure type to the new scene. Click on Poses. Select Sports Sets and Fencer and apply it to the scene. Now you'll give the fencer a sword.

Note: Even though the opening figure looks like the Male Casual figure, it is not and will not accept many features of the program properly. You must select a figure type before you start applying poses, hair, etc. to the figure.

3. Place the CD-ROM that accompanies the book in your CD-ROM drive.

4. Click on File/Import/3D_Studio. The 3D Studio box opens. Locate the file named sword.3ds in the Poser folder on the CD-ROM.

5. Click on the name sword.3ds in the large window under Look in: so that its name appears in the window File name.

6. Click on Open.

7. The Prop Import Options box opens. Here you can decide if you want the prop centered or placed on the floor; check Centered. You can also give it a percent of standard figure size. Different file types from different programs will import into Poser in very different sizes. This option lets you give the imported prop a size relative to a standard Poser figure so that you will have some idea of how large it will be when it appears. You can always scale it later to give it a more precise size.

    Enter a figure of 65 in the box to the right of Percent of standard figure size. Click on OK.

8. The sword appears at the feet of the figure in Poser. It is given the name OBJ_IMPORT_1 and is already selected.

9. Move and twist the sword around so that it is facing in the correct direction, and place it in the hand of the fencer.

10. Color the sword using Render/Surface Material:

    A. When the Color box opens, you can work with it much like you worked with the Color box earlier in 3D Studio MAX.
       1. You can define a color using the R,G,B and/or H,S,V boxes.
       2. You can click on a hue in the large rainbow-colored box and then define the white/black scale using the slider to the side of it.
       3. The Object Color is the base color. The Highlight Color is the color of the highlights. The Ambient Color should be set to black or grey.

    B. When you have your colors set, click on OK.

11. Save the scene as fig2b.pz3 to a location of your choosing using the Save As command. You can compare your work with the file Exer2b.pz3 on the CD-ROM.

REPLACING A BODY PART WITH A PROP

Any prop that can be imported into Poser can be used to replace a body part. You could replace a hand with a hook, for example, or import a strange-looking head to use in place of a regular head. The process for doing this is as follows:

1. Open Poser or click on File/New to start a new scene. If you haven't saved the old one, you will now be given an opportunity to do so.

2. Open the libraries, if they aren't already, and click on Poses. Select Creative Pose Sets and Fairy Dance. In the Figure library, select Male Nude. Turn Genitalia off if it is on—Figure/Genitalia. Click on Figure/Figure Height/Adolescent. Now you'll give the dancer a new head.

3. To keep this simple, just use a ball from the standard Poser props as a head. You could also import anything that you had drawn in AutoCAD, 3D Studio MAX, or other programs, following the import procedures outlined in the last part of this exercise.

   A. In the Props library, double click on the ball.
   B. After the ball appears at the bottom of the scene, scale it up to 110% using the parameter dial.

4. Move the ball into position so that it is in the same place occupied by the head of the figure:

   A. You should be able to do this using the Translate tool.
   B. You will probably need to look at it from a couple of different camera views to get it correct. The Main and Top cameras will certainly be necessary.

5. When everything is in position, select the body part you are replacing—the head. This is easiest to do using the Element pop-up under the main window.

6. Click on Figure/Replace Body Part With Prop. The Replace Part box opens.

7. Click on the box next to Prop: and select Ball_1.

8. Click on OK.

9. You will get a warning box that tells you about recommendations for how to work with the altered geometry. Read it and then click on OK.

10. Change the color of the ball using either the Color tool or the Render/Surface Material command on the pull down menu.

11. If you later decide that you want to go back to the regular head, click on Figure/Figure Type/Male Nude. The Keep Customized Geometry box opens. To restore to a regular head, leave all boxes unchecked and click on OK. You will also see this box if you decide later that you would like to change the figure type but keep the custom head. If you want to do this, place a check in the both of the small boxes and click on OK.

12. Save the file as fig2c.pz3 using the Save As command to a location of your choice. You can compare it to the file Exer2c.pz3 on the CD-ROM.

USING CAMERAS

You have already had some experience using the different cameras available with Poser, but this section will acquaint you with more of the details. You can switch to a different camera view in Poser anytime that you would like. You should be aware that when you do this, whatever camera you have selected will become the selected element. If you would like to work on a body part, you will have to reselect that body part after you have switched camera views. The cameras allow you to look at the scene from different points of view so that you can more easily work on various elements, compose the view that you want for a rendering, etc.

SELECTING THE CAMERA

There are four ways that you can select different cameras in Poser. The first way is to click on Display, then on Camera View, and then make a choice of Main, From Left, From Right, From Top, From Front, Face, Posing, Right Hand, Left Hand, Dolly, or Flyaround. The second way is to click on the Element pop-up at the bottom of the main window. When the pop-up menu appears, select the camera you want from the list. The third way is to use the pop-up by the camera controls on the screen. Click on the down arrow next to the title Camera Controls, and a pop-up menu appears that is identical to the one under Display/Camera View on the pull down menu. Click on the camera that you want to select that view. The fourth way is to make choices from the Camera Controls icons that appear on the screen. How these work will take a little more explanation and will be covered later in this section.

CAMERAS

The different cameras have different restrictions as to what can and cannot be done with each.

- Main, Posing, and Dolly Cameras: These can move anywhere. All of the Camera buttons will work with these cameras. They provide perspective viewpoints. The Main and Posing cameras move around the center of the scene space. The Dolly camera moves around itself. The Main and Dolly cameras can be used in animation. The Posing camera cannot.
- Top, Front, Left, and Right Cameras: These cameras are restricted in their movement to their own point of view. They provide a flat rather than perspective view of the scene. The Rotate and Translate In/Out buttons will not work with these cameras.
- Face, Right Hand, and Left Hand Cameras: These each provide a close-up view of the particular body part or element in their name. Other than that, they work like the Main camera.
- Flyaround Camera: This provides you with a rotating view of the figure. Click anywhere on the screen to stop the Flyaround view and return to the view in which you began.

EDITING TOOLS

After you have selected a camera, these editing tools will allow you to change the view through the camera. You can also perform these functions using the parameter dials. Different cameras will display different parameter dials depending upon what kinds of motion are possible.

 The Rotate Tool: This only works with the Main, Posing, and Dolly cameras. For the Main and Posing cameras, after this button is selected, click and drag to move the viewpoint of the camera. Drag up or down to change the view vertically. Drag left or right to change the view horizontally. As you move the camera, it will still point at the center of the scene. The Dolly camera moves around its own center.

 The Twist Tool: This only works with the Main, Posing, and Dolly cameras. This button rotates the Main and Posing cameras around the center of the scene. It rotates the Dolly camera around itself. Click and drag left or right.

 The Translate/Pull Tool: This tool works with all cameras. It moves any camera vertically or horizontally. Select the button and then click and drag to move the camera. Dragging vertically raises and lowers the camera. Dragging horizontally moves the camera from side to side.

 The Translate In/Out (ZTranslate) Tool: This only works with the Main, Posing, and Dolly cameras. It moves the camera closer to or farther away from the scene. Click and drag down to get closer to the scene. Click and drag up to get farther away.

The **Scale** Tool: This command zooms the camera. It works with all cameras. Click and drag to the right to get a closer view. Click and drag to the left to get a view from farther back.

CAMERA LIBRARY

There is also a collection of camera views in the library. Click on the **Camera** block in the library to see the **Camera Sets** menu. You can select any of these views by double clicking on them or clicking on them once and then on the check mark at the bottom of the library. If you find a view that you like by adjusting the camera you can also give it a name and save it here using the same procedures as for saving a pose.

CAMERA CONTROLS

The camera controls on the Poser screen represent another way to control what camera you choose and how to move about in the views from the camera. The camera controls appear on the screen as a set of icons when there is a check

**CAMERA
CONTROLS**

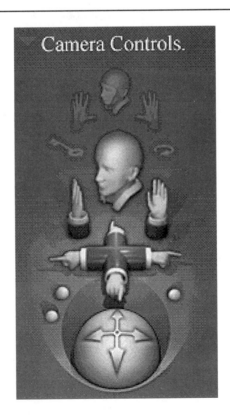

Camera Controls.

mark next to Camera Controls under the Window pull down menu. If you move the mouse over the icons in the Camera Controls area, the name of that particular icon will appear in the Camera Controls title area. Click on that icon to move to that view or activate that control function. The various icons in the Camera Controls area are, working from the top down:

Face Cam (looks like a small view of a face with a helmet): This switches you to a view of the figure's face.

Right Hand Cam: This switches you to a view of the figure's right hand.

Left Hand Cam: This switches you to a view of the figure's left hand.

Animating On/Off (looks like a key): This disables key framing for a camera.

Flyaround View (circular arrow): This turns the rotating view on and off.

Select Camera: Move the cursor over the large head when in From Front and a double-ended arrow will appear. Click and drag to change the icon and select From Top (icon is top view of head), From Left (icon is left view of head), From Right (icon is right view of head), Face Camera (icon is head with helmet on), Posing Camera (icon is figure with arms around legs), Right Hand Cam (icon is right hand), Left Hand Cam (icon is left hand) or Dolly Camera (icon is head with movie camera).

Note: The next three icons are used to restrict the camera movement. Click on one of these to allow the camera to move in only two of the three planes. Then use the appropriate editing tool to move the view from the camera.

Move Y and Z (icon is a side view of hand): This restricts camera movement to the Y and Z planes. The camera can only move backward, forward, up, and down.

Move X and Y (icon is a front view of hand): This restricts camera movement to the X and Y planes. The camera can only move vertically and horizontally.

Move X and Z (icon is shaped like a cross with a hand at each of the four ends): This restricts camera movement to the X and Z planes. The camera can only move forward, backward, left, or right.

Note: To the left of the large ball with four arrows in the middle are two dots. To the right of the ball there is one dot. The large ball is the rotation trackball. The three dots are the Scale, Focal Length, and Roll controls.

Rotation Trackball: It does not matter which editing tool is selected when you use the rotation trackball. Click and drag on the trackball itself to rotate the view. For most cameras, clicking and dragging on the trackball will rotate the camera around the outside of the studio. For the Main camera, it rotates around the center of the studio. For the Figure, Face, and Hand cameras, it rotates around the figure, face, or hands.

Scale: This acts like a zoom control. Click and drag right over the dot to zoom in. Click and drag left over the dot to zoom out.

Focal Length: This increases or decreases the focal length of the selected camera. Click on the dot and drag right to increase the focal length. Click on the dot and drag left to decrease focal length. Changing the focal length of the camera can create some extremely dramatic effects, like a fish-eye lens.

Roll: This tilts the view from the camera. Click on the dot and drag right to roll right. Click on the dot and drag left to roll left.

Parameter Dials

Whenever any camera is selected, there is also a set of parameter dials open for that camera. These dials can be used to obtain precise control over the view from the camera and are used like any other set of parameter dials. The dials will appear on screen if there is a check mark next to Parameter Dials under the Window pull down menu.

Camera Dots

The Memory Dots area also allows you to record changes that you have made to the view from a particular camera. Be sure that there is a check next to Memory Dots under the Window pull down menu for these to appear on the screen. Click on the down arrow and select Camera Dots from the pop-up that appears. After you have adjusted a view from a camera that you would like to save, click on a dot to save that view. Remember which dot you clicked on for that view. Whenever you would like to return to that view, simply click on the dot again. There are nine dots, each of which can be used to record a different view.

Using Lights

Poser has three lights that are a part of the program. Each of these lights may be controlled for direction, color, and intensity. Use the light controls that appear on the screen when there is a check next to Light Controls under the Window pull down menu. Three larger spheres and three smaller dots appear in the Light Controls area on the screen. The three larger spheres represent the three lights available in Poser. Click on one of these spheres to select that lighting instrument. The three dots represent the shorthand color control for that particular lighting instrument. More precise color control can be achieved through the use of the parameter dials once a lighting instrument has been selected. The three lighting instruments can also be selected by clicking on the Element pop-up menu just under the document window.

**THE LIGHT
CONTROLS**

ADJUSTING THE DIRECTION

Click on the first light sphere in the Light Controls area. You will see a circle with three arrows coming from one side appear in the document window. The arrows represent the direction from which the light is coming. When you move the cursor into the document window, you will see the cursor change into the double-curved arrows of the Rotate tool. You can click and drag in the window to move the circle with the arrows. This will change the direction from which the light is coming. If you watch the figure closely, you will see the effect of the light on the figure. Also watch the sphere up in the Light Controls area. As you move the cursor, the direction of the light displayed on the sphere will change, representing the direction from which the light is coming by a bright spot on the sphere. You can also move the cursor over the sphere in the Light Controls area. When it is over the sphere it will change into a dot and a curved arrow. Click and drag over the sphere to adjust the direction from which the light is coming.

In the Parameter Dials area of the toolbox, there are X, Y, and Z Rotation dials. You can also adjust the position of the light by using these dials. Click on the second light sphere to adjust the second light and the third light sphere for the third light.

ADJUSTING THE COLOR

Immediately next to each of the light spheres that represents one of the three lights is a small dot. Click on this dot and continue to hold the mouse button down to use the shorthand method of adjusting the color of that light. The Color box will open and you can move the cursor around in that box while still holding down the mouse button to choose a color. Release the mouse button to select the color. This is an extremely annoying and imprecise way to select colors, but you can also use the Red, Green, and Blue parameter dials to select the color. If you are not already familiar with additive color mixing, I suggest that you learn about it so that you can control the color of your lights more accurately through the use of the parameter dials.

ADJUSTING THE SCALE

The Scale dial in the Parameters box controls the size of the beam of light. You can increase and decrease it by scrolling it down to less than 100 percent or up above 100 percent. The 100% mark on the scale represents a light just large enough to cover any figures in the scene.

ADJUSTING THE INTENSITY

The intensity of the light is adjusted by using the Intensity parameter dial.

USING THE LIGHT PROPERTIES BOX

Open the Light Properties box by clicking on Edit/Properties while one of the three lights is selected. In the Light Properties box, you can:

- turn the light on or off by checking or unchecking the boxes,
- make it Animating or Not by checking or unchecking the boxes, or
- have it Cast Shadows or Not by checking or unchecking the boxes.
1. When you have made your selections for that light, click on OK.
2. Select another light and then return to the Edit/Properties box for it to make the same choices if desired.

USING THE SHADOW DIAL

The Shadow dial in the Parameters box also lets you control the strength of the shadow cast by that light. The scale runs from 0—no shadow—to 1—strongest shadow.

USING THE MAP SIZE DIAL

The Map Size dial in the Parameters box controls the size of the shadow map for the shadow cast by that light. The larger the map size, the more detail in the shadow. Larger map sizes, however, take up a considerable amount of RAM. Rendering will take longer as you increase the map size, as will renewing the view of the scene each time you make changes.

USING THE LIGHTS LIBRARY

The Lights library contains a number of preset lighting combinations that you can try out. These are available in the library when you click on the Lights bar. If you come up with a lighting combination on your own that you like, you can save that under Lights in the library as well.

RENDERING

You have already done some basic rendering with Poser. This section will make you aware of the more advanced options available in the program. First, review the basic options for rendering accessible under the pull down menu Render.

THE RENDER MENU

The Render pull down menu lets you render a final view of a scene and control the appearance of that rendering.

Render: This creates a rendering of the scene that uses all of the choices you have made under Render Options and Surface Material below.

Preset Render: This gives you a choice of a fast or a clean rendering. Both of these are "preset" and do not use the rendering options. The fast rendering tends to create jagged edges but is quick. The clean rendering eliminates the jagged edges but is slower.

Smooth Render: This is another render method with choices made by the program. You also have a fast or clean option much like the Preset Render options. This method is faster than the Preset Render functions because it does not apply bump or texture maps to the figure.

Render Options: This opens the Render Options box, where you can specify the size and details of your rendering.

Render to: This lets you specify the window in which the rendering will occur.

Main Window: This is faster and keeps the desktop from becoming cluttered with extra windows. There is only one size that can be rendered with this option: 350×350.

New Window: This creates the rendering in a different window from the main window. It allows you to choose different window sizes and specify the dimensions in pixels, inches, or centimeters. It also lets you specify the resolution. Click on the down arrow in the appropriate box to select the scale. Click to the right of the number in the Width, Height, or Resolution box and then drag to the left to change the size or resolution. After the number is highlighted, type in the new number. You can also just click to the right and then use the Backspace key before entering a new number. When you change width or height, the size of the other will automatically change to maintain the standard aspect ratio used by Poser: width/height = 1.333.

Surface Detail: This gives you choices about how the surface of the figure is rendered.

Anti-Aliasing: Select this for softer, smoother edges.

Use bump maps/Use texture maps: If you have applied bump or texture maps to the surface of the figure, selecting these options will let you see them in the rendering.

Cast shadows: If this is selected, the program will show shadows in the rendering. Shadows take longer to render. If you are in a hurry, you might want to deselect this option.

Render Over: This lets you choose the background for your rendering.

Background Color: This renders over the background color selected in general preferences—Edit/General Preferences. The default is black unless you change it.

Black: This creates a rendering with a black background even if you have a different background color or have imported a background picture.

Background Picture: If you have imported a background image, this option will render over that image. See the section later on importing background images (see page 183).

Surface Material: This lets you control the bump maps, texture, and color of objects in the rendering.

Object Pop-Up: At the top of the Surface Material box is a button with the name of the currently selected "object," or figure, such as Figure 1, Figure 2, etc. If there is more than one figure in the document window, click on this button to select each figure in turn.

Material pop-up: Underneath the Object pop-up is the Material pop-up. Click on this button and a pop-up will appear with the name of all of the materials in the scene, such as pants, shirt, skin, etc. Select the material for which you want to choose surface materials and then make selections in the rest of the box. When you are finished with that material, go on to the next material. After you have completed making selections for all the materials in the scene, click on OK.

Bump Map: A bump map adds surface relief to an object. In the Bump Map area of the Surface Material box are options that let you select an already loaded map, import one from outside, and control the strength of the map. See the section later on creating your own bump maps (see page 184).

Down Arrow Button: This button opens a list of already loaded bump maps for you to select.

Load Button: This button opens the Open box so you can load a bump map from another source.

Strength Slider: Click and drag on the slider to change the strength of the bump map.

Texture Map: A texture map wraps an image around an object. Texture maps are like painting on the surface of your figure. There are some standard texture maps available with Poser, and you can use Painter to create your own. See the section later on creating your own texture maps (see page 186).

Down Arrow Button: This button opens a list of already loaded texture maps for you to select.

Load Button: This button opens the Open box so you can load a texture map from another source.

Strength Slider: Click and drag on the slider to change the strength of the texture map.

The Object Color Button: Click on the Object Color button to change the basic color of the current object. This opens a good-quality Color box like the one available for foreground and background color under the pull down menu. The object color does influence the color of any texture map that is applied. Select an object color of white if you don't want to change the color of a texture map.

The Highlight Color Button: Click on the Highlight Color button to change the highlight of the current object. Highlights are the brightest parts of the object where light is reflected directly back to the eye.

The Ambient Color Button: Click on the Ambient Color button to change the ambient color of the current object. The ambient color is one that is given off without regard to light positions or colors. Too much ambient color will flatten shadows and highlights. It is usually best to keep this low—set to black or grey—unless you want to create a more two-dimensional looking figure. If you want to emphasize two-dimensionality, then set the ambient color to white or a bright color.

IMPORTING BACKGROUND IMAGES

If you would like to use a background behind your figure in Poser, you can import an image from Painter or another source. This image must be a .bmp or a .tif file. If you have an image that you would like to scan and use, be sure that it is saved as one of these two formats. Make a note of the file name and location so that you will know where to find it when it is time to import it into Poser. If the set designer on the show creates a rendering of the set in Painter, that can be saved as a .tif or .bmp file and imported to use as a background. Similarly, a rendering from 3D Studio MAX can be saved as a .tif or .bmp file and used as a background in Poser. A manually created rendering could also be scanned into a .tif or .bmp file and used as a background in Poser. See the sections on each of the programs for information on saving renderings, or see the information that came with your scanner for how to save scanned objects as particular file types.

To Import a Background Image

1. Click on File/Import/Background Picture. The Open box appears. Here is where you find the file name and location of the image that you have scanned in or previously saved in another program.
2. Under Files of type:, select the file type of the image that you want to import—either .bmp or .tif.

Note: It is very important that when this file was saved, it was given the appropriate extension to the file name. Otherwise, you will have much more trouble finding it. This function of the box will filter out all files that have not been given the appropriate extension. If the file was saved without an extension, you must select All Files here, and it will be more difficult to locate the file you're looking for.

3. In the Look in: area, select the drive and folder where the file is located.
4. When the file name appears in the large box under Look in:, click on it so that its name appears in the File name: area. Click on OK.
5. If the height and width of the image are different from the current main window, a box will open asking you if you want to change the size of the current window. Click on YES.
6. The background image will appear on the screen with the figure in front of it. At this point you may want to choose another display method such as Lit Wireframe or Flat Shaded for the figure so that it will be easier to see. You usually will also need to scale the size of the figure so that it appears in proper proportion in front of the background.
7. When it is time to render the scene, you also need to change your render options to Render Over the Background Picture.
8. You will also need to change the lighting in Poser to match the lighting in the background picture.

CREATING BUMP MAPS

Bump maps add surface texture to an object or figure in Poser. Think of using them as creating highlights and shadows on the figure. There are two bump maps already available in Poser—one of Male Muscle and another of Female Muscle. These work fine with the Male and Female Nude figures but look pretty silly on most of the other figure types. If you want to create your own bump map that can be used with the Casual, Business, or other figures, there are templates available that you can use for doing this. Bring the template into Painter or Adobe Photoshop to create the bump map. This bump map must be saved out of the other program as a .bmp or .tif file before it can be loaded into Poser.

To Create and Load a Bump Map

1. Open Painter or Adobe Photoshop.

2. Open a template from Poser. Its exact location will depend upon the version of the program. In Poser 3, it is located in the Texture folder inside the Runtime folder under the main Poser directory. There are actually a variety of templates there for different male and female figures. There are also textures located under the Poser3 Textures folder located under the Texture folder. Select the Male Muscle Texture.tif template so that in the next example you can see what the texture map that works with it looks like. The template will appear as a sort of shadow drawing.

3. Immediately use the Save As command on this file and give it a different file name. Do *not* save any changes that you make to the original file you opened from Poser. If you save any changes to the original file, you will be changing that file permanently and will not be able to recover that texture. Be sure that you do save the file as a .tif or .bmp file type and give it a .tif or .bmp extension. You may also want to save it to a different location.

4. In Painter or Photoshop, you create shadows where you want them to appear on the figure's "skin." You are drawing the folds, wrinkles, blemishes, etc. in the skin. You can even create a whole new skin type for an "alien" or "extraterrestrial." See the section in the Poser manual on creating a custom bump map for tips on the painting technique.

5. After you have created your new bump map, you will need to save it as a .tif or .bmp file with a name and location where it can be located. Don't forget to add the .tif or .bmp extension to the file name when you save it.

6. Load the bump map in Poser:
   A. Open the program.
   B. Select the figure type and pose that you want.
   C. Click on Render/Surface Material. Check that the proper figure is selected in the Current Object pop-up if more than one figure is in the scene.
   D. In the Bump Map area, click on Load. The Open box appears.
   E. Locate the file that you created and click on it so that its name appears in the File name: window.

F. Click on Open.

G. You will be prompted to convert a .pict or .bmp file into a .bum file. Go ahead and do so. This will save you time the next time that you want to use this bump map. The next time that you want to use this bump map, select the .bum file that is already there and you won't have to load the .pict or .bmp file again.

H. Click on the arrow button under Bump Map and select the file you just loaded.

I. Click on the OK button to exit the Surface Material box.

CREATING TEXTURE MAPS

Texture maps are images that are "painted" onto the surface of the figure. These can represent clothing, skin colors, etc. Think of these as the costume rendering that goes on top of the bump map. The folds and 3-D details of the costume are a part of the bump map. The fabrics and colors are represented on the texture map. Texture maps may be created in Painter or Adobe Photoshop based on a texture map that is available in Poser, but they must be saved as .tif or .bmp files to be used in the program. When you open one of these texture maps, some of the differences between a bump map and a texture map should become clearer.

You can create and use texture maps that aren't as detailed as the one in the method outlined below. You can create a texture map, for example, of a lizardlike skin that is applied over the entire figure to create an "alien."

To Create and Load a Texture Map

1. Open Painter or Adobe Photoshop.
2. Click on File/Open. The Select Image box appears.
3. Locate the Poser directory—usually under Program Files—and open the Textures folder under the Runtime folder as you did above in locating a bump map.
4. Click on Male nude texture.tif so that it appears under File name:.
5. Click on Open.
6. This is a texture map that you can select and place on the Male Nude Figure in Poser and accompanies the Male Muscle Texture.tif bump map that you saw under the bump map section. Costume designers will immediately recognize this as a sort of "skin" or costume that has been slit and laid out flat. Think about how the image that you see here would be wrapped around the figure in Poser, and you will have a better idea of how texture maps work.

7. Immediately use the Save As command on this file and give it a different file name. Do *not* save any changes that you make to the original file you opened from Poser. Be sure that you do save the file as a .tif or .bmp file type and give it a .tif or .bmp extension. You may also want to save it to a different location.

8. Now you can begin working on the new file in Painter or Photoshop to create a new rendering of the skin or to create an entirely new skin. See the section on creating a custom texture map in the Poser manual for tips.

9. When you have completed your changes, save the file. Make a note of its file name and location so that you can locate it when you load it into Poser.

10. Load the texture map in Poser:
    A. Open the program.
    B. Select the figure type and pose that you want.
    C. Click on Render/Surface Material. Check that the proper figure is selected in the Current Object pop-up if more than one figure is in the scene.
    D. In the Texture Map area, click on Load. The Open box opens.
    E. Locate the file that you created and click on it so that its name appears in the File name: window.
    F. Click on Open.
    G. Click on the arrow button under Texture Map and select the file you just loaded.
    H. Click on the OK button to exit the Surface Material box.

Examine the other bump and texture maps that exist in Poser. The male and female casual and business maps can be modified in Painter or Photoshop to create entirely new costume designs for the figures. Always be certain, however, that you first save the file under a different name before applying any modifications to it. It is usually a good idea to save it to a new location as well.

Exercise No. 3: Rendering with Cameras, Lights, Background, and Textures

The renderings that you have created so far have all been quick, simple renderings. This exercise will take you through the steps of creating a complete rendering using the cameras, lights, a background, bump maps, and textures.

1. Open Poser. Make sure that the following have a check mark by them under the Window pull down menu: Camera Controls, Document Tools, Preview Styles, Editing Tools, Light Controls, Memory Dots, Parameter Dials, and Tool Titles.

2. Choose the figure type of Male Casual.

   A. From the Standing Set in the library, give the figure the Conversation pose.

   B. Give the figure some hair.

   C. Use the Color tool to change the pants to blue jeans and the shirt to a light brown color.

3. Import a background:

   A. Click on File/Import/Background Picture. The Open box appears.

   B. From the Poser folder of the CD-ROM that accompanies the book, select Proj9b.tif so that its name appears in the File name: window, and click on Open. This background should look familiar. It is a rendering of one of the exercises that you worked on in 3D Studio MAX saved as a .tif file. You could also go back and save a rendering of one of your files from the work you did in the program as a .tif file and use it instead.

   C. A prompt appears asking if you want to change the window to match the background in size. Click on YES.

   D. You will find that the document window is now about 467×350 pixels in size. You will probably need to move it and maybe some of the other controls and/or tools around the screen to fit them all in. Remember that you click and drag on the title of the window or control to move it. To move the document window, for example, you would click and drag on Untitled until this document has been saved and assigned a file name.

4. Scale the body to about 65% so that it is in proportion to the background.

5. Drop it to the floor. Using the Translate/Pull tool, move it to a good location against the background.

6. Select the Main camera and use the editing tools to move the camera around to achieve a nice composition. You'll notice that the background does not move when you move the camera. If you change the position of the camera radically, you will probably also have to move and resize the figure to fit the new view.

7. Use the light controls to match the lighting on the figure as close as you can to the lighting on the background. The original scene for the background in 3D Studio MAX was lit with a down light from the practical that was very dim and had a color of R: 211, G: 211, B: 180 and a light

from stage left that was much brighter and had a texture map applied. You won't be able to get a color scale reading off of the texture map, so you will have to try to match its color visually. You may want to stop periodically to do a quick render to see how your lighting is coming along.

> *Hint:* Set up one of the lights in Poser coming from stage left with a red-orange color as the brightest light source. Set up a second light coming from overhead with the RGB readings given above for the practical and take its intensity down. Then set up the third light as a fill coming in from stage right with a low intensity and a grey color.

8. Check that a texture has been applied, and adjust the colors of all of the elements of figure.
   A. Click on Render/Surface Material.
   B. Be sure that Figure 1 is selected in the Object pop-up.
   C. In the Texture Map area, check to see that Casual Man Texture has been selected. If it hasn't, click on the down arrow in the box under Texture Map and select it.
   D. Click on the box with the down arrow in it next to Material:.
      1. Select each of the materials such as skin, pants, etc. in turn.
      2. As each material is selected, you can change the color of that material by clicking on the Object Color and Highlight Color buttons. This will allow you to control the color of these materials much more precisely than you were able to using the Color tool in the document window.
   E. Click on OK. You won't really see these changes show up until you render.

9. Set the Render Options:
   A. Click on Render/Render Options.
   B. In the Render to: settings, choose the following:
      1. New Window
      2. Width: 467 pixels
      3. Height: 350 pixels
      4. Resolution: 72 pixels/inch
   C. In Surface detail: check all boxes.
   D. In Render over: choose Background picture.

10. If you didn't want to create the rendering right now, you could click on OK to save the settings for later, but go ahead and click on the Render Now button to see the rendering and save the settings. If it doesn't look quite like what you want, you may have to go back and readjust the lighting on the figure. Pay attention to the direction of the light so that

the shadows will fall properly. You may also want to try adjusting some of your render options to see the role that they play in the rendering.

If you don't want to save the Render1 that you create, click on the X in the upper right-hand corner to close the rendering window and then click on **Don't Save** in the box that opens.

Note: One glitch that you will sometimes encounter in Poser 3 is a rendering that has a white space in it. If this should happen, click and drag on the blue bar at the top of the render window. This will usually clear the white space and reveal the entire rendering.

11. After you have created a rendering that looks like what you want, make some more changes to the figure:
    A. Reset the figure type to **Business Man**. Be sure that you keep the modified geometries, the props (hair) attached to the figure, and the current proportions. You will be prompted for all of these when you try to change the figure type.
    B. Reset the surface texture and colors:
       1. Click on **Render/Surface Material**.
       2. Be sure that **Figure 1** is selected in the **Object** pop-up.
       3. Be sure that **Biz Man Texture** is selected in the **Texture Map** pop-up.
       4. Click on the **Material** pop-up to select the different materials such as shirt, jacket, tie, etc. and then use the **Object Color** and **Highlight Color** buttons to change the colors of the materials to what you would like.
       5. Click on **OK**. You won't really see these changes show up until you render.
12. Click on **Render/Render**. This will create the rendering using the present settings in the Render Options box. If you don't like what you get, you can open the Render Options box again and reset those settings or go back and work with the lights, surface material, etc.

SAVING THE RENDERING

If you like the rendering that you have created you can save it as either a .tif or .bmp file that can then be used in a variety of other programs. The following is the procedure for saving the rendering as a file while the rendering is still open.

If you have rendered to the main window:

1. Click on File/Export/ and then either on TIFF or BMP depending upon which file type you prefer. The Save Image As box appears.
2. Give it the file name render1 with the extension of either .tif or .bmp or any other name of your choice.
3. In the Save as Type: area, select either .tif or .bmp depending upon which extension you have given the file above.
4. In the Save In: area, select the location on your hard drive, floppy drive, etc. to which you would like to save the file.
5. Click on Save.
6. Close the render window by clicking on the X in the upper right-hand corner.

If you have rendered to a new window:

1. Click on File/Save As. The Save File As box opens.
2. In the Save as Type: area, select either .tif or .bmp for the file type.
3. In the File name: area, name the file render1.tif or render1.bmp or any other name of your choice.
4. In the Save In: area, select the location on your hard drive, floppy drive, etc. to which you would like to save the file.
5. Click on Save.
6. Close the render window by clicking on the X in the upper right-hand corner.

SAVING THE POSER FILE FROM WHICH THE RENDERING WAS MADE

If you like the scene that you have created, you can save it as a Poser 3 (.pz3) file so that you can work with it some more or call it up anytime that you would like. When you reopen it, you will not see the rendering. You will also have to reset the render options before you can get the rendering to look like it did when you saved it. The following is the procedure to follow to save the scene as a Poser file. This cannot be done while a rendering is still open.

1. Click on File/Save As. The Save Pose As box appears.
2. Give it a file name of Fig3.pz3.
3. Select a location for the file to be saved in the Save In: area.
4. Click on Save.

A warning about file size: If you are planning on saving these files to a floppy disk, the .pz3 file format is much larger than the .tif format file. This is exactly the reverse of what is true with the older .pzr files that are used in Poser 2. In this size image—467 × 350 pixels—the .pz3 file is about 986 KB. The .tif file is about 642 KB. The two files will not fit on a single floppy disk. Remember, though, that the .tif file is simply an image. The .pz3 file is the entire Poser scene with all of its settings. You can open the .pz3 file at any time in Poser 3 and make changes to it.

PRINTING FROM POSER

You can print directly from Poser if you would like. There are a couple of things to keep in mind. You will print what you see inside the currently active window. If you have rendered to the main (document) window, that is what you will get. If you have rendered to another window, but the main window is active, you will get what is in the main window. The currently active window has a blue bar on top. The inactive window has a grey bar. Click on the grey bar on top of the inactive window to make it active.

Poser prints to the page size that is set for your printer. Even if you have a small window size, it will still print to whatever page size your printer is set for. If you want a smaller print, you will have to reset the page size on the printer.

In a wireframe display with a black background, Poser will automatically reverse the colors so that it is not printing to a black background.

To Print from Poser:

1. Click on File/Print Setup. This opens your Printer Control box. Make any changes that you would like in the setup of your printer such as switching from greyscale to color, changing the paper size or orientation, etc.
2. Click on File/Print.

EXPORTING POSER FILES TO OTHER PROGRAMS

Poser files can be exported in a variety of formats for use in other programs. Different programs have different requirements as to file type, however. If you want to use the file in AutoCAD, it will have to be exported as a .dxf file. The .dxf files from older versions of Poser seem to create problems for AutoCAD, but the .dxf files from Poser 3 seem to work well. 3D Studio MAX can import either .dxf files or 3D Studio (.3ds) files, but the .3ds files come in much easier and faster. Painter can open either .bmp or .tif files. Adobe Photoshop can only open .tif files.

You also need to keep in mind what kind of file you will be bringing into these programs and how it is going to be used. In Painter and Photoshop, you will be importing 2-D files that will serve as the beginning of a rendering that you are going to create. Depending upon what was in the active window when you exported the file, you will be working from just an image of a figure or an image of a figure with a background. If you exported from a rendering, you will have a file that looks like the rendering. If you exported from the working window, you will have a file that looks like that window. In AutoCAD and 3D Studio MAX, you will be importing a 3-D representation of a figure with no background. This will have to be moved, rotated, etc. like any other object in the program.

With these restrictions in mind, here is how to export a file from Poser for use in another program:

1. Click on File/Export.
2. A side box will open with a list of file types. Click on the file type that you want to create. The options include:
   A. BMP: This can be used in Painter.
   B. TIFF: This can be used in Painter or Photoshop.
   C. DXF: This can be used in AutoCAD or 3D Studio MAX.
   D. 3D Studio: This can be used in 3D Studio MAX.
3. The Export as File Type: box will open. The name of the file type will be what you have selected.
4. In the File name: box, enter the name that you want to give the file followed by a period and the three-letter file type extension—.dxf, .3ds, .tif, .bmp.
5. In the Save in: area, select a location for the file to be saved. Make sure that you remember this so you can find the file later.
6. Click on Save.

IMPORTING POSER FILES INTO OTHER PROGRAMS

IMPORTING A .tif OR .bmp FILE FROM POSER INTO PAINTER

This is the easiest one of the lot, because both programs are made by MetaCreations, which was formerly Fractal Design.

1. Open Painter.
2. Click on File/Open. The Select Image box opens.
3. Locate the file in the Look in: windows.
4. Click on the file so that its name appears in the File name: window.
5. Click on Open.

Importing a .3ds File from Poser into 3D Studio MAX

This is not quite as easy; it requires a little more thought.

1. Open 3D Studio MAX.

2. If you want to bring the figure into a scene that you have already created, open that scene.

3. Click on File/Import. The Select File to Import box will open.

4. Make sure that under File of type:, either 3D Studio Mesh (*.3ds) or All Files is selected.

5. Locate the file in the Look in: windows.

6. Click on the file so that its name appears in the File name: window.

7. Click on Open.

8. The 3DS Import box opens. Select Merge objects with current scene and click on OK.

9. The figure comes into the scene, and your first thought is probably "Where in the heck is it?" It is there, but it is so small that you can't see it. Look closely, and you will see that an X,Y,Z axis has appeared in all of the viewports. This represents the figure from Poser. Look over to the right in the command panel, and you will see that the Create button is active and that in the Name and Color window is the name Object_1. This is the name of the figure. Immediately change the name of the figure to something that will identify it for you if you accidentally deselect it. If you should accidentally deselect it, the only way that you will find it again is by using the Select by Name button.

10. Another good idea at this point is to click on the Lock Selection Set button on the status bar. This will keep you from deselecting the figure.

11. Working in the Left viewport, zoom down to the figure using Region Zoom. Get right at the corner of the X,Y axis and make a tiny window. If you made it tiny enough, you will see a small white lump at the corner of the X,Y axis.

12. Use Region Zoom again and make another tiny window around the small white lump. If you made this tiny enough, you will see a small representation of the figure lying on its back. If not, keep using Region Zoom to get down smaller and smaller until you can see a reasonably sized figure in the Left viewport.

13. Now is a good time to click on the Min/Max Toggle button to maximize the size of the Left viewport.

14. Choose the Select and Uniform Scale option from the Select and Scale button. You are going to scale the figure up to a size that is proportional with the rest of the scene.

15. Click and drag upward to increase the size of the figure. Click and drag up several times so that about all that you can see on the screen is the heel of the figure's foot.

16. Click on the **Zoom Extents** button. This gets you back to a full scene view.

17. Again click on the **Select and Uniform Scale** button. Scale the figure up to a size that looks close to what you want.

18. Click on the **Rotate** button and rotate the figure upright.

19. You may need to scale it again to get it closer to the size that you would like.

20. Now you can move it about, apply color and texture maps, and do whatever else you would like to the figure.

IMPORTING A .dxf FILE FROM POSER3 INTO AUTOCAD

I have not experienced any difficulties importing .dxf files from Poser 3 into AutoCAD. However, I have found importing .dxf files from earlier versions difficult. If you have any problems with importing Poser .dxf files into AutoCAD, take a look at the instructions for Poser 2 that are included on the CD-ROM that accompanies this book.

1. Export a .dxf file of the figure from Poser.
   A. When exporting, select an export range of **Single Frame**.
   B. Under **Export Options**, do not export object groups for each body part.
   C. Close Poser after you've finished exporting.

2. Open AutoCAD R12. For R13 or R14, skip to step 10.

3. Open the AutoCAD file into which you would like to import the figure.

4. Click on **File/Import/DXF In**. The **Select DXF File** box will open.

5. Locate the file that you want to import under **Directories:**. When the file name appears in the large box under **File Name:**, click on it so that it appears in the small box under File Name:.

6. Click on **OK**.

7. The Command line reads: **dxfin Regenerating drawing**.

8. Look around the screen. You probably will not see the figure. Don't worry. It's usually in the lower left-hand corner of the screen and extremely small. You will most likely have to zoom down to it several times in order for it to really be visible. Look for a small red dot in the lower left-hand corner of your screen. You will probably have to zoom down to it and pan over a little as well.

9. Now you should see the figure. From here you can move it around the drawing as you like and use any other AutoCAD command with it. It is

highly likely that you will have to scale it up to a size that is in proportion to the rest of your drawing and will have to rotate it as well. Poser 3 figures seem to come into AutoCAD lying down on their faces.

10. For R13: Click on **File/Import**. The **Import File** box opens. Under **List Files of Type:**, click on .dxf. Locate the file name and click on **OK**.

    For R14: Click on **File/Open**. The **Open File** box opens. Under **Files of Type:**, select .dxf. Locate the file name and click on **Open**.

Using Advanced Techniques

Poser is a very simple program to learn. Most of the techniques used in the program have been covered completely in this book, with the exception of animation. If you are interested in animation and have explored the area in 3D Studio MAX, then it will be quite easy for you to pick up the way that it is handled in Poser. The Animation palette of Poser is extremely similar to the track view of 3D Studio MAX. You can also import animation files from 3D Studio MAX into Poser to use as backgrounds. You can, for example, bring in the lighting cue file that you created in 3D Studio MAX and use it behind an animation file in Poser. The animation file in Poser can easily be set up to use the same lighting as the file from 3D Studio MAX so that the lighting on the figure and the lighting on the background are identical and change at the same rate.

Another area of Poser that would be worth examining would be further exploration of the more detailed use of bump and texture maps with the figures. Pushing bump and texture maps to their limits in modifying the geometry and look of the figures could create some intriguing possibilities. Using Painter to create new bump and texture maps would be worth the time spent learning the process better. The possibilities for creating 3-D costume renderings and characterizations are extremely interesting. The chapter in the instruction manual on surface materials does offer more help in this regard than the equivalent section does in Poser 2.

The Help Material available in Poser 3, while considerably more complete than in earlier versions, is still minimal. You will, for example, find terminology used in the program itself that is not in Help or the index for the instruction manual. The instruction manual covers the basic techniques in easy-to-understand language but has some major gaps and even some errors. Newer versions of the program will hopefully correct these errors and fill in some of these gaps. In the meantime, updates, useful files, and information on Poser is available at the MetaCreations home page on the World Wide Web at *http://www.metacreations.com/*.

PAINTER

INTRODUCTION

Painter is different in many ways from the other programs in these books. The other programs tend to be based on geometrical thought processes, while Painter is looser and based more on freehand concepts. Painter demands that you have already developed or are in the process of developing your skills as a freehand artist. If you can't draw, Painter won't help you draw any better. If you can draw, Painter will help you draw more easily and faster and will open up a whole new set of opportunities in drawing for you. Designers who have spent years developing their drawing and painting skills will feel very comfortable in Painter after a short learning process. They will be able to utilize these hard-earned skills in a very direct way. All of the tools in the program are given names and work in ways directly similar to the artist's tools with which designers are already familiar. Brushes, pencils, charcoal, watercolor, airbrushes, etc. are called exactly that and work pretty much like the real thing—sometimes even better. Watercolor, for example, doesn't "dry" until you tell it to. You can keep it "wet" until the drawing is finished if you like.

While the most common use of Painter by theatrical artists will be as a rendering program, there are numerous ways that it can be used with the other programs in this book. It can be used to create and modify textures and maps for 3D Studio MAX as well as to create "gobos" and projections for the lighting instruments. A painter's elevation for a backdrop can be drawn in Painter, printed out for use by the scenic artist, and also saved as a file that can be placed in a 3-D model in 3D Studio MAX to demonstrate its use with three-dimensional elements of the show. By using the two programs together, you can see how the backdrop will look on stage surrounded by all the rest of the scenery and under lighting. All of the scenery can be given actual surface treatments in the model created in 3D Studio MAX so that color and spatial relationships can be worked out on the computer before construction ever begins. Costume renderings done in Painter can be brought into the set renderings and examined in scale with one another before fabric buying and cutting has even started. It is exactly this kind of integration of the various theatrical artists' work through the use of these programs that this book is intended to help you understand in addition to the uses of the programs by the separate disciplines. The sections of the book dealing with importing and exporting are the key to this integration.

Painter is a complex program not because it is difficult to learn how to use, but because it does contain almost all of the traditional artistic tools and materials along with a number of others that cannot be purchased at your local art store. The most time-consuming aspect of the "learning curve" for Painter is remembering where each of the tools and materials is located and how to put it into use. After the skilled artist has mastered those parts of the program, he or she will usually find it as easy to use as working with the usual sets of brushes and pencils.

Painter is also the one program in this group that requires the use of a drawing or graphics tablet along with the program. While everything in the three other programs can be done with the mouse and keyboard, in Painter it is impossible to achieve the delicacy of stroke required by the skilled artist without having a drawing tablet. The drawing tablet transfers your "stroke" to the program and lets you control pencil or brush pressure in much the same way that you do with the real thing. Trying to do a watercolor wash with a mouse in Painter is about the equivalent of trying to do it with a palette knife on a canvas. You do not have to purchase a drawing tablet that is as large as the "paper" on which you are working, however. You will quickly develop a feel for the size of the tablet relative to the size of the screen, or "paper." It is perfectly possible to achieve all of the effects in the program by using a 4- × 5-inch tablet available for around $100. The 6 × 8-inch size is probably best for theatrical use. Larger sizes are available but will run considerably more in cost. Read the instructions for installing and using your graphics or drawing tablet carefully. Pay special attention to how you have to use the tablet to "click" or "double click" in a program, as you will need to know how to use it for this function as well as for making strokes.

Painter works slightly differently in PC and Mac formats. The major difference of which you need to be aware is the use of the Control, Alt, Command, Backspace, Delete, and Shift keys. Throughout the text that follows, you will see keys designated in the following format: Ctrl/**Command**. The key given before the / is the key that you will use in the PC version of Painter. The key given after the / is the key that you will use in the Mac version of Painter. Do not confuse this with the slash being used as it has throughout the book to separate commands on the pull down menus. File/**Open**, for example, still means that you should click first on File and then on **Open** on the pull down menu that appears under File.

Let's take a look at how the program is laid out and where the tools and materials are located.

BECOMING FAMILIAR WITH THE OPENING SCREEN

When you first open Painter, there will be some familiar elements on the screen such as the pull down menu bar across the top. There will also be a number of boxes located on the screen that will not be as familiar such as the Brushes, Art Materials, and Controls boxes. Exactly which boxes you see when you open the program is controlled by the pull down menus, so this is a good place to start in a tour of the program.

THE PULL DOWN MENU BAR

Just below the blue bar with the name of the program and the Minimize, Maximize, and Close buttons is a grey bar that contains the pull down menus. Many of the program commands are located here along with the controls that let you specify what other floating boxes or program elements you want to see displayed. More details on how to use specific commands will be given later in

THE OPENING SCREEN

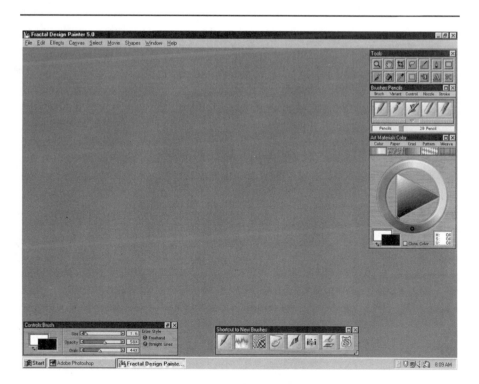

the book. Some of the elements of the pull down menu of particular interest to theatrical users are the following.

File

New: This opens the New Picture box, where you can specify the size, resolution, and background color of a new drawing space.

Open: This opens the Select Image box, where you can open an already created image.

Place: This lets you bring another image into an already open image. If you have an image of the scenery from the play opened and you would like to bring in an image of a costume rendering, this is the command you would use. The Select Image box opens to let you locate the image file. After you have selected the file, the Place box opens to let you control the position and size of the "floater" that is created from the imported image.

Close: This closes an opened image. It will prompt you as to whether you want to save any changes if you haven't already.

Clone: This creates a clone of an image. You can then work over the top of the clone on tracing paper, place it on a new material, and do a variety of other things with it. If you have opened an image from another source such as a figure from Poser, a rendering from 3D Studio MAX, a perspective image of a set from AutoCAD, or an image that has been scanned in, this allows you to work with it in a wide variety of ways while creating your rendering.

Save: This lets you specify the name, file type, and location when you are saving an image for the first time, or it saves any changes to the name, file type, and location previously specified.

Save As: If you want to give an image a new name, file type, or location without changing the old image, use this command.

Revert: If you have made changes to a file after saving, this command restores the last saved version of the file.

Page Setup: This accesses your printer's command box to make changes before printing.

Print: This prints a file directly from Painter.

Exit: This closes Painter.

Edit

Undo: This function will undo up to the last five commands one at a time.

Redo: This restores the last Undo command.

Fade: This opens the Fade box. In this box you can fade down the intensity of the last brush, pencil, etc. stroke. Choose a percentage to be faded and click OK.

Cut: This removes an item or items that have been selected.

Copy: This copies an item or items that have been selected to the clipboard.

Paste: This pastes anything in the clipboard into the drawing.

Clear: This cleans the contents of a mask.

Preferences: This opens the Preference boxes for General, Brush Tracking, Function Keys, Interface, Plug-Ins, Undo, Shapes, Internet, and Windows so that you can change or customize the way that these items work.

Effects

The first two categories that you see under Effects are the last two selected from the Tonal Control, Surface Control, Focus, and Esoterica submenus below. If you choose an effect from one of these submenus, it will show up here the next time that you click on Effects.

Orientation: Select an item or part of the image. This command will let you rotate, scale, distort, or flip the selected item.

Fill: Select an item or part of the image. This command will let you fill the selected item or image part with a color, pattern, gradation, or weaving.

Tonal Control: This lets you change color and tone specifications.

Surface Control:

Apply Surface Texture: This opens the Apply Surface Texture box. In this box you can change aspects of the surface of the material on which you are currently drawing such as shine and reflection. This box also lets you control aspects of lights such as color, direction, and intensity.

Apply Lighting: This lets you add lighting effects to your image.

Focus: This lets you control aspects of the camera in animation.

Esoterica: This contains a variety of special effects such as Marbling, Custom Tile, Grid Paper, Auto Van Gogh, Blobs, Pop-Art Fill, and more.

Objects:

Create Drop Shadow: This lets you add a dropped shadow to lettering.

Align: This lets you align selected items with one another.

Canvas

These commands all have to do with the canvas or the drawing space.

Resize: Use this to change the canvas, or image, size of the current image. This box will maintain the aspect ratio—width/height—of your current canvas size.

Canvas Size: Use this box to add on to one side of the canvas, changing the aspect ratio.

Make Mosaic: Click here to open the Make Mosaic box. You set the specifications for drawing in mosaics in this box and then draw with the box open.

Make Tessellation: Click here to open the Tessellation box. You set the specifications for drawing in tessellation in this box and then draw with the box open. A tessellation is a mosaic with nonrectangular lines.

Wet Paint: Use this with watercolor. When you are drawing in watercolors, there will be a check by Wet Paint. You can suspend painting in watercolors by removing the check without drying the paint.

Dry: This "dries" the watercolor. After it has been dried, it cannot become "wet" again.

Tracing Paper: Use this to turn on tracing paper, which allows you to trace over an image without changing the original image.

Set Paper Color: If you have already set a paper color when you opened a new drawing, you can use this command to set a paper color underneath that one. When you erase the top color, the color underneath will show through. This command will set the currently active color in the color box as the color underneath.

Rulers: This function lets you display rulers along the side of your drawing, snap to the ticks on the rulers, and set the options, or scale, of the rulers.

Guides: If you click at a point on a ruler, a guide will appear on the screen. The guide is a horizontal or vertical line across the screen at that point. The Guides menu lets you show or hide the guides and snap or not snap to them.

Grid: This lets you show the grid, snap to the grid, and under Grid Options, set up the spacing on the grid.

Select

These commands all have to do with selecting objects and areas in your drawing and what happens to those selections. After you have selected an object or an area, there are a variety of things you can do to it.

All: This selects the entire drawing.

None: This deselects everything selected.

Invert: If something is selected, this will deselect it and select everything else.

Reselect: Changed your mind? If you'd like to select back what you just deselected, click here.

Float: This turns anything selected into a floater. Floaters can be moved around and have numerous other properties as well.

Stroke Selection: This is used with mosaics. It creates a single wide set of tiles along a path traced with the cursor.

Feather: This feathers or softens the edges between a selected area and the area around it. The Feather Selection box lets you choose the width of the feather in pixels.

Modify: This lets you widen, contract, smooth, or create a border around something selected.

Auto Select: This lets you make a selection using different image characteristics as the basis.

Color Select: This lets you make a selection on the basis of color.

Convert to Shape: This lets you turn a selection into a shape that can then be modified for height, width, etc. Under the Shapes pull down menu is the Shape to Selection command, which reverses the process and converts a shape back to a selection.

Show Marquee/Hide Marquee: In this program, dotted lines—a marquee— are used to indicate a selection. You can turn the dotted lines on or off using this command.

Movie

These commands control the animation functions of Painter.

Shapes

In addition to drawing freehand in Painter, you can also create shapes. Shapes are vector-based forms that can be edited precisely. If you need precise curves or dimensions in parts of your drawing, shapes can provide them. Shapes are Painter's equivalents of the precision drawing tools of AutoCAD or 3D Studio MAX. The commands in this area are concerned with things that you can do to shapes.

Join Endpoints: This lets you join the end points of two shapes.

Average Points: This is used before joining two points. If you average the two points, a new point will be created between the two points to be joined. If you don't average, the two points will just be joined by a line.

Make Compound: Use this to create "holes" in shapes. Draw the first shape, then draw the "hole." Use the Make Compound command to create a shape with a hole in it.

Release Compound: This turns a hole created by the Make Compound command back into a separate object.

Set Duplicate Transform: This allows you to specify parameters when you copy (duplicate) a shape.

Duplicate: Use this to copy a shape.

Convert to Floater: This converts a shape to a floater.

Convert to Selection: This converts a shape to a selection.

Set Shape Attributes: This allows you to control aspects of shapes such as line width, opacity, kind of corner, etc., and it allows you to name the shape.

Blend: Blending "morphs" two shapes into a new one and lets you control shading on irregular shapes.

Window

This pull down menu is used to control which of the "floating boxes" or palettes appear on the screen. These boxes give you access to the tools, materials, etc. of Painter. Each of the commands below will be preceded by the word Show or Hide in the menu. Click on a Show command for a particular box to make that box appear on the screen. Click on a Hide command for a particular box to make that box disappear from the screen. These boxes can be arranged once they are on the screen by clicking and dragging on the name bar on the top of the palette. If the name bar is blue, the palette is active. If the name bar is grey, the palette is inactive.

Palettes: This makes all of the boxes appear or disappear.

Arrange Palettes: This lets you save or delete a palette layout that you have created.

Zoom In, Zoom Out, Zoom to Fit: These commands let you change the view of the canvas by zooming in, out, or to fit the size of the available space. When the Controls box is also open and you click here, you can control the size of the view in percentages by clicking on the Zoom Level window in the Controls box.

Tools: This opens and closes the Tools palette, where you can select from the tools available in Painter.

Brushes: This opens and closes the Brushes palette, where you select drawing tools such as brushes, erasers, pencils, charcoal, pastels, etc.

Art Materials: This opens and closes the Art Materials palette, where you select papers, gradations, patterns, and weaves. This palette also contains the color wheel, where you can select colors for backgrounds and drawing tools.

Objects: This opens and closes the Objects palette, where you can control floaters and masks.

Controls: The Controls palette is one that you will almost always want to have open. You can set parameters for and make choices about whatever you are doing with one of the other palettes here.

Color Set: The Color Set palette offers another way to choose colors besides the color wheel in the Art Materials palette. This is a selection of small color boxes arranged in a gradation. Click on one of the small boxes to select a color. You can also create custom color sets.

Custom Palette: This lets you organize by adding new palettes. It also allows you add new palette commands. If you have Painter 5, you will already find a Shortcut to New Brushes under this submenu that allows you to turn new brushes available with that version on and off.

Screen Mode Toggle: Around the sides of the drawing window area are scroll bars that let you scroll around the drawing if you have zoomed in and buttons that let you control certain commands such as grid and tracing paper. This command toggles those scroll bars and buttons on and off.

SAVING YOUR WORK: FILE TYPES

The way that a drawing or file is saved in Painter is not very much different from the way that files are saved in any of the other programs in this book. You click on File/Save As the first time that you save the drawing and fill in the parts of the Save Image As box in much the same way. Type in the name of the file and the extension in the File name: area. Select the location where you would like the file to be saved in the Save in: area. Select the file type that you would like the file to be saved as in the Save as type: area, making sure that the extension on the name matches the file type extension you chose, and click on Save. Similarly, to save changes that you have made to a drawing that has already been saved once, you simply click on File/Save.

If you want to use the drawing in another program, however, it is important that you understand the file types that are available for files to be saved as in Painter. There are a couple of new ones that you have not encountered in the other programs. Before you decide what file type to use and assign an extension to the file name, consider the options that are available and in what programs they might be used.

Painter File Types and Extensions

RIFF Files (*.rif): RIFF files are exclusive to Painter. If you save a file as a RIFF file, you will not be able to use it in any of the other programs in this book. If, however, you are going to use it just in Painter or you are going to store it on a floppy disk, there are a number of advantages to using a RIFF file type. It is a highly detailed file type, but still compact. If you need to save space it might be a good idea to save the file as a RIFF file and then convert it to another file type in Painter before you use it in another program. There are a number of special techniques used in Painter such as floaters that will only be saved if the file is saved as a RIFF file.

TIFF Files (*.tif): TIFF files are large, detailed files that can be imported into a wide variety of other programs. TIFF files can be imported into Poser for use as backgrounds and bump maps and texture maps. They can also be used in 3D Studio MAX as textures and bitmaps. They can be opened in Adobe Photoshop as well.

PICT Files (*.pct): This file type is common to Macs. It can be opened in Adobe Photoshop, but cannot be used in Poser or 3D Studio MAX.

Photoshop Files (*.psd): This is an Adobe Photoshop file type. It cannot be opened in Poser or 3D Studio MAX.

Bitmap Files (*.bmp): A large file type, this is often used on computer-screen graphics. These files can be used as backgrounds, bump maps, and texture maps in Poser, but cannot be used in 3D Studio MAX. They cannot be opened in Photoshop.

PC Paintbrush (*.pcx): This file type is common in PC graphics programs. It cannot be used in Poser, 3D Studio MAX, or Photoshop.

Targa Files (*.tga): This is another relatively large file type that is used in many graphics programs. It can be used as a texture or bitmap in 3D Studio MAX. It cannot be used in Poser. It can be opened in Photoshop.

GIF Files (*.gif): The most common graphic file type used on the World Wide Web, this type is compact in size. It can be used as a texture or bitmap in 3D Studio MAX. It cannot be used in Poser. It cannot be opened in Photoshop but can be created there.

JPEG Files (*.jpg): This is another graphic file type often used on the World Wide Web. It is also compact in size. It can be used as a texture or bitmap in 3D Studio MAX. It is commonly used as a rendering file in 3D Studio MAX. It cannot be used in Poser. It can be opened in Photoshop.

Postscript Files (*.eps): This file type is often used in commercial graphics. It cannot be used in Poser or 3D Studio MAX. It can be opened in Photoshop.

USING THE PALETTES, OR "FLOATING BOXES"

The palettes, or "floating boxes," are the heart of your control system for Painter. These are where you will be making the majority of choices in the program such as what kind of paper you want to draw on, what kind of pencil, brush, etc. you want to draw with, and what kind of tools you want to use. The palettes are turned on and off under the Windows pull down menu and can be moved around the screen by clicking and dragging on the name bar at the top. You can also turn them off by clicking on the X in the upper right-hand corner of the name bar. You need to learn which items are available in which palette so that you can locate them easily when desired.

THE TOOLS PALETTE

In most cases you will need to select the tool that you want to use in the Tools palette before you do anything else. For example, if you want to choose a

THE TOOLS PALETTE

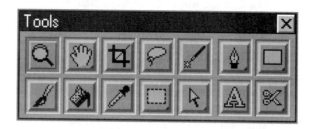

brush—any drawing tool such as a pencil, brush, airbrush, etc. is called a brush—you must first click on the Brush tool in the Tools palette before you go to the Brushes palette to make a selection. Some of the buttons in the Tools palette have a small detent at the lower right-hand corner. These indicate that there are pullouts underneath that button that can also be selected by clicking and holding on the button. If you place the cursor over a button and hold it there for a couple of seconds, the name of the button will appear on the screen. If you click on a button, it will be outlined in red to indicate that it has been selected. The buttons on the Tools palette, working from left to right, are described below.

Upper Row

The Magnifier Button: Click on this button and then click, drag, and release in the drawing window to zoom in to the window defined by the click and the release. Also look in the Controls palette. If you click on the box right under Zoom Level, you will open a pop-up menu that lets you select a zoom percentage for the magnifier.

The Grabber/Rotate Page Buttons: The Grabber button, which looks like a hand, lets you pan about the image in the drawing window. Underneath the Grabber button is the Rotate Page button, which looks like a circular arrow. This button lets you turn the entire drawing window at an angle so that you can draw at a more natural angle on your drawing pad. The Controls palette will show you the rotation angle that you have chosen.

The Crop Button: The Crop button lets you make a rectangular selection for cropping, or trimming the image. Click and drag to make the selection. A flashing rectangle will appear. Move the cursor over the corners or sides of the rectangle, and double-ended arrows will appear. Click and drag to change the size of the selection. Move the cursor inside the rectangle, and clicking scissors will appear. Click inside the rectangle to crop to your selection. If you have made a mistake in your cropping, use the Undo command to restore the old image and try again. In the Controls palette, you can specify an aspect ratio—width/height—for the crop and see the size and location of the crop in pixels.

The Lasso Button: The Lasso button lets you create an irregularly shaped selection in the drawing window. Click and drag in the drawing window to create the shape of the selection. Be sure that you finish at a point close to the start point that crosses the line you have drawn. A flashing dotted line will outline your selection. Using Edit commands, the selection can be cut, copied, or pasted into a new image. Using the Select command, it can be converted to a shape. Move the cursor inside the selection, and a pointing finger will appear. Click inside the selection to convert it into a floater. Using the floater adjuster, it can be moved around the drawing window. Using the Orientation commands under Effects, it can be rotated, scaled, distorted, or flipped. It will also appear on the Floater list in the Objects palette, where further operations can be performed on it.

The Magic Wand button: The Magic Wand button is another method of making a selection. It lets you select a group of continuous pixels based on color. If you have drawn a line in one color, for example, clicking anywhere on the line with the magic wand will select the entire line. The Controls palette lets you control the tolerance and feathering of the selection. Tolerance gives the program a range of similar colors to use in the selection. Increase the feathering to select a number of pixels around the edge of the selected color. In the Controls palette, choose whether this is a selection or a mask before using the wand. A selection can have all of the things mentioned under Lasso done to it and is indicated by a dotted outline. A mask is used to store a selection for later use. You can store up to 32 masks in Painter.

The Pen/Quick Curve Buttons: These buttons are used for drawing shapes. The Pen button is used to draw straight lines and bezier curves. Click on points to draw straight lines. Click and drag to draw bezier curves. The Quick Curve button is used to draw freehand curves.

The Rectangular Shape/Oval Shape Buttons: These buttons are used for drawing square, rectangular, circular, and oval shapes. Click, drag, and release to create the shape.

Lower Row

The Brush Button: This activates the Brushes palette. You can then choose the type of brush, eraser, pencil, etc. that you want. Use this to draw strokes with the drawing tools in the Brushes palette. Hit the b key on the keyboard for freehand strokes. When the b key is toggled, click and drag to make a freehand stroke. Hit the v key on the keyboard for straight lines. When the v key is toggled, click on points, and a line will be drawn between them.

The Paint Bucket Button: This fills an enclosed area or the background with the color selected on the color wheel, a gradation, or a weave. Select which to use in the Controls box. You can also adjust the fill for tolerance and feather in the Control box.

The **Dropper** Button: Use this to select a color from the drawing window. Click on a colored area in the drawing window to make that color the current color. The **Controls** box shows you the RGB and HSV values for that color.

The **Rectangular Selection/Oval Selection** Buttons: Use these to make rectangular or oval selections. You can then do any of the things mentioned in the **Lasso** menu with those selections. The **Controls** box shows the location and size of the selection.

The **Floater Adjuster, Selection Adjuster,** and **Shape Selector** Buttons: These three buttons are stacked on top of one another. The **Floater Adjuster** button lets you move a floater around the drawing space. Click and drag to move. The **Selection Adjuster** button lets you move a selection around the drawing space. Click and drag to move. The **Shape Selector** button lets you select and move a shape. Click to select. Click and drag to move.

The **Text Tool** Button: The **Text** tool lets you create text in your drawing window. Use the **Controls** box to set the point size and font for the text. It can use any Adobe Type 1 or True Type font loaded in the **Fonts** area of your computer. Click at the start point of the text in the drawing window and then type in the text that you want. Text is a shape and can be moved and modified like any other shape. Each letter of the text is a separate shape and can be treated as such. You can select a letter of text and use the **Create Dropped Shadow** command under **Effects/Objects** to make a dropped shadow for each text letter.

The **Scissors, Add Point, Delete Point,** and **Convert Point** Buttons: These are all shape editing tools that are stacked underneath one another. The **Scissors** tool cuts path segments between points to break a shape into two parts. The **Add Point** tool adds a control point between two other points so that you can change the shape of a line or curve. The **Delete Point** tool deletes a control point. The **Convert Point** tool lets you change smooth points to corners and vice versa.

THE BRUSHES PALETTE

The **Brushes** palette allows you to choose and modify the drawing tool that you want to use in Painter. There are a wide variety of brushes, pens, pencils, erasers, watercolors, oils, acrylics, airbrushes, and other equipment available as well as a selection of new brushes if you have Painter 5 or higher. All of these can also be modified for specific needs. The modifications can be saved and given a name so that you can locate them later when you may need them again. Navigating and using the Brushes palette can take time to learn, primarily because there is so much available and so many ways that you can modify what is available. A later exercise will work you through the use of the Brushes palette.

The Brushes palette that you see in the figure labeled The Brushes Palette is the expanded version that includes the **Brush** library. Click on the bar with the arrow on it just below the top row of icons to display and hide the library. The top row of five icons represents the brushes that are immediately available. The one selected will appear with a red outline around it. Click on any of the five to select it. The brushes in the lower section—the library—are not available until they have been brought up to the top row. To bring a brush up from the library to the top row, just click on the brush that you want in the library. It will come up to the top row, replacing the brush that has been least used recently.

You can identify a brush by holding the cursor over the top of its icon for a couple of seconds. A label with the name of the brush will appear.

At the bottom of the palette are two pop-up windows. The window on the left identifies the currently active brush. Click on that window and you will see a pop-up showing all of the available brushes. Clicking on any of them will select that brush and bring it up to the top row if it isn't there already. At the bottom of this pop-up is the **Load Library** command. Click there to load new brush libraries. You can also access the new brushes through the shortcut, which is located under **Window/Custom Palette/Shortcut to New Brushes**. The window on the right at the bottom of the palette is the **Brush Variant** pop-up window. Click here to see the variations on the brush that you have already selected. Click on any of these variations to select it. At the top of the palette is the pull down menu. Click on any of the words in the following list to open more options and commands.

Brushes Palette Pull Down Menu Options

Brushes: These commands are used to build new or custom brushes.

Variant: These commands are used to build new or custom variants on a brush.

Control: These commands let you change the parameters of a selected brush and variant. Note that some of these commands as well as other Control commands are also available in the Controls palette.

Nozzle: Nozzles let you duplicate images as though they were popping out of a hose. On this pull down menu, you access the Nozzles palette and its controls.

Stroke: These commands let you record and play back brush strokes.

Exercise No. 1: Working with Brushes

This exercise will work you through how to use, modify, and control some of the brushes that are available in Painter. After you understand the basic principles involved, you should experiment with other brushes on your own. The variations available are almost infinite.

1. Before doing anything else with brushes, you are going to set your own pressure sensitivity. This is an adjustment that you make in the program when you are working with a stylus or drawing pad. It sets the stylus sensitivity to your own stroke or brush pressure. Do not try this if you are working with a mouse rather than a stylus or drawing pad.
   A. Open the Brush Tracking dialogue box by clicking on Edit/Preferences/Brush Tracking.
   B. Using your stylus, draw in the "scratch pad" that appears using your normal drawing stroke. Watch how the brush stroke "tracks" your stroke.
   C. If this is not how you would like the brush to track, make adjustments to the Velocity Scale, Velocity Power, Pressure Scale, and Pressure Power sliders.
   D. Try the stroke again.
   E. If this is still not how you would like the brush to track, make further adjustments to the sliders.
   F. When you have the brush stroke that appears in the scratch pad adjusted the way that you would like, click on the OK button.

2. Next, open a new drawing space or picture:

   A. Click on File/New. The New Picture box opens.

   B. Click on the button to the right of the Width: window to select units. Your choices are pixels, inches, CM, points, picas, or columns. Select inches. Do the same in the Height window.

   C. Click on the button to the right of the Resolution: window to select units. Select pixels per inch.

   D. Enter a width of 7 inches and a height of 7 inches in the windows. Leave the resolution at 72 pixels/inch.

   E. Click on the box above Paper Color to select a background color. You can enter numerical values in the RGB and HSV scales or click anywhere in the rainbow-colored Hue box and then use the Black/White slider to its side to select a color. For now, leave the color as white. Exit the box by clicking on OK to create a background of the color that you have chosen or Cancel to leave the background color the same.

   F. Click in the circle next to Image under Picture Type.

   G. Click on OK to create a new drawing space.

Note: If during the middle of the following exercise you start filling up the drawing space with strokes and can't see what you are doing anymore, just close the old space and open a new one:

   • Click on the X in the upper right-hand corner of the blue bar on the drawing space. Painter will ask you if you wish to save the changes, click on No.

   • Repeat steps 2A–2G above or just click File/New and then click on OK to create the same space size again.

3. The new drawing space appears on the screen.

   A. Move the cursor over the detent in the lower right-hand corner of the border surrounding the drawing space. A double-sided arrow will appear. Click and drag on the detent to expand and contract the border surrounding the drawing space.

   B. On the left side and bottom of the border surrounding the drawing space are scroll bars and arrows. You can click on these arrows or click and drag on the button in the bar to move the drawing space around inside its border.

   C. On the blue bar at the top of the drawing space is the name of the current file—at this point Untitled—and the buttons that let you minimize, maximize, and close the drawing space.

    D. Just above the scroll bar on the right of the drawing space are three buttons.

        1. The top button is the **Tracing Paper** button. This is used to place tracing paper over the top of a clone so that you can draw over the image. There will be more on this later.

        2. The middle button, with blue lines on a white background, is the **Grid** button. This places a transparent grid over the image. Using the commands under the **Canvas** pull down menu, you can control the size of this grid and snap to it if desired.

        3. The bottom button is the **Output Preview** button. This button lets you see how your image will look when printed. If you are working on tracing paper, for example, the clone image underneath the tracing paper will disappear.

        For now, do not click on any of these buttons.

    E. Just to the left of the scroll bar on the bottom border are two more buttons.

        1. The left button that looks like a brown splotch controls where in the drawing space you are able to draw. Click on it, and three pop-up buttons will appear.

            a. left one of these—a large brown splotch—is the **Draw Anywhere** button. Click on this button to be able to draw both inside and outside of selections.

            b. The middle of these—a splotch with a white hole in the middle—is the **Draw Outside** button. Click on this button to draw only outside of selections.

            c. The right one of these—a small brown splotch—is the **Draw Inside** button. Click on this button to draw only inside selections.

            d. Select the **Draw Anywhere** button.

        2. The right button (i) is the **Image Information** button. Click and hold on it to display the height, width, and resolution of the current drawing space.

4. Click on the **Brushes** button in the **Tools** palette. This activates the Brushes palette. If either of these palettes does not appear on the screen, click on **Show Tools** or **Show Brushes** under the **Window** pull down menu.

5. The Brushes palette has several parts with which you need to be familiar. This layout will be similar to other palettes in Painter.

    A. The Name Bar: Across the top of the palette is a blue bar with the name of the palette on it. To the right side of this bar is a **Minimize/ Maximize** button, with one or two rectangles in it, and a **Close** button with an X in it. Click on the Minimize/Maximize button to display extra controls. The extra controls are displayed when the button shows two rectangles. This is where you want it to be for this exercise.

B. The Pull Down Menu: Just below the name bar is the pull down menu. Here the words Brush, Variant, Control, Nozzle, and Stroke appear. Clicking on any of these words will open pull down menus beneath them with more commands.

C. The Brush Selection Buttons: Immediately below the pull down menu are the five Brush Selection buttons. These icons let you select a particular brush type. Hold the cursor over the top of a button for a second or two, and the name of the brush will appear.

D. The Drawer Pushbar: Just below the five Brush Selection buttons is the drawer pushbar. This is a blue bar with an arrow in the middle of it. Click on this bar to "open" the Brush drawer and display more brushes that are available. Hold the cursor over the top of each button in the drawer and the name of the brush will appear.

E. The Brush Pop-Up and the Brush Variant Pop-Up: Just below the Brush drawer are two white windows with words in them. The one on the left is the Brush pop-up. Click on this to select brush types by name. The one on the right is the Brush Variant pop-up. Click on this to select variants on the brush type by name.

F. The Method and Subcategory pop-ups: If the Brushes palette is maximized, you will also see two white windows below the Brush and Brush Variant pop-ups. These define the ways that the brushes work. The Method pop-up displays a variety of general categories. The Subcategory pop-up displays variations on the method selected.

6. First just get a feeling for drawing in Painter by using several pencils:

A. Click on the Brush pop-up at the lower left corner of the Brushes palette and select Pencils.

B. Click on the Brush Variant pop-up to the right and select 2B Pencil.

C. Make some strokes in the drawing space.

D. In the Brush Variant pop-up, select the 500 lb. Pencil.

E. Make a stroke in the drawing space.

F. In the Brush Variant pop-up, select the Thick and Thin Pencil.

G. Make curved strokes and loops in the drawing space. Notice how this one acts like a calligraphy tool.

H. Try out each of the other variants.

I. Go back to the 2B Pencil.

7. If the Controls palette is not open, click on Show Controls in the Window pull down menu. Examine the Controls palette.

Note: If you have Painter 4 or an earlier version of the program, read step 10 on page 217 before starting this part.

A. Under **Draw Style,** you should have **Freehand** already selected—this is the default. Freehand lets you use the stylus for your drawing pad just as you would a pencil or brush. Select **Straight Line** instead.

   1. Click on two points in the drawing space. A straight line will connect the two points. Click on another point. A straight line will connect from the last point to this one. You will continue to connect to subsequent points until you toggle **Straight Line** off and **Freehand** on.
   2. **Straight Line** can be toggled on by clicking on **Straight Line** in the Controls palette or by hitting the **v** key on the keyboard.
   3. **Freehand** can be toggled on by clicking on **Freehand** in the Controls palette or by hitting the **b** key on the keyboard.
   4. Toggle Straight Line off and Freehand on.

B. The **Size** bar in the Controls palette lets you change the size of the pencil in pixels.

   1. Click on the arrows or click and drag on the slider to increase or decrease the size of the pencil. You can also click to the right of the number in the window to the right of the slider and enter a new number using the keyboard.
   2. Try out several different sizes.

C. The **Opacity** bar in the Controls palette lets you change the translucency of the pencil in percentages.

   Try out several different opacities. When using a pencil, you will have to set a pretty low figure to see a visible difference. This is not the case with some of the other brushes.

D. The **Grain** bar on the Controls palette will only show an effect if you are using a paper with grain on it. It will increase and decrease how much grain from the paper appears when you draw. I will cover selecting different papers later in the exercise on art materials.

E. The two boxes to the left of the Size, Opacity, and Grain bars are the **Color** boxes. They let you select a primary and a secondary color.

Note: These are Painter's names for two colors that are available for you to use when drawing. They have nothing to do with the primary and secondary colors of color mixing systems. Do not get confused by the terminology. If the names are a problem, think of them as your number one and number two colors. The primary color is the box on top. The secondary color is the box underneath. You will always be drawing in the primary color, but you can switch colors by clicking on the double-ended arrow that points to both boxes.

1. Make sure that the **Art Materials** palette is opened. If it isn't, open it by clicking on **Show Art Materials** in the **Window** pull down menu.
2. Make sure that **Color** is selected in the Art Materials palette. If there is not a red outline around the rainbow button under the word **Color** in the Art Materials palette, then click on that button.
3. You change the colors in the **Controls** palette using the **Art Materials** palette. In the Art Materials palette, click on the **Color** box in the lower left-hand corner that you want to change. You can select either the primary or the secondary color.
4. Change the primary or secondary color by using the Art Materials palette. Use the color wheel in the Art Materials palette to change colors.
   a. The multicolored ring, or **hue ring**, is where you select a hue. You click in the hue ring or click and drag the black circle around the ring to select a hue. Select a new hue.
   b. The triangle, or **saturation/value triangle**, in the middle of the hue ring is used to select a black/white scale. You click in the saturation/value triangle or click and drag on the white circle to select a new saturation and value. Select a new saturation and value.
   c. Notice that as you do this, the color in the Controls palette Color box changes.
5. If you changed the secondary color, you will have to make it the primary color before you can draw with it. Click on the double-ended arrow to change the primary and secondary colors.
6. Draw a line in the new color.
7. Change the secondary color by using the Art Materials palette.
8. Click on the double-ended arrow in the Controls palette to make the new secondary color the primary color.
9. Draw a line in the new color.
10. Work with the color wheel in the Art Materials palette and the Color boxes in the Controls palette to create and draw in a variety of colors till you get a feeling for how these tools operate.

8. Recording and playing back strokes: In Painter it is possible to record a stylus stroke and to play it back. In effect, this is a way to precisely copy a stroke that you make over and over again.

A. In the **Brushes** palette, click on **Stroke/Record Stroke**.

B. Make a stroke in the drawing space.

C. In the **Brushes** palette, click on **Playback Stroke**.

D. Click anywhere in the drawing space. The last stroke will be repeated where you clicked.

E. Auto Playback Stroke will keep repeating the stroke again and again until you click in the drawing space to stop the playback.

F. You will stay in Playback Stroke mode until you click again on Record Stroke.

G. Record and play back a stroke.

9. Experimenting with brush methods: If you have the Brushes palette maximized, you will see the labeled Method and Subcategory pop-ups underneath the Brush and Brush Variant pop-ups. These let you choose how brush strokes interact with color. You choose methods by clicking on the method pop-up and then selecting a method. Each method has subcategories that can be selected in the Subcategory pop-up. The default method and subcategory will change with each brush selected, but you can still change methods and subcategories when using that brush. Try out several different methods and subcategories.

A. Select Pencils in the Brush pop-up. Select 500 lb. Pencil in the Brush Variant pop-up.

B. Take a stroke in the drawing space in one color. Change colors and take another stroke that crosses the first. Repeat the second stroke several times and watch the pigment build up.

C. Select Cover in the Method pop-up and Soft Cover as the subcategory. Take a stroke in one color. Change colors and take another stroke that crosses the first one. Notice that instead of building up, the stroke completely covers the first one.

D. Select Eraser in the Method pop-up and Soft Paint Remover as the subcategory. Take a couple of strokes over lines that are already in the drawing. You are erasing what is there.

E. Select Plug-In in the Method pop-up and then try out a number of the different subcategories. Most of these are special effects of different kinds. Some of them work over already existing lines. Others create strokes of their own.

F. Some of the methods available here such as Eraser or Clone are similar to brush types that you will find in the Brushes palette and will be explained in more detail later.

G. When you have tried out a number of different methods and subcategories, restore the method of Buildup and subcategory of Grainy Hard Buildup.

10. Building a brush: If you have version Painter 4 or earlier, you may need to "build" a brush every time that you change a parameter such as size. To build a brush, click on the Brush pull down menu on the Brushes palette, then click on Build Brush. In Painter 5, there are only certain

parameters that require building a brush before it can be used. Step 5 of this exercise can be done in Painter 5 without having to build a brush. Other parameter changes may require it. In Painter 5, click on the **Brush** pull down menu on the **Brushes** palette, then click on **Auto Build Brush**. In Painter 5, after Auto Build Brush is selected, you won't have to worry about building brushes again in that session. In Painter 4 and earlier versions, every time that you change parameters on a brush, it has to be rebuilt. In any version, if you try to use a brush that must be built, the program will ask you if you want to build the brush. If you have Painter 5, go ahead and click on **Auto Build Brush** now.

11. The **Control** pull down menu: Use more brush parameters: In addition to the controls for size, opacity, and grain on the Controls palette, there are other brush controls located under the **Control** pull down menu on the **Brushes** palette.

Note: In Painter 4 or earlier, or if you have not selected **Auto Build Brush** in Painter 5, you will have to build the brush before you can try out the following changes.

A. Click on **Control/Size** to open the **Brush Controls Size** palette.
1. The large window shows you the current brush size.
2. The buttons to the right of the large window display a variety of tip styles.
   a. Click on several of these buttons and try strokes in the drawing space with the different tips to see the effect.
   b. Reselect the rounded tip in the left-hand corner of the lower row.
3. The **Size** sliders control the size of the brush tip.
   a. The **Size** slider defines the basic tip size. This shows up as a black dot in the large window.
   b. The **+−Size** slider defines the difference between the smallest and widest part of the tip. On the thick-thin pencil, for example, this will determine the difference between the thin stroke and the thick stroke. This difference will show up as a grey area surrounding the black dot in the large window. This difference will also register when using a symmetrical brush as a fading of the color as you get away from the tip. If you are using a drawing pad, the pressure of your stroke on the pad will determine how much of this +− area is conveyed to the drawing window.
   c. The **Step Size** slider controls how much larger or smaller each of the above sizes will get each time that you click on an arrow at one side of the slider.

    d. Try using several different sizes and +−sizes to see the effect with different tips.

4. The Angle Control sliders affect the angle and the roundness of the brush.

    a. The Squeeze slider determines the roundness of the brush. If this is at 100%, you have a round brush. Moving the slider to a lower percentage gives you a less round brush.

        1. Move the Squeeze slider up and down to create more or less round brushes and try them out in the drawing space. At the lower settings you turn the 2B Pencil into a Thick-Thin Pencil.

        2. Set a Squeeze number of around 25%.

    b. The Angle slider determines the angle of the thin and thick sides of the brush relative to how you are holding the stylus on your drawing pad. Move the Angle slider, and you will see the angle change in the large window.

        1. Try out several different angles in the drawing space.

        2. Return the Squeeze setting to 100% and the Angle setting to 25 degrees.

5. The dab types control the look and feeling of the line you get out of the brush.

    a. Set Size at about 15 pixels. Set +−Size at about 1.5.

    b. Select the 1-pixel dab type. Draw a line in the drawing space. You get a series of 1-pixel dots.

    c. Reset Size to 5 pixels. Draw a line in the drawing space. The dots are closer together.

    d. Reset Size to 15 pixels.

    e. Select the Bristle dab type. Draw a line in the drawing space. You get a bristly looking line.

    f. Select the Circular dab type. Draw a line in the drawing space. You get a regular-looking line.

    g. Reset Size to 5 pixels.

6. Close the Brush Controls: Size box by clicking on the X in the upper right-hand corner. If you wanted to leave it open, you could click and drag on the blue bar at the top of the box to move it to another part of the screen.

B. Spacing: Click on Control/Spacing on the Brushes palette to open the Brush Controls: Spacing palette.

    Most brush strokes consist of a series of dabs. This box lets you control the spacing of the dabs.

1. Change the Spacing Size to 100%. Make a stroke in the drawing space. Notice that the dabs have become a little more spaced out.

2. Change the Mn Spacing to 20. Make a stroke in the drawing space. Notice that the dabs have become a lot more spaced out.

3. Click on the Stroke Type window and change it to Multi. Make a stroke in the drawing space. Notice that the dabs have become darker. That is because you are now taking multiple dabs at each point. The number of dabs taken at each point is determined by the slider underneath the Stroke Type window.

4. Return Spacing Size to 50% and Mn Spacing to 1.0.

5. Rake and Hose apply to other brush types that will be covered later.

6. Close the Brush Controls: Spacing palette.

C. Sliders: Click on Control/Sliders on the Brushes palette to open the Advanced Controls: Sliders palette.

The Sliders palette lets you set multiple parameters out of the same box. It will also allow you to control how much the pressure of your stylus on your drawing pad affects these parameters.

1. Line up the Size slider with Pressure. More pressure on your stylus will change the size of the line drawn. Return Size to None. Pressure on the stylus does not change the size of the line.

2. Line up the Color slider with Velocity. Change the speed at which the stylus moves in the middle of a stroke. The color will change from the primary color to the secondary color with the speed.

3. Line up the Color slider with Direction. Change direction in the middle of a stroke. The color changes from the primary to the secondary as you change direction.

4. Try out several different combinations of slider positions. Some of these effects will vary with the particular brush and/or art material that is being used. Bleed, for example, becomes more important when working with the watercolor brush. Grain will show no difference except when a paper with grain is being used as an art material. When finished, return all sliders to None, except for Opacity and Grain, which should be set on Pressure.

5. Close the Sliders box by clicking on the X in the upper right-hand corner.

12. Saving variants of brushes: If you have created a variant of a brush that you would like to use again later, you can give it a name and save it in Painter. If you have made changes to a variant under the Controls palette or in some of the other areas, those changes will disappear when you select a new brush or variant. If you don't save the variant to a new name, your changes will be lost. If you save it as a variant, it will be available on the Brush Variant pop-up when the type of brush—pencil, watercolor, eraser, etc.—is selected.

Saving a Brush Variant

To save a variant of an already existing brush, use the Variant pull down menu on the Brushes palette. Let's work with a variant of the 2B Pencil that you will create. This same process will apply to any variant of a brush that you create.

   A. In the Brushes palette select the 2B Pencil.

   B. In the Controls palette, give it a size of 5 pixels and an opacity of 30%.

   C. Draw a couple of lines with the brush you have created.

   D. Click on Variant in the Brushes palette pull down menu.

   E. Click on Save Variant. The Save Variant box opens.

   1. Enter a new name in the Save As: box. Type in Test Pencil. **Warning:** Always enter a new name when using this box. If you don't, the basic pencil or brush type that you were working from will change to the new settings permanently.

   2. If you wanted to save the primary and secondary colors along with the new variant, you could click in the Save Current Colors box.

   3. Click on OK.

   4. You have just created a new pencil called Test Pencil. Notice that the name in the Variant pop-up has changed to Test Pencil. It will now be available until it is deleted.

   F. Take a couple of strokes with the new pencil.

   G. Select the 500 lb. Pencil and take a stroke or two with it.

   H. Reselect the Test Pencil and take a stroke with it.

Deleting a Brush Variant

   A. Make sure that Test Pencil is selected in the Variant pop-up.

   B. Click on Variant/Delete Variant.

   C. A box will open asking you if you really want to do this. Click on Yes.

13. Using the erasers: Erasers in Painter are brushes and can be found on the Brushes palette. The general brush type of Eraser includes a whole category of items that you may not think of strictly as erasers such as Bleaches and Darkeners. If your drawing space doesn't have a lot of strokes in it right now, make several using different colors and sizes of pencils.

   A. Click on Eraser in the Brush pop-up of the Brushes palette.

   B. In the Variant pop-up, select Fat Eraser.

   1. Click and drag across several lines to see how the fat eraser works.

   2. In the Controls palette, take the size down to 5 pixels and the opacity down to 25%.

   3. Use the fat eraser again and notice the difference.

C. In the Variant pop-up, select **Medium Bleach**. Use it across several strokes to see the effect. Do not bleach the lines all of the way out.

D. In the Variant pop-up, select **Medium Darkener**. Use it across the lines that you did not bleach completely away as well as several of the other lines. Notice the effect.

14. Using Watercolors: Watercolors employ some commands that aren't used with other brushes. You will explore some of those in this part of the exercise. If you haven't closed this drawing space and created a new one in a while, this would be a good time to do so. Do not save the old drawing.

A. Select the **Water Color** brush in the **Brush** pop-up of the **Brushes** palette.

B. Select the **Simple Water** variant. Take a couple of strokes with it in the drawing space.

C. Click on **Control/Water**. The **Advanced Controls: Water** box opens.

   1. Change the **Diffusion** setting to 10. Take a stroke. Notice how much the stroke spreads out and blurs. The diffusion scale lets you control this in watercolors.

   2. Change diffusion back to 0.

   3. Change the **Wet Fringe** setting to 0. Take a couple of strokes.

   4. Change the **Wet Fringe** setting to 100%. Notice that the edges of all the strokes taken at the lower diffusion setting change. Actually, even the strokes taken at the higher diffusion setting are changing, but you just can't see it because of the high diffusion. The Wet Fringe mode determines how much the color pools at the edges of the stroke.

   5. Change the wet fringe setting back to 22%.

D. Select a new color for drawing in the Art Materials Color palette.

E. In the **Controls** palette, change the opacity to 10%.

F. Take a stroke that crosses one or more of the old strokes. Repeat the same stroke several times.

G. Change the opacity back to 29%.

H. Take a stroke with the current color.

I. Change the color and take another stroke right next to the last one. The two should touch in spots along their length.

J. Select the **Pure Water** variant.

K. Take a stroke on the line between the two colored strokes you just drew. Notice that at first you only see a line of dots, and then the water diffuses the two colors. Take a few more strokes in the same place and slightly to the side. Notice the effect.

L. Change the diffusion to 10 and take another stroke using the Pure Water mode.

M. Try out several more of the variants available in the Variant pop-up such as **Splatter, Diffuse,** and **Large.** Remember that you can change the size, opacity, diffusion, and wet fringe on all of these.

N. Perhaps you've decided that you like what you see, and you want to dry your watercolor. After it is dried, you will not be able to blend using the Pure Water mode again. Click on **Canvas/Dry.** Try using the **Pure Water** variant again. It doesn't have any effect.

O. Watercolors work on their own layer in the drawing until they are dried. When you are working with them wet, they will not affect other pigments such as pencils or other paints except that you will be able to see the other pigments through the translucency of the watercolors. When the watercolors are dried, they are "lowered" onto the same layer with the other pigments at the same time that they are dried.

15. Using water: The Water brush is a different brush from the Water Color brush. It does not work on the wet watercolor layer. It works on the layer where the other pigments are located. This the same layer to which watercolors are moved when they dry.

A. Select **Water** in the **Brush** pop-up of the **Brushes** palette.

B. Select the **Just Add Water** variant. Take a couple of strokes across the dried watercolors. It's like working with the Pure Water mode back on the wet watercolor layer.

C. Water, however, will work on any pigment.

D. Select **Pencils** and the **500 lb. Pencil** variant. Take a stroke or two.

E. Select the **Brush** icon in the Brushes palette.

   1. Select the **Camel Hair** brush variant. Take a stroke or two in a different color.

   2. Select the **Oil Paint** variant. Take a stroke or two in a different color.

   3. Select the **Big Dry Ink** variant. Take a stroke or two in a different color.

F. Select **Water** and the **Just Add Water** variant. Take several strokes across the above pigments. The water works on all of them.

G. Try out several other water variants like the **Water Rake, Water Spray,** and **Frosty Water.**

16. Try out the Clone brush: The Clone brush works with patterns. It will let you add a pattern to the drawing.

A. Select **Cloners** in the **Brush** pop-up of the **Brushes** palette.

B. In the Art Materials palette, click on the Pattern icon underneath the word Pattern. This opens the pattern selector. Click on the drawer pushbar—the light blue bar with an arrow on it. The different patterns available are displayed. The white pop-up window underneath will also display the names of the patterns when you click on it.

C. Select a pattern.

D. Go back to Brushes palette.

E. Select the Soft Cloner in the Variant pop-up. Take several strokes right next to one another across the colors that are already in the drawing space. The pattern starts to appear underneath the colors. More strokes over one another will sharpen the pattern.

F. Try out several of the other cloner variants such as the Straight Cloner and the Impressionist Cloner.

G. You can also create your own patterns in Painter and use them as patterns. I will cover this process in a later section of the book.

17. Try the image hose: The image hose works with nozzles. A nozzle is an image file. Painter has a selection of nozzles that you can use right away, and later in this book you will learn how to import images into Painter and create your own nozzles.

A. Click on the Image Hose brush in the Brushes palette.

B. Select 3 Rank R-P-D as the variant.

C. In the Brushes palette, click on Nozzle/Nozzles. . . .

D. The Brush Controls: Nozzle box opens. Here you can select a nozzle. Click on the light blue drawer pushbar to see the nozzles available. The white pop-up window underneath also lets you select a nozzle by name.

E. Select a nozzle.

F. Take a stroke across the drawing window. The images will appear.

G. Try out several different nozzles along with several different variants on the image hose.

18. Use the Brush brush: Just to keep you thoroughly confused, since all of the tools that have been covered in this exercise are called brushes in Painter, there is also a brush with the name of Brush. It includes a wide variety of types and pigments such as Camel Hair, Inks, Oils, Washes, and even a Brush brush variant called Brushy. At this point the redundancy of Painter's naming system seems to have been carried to its ultimate extreme. Nevertheless, there are some extremely useful brushes in this category.

A. Click on the Brush pop-up and select Brush.

B. Click on the Variant pop-up and select Oil Paint.

    C. Take a couple of strokes with the Oil Paint brush to see how it works. You can, of course, as with any of the others, change the settings in the Controls palette to create variations. Change the color and take a stroke across the earlier ones, and you will notice that it covers the previous strokes completely.

    D. Try out several of the variants to see how they differ.

19. Try the Artists brushes: This category of brushes is named after artists and artistic techniques. Variants include Seurat, three Van Goghs, Impressionist, Flemish Rub, and Piano Keys.

    A. Click on the Brush pop-up and select Artists.

    B. Click on the Variant pop-up and select Seurat.

    C. Take a stroke with the Seurat brush. Notice the Pointilistic technique. You do not even get all the same color, but a selection of related colors. Change colors and take another stroke.

    D. Try out the rest of the Artists brush variants and you will understand how they got their names.

20. Use the Liquid brushes: Most of the Liquid brushes create distortion effects. You can use them to drag, smear, and distort brush strokes that have already been applied.

    A. Click on the Brush pop-up and select Liquid.

    B. Click on the Variant pop-up and select Distorto.

    C. Drag the Distorto brush across some strokes already on the drawing space.

    D. Try the same sort of stroke with Smeary Mover.

    E. Try out several more of the Liquid brushes.

21. Try the Pens brushes: The Pens brushes imitate some of the techniques that you may be used to using with ink.

    A. Click on the Brush pop-up and select Pens.

    B. Click on the Variant pop-up and select Single Pixel.

    C. Try a stroke with it. This is the smallest brush that you can select. It creates a line one pixel in width.

    D. Try out the Scratchboard Rake, Pixel Dust, Calligraphy, and Leaky Pen variants.

22. Use the Airbrush: This brush imitates the effects that can be achieved with a real airbrush.

    A. Click on the Brush pop-up and select Airbrush.

    B. Click on the Variant pop-up and select Fat Stroke.

    C. Try out the Fat Stroke airbrush. Notice that there is one important difference between Painter's airbrush and a real one: If you hold a real airbrush in place for more than a second, it will quickly build up. Painter's airbrush stops spraying when you stop moving the stylus.

D. Try out several of the other Airbrush variants.

23. Open the file **Exer1**.rif from the CD-ROM to see some of the examples of brush strokes and types that have been covered in this exercise.

24. This exercise has given you a look at most of the brushes available in Painter. It has not covered all of them, however. Take the time to work with **Charcoal**, **Chalk**, **Felt Pens**, and **Crayons** and to explore how some of the controls both in the **Controls** palette and the **Control** pull down menu change the way that these and other brushes work. As I mentioned earlier in the exercise, the variations that can be achieved with brushes in Painter do approach infinity. You will quickly learn which brushes fit your style and what controls you need to change to get the effects that you would like with them. That will be the time to start saving some variants of your own so that they will be available for later use. You will probably not want to save the final screen from this exercise. It was intended to acquaint you with the brushes available in Painter and how to create variations on them. If you should, however, please refer to the earlier section on saving a drawing.

USING ART MATERIALS

You have already learned how to use the Color palette in Exercise No. 1. The Color palette is just one of several palettes that are available on the Art Materials palette. This is also where you can choose paper types for your drawings and find and construct gradations, patterns, and weaves for use in the drawings. If the Art Materials palette does not appear on your screen, you can make it appear by clicking on **Window/Show Art Materials**. The exact appearance of the Art Materials palette will change depending upon which of the other palettes found there happen to be open, but the general layout is as follows.

The Name Bar: Running across the top of the Art Materials palette is the name bar. It will be blue in color when the palette is available and will say **Art Materials**: and then the name of the palette that is currently open, such as **Color**, in the upper left-hand corner. Click and drag on the blue bar to move the palette about the screen. On the right side is the minimize/maximize button—showing one or two rectangles—and the **Close** button, with an X on it. When the Min/Max button shows two rectangles, additional parameters will appear at the bottom of the palette.

The Pull Down Menu Bar: Just below the name bar is the grey pull down menu bar with the words Color, Paper, Grad, Pattern, and Weave. You can click on the names on this bar to open additional controls for the specific palettes.

The Palette Buttons: Just below each name on the pull down menu bar is an icon for opening the palette associated with that name. Click on the Color icon to open the Color palette, the Paper icon to open the Paper palette, etc. The appearance of the Art Materials palette below these icons depends upon which palette is open.

The Palette Controls: The large area immediately below the Palette buttons will show the controls and selection choices for the palette that is currently opened on the Art Materials palette. Click on the Color icon and this section will let you choose colors for use in your drawing, for example.

The Palette Parameters: Immediately below the Palette Controls section is the Parameters section. This section will only appear when the palette has been maximized and the Min/Max button on the name bar shows two rectangles. This section displays additional controls or parameters for the palette that is currently open.

COLOR PALETTE

With the Art Materials palette open, you can open the Color palette by clicking on the Color icon. Here is where you can select colors for use in your drawing. Let's review how to select colors and then go over some of the other uses of the Color palette.

Parts of the Color Palette

The Color Wheel (Ring and Triangle): You change colors by using the hue ring and saturation/value triangle in the Color palette. Click on the hue that you would like on the ring and then select the saturation/value that you would like by clicking in the triangle. You can also click and drag on the small ring in each of these areas to select the hue or saturation/value.

The HSV/RGB Square: Just below the color wheel to the right is the HSV/RGB square. This is a small box where the HSV or RGB values of the color that you have chosen are displayed. Click in the box to toggle between HSV and RGB values.

The Primary and Secondary Color Boxes: Just below the color wheel to the left are two boxes that display the primary and secondary color choices. The top box is the primary color, which is the active drawing color. The bottom box is the secondary color, which is available, but is not the active drawing color. You can switch the colors in the Primary box and the Secondary

**THE COLOR
PALETTE**

box by clicking on the double-ended arrow that points to both boxes. Only the color that appears in the primary box can be used when you are drawing. If you click on either the Primary or the Secondary box, a black outline will appear around it. You can change the color in the box with the black outline using the color wheel. These same Primary and Secondary Color boxes also appear in the Controls palette.

The Clone Color Box: To the right of the Primary Color box is the small Clone Color box. You can click here to tell the brush to paint with colors from a clone source.

The Color Variability Parameters: The section underneath the main Color palette section is the Parameters area. This is the area that is only open when the palette is maximized. When the Color palette is open, this contains sliders that let you control the HSV values of the color.

The **Color** Pull Down Menu: Clicking on the word **Color** in the pull down menu on the palette opens the choices and commands available with the Color palette. Your options are:

Color Picker: This gives you the options of **Standard**, **Compact**, and **RGB** colors.

> **Standard**: This displays the hue ring and saturation/value triangle.

> **Compact**: This displays a more compact version with a hue bar and the saturation/value triangle.

> **RGB**: This displays a set of RGB scales that can be used for selecting hue.

Display as HSV/Display as RGB: This option toggles the HSV/RGB square to display one or the other set of values.

Use Clone Color: Choosing this has the same effect as checking the Clone Color square. It tells the brush to use colors found on the clone.

Load Color Set: This lets you load additional color sets. In the main Painter directory on your hard drive—usually located under Program Files—for example, there is a set of Pantone colors available. You can load this color set by clicking on **Load Color Set**. In the **Select Color Set** box that opens, double click on the **Extra Art Materials** folder. Then double click on **Pantone Colors.txt**. The Pantone color set will appear on the screen.

Adjust Color Set: Clicking here opens the **Art Materials: Color Set** box. This box allows you to change the way that a color set such as the Pantone color set is displayed on the screen. You can change the size of the color squares displayed and in how many rows and columns they are displayed.

THE PAPER PALETTE

The **Paper** palette on the Art Materials palette is where you choose the paper, or texture, on which you draw. With some brushes, the texture of the paper will make a big difference in the appearance of the drawing. You can also draw a stroke with one texture of paper, change papers, and make another stroke. The first stroke will maintain the texture of the paper on which it was drawn, while the second stroke will take on the texture of the new paper. The illustration labeled The Paper Palette shows the palette with the **Paper** drawer opened.

Parts of the Paper Palette

The **Paper** Icons: Just below the pull down menu bar are the five **Paper** icons. The one with the red outline around it is the currently selected paper type.

Click on one of the others to select a different paper type. Hold the cursor over the top of the icon for a second or two, and the name of the paper type will appear.

The Drawer Pushbar: Just below the five Paper icons is the light blue drawer pushbar. Click on this to open the Paper drawer underneath and display icons for additional paper types. With the paper drawer closed, you can also toggle the Min/Max button to display and change parameters of the currently selected paper type. This display shows you a detailed picture of the paper and lets you invert the texture and change the scale of the paper.

The Paper Pop-Up: Below the paper drawer is the Paper pop-up. It displays the name of the current paper type. Click on it and the pop-up will open where you can select paper types by name.

The Pull Down Menu Bar: If you click on Paper on the pull down menu bar, you will be able to select commands and choices that you can make with the Paper palette.

   Capture Paper: The Capture Paper command lets you take a part of an image in the drawing space and turn it into a paper texture.

   Make Paper: The Make Paper command lets you create paper from a pattern.

   Invert Paper: The Invert Paper command reverses the highs and lows in the texture of the paper.

   Paper Mover: This opens the Paper Mover box, which lets you move papers from one library to another and delete them.

THE GRADATION (GRAD) PALETTE

Gradations can be used in Painter with the Fill tool to fill selections, floaters, or masks. The Grad palette lets you select already existing gradations and create new ones.

Parts of the Grad Palette

The Gradation Icons: These five icons display the gradations currently available for use. The active Gradation icon has a red outline around it. Hold the cursor over the top of the icon to display the name.

The Drawer Pushbar: Click on the light blue bar below the icons to open the drawer and display the current Gradation library to select more gradations. Close the drawer and click on the Min/Max button to display the larger area shown in the figure labeled The Grad Palette where you can change the angle of the grad and select a grad type. The smaller areas below that shown

**THE GRAD
PALETTE**

in the figure are the Order buttons, which you can use to change the order of the colors in the gradation.

The Gradation Pop-Up: The Gradation pop-up is the white bar with the name of the current gradation. It is either located below the drawer when the drawer is open or below the drawer pushbar when the drawer is closed. Click on it to select a gradation by name.

The Pull Down Menu: Click on Grad on the pull down menu to display the commands available with the Gradation palette.

Capture Grad: Select an area in the drawing space. Click on Capture Grad and the colors in the area will be turned into a gradation.

Express in Image: This option opens the Express in Image box, which lets you apply the gradation to the entire image in the drawing space or a selected part of it based on the luminance values of the image itself.

Edit Grad: This lets you edit the currently active gradation.

Save Grad: After you have created a new gradation, this opens the Save Grad box to let you give it a name and save it in a library.

Grad Mover: This lets you delete, change the name of, and move gradations from one library to another.

**THE PATTERN
PALETTE**

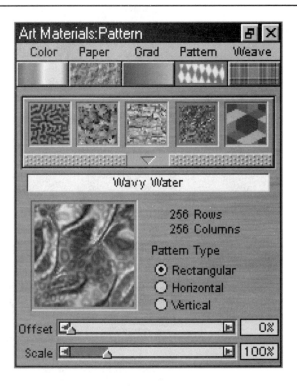

Patterns can be used in Painter with the Fill tool to fill selections, floaters, or masks. The **Pattern** palette lets you select already existing patterns and create new ones.

Parts of the Pattern Palette

The **Pattern** Icons: The five icons immediately below the pull down menu are all patterns available for use. There is a red outline around the currently selected pattern. Hold the cursor over the top of an icon to display the name.

The Drawer Pushbar: Click on the light blue drawer pushbar to display more icons of available patterns. Click on the **Min/Max** button to display controls for the selected pattern. These controls let you change the pattern type, offset, and scale.

The **Pattern** Pop-Up: The white box with the name of the currently selected pattern in it is the **Pattern** pop-up. Click here to select patterns by name.

The Pull Down Menu: Click on **Pattern** on the pull down menu to choose commands that let you create, modify, and store patterns.

Capture Pattern: Select a part of the drawing area to be turned into a pattern. Click here to do so.

Define Pattern: This option lets you give an image or a selected part of an image patternlike characteristics. For example, if you drag a brush stroke off of the screen, it comes back in on the other side. This can help in creating patterns since they are tiled and one side must match up with the other.

Make Fractal Pattern: This command opens the **Make Fractal Pattern** dialogue box. Here you can define parameters for the fractal pattern generator to create unusual patterns.

Add Image to Library: This lets you add a new pattern that you have created to a Pattern library.

Check Out Pattern: This opens the selected pattern in a drawing window so that you can see it in a larger size and use any Painter tool or brush on it for modifications.

Pattern Mover: This lets you delete, change the name of, or move a pattern from one library to another.

Weaves can be used in Painter with the Fill tool to fill selections, floaters, or masks. The **Weave** palette lets you select already existing weaves and create new ones.

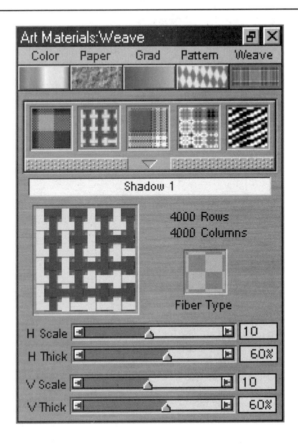

Parts of the Weave Palette

The **Weave** Icons: The five icons represent weaves that are available for selection. A red outline surrounds the active weave. Hold the cursor over the top of the icon to display the name.

The Drawer Pushbar: Click on the light blue bar to open the **Weave** drawer to see more available weaves. Click on the **Min/Max** button to display controls for the selected weave. These controls let you change the fiber type, the horizontal scale and thickness, and the vertical scale and thickness.

The **Weave** Pop-Up: The white box that contains the name of the selected weave. Click here to select a weave by name.

The Pull Down Menu: Click on **Weave** on the pull down menu to see the commands and available choices that you can use with weaves.

> **Get Color Set**: This opens the color set for the selected weave. You can then change these colors using the Color palette.

Put Color Set: After you have changed the colors in a weave color set, use this command to apply the new colors to the preview window in the Weave palette. Then when you apply the weave to a drawing, it will use the new colors.

Edit Weave: This opens the Edit Weave box, where you can change the pattern of a weave and create a new one.

Save Weave: Use this to name a new weave. If you don't give the new weave a name, Painter will replace the old weave with the new one but not give it a new name. The old weave will be lost.

Weave Mover: This lets you delete, change the name of, or move a weave from one library to another.

Exercise No. 2: Using Art Materials

This exercise is designed to help you understand how to work with art materials: colors, papers, gradations, patterns, and weaves.

Working with Color

1. Start a new drawing space.
2. Select a brush.
3. Open the Color palette if it isn't open by clicking on the Color icon on the Art Materials palette.
4. On the Art Materials palette, click on Color on the pull down menu.
5. Click on Color Picker/Compact Colors. Create and draw with several colors using the compact version.
6. Click on Color Picker/RGB Colors. Create and draw with several colors using the RGB version.
7. Click on Color Picker/Standard Colors to return to the Standard color picker.
8. Open the Pantone color set. This is a selection of colors coded to the Pantone scale:
   A. Click on Color/Load Color Set. The Select Color Set box opens.
   B. In the Files of type: area, select All Files.
   C. In the Look in: area, locate and open the main Painter folder. This is usually under Program Files.
   D. Open the Extra Art Materials folder.
   E. Click on Pantone Colors.txt in the Extra Art Materials folder. The name should appear in the File Name: area.

F. Click on the **Open** button.

G. The **Pantone** color set will open. Click on the blue bar on top and move the set to a convenient location on the screen.

  1. Scroll up and down in the set and locate a color that you like.
  2. Click on that color. It will appear in the color picker.
  3. Draw a stroke with the Pantone color.
  4. Select and draw with another Pantone color.

9. Use the dropper to reselect a color that you have already used. The **Dropper** tool in the **Tools** palette lets you duplicate a color that was used earlier:

  A. Click on the **Dropper** in the Tools palette; click on **Window/Show Tools** if the palette isn't open.

  B. Move the cursor over a color in the drawing space that you used earlier. Click on that color.

  C. The color will reappear in the color picker.

  D. Click on **Brushes** in the Tools palette and draw a stroke with the color.

10. Close the drawing space without saving and open a new one.

Note: Any time that your drawing space gets too crowded with strokes in the exercise, close the old one without saving and open a new one.

Working with Paper

The Paper palette lets you select and create different paper types or textures. This is like drawing on top of a textured piece of paper. With certain brushes, the texture will show through; with others it will not.

1. Open the **Paper** palette in the **Art Materials** palette by clicking on the **Paper** icon.

2. Open the **Paper** drawer by clicking on the light blue **drawer pushbar** underneath the icons. This displays additional paper types.

3. Move the cursor over the top of several of the icons and hold it in place for a second or two to display the name of the paper type that corresponds with each icon.

4. Click on the **Paper** pop-up and select **Hatching** as the paper type.

5. Go to the **Brushes** palette and select **Water Color** as the brush type and **Broad Water Brush** as the variant. This brush will really show the texture of the paper.

6. Take a stroke in the drawing space with the brush.

7. Go back to the Paper palette and select **Crackle** as the paper type.

8. Take a stroke in the drawing space with the brush. Notice the different texture. Notice also that the paper texture under the old stroke has not changed. You can change paper types to get different textures for different strokes.

9. Click on the Min/Max button on the Art Materials: Paper name bar. This closes the drawer. Click again. This opens the controls area in the palette for the Crackle texture. You will see a large window displaying the current paper type.

    A. Click in the box by Invert Paper. Take a stroke in the drawing space. Notice the difference from the last stroke.

    B. Move the Scale down to 50%. Take a stroke in the drawing space. Notice the difference from the last stroke.

10. Try out a couple of other paper types.

11. Create a new paper texture.

    A. In the Art Materials palette, click on Paper on the pull down menu and then on Make Paper.

    B. The Make Paper box opens.

        1. Click on the Pattern button in the Make Paper box and select Diamond from the pop-up menu.

        2. Change the Spacing to 10 and the Angle to 15 degrees.

        3. Double click to the right of Untitled in the Save As: box so that it is highlighted.

        4. Give the paper type a name: Type in Test.

        5. Click on OK. Your new paper type appears in the sample window of the Paper controls area.

        6. Take a stroke in the drawing space using the new paper type.

12. Use the Paper Mover tool to delete the new paper type:

    A. In the Art Materials palette, click on Paper on the pull down menu and then on Paper Mover.

    B. In the window on the left side of the box, click on the icons until you locate the one named Test. It should be the last one. In the middle section under Current Paper, it should read Test.

    C. Click on the Delete button.

    D. Click on the Quit button.

13. Close the old drawing space without saving and open a new one.

Working with Gradations

Gradations can be used to fill selections, masks, and floaters or the entire drawing. This part of the exercise will show you how to use and create gradations. A later exercise will cover selecting areas and using masks and floaters in more detail.

1. Click on the Grad icon in the Art Materials palette to open the Gradation palette.

2. Click on the light blue drawer pushbar to open the Gradation drawer. Hold the cursor over the top of several of the icons to display the name of the icons.

3. Choose a gradation by clicking on one of the icons. If it is in the drawer, it will move up to the icon row and be outlined in red.

4. Next you will make a selection and fill it with the gradation:

    A. Go to the Tools palette and click on the Rectangular Selection tool. This is just one way of making a selection.

    B. In the drawing space, click on a point and then drag the cursor diagonally to define a rectangle. Release the mouse button when you have the rectangle defined. The selection will be outlined in a flashing dotted line.

    C. Go to the Tools palette and click on the Fill tool, which looks like a paint bucket.

    D. In the drawing space, click in the middle of the rectangle that you defined.

    E. It will fill with the gradation that you selected earlier.

5. Go back to the Grad palette and choose the Browns gradation by using the pop-up.

6. Select another area and fill it with the Browns gradation.

7. Return to the Grad palette and choose the Two-Point gradation.

8. Click on the drawer pushbar to close the drawer. If the gradation does not appear in a large square surrounded by a circle where the open drawer used to be, click on the Min/Max button until it does. This is the Gradation controls area. The gradation is surrounded by a circle and there are four other boxes to the side. The gradation also appears on a long bar underneath. Below the long bar are six buttons.

    A. If you do not see a gradation in the areas mentioned above, it is because your primary and secondary colors are the same color. Open the Color palette and choose different colors for the primary and secondary colors. The gradation will reflect the colors that you have chosen. If you don't like the colors of the gradation, open the Color palette and choose two different primary and secondary colors.

    B. Return to the Gradation palette. These are the controls:

        1. The circle surrounding the gradation preview window is the grad angle ring. Click and drag on the dot on the circle to change the angle of the gradation.

2. The four boxes to the right of the grad angle ring are the Grad Type boxes. Click on each of them and watch the gradation in the gradation preview window change.

3. Underneath the gradation in the long bar are six control buttons. Hold the cursor over each of them and the name of the button will appear. Click in turn on the Left to Right Grad, Mirrored Left to Right Grad, Right to Left Grad, Double Left to Right Grad, Mirrored Right to Left Grad, and Double Right to Left Grad buttons and see how the gradation changes.

C. Select another area in the drawing space and fill it with a gradation that you have created using the controls in steps B1–B3 above.

D. Click on Select/None on the main pull down menu to remove the flashing dotted lines from around the selection.

9. Now you'll explore some of the options available using the commands that appear under the Grad pull down menu.

A. The Capture Grad Command: The Capture Grad command uses a selection of pixels from the drawing space to form the colors of a gradation. This lets you create a gradation using many different colors.

1. Open the Color palette. Click on Brushes on the Tools palette. Choose a brush such as 500 lb. Pencil and choose a color in the Color palette. Make a stroke in the drawing area. Choose a second color and make a stroke with it in the drawing area right next to the first one. Choose a third, fourth, and fifth color and make a stroke with each of them right next to the others.

2. Select the Rectangular Selection tool in the Tools palette. Make a selection that is a skinny rectangle either horizontally or vertically. This rectangle should cross all of the color strokes that you made with the brush. The program will choose the first row of pixels horizontally or vertically, depending upon the shape of the rectangle, to make up the gradation. If, instead of crossing the five color strokes, you were making a selection in a complex drawing, the color choices would be determined by the placement of your rectangle.

3. On the pull down menu of the Art Materials palette, click on Grad/Capture Grad.

4. The Save Grad box will open.
   a. Type in a new name for the gradation such as Test.
   b. Click on OK.
   c. Open the Grad palette and you will see the gradation displayed in the preview window. You can use the controls to change the gradation.
   d. Click on Select/None to remove the rectangular selection window from the screen.

B. The Express in Image Command: This command lets you apply a gradation to an image or part of an image using the luminance values of the image. That means you won't see the gradation as a swirl or linear gradation like you have to this point unless part of your selection is a swirl or linear gradation. The values of the image determine how the gradation is distributed. If you select an area of solid color, the gradation will appear as one color. If you select an area with different textures and colors, then the gradation will use the values created by those different textures and colors to distribute the gradation. The colors in the selected area will not be the colors of the gradation but are used to determine values.

This would be a good time to close this drawing space and create a new one.

1. Choose a paper.
2. Click on the Brush tool in the Tools palette.
3. Choose a brush that will let the texture of the paper show through.
4. Choose a color.
5. Make a stroke in the drawing area.
6. Choose a new paper and color. Make another stroke in the drawing area right next to the last one.
7. Repeat the previous step several times. You want to get different colors and textures right next to one another in the drawing area so that you will have a good example of how this command works. You are using paper texture and different colors to create a variety of values in the drawing area.
8. Open the Grad palette and choose a gradation.
9. Click on the Rectangular Selection tool on the Tools palette and select a rectangular area that cuts across all of the strokes that you drew.
10. On the Art Materials palette pull down menu, click on Grad/Express in Image.
11. The Express in Image box opens. Change the Bias setting to see how that affects the image.
12. Click on OK.
13. On the main pull down menu, click on Select/None.
14. If you had not selected part of the image in step B9 above, the command would have been applied to the whole drawing area.

C. The Edit Grad command: The Edit Grad command lets you edit existing gradations to create new ones.
1. Go to the Color palette and choose a primary and secondary color that you would like to see expressed in a gradation.

2. Go to the **Grad** palette and choose the **Two-Point** gradation. You can use the **Edit Grad** command with any gradation. This is a simple example that may help you understand the editing process more easily.

3. In the pull down menu of the Art Materials palette, click on **Grad/Edit Grad.**

4. The **Edit Grad** box opens.

    a. Click in the middle of the colored gradation bar. This will divide it into two parts. You can click anywhere in the colored gradation bar to create as many divisions as you want. Create a few more divisions. If you create too many divisions, you can click and drag on one of the pointers below the colored gradation bar so that it is on top of another.

    b. Click on one of the square boxes above a division. The **Color:** button will appear. Click on the **Color:** button and select **RGB, Hue Clockwise,** and **Hue Counterclockwise** each in turn to see how they change that division. Also click on the **Linear** box each time to see how that affects the image. Make some changes in the divisions.

    c. If the Edit Grad box is blocking your access to the Grad palette, click and drag on the blue name bar to move it out of the way.

    d. Make changes to the controls in the Grad palette and see how these affect the image. When you have the gradation in the preview window looking the way that you would like, click on **OK** in the Edit Grad box.

5. In the pull down menu of the Art Materials palette, click on **Grad/Save Grad.** The **Save Grad** box opens. Enter a new name like **Test2** in the **Save As:** area and click on **OK.**

Note: The Save Grad command does not have to be used just with the **Edit Grad** command. Any time that you are creating a new grad by using the controls or any other method, you can save those changes to a new name using the **Save Grad** command. This will let you recall a modified grad without having to make the changes again.

D. The **Grad Mover** tool: The **Grad Mover** tool lets you delete grads from the current library, move grads between libraries, and create new libraries.

1. In the left window, click on the icons until you find the new grad **Test.** You will probably have to use the scroll bar on the side of the window to locate it. It will be at the bottom.

2. When the name **Test** appears under **Current Grad:** in the middle section, click on **Delete.**

>   3. Delete the grad Test2.
>   4. Click on Quit.

10. Close the drawing space without saving it and create a new one.

Working with Patterns

Patterns are applied to selections in the drawing in the same manner that gradations are applied. This section of the exercise will help you to understand how to use, modify, and create patterns.

1. Click on the Pattern icon on the Art Materials palette to open the Pattern palette.
2. There are five Pattern icons displayed for your choice. Click on the light blue drawer pushbar to display more Pattern icons. Hold the cursor over the top of the Pattern icons to display the names of the patterns. You can also choose a pattern by name by clicking on the pop-up menu and then selecting the name that you want. The selected pattern appears outlined in red on the top row of icons.
3. Choose the Vines pattern.
4. Use the Rectangular Selection tool to select an area in the drawing space.
5. Use the Fill tool to fill the area with the Vines pattern.
6. Click on Select/None on the main pull down menu to deselect the area.
7. Click on the drawer pushbar and the Min/Max button until the control area with the large pattern preview window appears where the Pattern drawer used to be. Here you can make changes in the pattern.
   A. Change the Scale to 50%.
   B. Scroll the Offset pointer to higher and lower percentages.
   C. Watch the preview window to see what happens to Vines. There are other patterns for which changing the offset will not produce a noticeable effect.
   D. Change the pattern to Checkers.
   E. Change the Scale to 50%.
   F. Click on the circle next to Horizontal. Click and drag the pointer under the Offset scale left and right.
   G. Click on the circle next to Vertical. Click and drag the pointer under the Offset scale left and right.
8. Try making modifications in a couple of other patterns.
9. Work with the Pattern Pull Down Menu.
   A. The Capture Pattern command: The Capture Pattern command is used to select a part of an image or a whole image as a pattern.
      1. Click on the Brushes tool in the Tools palette.

2. Using different brushes, colors, and papers, if you like, create a drawing in part of the drawing space that you are going to use as a pattern that can be tiled or repeated vertically and horizontally. Keep it simple for now, but think about how it will look when it is repeated vertically and horizontally.

3. Use the Rectangular Selection tool to select the part of the drawing that you would like to turn into a pattern.

4. On the pull down menu in the Art Materials palette, click on Pattern/Capture Pattern.

5. The Capture Pattern box opens.
   a. Click on Rectangular Tile and move the Bias slider.
   b. Do the same with Horizontal Shift and Vertical Shift.
   c. Work with the three above choices and the Bias slider to get the pattern looking the way that you want.
   d. Double click on the right side of the name box to highlight Untitled and then type in a new name for the pattern, such as Test.
   e. Click on OK.

6. Click on Select/None on the main pull down menu to clear the rectangular selection.

7. Open the Pattern palette.

8. In the controls area of the palette, change the offset and scale to your liking.

9. Use the Rectangular Selection tool to select a part of the drawing, and then fill it with your pattern.

10. Click on Select/None to clear the rectangular selection.

B. The Define Pattern command: The Define Pattern command is used to give an image patternlike characteristics. It makes two changes to the way that the drawing space works to help you create patterns. First, when you are drawing in the drawing space with Define Pattern checked, if you draw out one side of the screen, the stroke comes in on the other side. This helps you match up patterns at the edges. Second, when you depress and hold the Shift key, the image in the drawing space is tiled like a pattern. You won't notice this until you use the Grabber tool, which looks like a hand, to move the image around. Then you will be able to align the image the way that you would like in the drawing space. Both of these changes may be a little easier to understand when you see them in action.

   1. Close the old drawing space without saving and create a new one with smaller dimensions: 2 inches × 2 inches.

   2. Move the whole drawing space so that there is room around all sides of it. This is so that you can take advantage of the wraparound effect of the Define Pattern command.

3. Choose the **Brushes** tool on the **Tools** palette and select a smaller brush like the **2B Pencil** and a color that you like. You want to create a simple pattern for the sake of the demonstration.

4. In the **Art Materials** palette pull down menu, click on **Pattern/Define Pattern**.

5. Make a diagonal stroke that starts at the middle of the drawing space and goes to a corner. When you get to the corner, keep moving the brush. The stroke will appear at the opposite corner and continue back to the middle again if you keep moving the stylus in the same direction. This is the wraparound effect of the Define Pattern command. When the stroke leaves the drawing space, it will continue on the opposite side of the drawing space.

6. Make a few more strokes that utilize the wraparound effect.

7. Now, let's examine the tiling effect. Click on the **Grabber** tool (the hand) in the **Tools** palette.

8. Click and drag with the Grabber tool in the drawing space. Notice that the whole drawing space moves inside its border. Recenter it again in the border.

9. Hold the **Shift** key down. With the Shift key depressed, again click and drag with the Grabber tool. The drawing space has been tiled. You can now move the tiled space around to select the exact position of the pattern that you would like within the drawing space. As you move the tiled drawing space around with the Grabber tool, remember that when you release the Grabber, that will be the look of the pattern that you are creating.

10. On the main pull down menu, click on **Select/All**.

11. On the pull down menu on the **Art Materials** palette, click on **Pattern/Capture Pattern**.

12. The **Capture Pattern** box opens. Give it a new name such as **Test2**. Make any other changes that you would like in the Capture Pattern box and then click on **OK**.

13. If the **Pattern** palette is not open, click on the **Pattern** icon on the **Art Materials** palette to open it.

14. Open the controls area of the Pattern palette and make any adjustments to **Scale**, **Offset**, etc. that you would like in the pattern.

15. Close the current drawing space without saving it and open a new one that is 7 inches × 7 inches.

16. Use the **Rectangular Selection** tool to select an area in the drawing space and then the **Fill** tool to fill it with the new pattern.

17. In the main pull down menu, click on **Select/None** to clear the rectangular selection.

C. The Make Fractal Pattern command: Fractal generators are very useful in pattern creation because they produce random images. By controlling the parameters of the fractal generator in Painter, you can create a wide variety of patterns. Let's use Painter's fractal generator to create a pattern.

1. In the Art Materials palette pull down menu, click on Pattern/ Make Fractal Pattern.

2. The Make Fractal Pattern box opens.

3. Choose a size of 256. The fractal pattern that you are designing will be created in a new drawing space over the top of the old drawing space. This will give it a smaller space so that you will understand what is happening when the new space appears.

4. Move the Power, Feature Size, Softness, Angle, and Thinness sliders around to change the parameters of the fractal generator.

5. Click on the Channel button to change between Surface Normal, Gradient Bearing, and Height as Luminance.

6. When the preview window looks the way that you would like, click on OK.

7. The new drawing space appears with the Pattern in it.

8. In the main pull down menu, click on Select/All.

9. In the pull down menu on the Art Materials palette, click on Pattern/Capture Pattern.

10. The Capture Pattern box opens. Give the pattern a new name such as Test3. Change the Bias, Shift, and Tile if you would like. Click on OK.

11. Close the new drawing space that contains the pattern. You do not need to save the changes.

12. Use the Rectangular Selection tool to select an area in the old drawing space and then use the Fill tool to fill it with the new pattern.

13. In the main pull down menu, click on Select/None to deselect the rectangular space filled with the new pattern.

D. The Pattern Mover tool: The Pattern Mover tool is used to delete patterns, move patterns to a different library, and create new libraries.

1. In the Art Materials palette pull down menu, click on Pattern/Pattern Mover.

2. Locate the patterns Test, Test2, and Test3 and delete them like you did with the Grad and Paper Mover tools.

3. Quit the Pattern Mover function.

4. Close the old drawing without saving and start a new one.

Working with Weaves

Weaves, like grads and patterns, are used to fill selections, masks, and floaters. Modifying and creating them is a little different, however. This section will show you the basics of working with weaves.

1. Open the Weave palette by clicking on the Weave icon on the Art Materials palette.

2. The five icons that appear all represent already created weaves that are available.

3. If the Weave drawer with more icons is not open, open it by clicking on the light blue drawer pushbar.

4. Choose a weave by clicking on one of the icons or by clicking on the pop-up, where you can select one by name. Select the Shadow 1 weave. It should move up to the top five Weave icons and be outlined in red.

5. Click on the drawer pushbar again to close the Weave drawer. If the Parameters area with the weave preview window, fiber type, and the H and V scales is not present, click on the Min/Max button to make it appear. Now you can change the parameters for the Shadow 1 weave that is selected.

6. Click on the Fiber Type window. You have a choice between an open weave and a tight weave.

7. Change the H (Horizontal) Scale and Thickness values and the V (Vertical) Scale and Thickness values.

8. Use the Rectangular Selection tool to select an area in the drawing space and the Fill tool to fill it with the weave.

9. Click on Select/None to deselect the rectangle.

10. Use the Weave pull down menu:

    A. The Get Color Set command: This command lets you change the colors of the weave.

        1. On the Art Materials pull down menu, click on Weave/Get Color Set. The color set appears.

        2. Open the Color palette.

        3. Choose a new color for the weave in the Color palette.

        4. Hold down the Alt key and click on the color in the weave color set that you want to replace with the new color.

        5. Pick a second new color for the weave in the Color palette.

        6. Hold down the Alt key and click on the color in the weave color set that you want to replace with the new color.

        7. Click on Weave/Put Color Set in the Art Materials pull down menu.

        8. Open the Weave palette. The new colors are now in place on the weave.

9. Reselect the filled area using the Rectangular Selection tool and fill it with the new weave using the Fill tool.

10. Change the H and V Scale and Thickness values and fill the selection again.

11. Click on Select/None to deselect the rectangle.

B. The Edit Weave command: This command opens the Edit Weave box and lets you modify this weave or create a new one.

1. Click on Weave/Edit Weave in the Art Materials pull down menu. The Edit Weave box opens.

2. There are a bunch of formulas that you can enter in the boxes on the left, but the easiest way to change a weave or create a new one is to click in the squares in the box on the right that represents the pattern graphically. Click on a black square, and it will turn white. Click on a white square, and it will turn black. Black and white represent the two colors of the weave. Keep clicking until you get a pattern that you like.

3. Click on OK.

4. Click on Weave/Save Weave in the Art Materials pull down menu. The Save Weave box opens.

5. Give the weave a new name such as Test. Click on OK.

6. Go back to the Weave palette to change the H and V Scale and Thickness values.

7. Use the Get Color Set and Put Color Set commands to change the colors.

8. Select a new area in the drawing space and fill it with the new weave.

9. If you are really interested in advanced weaving, read the Weaving PDF file in the Documentation folder on the Painter CD-ROM that you used to install the program. You can literally use this like an eight-harness, eight-treadle loom to create patterns in multiple colors.

10. Click on Select/None to deselect the rectangular area.

C. The Weave Mover command: Use the weave mover command to delete weaves, assign weaves to libraries, or create new libraries.

1. Click on Weave/Weave Mover.

2. The weave mover opens.

3. Delete the Test weave as you did with the Pattern and Grad Mover tools.

4. Quit the weave mover.

11. Open the file Exer2.rif from the CD-ROM to see some examples of the kinds of things that can be done with art materials.

USING VIEW, CANVAS, SELECTION, AND MASK TOOLS

The Tools palette in Painter contains a number of tools that allow you to make selections, control your view of the drawing, and perform similar functions. Some of the other tools such as the Brush, Fill, and Dropper tools have already been covered in previous exercises. This section and the exercise that follows will cover the tools on the Tools palette that deal with controlling the drawing itself and making selections in the drawing.

 The Magnifier Tool: The Magnifier tool allows you to zoom in and out of a view of the drawing so that you can view it in greater detail or return to the full view. Click and drag to form a window, and you can zoom in to the view size that you want. Hold the Ctrl + Alt keys down and click to zoom out. Set the zoom level by clicking on the Zoom Level pop-up in the Controls palette.

 The Grabber and Rotate Tools: The Grabber and Rotate tools are stacked on top of one another in the Tools palette. Click and hold on the button to make the other one appear. Move the cursor to the tool that you want and click to select it. The Grabber tool lets you pan about the drawing. The Rotate tool lets you rotate the entire drawing to an angle. Click and drag with either.

 The Crop Tool: The Crop tool lets you decrease the size of the canvas on which you are drawing. Click and drag to define a new size. Move the cursor over one of the edges of the crop to move that edge by clicking and dragging. Click inside the crop to change the size of the canvas. On the main pull down menu, the Canvas/Canvas Size command will also let you decrease or increase the size of the canvas.

 The Lasso Tool: The Lasso tool lets you make a freehand selection from the drawing space. Click and drag to form the shape of the selection. Hold down the Shift key and click and drag again to add to the selection. Hold down the Ctrl key and click and drag again to subtract from the selection.

 The Rectangular and Oval Selection Tools: These tools are stacked on top of one another. Click and hold on one button to make the other one appear. Move the cursor to the tool that you want and click to select it. Click and drag with either to form the shape of the selection. Hold down the Shift key and then click and drag to form a square or circular selection.

 The Magic Wand Tool: The Magic Wand tool lets you make selections in the drawing space through the use of color. Click or click and drag to select a continuous group of pixels in the drawing of a similar color. Hold down the

Shift key and click to add neighboring colors or another area. Hold down the Ctrl key and click to delete neighboring colors from the selection. In the Controls palette, you can change the tolerance, feather, and anti-alias of the tool. Tolerance controls how much variance from the color clicked on will be selected. Feather controls the size of the edge of the selection. Anti-alias gives you a soft edge to the selection.

Selections and Masks

Making a selection in Painter is like picking part of an image. You can then do a number of different things to that selection. It can be filled with a color, a gradation, a pattern, or a weave as you have seen in the section dealing with those art materials. The selection can also be converted into a user mask. Masks are like selections that have been saved so that they can be used again. There can only be one selection at a time, and when that selection has been deselected, you have to go through whatever selection process was used originally to turn it into a selection again. Masks can be recalled using the Objects palette. When a selection has been converted into a mask, it can be combined with, subtracted from, added to, or intersected with another mask to create a new mask. These can all be very useful techniques for defining the precise part of an image that you would like to fill or paint over.

Exercise No. 3: Using View, Canvas, Selection, and Mask Tools

Viewing and Resizing the Drawing Space

1. Open a new drawing space that is 7 inches × 7 inches.

2. Click on the Brush tool and select a brush and color. Make a couple of strokes in the drawing space.

3. Click on the Magnifier tool.

   A. Open the Controls palette if it isn't open and click on the pop-up under Zoom Level. Move the cursor to the zoom level that you would like and click. The image will decrease or increase in size by the amount that you chose.

   B. Move the cursor over the drawing space. Notice that the cursor appears as a magnifier with a + inside it. This tells you that you are in the Zoom In mode and clicking the mouse will magnify the image. Click once to zoom in by one step. Click again to zoom in by another step. Each click will magnify the drawing by one of the steps in the Zoom Level pop-up.

C. You can also use the Zoom In mode to zoom to a specific part of the image. Click and drag to create a rectangle. The drawing window will zoom in to that part of the drawing space.

D. Hold down the Ctrl + Alt/Command keys and move the cursor over the image. Notice that the cursor now has a - inside it. This tells you that you are in the Zoom Out mode and clicking the mouse will decrease the size of the image. Click once while holding the Ctrl + Alt/Command keys. This will decrease the size of the image by one of the steps in the Zoom Level pop-up.

E. Zoom back to 100% using the Zoom Level pop-up in the Controls palette.

F. It is likely that the image will not be centered in the drawing space. It will be back at 100 percent but centered on the area that you last zoomed in on.

4. Click on Window/Zoom to Fit on the main pull down menu. This will make the image fit the size of the drawing space.

5. Click on the Grabber tool, which looks like a hand, on the Tools palette.

A. Move the cursor over the drawing space. It will appear as a hand.

B. Click and drag to pan about the image.

C. Zoom in to a tight view of part of the image.

D. Use the Grabber tool to move about the image.

E. Zoom to 100%.

F. Use the Grabber tool to center the image in the drawing space.

G. Zoom in to a tight view of part of the image.

H. Click on Window/Zoom to Fit to center the image in the drawing space and make it fit the space exactly.

6. Click on the Rotate tool, which is located underneath the Grabber tool on the Tools palette.

A. Click and drag to the left or right to rotate the entire image in the drawing space. This lets you rotate the whole image to an angle that may be more comfortable for use with your drawing tablet. The Controls palette will display exactly how much you have rotated the image.

B. After you have rotated the image, you may want to click and drag on the detent at the lower right-hand corner of the drawing space border to increase or decrease the size of the border so that your image will fit inside it rotated.

C. Rotate the image back so that it is lined up with the border of the drawing space. Notice the angle in the Controls palette. It should be at 0 degrees. This may not, however, be a true 0 degrees.

  D. To return the canvas to a true 0 degrees, hold down the Ctrl key and
      click in the drawing space. You may have to do this before you can use
      other tools such as Crop.

7. Click on the **Crop** Tool in the Tools palette.

  A. Click and drag to form a rectangle. The rectangle that you form will be
      the new cropped image. Most likely, however, you will not be able to
      do this. You will instead get a message that tells you that you cannot
      crop a rotated image—even if you did take the angle back to 0 degrees
      in step 6C above.

  B. Select the **Rotate** tool again. Click once in the image. This will return
      the image to no rotation. Now you will be able to use the Crop tool
      and a number of other tools that will not work on rotated images.

  C. Select the Crop tool.

  D. Click and drag to form the size and location of the image that you
      would like to crop.

  E. The image is surrounded by a moving, dotted outline.

     1. Move the cursor to a corner of the dotted outline. A double-ended
         arrow with a corner will form. Click and drag to move the position
         of that corner.

     2. Move the cursor to one of the vertical or horizontal sides of the
         dotted outline. A double-ended arrow with a straight line will
         form. Click and drag to move the position of the side.

     3. Move the cursor outside the dotted outline. A + forms. Click to
         deselect the crop area.

     4. Reform the crop area by clicking and dragging with the Crop tool.
         Move its corners and/or sides to the position that you would like.

     5. Move the cursor inside the dotted outline. Scissors will form. Click
         to crop the area that you have selected.

  F. Click on **Edit/Undo Crop** to restore the earlier sized image.

8. **Canvas** commands also allow you to resize the drawing space.

  A. Click on **Canvas/Resize**. The **Resize** box opens.

     1. Click on the **pixels** button next to the **Width** window to select **inches**.

     2. Click on the **pixels** button next to the **Height** window to select **inches**.

     3. Enter a new value for the width and height of the drawing space in
         the window next to them: 7.5 inches each.

Note: When you change the width, the height will automatically change to
maintain the same aspect ratio. Notice also that the number of pixels per inch
will decrease unless you remove the check from the **Constrain File Size** box.
If you do not allow Painter to create a larger file size by removing the check
from the Constrain File Size box, your resolution will rapidly decrease as you
increase the image size.

    4. Click on **OK**. The drawing space will be resized to the dimensions you chose.

    5. Resize the drawing space back to 7 inches × 7 inches. Make a note of the resolution.

  B. Click on **Canvas/Canvas Size**. The Canvas Size box opens. This box allows you to add size to a specific side of the drawing space. You can add additional drawing room on the top, the left, the bottom, or the right.

    1. The additional size must be added in pixels. Remember that the resolution you were working with was N *pixels/inch*. This means that for each additional inch that you want to add to a side, you must add N *pixels*.

    2. Add .5 inches to the right side of the drawing space by typing in the appropriate number of pixels in the **Add pixels to right** window.

    3. Click on **OK**.

    4. Click on **Window/Zoom to Fit** to see the additional space.

    5. Click on **Canvas/Canvas Size** to reopen the Canvas Size box.

    6. Subtract the same number of pixels from the right side of the drawing space by entering the same number that you used above in the window preceded by a minus sign.

    7. Click on **OK**. The number of pixels that you specified will be removed from the right side of the drawing.

Making Selections and Masks in the Drawing Space

The **Lasso** tool, the **Magic Wand** tool, and the **Rectangular and Oval Selection** tools can be used to create a selection or a mask in Painter. When any of these tools are activated, you will notice two boxes in the **Destination** area of the **Controls** palette labeled **Selection** and **User Mask**. If you check the appropriate box before making your selection, you will be creating either a selection or a mask. Selections can be turned into masks later, but the process is speeded up if you make the choice first.

1. Start a new drawing approximately 7 inches × 7 inches.
2. In the **Art Materials** palette, select a paper texture of **Impulse** for the drawing space.
3. Click on **Brush** on the **Tools** palette. Select the **500 lb. Pencil** and select a color using the **Color** palette in the Art Materials palette. Draw an **X** in the drawing space.
4. Use the **Magic Wand** tool:

  A. Click on the **Magic Wand** tool on the Tools palette.

  B. In the **Controls** palette, place a check in the **Selection** circle.

C. Click on the X using the Magic Wand tool.

Several things might happen depending upon the color and paper you chose. Most likely, the entire X will not be selected. This is because the brush and paper combine to create different "colors"—actually, saturation levels and values in this case. The Magic Wand tool selects a limited range of continuous colors based on the color of the pixel located where you clicked in the drawing. You can change the range that the magic wand selects, though, to select exactly what you would like out of the drawing.

1. In the Controls palette, click on the arrow on the right side of the **Tolerance** slider. This increases the color range that the Magic Wand tool will select.

2. Keep clicking on the arrow and watch the dotted outline of the selection. As the tolerance increases, more and more of the X will be selected.

3. You can also feather the edge of the selection by increasing the value of the **Feather** slider.

4. If **Anti-alias** is checked, you will get a soft edge on the selection.

5. Increase the value of the Tolerance slider, and use the Feather and Anti-alias sliders if necessary, to select the entire X.

6. You can also use the Magic Wand tool to invert the selection you made. This method sometimes makes it easier to select exactly the part of the drawing that you want.

7. Return the Tolerance and Feather sliders to 0.

8. Deselect the X by clicking on **Select/None** in the main pull down menu.

9. Click outside of the X with the Magic Wand tool. You have now selected the white area that surrounds the X. Click and drag on the detent at the lower right corner of the border around the drawing space. If you make the box just a little larger than the drawing space itself, you will see that the dotted lines indicating the selection run all the way around the edge of the drawing space.

10. Click on **Select/Invert** on the main pull down menu. The area that was not selected—the X—now becomes the selection. The area selected could now be filled with a new color, grad, pattern, or weave. It can also be used to block off that part of the drawing from the rest of the drawing.

5. Using the **Masking** buttons: Don't confuse the **Masking** buttons in the lower left-hand corner of the drawing space border with creating a mask in Painter. These buttons can be used with both selections and masks to block off part of the drawing space so that you cannot draw in it.

A. Click on the Masking button on the lower left-hand corner of the drawing space border—it is to the left of the I button and looks like a brown splotch. The three options appear. With the large brown splotch chosen, you can draw anywhere in the drawing space. With the splotch with the hole in it chosen, you can only draw outside the selection. With the small splotch chosen, you can only draw inside the selection.

B. Click on the Draw Outside button—the splotch with a hole in it.

C. Click on the Brush button on the Tools palette and select the 500 lb. Pencil again.

D. Choose a different color.

E. Draw a line across the X. Notice that the new color will not appear in the selected area, only outside of it.

F. Click on Edit/Undo Brush Stroke.

G. Click on the Draw Inside button—the small brown splotch.

H. Draw a line across the X. Notice that the new color only appears inside the selected area.

I. Click on Edit/Undo Brush Stroke.

J. Click on the Draw Anywhere button—the large brown splotch.

K. Draw a line across the X. Notice that the new color appears both inside and outside of the selected area.

L. Click on Edit/Undo Brush Stroke.

M. The Masking button can also be used to block off a selected area in order to apply effects to it.

N. Click on the Draw Inside button.

O. Click on Effects/Tonal Control/Posterize on the main pull down menu.
   1. The Posterize box opens.
   2. Set Levels at 8.
   3. Click on OK.
   4. The color range in the X has been limited to eight colors. Notice how the different color areas have been more precisely defined.
   5. Any of the effects available could be used in this way and applied just inside the selected area. If you had chosen the Draw Outside button, the effect would have been applied only outside of the X.

P. Click on the Draw Outside button.
   1. In the Patterns palette, choose the Vines pattern.
   2. Click on the Fill tool in the Tools palette.
   3. Click with the Fill tool on the area outside of the X.
   4. The Vines pattern fills the rest of the drawing space, but not the X.

  Q. Click on Edit/Undo Paint Bucket Fill.

  R. Click on the Draw Anywhere button.

6. Turning the selection into a mask: Remember that only one selection can be active at a time. If you have made a selection that you would like to use again later you can turn it into a mask, give it a name, and recall it when you need it.

  A. If the Objects palette is not visible, turn it on by clicking on Window/ Show Objects.

  B. Click on the Mask icon underneath the word Mask on the Objects palette. It will outline in red and the name bar on the Objects palette will read Objects: Mask List.

  C. Click on the Save Selection button on the Mask List palette.

  D. The Save Selection dialogue box appears.

    1. There is a pop-up button next to the words Save To:. Right now it says New. If you had already created another mask, you could click here to select an already named mask and save this selection to that name, replacing the mask that you had given that name earlier. If you had already created a mask you would also be able to choose one of the options available under the Operation area. For now, though, New is your only choice.

    2. Click on OK.

  E. In the Mask List palette, the line New Mask 1 appears.

  F. Double click on the line New Mask 1 in the Mask List palette. The Mask Attributes box appears. You could also open the Mask Attributes box for New Mask 1 by single clicking on the line New Mask 1 and then clicking on Mask/Mask Attributes in the pull down menu bar on the Objects palette.

    1. Type in a descriptive new name for the mask in the Name: area— call it X.

    2. Click on OK.

    3. Only the mask is now visible in the drawing space. You'll notice that it shows up as a black space in the shape of the X you drew.

    4. To make the whole drawing visible again, click on the RGB - Canvas line in the Mask List palette. Notice that the "eye" next to the line opens when you do this. The "eye" indicates what masks are visible in the drawing.

    5. The selection dotted lines should have disappeared when you turned the selection into a mask. If they haven't, click on Select/ None in the main pull down menu.

7. Using the Lasso Selection tool: The Lasso Selection tool lets you select a freehand area in the drawing.

   A. Click on the Lasso Selection tool on the Tools palette.

   B. Move the cursor over the drawing space. Notice that the cursor has turned into a circle with a dot in the middle.

   C. Click and drag with the cursor around the outside of the X in the drawing space. Do not try to follow the outline of the X exactly. Just outline a space around the X. When you release the mouse button, the selection space will form, outlined in a flashing dotted line. If you stopped where you started, this would enclose the entire space that you outlined. If you stopped somewhere other than where you started, the start and stop points would be connected by a straight line.

   D. Save this selection as a mask with the name of Outline.

   E. Make the whole drawing visible again by clicking on the RGB - Canvas line in the Mask List palette.

8. Using the Rectangular/Oval Selection tools: The Rectangular and Oval Selection tools are located on top of one another on the Tools palette. Click and hold on the button to make the other button appear. Then click on the button you want to select.

   A. Click on the Rectangular Selection tool on the Tools palette.

   B. Move the cursor over the drawing space. The cursor turns into a +.

   C. Click and drag with the cursor to define a rectangle that crosses the top half of the X. Do not cover the whole X with the rectangle.

   D. Note that if you hold down the Shift key while clicking and dragging, the tool will select a square space.

   E. Save the selection as a mask with the name of Rectangle.

   F. Make the whole drawing visible again by clicking on the RGB - Canvas line in the Mask List palette.

   G. Click on the Oval Selection tool on the Tools palette.

   H. Click and drag with the cursor to define an oval that crosses the bottom half of the X.

   I. Note that if you hold down the Shift key while clicking and dragging, the tool will select a circular space.

   J. Save the selection as a mask with the name of Oval.

   K. Make the whole drawing visible again by clicking on the RGB - Canvas line in the Mask List palette.

9. Using a mask: Once masks have been saved and named they must be loaded before they can be used.

   A. In the Mask List palette, click on the Load Selection button. The Load Selection box appears.

   B. Click on the pop-up button next to Load From:. Click on X to select the X mask.

   C. Under Operation, place a dot in the circle next to Replace Selection.

   D. Click on OK.

   E. The flashing outline around the X reappears. It is now the active selection.

   F. You could now fill it with something else by using the Fill tool or use the Masking button to draw inside or outside it, etc. It acts just like a selection.

   G. Click on Select/None on the main pull down menu to deselect the mask.

10. Combining, subtracting, and intersecting masks: Masks can also be combined, subtracted, and intersected to create new selections. Remember that the Outline mask that you created included both the X and area around the outside of it. Let's say that you wanted to change it so that it was just the area around the X, but not the X itself. Then you could use it as a selection with the Masking button to draw in just that area. This would be possible by subtracting one mask from the other.

    A. Subtracting masks:

       1. Load the mask from which you are going to be making a subtraction—in this case, the Outline mask:
          a. Click on the Load Selection button in the Mask List palette.
          b. On the Load From: pop-up, choose Outline.
          c. Choose Replace Selection.
          d. Click on OK.

       2. Choose the mask that is going to be subtracted from the Outline mask:
          a. Click on the Load Selection button in the Mask List palette.
          b. On the Load From: pop-up, choose X.
          c. Place a dot in the circle next to Subtract From Selection.
          d. Click on OK.
          e. You now have a new selection that is the outline without the X. You could fill this area, use the Masking button to draw inside or outside of it, etc.

3. If you want to save this selection as a new mask you can also do that.
   a. Save the selection as a new mask named Outlinew/oX.
   b. Make the whole drawing visible again by clicking on the RGB - Canvas line in the Mask List palette.

B. Combining masks:
   1. Load one of the two masks that you want to combine—in this case, the Rectangle mask:
   2. Click on Load Selection again.
      a. Select Oval from the Load From: pop-up.
      b. Place a dot in the circle next to Add To Selection.
      c. Click on OK.
      d. You now have a new selection that combines both the rectangle and the oval. You could fill this area, use the Masking button to draw inside or outside of it, etc.
   3. Save this selection as a new mask:
      a. Save the selection as a new mask named Rec/Oval.
      b. Make the whole drawing visible again by clicking on the RGB - Canvas line in the Mask List palette.

C. Intersecting masks: When you use the Intersect With Selection option, you are creating a new selection from a space that is common to two masks. The parts of the masks that do not overlap will not be in the new selection. Remember that I had you draw the rectangle so that it only covered the top half of the X. You will now use the Intersect With Selection option to create a new selection that will be only the part of the X that is inside the rectangle.
   1. Load the Rectangle mask.
   2. Click again on the Load Selection button.
      a. Choose X in the pop-up next to Load From:.
      b. Place a dot in the circle next to Intersect With Selection.
      c. Click on OK.
      d. You now have a new mask that is just the part of the X that is inside the rectangle. You could fill this area, use the Masking button to draw inside or outside of it, etc.
      e. Save this as a mask named Rec/NoX.
      f. Make the whole drawing visible again by clicking on the RGB - Canvas line in the Mask List palette.

11. Save the changes you have made to a file on your floppy or hard drive as proj3.rif. Compare it to the file exer3.rif in the Painter folder on the CD-ROM.

12. Use the masks that you have created in a variety of ways in the drawing. Fill inside or outside some of them with colors, patterns, grads, etc. Use the Masking button to draw and/or fill around them, inside them, etc. Play around until you have a good feeling for loading and deselecting masks and using them in various combinations. Subtract, intersect, and combine different combinations to create new masks and selections.

DRAWING WITH SHAPES

Shapes are objects in Painter that are drawn and edited with special tools. They can be filled like brush strokes, but they can also be edited like entities in AutoCAD or splines in 3D Studio MAX. Like the splines in 3D Studio MAX, they are vector-based. If you need precision in some of the objects in your drawing, shapes will give you that geometric exactness. Text is also a shape in Painter. The following are the tools in the Tools palette that let you draw, define, and edit shapes.

The Shape Design Tools

 The Pen Tool: This is located on the same button with the Quick Curve tool. It is used to draw shapes. It can draw either straight lines or bezier curves.

 The Quick Curve Tool: This is located on the same button with the Pen tool. It is used to draw freehand shapes.

 The Text Tool: This is used to add text to your drawing.

The Shape Object Tools

 The Rectangular Shape Tool: This is located on the same button with the Oval Shape tool. It is used to create rectangular or square shapes.

 The Oval Shape Tool: This is located on the same button with the Rectangular Shape tool. It is used to create oval or circular shapes.

The Shape Edit Tools

 The Scissors Tool: This is located on the same button with the Add, Delete, and Convert Point tools. It is used to cut path segments.

 The Add Point Tool: This is located on the same button with the Scissors, Delete, and Convert Point tools. It is used to add a control point to a shape.

The Delete Point Tool: This is located on the same button with the Scissors, Add, and Convert Point tools. It is used to subtract a control point from a shape.

 The Convert Point Tool: This is located on the same button with the Scissors, Add, and Delete Point tools. It is used to change a control point from a smooth to a corner point.

Image Window Controls That Are Useful with Shapes

When creating shapes, there are several aspects of the drawing space of Painter that can be extremely helpful. The grid, guide, and ruler options, for example, can help you get a better idea of the size of the lines that you are drawing. The ability to snap to the grid, guides, or ruler points can help you be more exact in your drawing. These commands are all located under the Canvas pull down menu. The grid can also be turned on and off by clicking on the Grid button in the upper right area of the border surrounding the drawing space.

The Grid: In the upper right part of the border surrounding the drawing space, you will see a button that is white with several blue lines on it. When you click on this button, the grid will appear in the drawing space. This grid will not be in any print that you do from the drawing nor will it appear when the drawing is saved as a file in any format other than .rif. The grid can also be turned on and off by clicking on Canvas/Show Grid or Canvas/Hide Grid. By clicking on Canvas/Grid Options, you will open the Grid Options box, where you can change the spacing of the grid, the type of the grid, and the color of the grid and the background. If you click on Canvas/Snap to Grid, you can also toggle on and off the Snap to Grid function. With Snap to Grid toggled on, points in drawing shapes will snap to the nearest grid intersection.

The Rulers: You can turn on the rulers by clicking on Canvas/Rulers/Show Rulers. You can set the ruler units by clicking on Canvas/Rulers/Ruler Options. This opens the Ruler Options box, where by clicking on the pop-up button next to Ruler Units:, you can select Inches, Pixels, CM, Points, or Picas. You can also snap to the ticks on the rulers by toggling Canvas/Rulers/Snap to Ruler Ticks on and off.

The Guides: Guides are lines that go all the way across the drawing space from a ruler. They are turned on by clicking on Canvas/Guides/Show Guides and off by clicking on Hide Guides. To create a guide, click at a point on a ruler. The guide line will appear if the guides are turned on. You can also move a guide by clicking and dragging on the black arrowhead that is at the end of the guide on the ruler. Guides can be snapped to by toggling Canvas/Guides/Snap to Guides on. Double click on the black arrowhead at the end of a guide and you will open the Guide Options box. In the window next to x=, you can reposition the guide by typing in a number. X in this case equals the distance from the 0 point on that ruler. This option allows you to position a guide more precisely than you can by just clicking on the ruler. In the Guide Options box, you can also change the color of that guide, specify the same color for all guides, lock that guide so that it cannot be moved, and delete all of the guides.

The Set Default Shape Attributes Box

The Set Default Shape Attributes box is where you set general parameters for the shapes that you are going to draw. It is opened by clicking on Shapes/Set Shape Attributes. There are three parts to the Shape Attributes box: the Strokes section, the Fill section, and the General section.

A stroke is a border around the edge of the shape. Click in the window next to the word Stroke if you want to have a border; leave it blank if you do not. The larger box to the right of Stroke is the color box. Double click here to select a color for the stroke. Below that are the Opacity and Width sliders. Here you can change the percent of the opacity and width for the stroke in pixels. You also use stroke to define the width of a shape that is a line. Below the Opacity and Width sliders are the End point and Corner selectors. Click here on the option that you would like for the end point of a line and the type of corner. Below those boxes is the Miterlimit slider. This slider lets you define how sharp the corner type you selected will be. The smaller the miterlimit, the sharper the corner.

In the Fill section you can determine what the inside of the shape is going to look like. Check the box next to the word Fill if you want the shape to be filled. Leave it unchecked if you do not. To the right of the word Fill is the Fill color selector. Double click here to change the color of the fill. You can still fill a shape with a color from the Color palette, a pattern, grad, etc. by using the Fill tool. To the right of the color selector are two stars. Select the solid star if

THE SET
DEFAULT SHAPE
ATTRIBUTES BOX

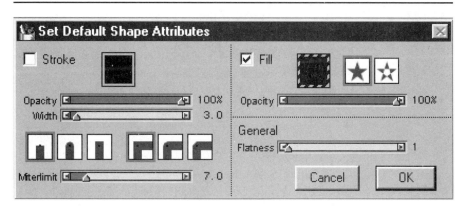

you want overlapping areas within the shape to be filled. Select the hollow star if you do not want overlapping areas within the shape to be filled. The Opacity slider determines the opacity of the fill.

The General section contains the Flatness slider. This determines how the curves on the shape will be represented when printing. Curves are actually drawn when printing by using a series of straight lines. The more straight lines used, the smoother the curve. The higher the setting on the Flatness slider, the more straight lines will be used to draw the curve and the smoother the curve.

Exercise No. 4: Drawing with Shapes

This exercise is designed to familiarize you with the commands and techniques used in drawing with shapes. Note that while it is possible to draw shapes using a stylus or drawing pad, it is much easier to do so using a mouse.

Drawing Lines Using the Grid

1. Create a new drawing space that is 7 inches × 7 inches.
2. Show the grid.
3. Toggle Snap to Grid on by clicking on Canvas/Grid/Snap to Grid on the pull down menu.
4. Open the Grid Options box and set the following parameters:
   A. Grid Type = Rectangular
   B. Horizontal Spacing = .167 Inches
   C. Vertical Spacing = .167 Inches

Drawing with the Pen Tool

1. Click on the Pen tool in the Tools palette.
2. Draw a straight line using the Pen tool:
   A. Click at a point close to a grid intersection.
   B. Click at another point close to a grid intersection.
   C. Hold down the Ctrl/Command key and click away from the line in the drawing space to complete the line and deselect it.
3. Draw a series of straight lines using the Pen tool:
   A. Click at a point close to a grid intersection.
   B. Click at another point close to a grid intersection.
   C. Click at another point close to a grid intersection.
   D. Click at another point close to a grid intersection.
   E. Hold down the Ctrl/Command key and click away from the line in the drawing space to complete the line and deselect it.

4. Create a closed shape using straight lines:

   A. Click at a point close to a grid intersection.

   B. Click at another point close to a grid intersection.

   C. Click at another point close to a grid intersection.

   D. Click at another point close to a grid intersection.

   E. Either click at the first point again or click on **Close** in the **Controls** palette.

5. Open the **Set Default Shape Attribute** box by clicking on **Shapes/Set Shapes Attributes** on the pull down menu.

   A. The last shape that you drew is still selected. The changes that you make in the Shape Attributes box will only affect that shape.

   B. Click in the **Fill** box to turn fill on and off. Leave it off.

   C. Click in the **Stroke** box to turn stroke on and off. Leave it on.

   D. Change the width of the stroke.

   E. Select a square end point and a square corner.

   F. Change the width of the stroke to 2 pixels.

   G. Click on the **Set New Shape Attributes** button. This sets these parameters for the next time that you draw a shape.

   H. Click on **OK**.

   I. Hold down the **Ctrl/Command** key and click away from the shape in the drawing space to complete the line and deselect it.

6. Draw a series of lines using a combination of straight lines and curves: As you have seen above, when you click at points, you draw straight lines using the **Pen** tool. If you click and drag at a point, you will instead create a curve.

   A. Click at a point close to a grid intersection.

   B. Click and drag at a point close to a grid intersection.

      Hold down the mouse button as you drag the cursor, and a curve will begin to form between the last two points. The direction and distance that you drag will determine the shape of the curve. Keep holding the mouse button down and drag in different directions and different distances to see the possibilities available. Release the mouse button when you have the curve that you want. Even if this is not the exact curve that you want, don't worry. Get as close as you can. Later you will learn how to edit this curve.

   C. Move the cursor to another grid intersection. Click and drag at that point to form another curve.

   D. Move the cursor to another grid intersection. Click and drag at that point to form another curve.

E. If you make a mistake and want to erase the last line segment that you drew, hit the **Backspace/Delete** key on the keyboard. Note that you can also erase up to the last five line segments that you drew by using the **Edit/Undo Pen Digitizing** command.

F. Move the cursor to another grid intersection. Click and drag at that point to form another curve.

G. Next, let's follow the curve with a straight line. This requires a little different technique. Move the cursor so that it is over the last end point; this end point is red on the screen. You'll notice that a small arrowhead forms. Click on the last end point. The blue bezier line will disappear. Move the cursor to the end point of the straight line that you would like to draw. Click on that point and a straight line will form between that point and the last end point.

H. Hold down the **Ctrl/Command** key and click away from the shape in the drawing space to complete the line and deselect it.

7. Start a line with a curved line: Making the first line that you draw a curved rather than a straight line requires a slightly different approach.

A. Click and drag from a point to form the blue bezier line. This line should be in the general direction that you will want the curve to be created.

B. Click and drag at a second point to form the curve.

C. Hold down the **Ctrl/Command** key and click away from the shape in the drawing space to complete the line and deselect it.

8. Add lines to any of the lines that you have already drawn.

A. Click on one of the points that you used to draw a line—an anchor point. You can select either end or any of the intermediate anchor points.

B. Click at a point to draw a line from the anchor point selected to that point. Click and drag at a point to form a curve from the anchor point selected to that point.

C. Hold down the **Ctrl/Command** key and click away from the shape in the drawing space to complete the line and deselect it.

9. Erase some of the lines that you have drawn.

A. Activate the **Shape Selection** tool: Click and hold on the button to the left of the Text button on the Tools palette. Three buttons will appear. Click on the button with the arrowhead. This is the Shape Selection tool.

B. Click on one of the points that you used to draw a line—an anchor point. That anchor point will turn red and the bezier lines will appear.

C. On the main pull down menu, click on Edit/Cut.

D. Use the Shape Selection tool and the Edit/Cut command to erase some of the lines that you have drawn.

Using the Quick Curve Tool to Draw a Freehand Shape

1. Turn off the grid and the Snap to Grid command.

2. Click and hold on the Pen tool on the Tools palette. The Quick Curve Tool button will appear. Click on the Quick Curve Tool button.

3. Click and drag to form a freehand shape in the drawing space. When you release the mouse button, the curve will appear.

4. Notice that the end points appear in red and the other anchor points for the curve that you drew also appear.

5. You can select either end point by holding down the Ctrl/Command key and clicking on the end point that you would like.

6. Add to the selected end point by clicking on it and dragging to form a curve that extends from that end point.

7. Complete and deselect the curve that you drew by clicking anywhere else in the drawing space.

8. Draw another curve using the Quick Curve tool. This time, though, create a solid shape by returning the cursor to the point where the curve began before releasing the mouse button.

9. Use the Shape Selection tool and the Edit/Cut command to erase one of the curves that you drew.

Drawing with the Rulers and Guides

1. Click on Canvas/Rulers/Show Rulers to activate the rulers.

2. Click on Canvas/Rulers/Ruler Options to open the Ruler Options box.

   A. Click on the pop-up next to Units: to select Inches.

   B. Click on OK.

3. Click on Canvas/Rulers/Snap to Ruler Ticks to toggle the Snap to Ruler Ticks mode on.

4. Use the Pen tool to draw a couple of lines.

5. Click on Canvas/Rulers/Snap to Ruler Ticks to toggle the Snap to Ruler Ticks mode off.

6. Use the Pen tool to draw a couple of lines.

7. Create some guides:

   A. Click on one of the rulers to create a guide. The guide will form at the point where you click on the ruler.

B. Create several more guides on both the horizontal and vertical rulers.

C. Double click on the black arrowhead at the base of one of the guides.
1. The Guide Options box opens.
2. Type in a new value in the x= box for the location of the guide. This lets you position the location of the guide more precisely than just clicking on the ruler.
3. You can lock this guide into position by checking the box next to Locked Guide.
4. You can also delete the guides by clicking on the Delete All Guides button, but do not delete the guides at this time.
5. Click on OK to exit the Guide Options box.

D. Click and drag on one of the guides to move its location. Note that you will only be able to do this with unlocked guides.

8. Click on Canvas/Guides/Snap to Guides to toggle the Snap to Guides mode on.

9. Use the Pen tool to draw several lines. Note that you have to be very close to the guides for the Snap to command to work.

10. Hide and show the guides by using the Canvas/Guides/Hide Guides and Show Guides commands.

11. Delete all the guides using the Guide Options box.

12. Use the Shape Selection tool and the Edit/Cut command to erase one of the shapes that you drew.

Using the Rectangle and Oval Shape Tools

Rectangular, square, oval, and circular shapes are most easily created by using the Rectangle and Oval Shape tools.

1. Click on the Rectangle Shape tool on the Tools palette.

2. Click and drag in the drawing space to form a rectangle.

3. Click anywhere outside of the rectangle to deselect the rectangle.

4. Hold down the Shift key and click and drag to form a square.

5. Click on the Oval Shape tool on the Tools palette. It is located underneath the Rectangle Shape tool. Click and hold on the Rectangle Shape tool to reveal the Oval Shape tool.

6. Click and drag in the drawing space to form an oval.

7. Click anywhere outside of the oval to deselect the oval.

8. Hold down the Shift key and click and drag to form a circle.

9. Click on Shapes/Set Shape Attributes to open the Set Default Shape Attributes box.

    A. You can change the width of the stroke, or border, by using the **Width** slider in the **Stroke** section. Do not change the width of the stroke at this time as you have already drawn a shape. You will change the width prior to drawing a shape in step 12 below.

    B. You can fill the shape by checking the **Fill** box. Check the **Fill** box.

    C. Click on **OK**.

10. Click anywhere outside the circle to deselect the circle.

11. Use the **Shape Selection** tool to select another shape.

12. Click on **Shapes/Set Shape Attributes** to open the **Set Default Shape Attributes** box.

    A. Change the width of the stroke.

    B. Fill the shape.

    C. Click on **OK**.

13. Use the **Shape Selection** tool and the **Edit/Cut** command to erase one of the shapes that you drew.

Using the Text Tool

The **Text** tool in Painter lets you add text to your drawing. Text is a shape just like the lines, curves, rectangles, etc. that you have been drawing so far in this exercise.

1. Click on the **Text** tool on the **Tools** palette.

2. In the **Controls** palette, use the **Point Size** slider to choose the size of the text.

3. Click in the window next to **Font** to select the font for the text. If you don't want one of the fonts that appears there, click on **Other Font** to open the **Choose Font** box, where you can select any font with an asterisk next to its name. Click on the font that you would like and then click on **OK**.

4. Click on the upper of the two superimposed boxes in the Controls palette and then go to the **Art Materials/Color** palette to select a color for your text.

    Note: You could have also used this box to select a color for any of the shapes that you drew earlier.

5. Click with the cursor in the drawing space where you would like the line of text to begin.

6. Type in the text, and it will appear. You can also use the **Backspace, Shift,** and **Enter** keys just like you would if you were working in a word processor, with the exception that once you start a new line by hitting the **Enter** key, you cannot get back to the line above it again. There is a method for editing text using the objects palette that you will learn about in the next section based on the fact that each letter of text is actually a separate object in Painter, but it is much easier to carefully check each line before hitting the enter key.

7. Click on the Shape Selection tool on the Tools palette to deselect the text that you have drawn.

Creating a Dropped Shadow on the Text

After you have drawn your text, you can also add a dropped shadow to it. Each letter of text is a separate shape, however, and the shadow must be added one letter at a time.

1. Click on the Shape Selection tool on the Tools palette.
2. Click on the letter of the text to which you would like to add a dropped shadow.
3. Click on Effects/Objects/Create Dropped Shadow on the main pull down menu.
4. The Drop Shadow box opens. Here you can set the X and Y offsets, opacity, radius, angle, and thinness of the dropped shadow. When you have these set the way that you would like, click on OK.
5. The Commit box will open, asking you if you want to commit this shape to an image floater. Click on Commit. The dropped shadow can only be added to a floater.
6. The dropped shadow for the letter you chose appears.
7. That letter is no longer a shape. It is now a floater. You will no longer be able to use the Shape Selection tool to select it.
8. Go ahead and add a dropped shadow to other letters in your text. Experiment with the different parameters in the Drop Shadow box. Leave a couple of letters without a dropped shadow.

Moving Text

After you have created text, it can be moved around the drawing space. The method for moving it depends upon whether it is still a shape or it has had a dropped shadow added to it, meaning it has been converted to a floater. To move text, following the instructions below.

1. Click on the Shape Selection tool in the Tools palette. You can use this tool to move text without dropped shadows.
2. Click and drag to form a rectangle around the text that you would like to move.
3. Click on the text and drag it to a new position.
4. Click anywhere else in the drawing space to deselect the text.
5. Click on the Floater Adjuster tool in the Tools palette. This is located under the Shape Selection tool and looks like a pointing finger without a dotted rectangle. You can use this tool to move text with dropped shadows.

6. Click on a single letter to select it or click and drag to form a rectangle around a group of letters to select them.

7. Click on the text and drag it to a new position.

8. Click anywhere else in the drawing space to deselect the text.

Cutting Text

Text can also be erased or cut after it has been created. Once again the method for doing this depends upon whether it is still a shape or it has been converted to a floater by having a dropped shadow added to it.

Cutting Text Without a Dropped Shadow

1. Click on the **Shape Selection** tool in the **Tools** palette. You can use this tool to select text without dropped shadows for cutting.

2. Text must be cut one letter at a time. You cannot use the rectangle selection method as you did for moving the text. Click on a letter of text without a dropped shadow to select it. Click on **Edit/Cut**.

Cutting Text with a Dropped Shadow

1. Click on the **Floater Adjuster** tool in the **Tools** palette. You can use this tool to select text with dropped shadows for cutting.

2. Click on a letter of text with a dropped shadow to select it. Click on **Edit/Cut**.

3. Cut—one letter at a time—some of the text from the drawing space.

Editing Shapes

Once shapes have been created, you can use a variety of tools to edit them and change the way that they look.

1. Use the **Pen** tool to draw a connected series of line segments. This time before you draw, use the top box of the two superimposed boxes in the **Controls** palette along with the **Color** palette to choose a color for the shape.

2. Use the **Quick Curve** tool to draw a freehand line.

3. Use the **Rectangle Shape** tool to draw a rectangle.

4. Use the **Oval Shape** tool to draw an oval.

5. Use the **Text** tool to add text to the drawing.

Using the Shape Selection Tool to Edit

1. Click on the **Shape Selection** tool.

2. Click in the middle of the oval shape. The anchor points will appear as red squares. **Note:** This will only work if the shape is filled. If it isn't filled, click and drag to form a rectangle that completely encloses the shape.

3. Click and drag on the middle of the oval shape to move it to a new location if it is a filled shape. If it is an unfilled shape, you must click and drag on one of the red anchor points to move it. **Note:** This will only work if *all* of the anchor points appear. Be sure that the window you use to select the shape completely encloses it.

4. Click outside the oval shape to deselect it.

5. Click on the stroke, or outline, of the oval shape near one of the anchor points.

6. That anchor point will reappear, but with blue control lines emanating from it.

   A. Click and drag on the anchor point to move it and change the shape of the oval shape.

   B. Click and drag on one of the blue dots at the end of the control line coming from the anchor point to change the shape of the curve.

7. Click and drag to form a rectangle that completely encloses the oval shape. All of the anchor points appear with their blue control lines.

   A. Click and drag in the middle of the oval shape to move it to a new location.

   B. Click and drag on an anchor point to move it.

   C. Click and drag on the end of a control line to change the shape of the curve.

8. Click outside of the oval shape to deselect it.

Using the Floater Adjuster Tool to Edit

The **Floater Adjuster** tool can be used on shapes even though they are not floaters. When you use the Floater Adjuster tool, there are different options available to you with the shape.

1. Click on the **Floater Adjuster** tool on the **Tools** palette.

2. Click on the rectangle shape that you drew earlier if it is filled. It will outline in black and yellow lines with black and yellow boxes at the corners and the middle of each side. If it isn't filled, click and drag to form a rectangle that completely encloses the shape.

   A. Click and drag in the middle of the rectangle shape if it is filled to move it to a new location.

   B. Click and drag on one of the corner boxes to scale the size of the shape up and down.

   C. Click and drag on one of the boxes on the middle of a side to move that side.

3. Click on Effects/Orientation/Rotate on the main pull down menu. The Rotate Selection box appears.

   A. Enter the number of degrees counterclockwise that you would like to rotate the rectangle shape.

   B. Click on OK.

4. Hold down the Ctrl/Command key and click and drag on a box at the corner of the shape. This lets you rotate the shape.

5. Hold down the Ctrl/Command key and click and drag on a box in the middle of a side. This lets you slant that side of the shape.

6. Click on Effects/Orientation/Distort on the main pull down menu. The Distort Selection box appears.

   A. Click and drag on any of the boxes on the black and yellow border surrounding the shape.

   B. You can move any of these boxes independently to distort the shape.

   C. As you move one or more of these boxes, smaller black boxes will appear on a light black outline around the shape. Once the smaller black boxes are away from the black and yellow outline, you will need to click and drag on the smaller boxes to continue distorting the shape.

   D. When you have finished distorting the shape, click on OK.

   E. Click anywhere outside of the shape to deselect it.

7. Click and drag to form a rectangle that completely encloses the text that you drew earlier. Each letter of the text is surrounded by a black and yellow outline with black and yellow boxes at the corners and sides. These boxes, however, are linked and can be used to move, scale, stretch, rotate, slant, or distort all of the letters of the text at one time.

   A. Experiment with the above commands on the text.

   B. Click outside of the text to deselect it.

Using the Shape Edit Tools

The Shape Edit tools on the Tools palette—Scissors, Add Point, Delete Point, Convert Point—can also be used to change shapes.

1. Click on the Shape Selection tool on the Tools palette.

2. Select the quick curve shape (the freehand line) by clicking and dragging to form a rectangle that completely encloses the shape. This will show you all of the anchor points and their control lines. You can also select the shape by clicking on it, but this may only display the control lines for the anchor points near where you clicked.

3. If all of the anchor points are selected, they will all appear as red boxes and you can click and drag on any anchor point to move the entire shape.

4. Click outside of the shape to deselect it.

5. Click on one of the end points of the shape. That end point appears as a red box. Click and drag on the red box to move the end point.

6. You can also now see the other anchor points as white boxes. Click and drag on any anchor point to move it.

7. When you click on an anchor point it turns to a red box. The blue control lines for that anchor point also appear. Click and drag on the blue dots at the ends of the control lines to change the curve of the shape.

Note: Before using any of the following tools, you must have already selected the shape with the Shape Selection tool.

Adding Anchor Points

1. Click on the Add Point tool.

2. Click on the freehand shape at a point where you would like to add an anchor point.

3. Click on the Shape Selection tool.

4. Click and drag on the new anchor point to move it or click and drag on the blue control line ends to change the curve.

Deleting Anchor Points

1. Click on the Delete Point tool.

2. Click on an anchor point on the freehand shape to delete that anchor point.

Cutting a Shape

The Scissors tool lets you cut a shape so that you can divide it into two parts, add a new shape between two existing points, or add another open shape between those two points.

1. Click on the Scissors tool.

2. Pick a point that is between two anchor points.

3. Place the cursor over that point so that the cross point of the scissors is located where you want to make the cut. Click the mouse button.

4. What looks like a new anchor point appears. This is actually two anchor points, one on top of another.

5. Click on the Shape Selection tool on the Tools palette.

6. Click on the "new" anchor point. This will select the top of the two anchor points. Use the Shape Selection tool to move that anchor point away from the one underneath.

7. You can now work with the two shapes separately, add another shape in between to reconnect them, etc.

8. Click outside of the two shapes to deselect them.

Converting a Corner Point to a Smooth Point or Vice Versa

1. Click on the Shape Selection tool.
2. Click on the shape that you drew using the Pen tool earlier. The anchor points should appear.
3. Click on the Convert Point tool.
4. Click on a corner anchor point that you would like to convert.
5. If you do not see any blue control lines emanating from that anchor point, click on the anchor point and drag outward to make them appear.
6. Click and drag on the ends of the blue control lines to change the angle.
7. You can also click on a smooth anchor point to convert it to a corner point or click on a start anchor point to change the line coming out of it from a straight line to a curve or vice versa.

Save the work that you have done as Proj4.rif on a 3.5-inch disk or to your hard drive. You can compare Exer4.rif in the Painter folder on the CD-ROM to the work that you have done in Exercise No. 4.

USING FLOATERS AND PLUG-IN FLOATERS

The Objects palette is where you deal with floaters in Painter. If you click on the Floater icon on the Objects palette, the Floater List palette will appear. As the name implies, floaters are images that "float" above the canvas in Painter. Floaters serve a number of different purposes. Selections, for example, cannot be "moved" around the canvas in the sense that we think of moving objects in AutoCAD or 3D Studio MAX. Floaters, however, can. Selections can be converted into floaters and then can be moved in the traditional sense. Because floaters are on a layer above the canvas, you can continue to draw on the canvas without affecting the floater. You can also draw in the floater. Floaters can be cut or copied from other drawings and then pasted into the current drawing. A number of special effects can also be applied to floaters by using the composite method in the Controls palette.

Floaters will only be saved as floaters if you save your file in the Painter .rif format. If you save the file in any other format, they will automatically be "dropped" onto the canvas and will no longer be floaters. While you are working with floaters in Painter, you can also choose to drop them onto the canvas by using the Drop button on the Floater List palette. After a floater has been

dropped onto the canvas, if you want to deal with it as a floater again, you will have to select it and then convert it into a floater.

Floater Types

Shapes: Shapes are automatically created as floaters so that they can be moved about the canvas and manipulated as you have seen in the section of this book on shapes.

Image Floaters: Image floaters are the type that you will deal with the most often. These are images or parts of images that are on a layer above the canvas. You can move them around, paint in them, and apply effects to them.

Reference Floaters: A reference floater is a temporary state that can be created for an image floater. When an image floater is changed into a reference floater, a number of different transformations can be performed on the floater. The resolution of the image will be temporarily lost when you do this. Reference floaters can be resized, rotated, or slanted. When you have finished the transformation, you can then convert the object back to an image floater to restore the resolution of the image.

Plug-In Floaters: Plug-In floaters are special floaters available in Painter that create effects over already existing images. Some of these work with image floaters and others work with parts or all of images on the canvas underneath them.

The Floater List Palette

Working in the Floater List palette, you can layer floaters so that they will appear on top of one another in whatever order you desire. The Floater List palette also allows you to select, hide, lock, name, and group floaters.

Floater Special Effects

By using the Controls palette for the Adjuster tool, you can select composite methods for a floater. The composite method affects the way that the floater relates to the layer below it in the drawing by changing the relationship between the colors of the floater and the colors beneath it. Most of these special effects will only work if there is an image beneath the floater. They will usually not work on a plain black or white background.

Exercise No. 5: Working with Floaters

This exercise is designed to familiarize you with how floaters work in Painter. By using floaters you greatly increase the range of effects that you can use in your drawing and give yourself the ability to change the composition of the drawing by moving parts of it around and transforming those parts. The Floater List palette and the Controls palette are the two most important areas where you will work with floaters. This exercise will cover the use of both of those areas in detail.

Part 1: Preparing a Drawing Space

1. Open a new drawing space 5 inches × 5 inches in size.
2. Be sure that the Controls palette and the Objects palette are open.
3. Click on the Floater icon on the Controls palette to open the Floater List palette if it isn't already open.
4. Create a background color and texture so that you can see some of the floater effects better.
   A. Go to the Art Materials palette and click on the Paper icon.
      1. Select Handmade Paper.
      2. Expand the palette by clicking on the Min/Max button if necessary so that you can see the Scale slider and increase the scale to 400%.
   B. Go to the Color palette and select a light tan or cream color.

C. Click on Effects/Surface Control/Color Overlay. This will open the Color Overlay box so that you can lay in color and paper texture simultaneously over the entire drawing space. In the Color Overlay box:

1. In the pop-up next to Using:, select Paper.
2. Set the Opacity slider to 100%.
3. Place a dot in the circle next to Dye Concentration.
4. Click on OK.
5. The entire drawing space will be filled with the paper texture and color.

5. Save this drawing space as Floatest.rif in a location where you can find it later to delete it or reopen it. Leave it open after you have saved it.

Part 2: Creating a Floater from a Selection, a Shape,
and a File Using the Floater List

You are now going to create a floater in another drawing space and drag it over to the Floatest drawing. You could also create the floater in the current drawing space, but as you will see in the first part of the exercise below, this would include part of the background in the floater.

1. Create a floater from a selection in the current drawing space:

A. Select the Brush in the Tools palette.

B. In the Brushes palette, select the 500 lb. Pencil.

C. In the Color palette, select a saturated red color.

D. In the Controls palette, change the size to about 10 Pixels.

E. Draw a small X in the drawing space.

F. Select the Magic Wand tool in the Tools palette.

G. Click on the X with the Magic Wand tool.
   Change the Tolerance, Feather, and Anti-Alias values in the Controls palette until it looks like you have selected all of the X.

H. Click on Select/Float. This will convert the selection into a floater. It will be surrounded by a rectangle enclosed in a black and yellow line to indicate that it is a floater. Notice that in the Floater List, a line labeled Floater 1 appears. This is the control line for the floater that you just created. Later you will learn how to use this control line to work with the floater.

I. Click on the Floater Adjuster tool in the Tools palette.

J. Use the Floater Adjuster tool to drag the floater away from its present location in the drawing. Notice that there is a white space left where the floater used to be. This is because the Magic Wand tool selected both the red X and the background. They were both on the same layer, and it selected everything on that layer.

    K. Click on Edit/Undo Floater Move.

    L. Click on Edit/Undo Float.

    M. Click on Edit/Undo Magic Wand.

    N. Click on Edit/Undo Brush Stroke.

    O. Click on Edit/Undo Brush Stroke.

    P. This gets rid of the floater and the brush strokes. Remember that you can only back up five steps with Undo.

2. Now let's create a floater in a different drawing space and paste it into the current drawing space so that you can move it around on top of the background. Do not close the old drawing space labeled Floatest.

    A. Click on File/New and create a new drawing space 1 inch × 1 inch in size.

    B. Select the Brush in the Tools palette and select the 500 lb. Pencil in the Brushes palette.

    C. Change the size to about 10 Pixels in the Controls palette and choose a saturated red color in the Color palette.

    D. Draw an X in the new drawing space.

    E. You could select the X using the Magic Wand tool just as you did before and change it into a floater, but instead you are going to use a different method of selection that will help demonstrate some of the options available using the Composite Method process with a floater.

        1. Click on Select/All to select the entire new drawing space.

        2. Click on Edit/Copy to copy it to the clipboard.

        3. Click on the X button in the upper right-hand corner of the border around the new drawing space to close it. Do not save it when the prompt appears asking you if you want to save it.

        4. The title line at the top of the Floatest.rif drawing space should now be blue, indicating that it is active.

        5. Click on Edit/Paste/Normal.

        6. The entire drawing with the red X in it will appear in the drawing space as a floater. Notice that a line labeled Floater 2 appears in the Floater List. This is the control line for the new floater.

    F. Click on the Floater Adjuster tool in the Tools palette.

    G. Use the Floater Adjuster tool to move the floater around the drawing space.

    H. Go to the Controls palette.

        1. Click on the pop-up next to Composite Method.

        2. A long list of options will appear. Click on each of these options one at a time to see how each affects the relationship between the floater and its background. With some of them there will be no

noticeable difference. Different backgrounds will affect these options in different ways. You can also move the floater around to different parts of the background using the Floater Adjuster while you are trying out these options. Finally, choose either Gel or Darken to give you the red X over the already created background. You could have used the Composite Method options with a floater created by using the Magic Wand tool in the new drawing space, but the effect of the options would not have been as easy to see.

3. Using the Floater List: There are a number of things that you can do to the floater by using the control line in the Floater List.

   A. Double click on the name of the floater in the Floater List. This opens the Floater Attributes box.

      1. Change the name of the floater to X Floater. You can give a floater whatever name you would like to help you locate it later in the Floater List when you have a lot of them.

      2. Click on OK.

   B. Click on the small lock next to the name of the floater in the Floater List. This locks it in place so you cannot move it using the Floater Adjuster. Click on the small lock again to unlock it.

   C. Click on the open eye next to the lock. The floater disappears. It is not really gone, it just isn't visible anymore. Click on the closed eye and the floater will reappear.

   D. If there were another floater in the Floater List, you could click and drag on the star to change the position of this floater in the Floater List. The top position in the list corresponds to the top position in the drawing. Floaters will appear to be layered on top of one another depending upon their position in the list. After you create another floater, the options will be demonstrated to you visually in the drawing space.

   E. You will also notice that there are buttons at the bottom of the Floater List. These buttons let you perform other functions on a floater that has been selected. Do not click on any of them now. They perform the following functions.

      1. The Drop button would drop the floater onto the canvas. The object would no longer be a floater, but it would appear in the drawing as a red X.

      2. The Delete button would eliminate the floater from the drawing completely. The red X would completely disappear.

      3. The other buttons will be covered later in this exercise.

4. Next let's import as a floater a file that already exists. In the CD-ROM accompanying this book, you will find a file labeled Ofloater.tif under the Painter section. You are going to import it as a floater.

    A. Click on File/Open and then locate the file Ofloater.tif on the CD-ROM that accompanies this book.

    B. Click on Open. The file will appear as a new drawing window. It will be a green O with a white background.

    C. Follow the numbered steps outlined in section 2E above. The floater will be labeled Floater 3 on the Floater List.

    D. Rename it O Floater on the Floater List.

    E. Change the composite method for it to Darken.

    F. Use the Floater Adjuster tool to move it where you would like in the drawing.

5. Next let's create a shape. It will also appear on the Floater List after it has been created.

    A. Click on the Quick Curve button on the toolbar.

    B. Set your color to a saturated blue in the Color palette.

    C. Use the Quick Curve tool to draw an irregular, enclosed shape that will be filled with the color blue you selected.

        1. It will appear on the Floater List as Shape 1.

        2. It will have a red circle and yellow triangle to the left side of its line to indicate that it is a shape instead of an image floater. You will still be able to treat it like any other floater. You can use the Floater Adjuster tool to move it about the drawing space, for example. You can also rename it and change the position of its layer using the Floater List.

6. Adjusting position on the Floater List: The Floater List can also be thought of as indicating the height or level of the floaters above the background, with the first line being the highest floater and the bottom line being the lowest floater. You can adjust this position to place one floater on top of another as desired.

    A. Select the Floater Adjuster tool from the Tools palette.

    B. Select the O floater by clicking on it in the drawing with the Floater Adjuster. Change its composite method to Default in the Controls palette.

    C. Select the X floater by clicking on its name in the Floater List. Change its composite method to Default in the Controls palette.

    D. Using the Floater Adjuster, arrange the three floaters so that they overlap one another.

    E. You will notice that the opaque portions of the floaters block out parts of one another.

    F. Click and drag on the circle and triangle to the left of Shape 1 on the Floater List and drag it down to the bottom of the list.

G. Click and drag on the star to the left of O floater on the Floater List and drag it up to the top of the list.

H. Notice how this changes which parts of which floaters block your view of the other floaters. Rearrange the order of the Floater List so that you have an idea of how the position on the list affects which floater is on top of other floaters.

I. You can also use the buttons on the Controls palette when the Floater Adjuster is selected to change the order of the Floater List. If a floater is selected and you click on the Front button on the Controls palette, it will move it to the top of the list. Click on the Back button to move it to the bottom of the list. The >> button will move it up one position on the list. The << button will move it down one position on the list.

J. Move the floaters around so that they do not overlap, and change the composite method for the O floater and the X floater to Darken.

Part 3: Changing the Opacity of Floaters

1. Select the O floater.
2. On the Controls palette, change the Opacity slider to 50%.
3. In turn, select the X floater and Shape 1 and change their opacities to 50%.
4. Move the floaters around on top of one another to see how they appear with these new opacities.

Part 4: Grouping and Ungrouping Floaters

If you have a spatial arrangement of floaters that you would like to keep so that you can move them all around together as a group, you can do this by grouping floaters. This can be especially useful, for example, when working with text. Remember that text is a shape and hence can be treated as a floater. Each letter of text is a separate shape, so grouping words together can also save time when moving them around.

1. Click on the Text tool on the Tools palette.
2. In the Controls palette, set the point size to 50 and the font to Arial or any other simple font.
3. Set the color to a color that you would like on the Color palette.
4. Click in the drawing space where you would like the text to start and then type Test.
5. Notice that the letters T, e, s, and t all appear on the Floater List as separate shapes and they are all highlighted.
6. Click on the Group button on the bottom of the Floater List. The separate lines for T, e, s, and t disappear and a new line labeled Group 1 appears.

7. Double click on the Group 1 line and rename it **Test**.

8. You can now use the Floater Adjuster tool to move the whole word around together. You can use the Controls palette to change the opacity and composite method, and you can use the Floater List or the Controls palette to change its position on the Floater List.

9. To ungroup the word **Test**, you would select it with the Floater Adjuster or on the Floater List and click on the **Ungroup** button. It will break down into its separate letters. Do not ungroup it now.

10. You can also open and close a group to gain access to individual floaters within the group.
    A. To the left of the **Test** group on the Floater List, there is a triangle with the point facing right.
    B. Click on the triangle to open the group.
    C. You can then select and work with individual floaters within the group.
    D. Click on the downward-pointing triangle to the left of the **Test** group to close the group.

11. If you have decided that you will never want to work with any of the individual floaters within a group again, you can collapse the group into a single floater. After a group is collapsed, it cannot be separated into its individual parts again.
    A. Make sure that the group that you want to collapse is selected and closed.
    B. Click on the **Collapse** button at the bottom of the Floater List.
    C. You will be asked if you really want to do this. Click on the **Commit All** button.

Part 5: Working with Floaters

This section of the exercise will cover some of the other things that can be done with floaters.

1. Trimming a floater: When a floater is created, it may encompass a larger space than you would like. You can trim it down to a smaller space by using the **Trim** button on the bottom of the Floater List.
    A. Select the **Test** floater.
    B. Click on the **Trim** button on the Floater List.
    C. The floater is trimmed to the smallest size possible.

2. Adding a dropped shadow: You have already seen how to add a dropped shadow to text as single letters. You should know, however, that you can also add them to text that has been grouped or collapsed into a single floater. Dropped shadows can be added to any floater.

    A. Select the **Test** floater.

    B. Click on **Effects/Objects/Create Dropped Shadow**.

    C. The **Drop Shadow** box opens.

        1. The **X** and **Y Offset** values determine the distance that the shadow is offset from the center of the floater.

        2. The **Opacity** value determines the darkness of the shadow.

        3. The **Radius, Angle,** and **Thinness** values control the amount of blurring of the edges of the shadow.

            a. **Radius:** 0 produces a sharp edge; increase the radius for a softer edge.

            b. **Angle:** This sets the direction in which the blurring occurs.

            c. **Thinness:** If streaks occur, increase the thinness to soften the streaks.

    D. Try out some settings for a dropped shadow on the **Test** floater. Click on **OK** when all settings are what you want.

    E. Click **Edit/Undo Create Dropped Shadow** and try out some different settings until you get one that you like.

    F. Notice that the name of the floater on the Floater List has changed to **Test and Shadow**.

3. Changing the size of a floater: You can change the size of a floater very precisely and in the direction that you would like by using the **Floater Size** command.

    A. Select the **X** floater.

    B. Click on the **Floater** pull down menu on the **Objects** palette.

    C. Click on **Floater Size**.

    D. You can adjust the size by adding pixels to the **Top, Left, Bottom,** or **Right**.

    E. Use numbers of pixels to increase the size. Place a minus sign in front of the number to decrease the size.

    F. Decreasing the size of the floater can actually crop part of it away, cutting off that part of the image.

    G. Try placing a -36 in the **Top** window. Click on **OK**.

    H. Notice that you have cut off the top half of the X.

    I. Click on **Edit/Undo Crop** to restore it.

4. Filling a floater: Floaters can be filled with colors, gradations, patterns, weaves, etc. It is important to remember, however, what the shape of the original floater was. Many floaters are created from rectangular or square selections. If this is the case, the entire rectangle or square will be filled. The X floater and the O floater, for example, were created by selecting all

of a square-shaped drawing space, so if you filled them with a color, the entire square-shaped space would be filled. Step I in this section of the exercise shows you how to use the Magic Wand tool to overcome this problem.

A. Select the **Test and Shadow** floater.

B. Go to the **Art Materials** palette and open the **Grad** palette.

C. Select the **Sunset** grad.

D. Select the **Fill** tool on the **Tools** palette.

E. Click inside the **Test and Shadow** floater. It will fill with the Sunset grad.

F. Go to the Floater List and select **X Floater**.

G. Fill it with the **Sunset** grad. Notice that it fills the entire square.

H. Click on **Edit/Undo Paint Bucket Fill**.

I. Now let's try creating a floater using the **Magic Wand** tool.

   1. Create a new drawing space 1 inch × 1 inch in size.

   2. Click on the **Brush** tool on the Tools palette.

      a. Select the **500 lb. Pencil** in the **Brushes** palette.

      b. Change the size to about **10 Pixels** in the **Controls** palette.

      c. Select a color of magenta in the **Color** palette.

      d. Draw an **X** in the new drawing space.

   3. Click on the **Magic Wand** tool in the Tools palette.

   4. Click on the X in the new drawing space.

   5. Change the tolerance, feather, and anti-alias in the **Controls** palette until all of the X is selected.

   6. Click on **Edit/Copy**.

   7. Close the new drawing space by clicking on the X in the upper right-hand corner of the border around it. Do not save the changes.

   8. Click on **Edit/Paste/Normal**. The magenta X appears as a new floater.

   9. Rename the new floater as **X2 Floater**.

   10. Select the **Sunset** grad from the Grad palette.

   11. Use the Fill tool from the Tools palette to fill the X2 floater. Notice that just the X is filled and not the square around it.

5. Painting in a floater: If a floater is selected, you can paint in it; if no floater is selected, you can paint on the canvas as usual without painting on the floater. You can only paint across a floater group, however, after it has been collapsed.

   A. Click on the **Floater Adjuster** tool on the **Tools** palette.

   B. Click on the canvas away from any floater to deselect all floaters.

C. Select the **Brush** tool in the Tools palette.
   1. Select **2B Pencil** in the **Brushes** palette.
   2. Select blue or another dark color in the **Color** palette.
D. Draw a line that crosses the O floater.
E. Click on the **O Floater** line in the Floater List. This selects the floater and activates the Floater Adjuster.
F. Move the floater away from the line that you drew. Notice that the line stays where it was drawn, but it is not present in the floater.
G. On the **Objects** palette, click on the **Floater** pull down menu.
   1. Click on **Floater Attributes**.
   2. In the Floater Visibility Mask area, select **Disabled**.
   3. Click on **OK**. If you don't do this, you will be painting on the mask instead of the floater.
H. Click on the **Brush** tool in the Tools palette.
I. Draw a line across the O floater. Notice that you can draw in the floater, but not outside of it.
J. Click on the **Floater Adjuster** tool in the Tools palette.
K. Move the O floater. Notice that the line moves with the floater.

6. Editing a floater's mask: When you create a floater, you also create a mask for the floater at the same time. If you change the mask for the floater, you will change how much of the floater is visible in the drawing. This can be a way to make part of the floater image disappear. The easiest way to edit the floater mask is to paint in it in greyscale. White removes the mask, which makes more of the image invisible. Black adds to the mask, which makes more of the image visible. Various shades of grey make that portion of the mask more or less transparent. You must use a brush method of **Mask** to work on the floater mask. You can only work on the mask of the currently selected floater.
   A. Select the X floater.
   B. On the **Objects** palette, click on the **Floater** pull down menu.
      1. Click on **Floater Attributes**.
      2. In the Floater Visibility Mask area, select **Normal**.
      3. Click on **OK**. If you don't do this, you will be painting on the floater instead of the mask.
   C. On the Objects palette, click on the icon under the word **Mask** to open the **Mask List**.
   D. On the left side of the **X Floater Mask** line is a closed eye. Click on the eye to open the eye and reveal the mask.
   E. It is easiest to see what you are doing, however, if you work with the mask unrevealed. Then you can see the parts of the image disappear as

you paint over them. It can also sometimes be difficult to "paint" on the mask itself. Click on the X Floater Mask eye again to close the eye.

F. Click on the **Brush** tool on the Tools palette. The airbrush is the best tool for working on masks. Select the **Airbrush** on the **Brushes** palette and select the **Thin Stroke** variant.

   1. Click on the **Min/Max** button on the Brushes palette to reveal the **Method** and **Subcategory** pop-ups if they are not already revealed.

   2. Select a method of **Mask (Cover)** and a subcategory of **Soft Cover**.

G. On the **Color** palette, select white.

H. Take a stroke across the floater. Notice that the you have in effect "erased" the part of the X that you crossed with the stroke. This is because the white color is removing the mask.

I. On the Color palette, select black.

J. Take a stroke across the previous white stroke. Notice that the floater is reappearing. This is because the black color is reapplying the mask.

K. Click on the icon under the word **Floater** on the Objects palette to reveal the Floater List again.

L. Click on **Edit/Undo Brush Stroke** and then again on **Edit/Undo Brush Stroke** to remove the mask change.

7. Using effects on a floater: There are also a number of effects that can be applied to floaters.

A. In the Floater List, select the **X2 Floater**.

B. Click on the **Effects** pull down menu. Click on **Orientation/Flip Horizontal**.

C. Click on the **Effects** pull down menu. Click on **Orientation/Flip Vertical**.

D. In the **Orientation** area, you can also rotate, scale, and distort the floater.

E. Experiment with rotate, scale, and distort. After you have applied each of these effects, click on **Edit/Undo** to undo the effect.

F. Click on the **Effects** pull down menu. Click on **Esoterica/Apply Marbling**.

G. Experiment with several of the other effects that are available. After applying each effect, click on **Edit/Undo** to undo that effect.

8. Creating a transparent floater: It is also possible in Painter to create a transparent floater and paint into it. If you would like to paint directly over the canvas into a blank floater, this is the way that you go about it.

A. Click on the **Floater Adjuster** tool on the **Tools** palette. Click away from any floaters on the canvas to deselect all floaters.

B. If you would like to create a transparent floater that is the size of the whole canvas, then click on Floater/Transparent Layer in the pull down menu on the Objects palette. If you would like to create a smaller transparent floater, you must use the Rectangular Selection tool to select an area of the canvas. After you make the selection, click on Floater/Transparent Layer in the pull down menu in the Objects palette. This converts that selection into a transparent floater.

1. Click on the Rectangular Selection tool on the Tools palette.
2. Click and drag to create an area about 1 inch square on the canvas.
3. Click on Floater/Transparent Layer in the pull down menu in the Objects palette.
4. You have now turned the area that you selected into a transparent floater. It appears on the Floater List as Transparent Layer.

C. Rename the transparent layer to T Floater.

D. Click on the Brush tool in the Tools palette. To draw on a transparent floater, you must use a Transparent Layer brush. Almost any brush that you would like to use can be converted into a Transparent Layer brush by using the Method and Subcategory pop-ups on the Brushes palette.

1. Select the 500 lb. Pencil.
2. In the Controls palette change the size to about 10.
3. If the Method and Subcategory pop-ups are not visible on the Brushes palette, click on the Min/Max button to make them appear.
4. Select a method of Plug-In and a subcategory of Transparent Layer Brush.

E. Select the color purple on the Color palette.

F. Draw a T on the T floater.

G. Click on the Floater Adjuster tool on the Tools palette.

H. Move the T floater to a new location.

Part 6: Creating and Using a Reference Floater

A reference floater is a special state to which a floater can be converted in order to perform a variety of transformations. This is simply a technique that Painter uses to speed up the transformation process. The floater is converted into a low-resolution entity so that the transformations can take place more quickly. After you have performed the transformations, the floater is converted back into an image floater. Reference floaters are just for transformations; you cannot draw in a reference floater.

1. Creating a reference floater:

A. Select the X floater by clicking on it with the Floater Adjuster tool or clicking on its line in the Floater List.

B. In the Controls palette, change its opacity to 100%. This is just so that you will be able to see some of the transformations better.

C. In the main pull down menu, click on Effects/Orientation/Free Transform. On the Floater List, the X Floater line shows an icon with the same eight handles that appear around the floater box on the canvas. This indicates that it has been converted into a reference floater. Now you can perform transformations on the floater.

2. Transforming a reference floater:

A. Resize:

1. Click and drag on a corner handle to resize the floater.
2. Hold down the Shift key while you click and drag to maintain the proportions as you resize.

B. Rotate: Hold down the Ctrl/Command key and click and drag on a corner handle to rotate the floater.

C. Skew (Slant): Hold down the Ctrl/Command key and click and drag on a side handle to skew the floater.

D. Use the Set Transform dialogue box:

1. On the main pull down menu, click on Effects/Orientation/Set Transform. This opens the Set Transform dialogue box.
2. In the Set Transform dialogue box you can specify any of the transformations numerically. This box will also let you return to the original image after you have used the Resize, Rotate, and Skew commands above.

   a. In the Scaling area, change both Horizontal and Vertical to 100%. This will change the Resize command back to its original size.
   b. In the Rotation window, change the value to 0. This will change the rotation back to the original.
   c. In the Slant window, change the value to 0. This will change the skew back to the original.
   d. Click on OK. This will restore the original image.

3. Open the Set Transform box again and make some changes to the floater using numerical entries.

3. Converting a reference floater back to an image floater: After you have made all of the transformations that you would like to the reference floater, you can convert it back into an image floater by clicking in the main pull down menu on Effects/Orientation/Commit Transform. Go ahead and convert the reference floater back to an image floater. Notice that the handles in both the canvas and on the Floater List have disappeared.

Part 7: The Floaters Portfolio: Saving and Reusing Floaters

If you have created a floater that you would like to use later, you can store it on the Floaters Portfolio palette. Floaters can also be moved from the Floaters Portfolio palette onto the canvas.

1. Saving a floater:
    A. Open the Floaters Portfolio palette by clicking on Floater/Floaters Portfolio on the Objects palette pull down menu.
    B. Click on the Floater Adjuster on the Tools palette.
    C. Select the floater that you would like to store by clicking on it with the Floater Adjuster or clicking on its line in the Floater List. Click on the X2 floater.
    D. Hold down the Alt/Option key and then click and drag the X2 floater onto the Floaters Portfolio palette. The Save Floater box will open. You can rename the floater now if you would like.
    E. Click on OK. The X2 floater has now been added to the Floaters Portfolio palette.
    F. If you want to remove the floater from the canvas at the same time that you save it to the Floaters Portfolio palette, do not hold down the Alt/Option key when you click and drag it onto the Floaters Portfolio palette.

2. Reusing a floater:
    A. Locate the Hand floater on the Floaters Portfolio palette.
    B. Click and drag it onto the canvas.
    C. It appears on the Floater List as the line Hand.
    D. Close the Floaters Portfolio palette by clicking on the X in the upper right-hand corner.

Part 8: Using Plug-In Floaters

If you have Painter 5, there are a number of plug-in floaters that you can use. These are not available with earlier versions of the program. Plug-in floaters are really another category of special effects that can be applied to floaters. They fall into three general types: a plug-in floater that creates a new floater; a plug-in floater that alters an existing floater; and a plug-in floater that alters the images underneath the floater. If you save your drawing in a .rif format, the plug-in floaters remain active and can be changed again at any time. If you save your drawing in another format, the plug-in floater is set and cannot be altered. The way that each plug-in floater works will vary. I will talk you through using several of them below. For more information on plug-in floaters, refer to "Working with Plug-In Floaters" in your *Painter Users Guide.*

1. Using a plug-in floater that alters an existing floater:
   A. Open the **Plug-In Floater** palette by clicking on the **P. Float** icon on the **Objects** palette.
   B. If the **Hand** floater is not active, select it by using the **Floater Adjuster** tool from the **Tools** palette.
   C. Click on the pop-up at the bottom of the Plug-In Floater palette and choose **Impasto**.
   D. Click on the **Apply** button.
   E. The **Impasto Options** box opens. If the Options box is covering the hand on the canvas, click and drag on the blue bar at the top of the box to move it to the side so that you can see the hand as you make changes in the box. You are going to use the Impasto option to create wrinkles on the hand by pulling up texture from the paper underneath the drawing.
      1. Uncheck the box next to **Draw with Color** if it is checked.
      2. Check the box next to **Draw with Depth** if it is unchecked.
      3. In the **How Depth is Drawn** pop-up, select **Paper**.
      4. In the **Brushes** palette, select **Airbrush** and **Thin Stroke**. You may have to move the Plug-In Floater palette around the screen to access the Brushes palette and then move it again so that you can see the hand in the drawing space.
      5. Draw on the hand with the airbrush. The paper texture underneath will rise up to the hand, creating wrinkles on the hand. If you don't like one of the strokes that you make, you can use the **Edit/Undo** command to remove it. Remember that you can only undo back five strokes. Use the airbrush to create a hand that looks aged from the wrinkles.
      6. Click on **OK**.
   F. Click on the **Floater** icon on the Objects palette to reveal the Floater List. Notice that there is a **Plug-In** icon next to the **Hand Floater** line on the list. This tells you that a plug-in floater has been applied to the Hand floater.
      1. Open the Impasto Options box again by double clicking on the name of the **Hand Floater** on the Floater List.
      2. Click on **Clear Depth Layer** in the Impasto Options box to remove the wrinkles.
      3. Click on **OK**.
      4. On the pull down menu on the Objects palette, click on **P. Float/Revert to Original** to completely eliminate the plug-in floater.
   G. Plug-in floaters are what Painter refers to as "dynamic." This means that they can be changed any time that you would like by reopening

the Options box as you did in 1A–1D above. If you decide that you want to permanently keep the effect that you have created, you can also convert to an image floater by clicking on the **Commit** button at the bottom of the Objects palette while that floater is selected. Once a plug-in floater is committed, it cannot be changed. There are a number of other actions that will also commit the plug-in floater:

- saving the drawing in a format other than .rif,
- painting in the floater, except for Impasto,
- applying an effect to the floater,
- applying another plug-in floater to the floater,
- dropping the floater, or
- collapsing a group that contains a plug-in floater.

2. Using a plug-in floater that alters the images beneath it:

   A. Click on the **Floater Adjuster** on the **Tools** palette.

   B. Click somewhere on the canvas other than on a floater to deselect all floaters.

   C. Click on the **P. Float** icon to open the **Plug-In Floaters** palette.

   D. Select the **Brightness and Contrast** plug-in floater.

   E. Click on the **Apply** button. This opens the **Brightness/Contrast** dialogue box and applies the plug-in floater to the entire drawing space.

   F. Click on the **OK** button on the Brightness/Contrast dialogue box to close it. You are now going to resize the floater so that its effects will apply to just part of the drawing space.

   G. On the **Objects** palette pull down menu, click on **Floater/Floater Size.** This opens the **Floater Size** box.

      1. In the **Adjust Size** section, add -150 Pixels to the top.
      2. In the **Adjust Size** section, add -150 Pixels to the left.
      3. In the **Adjust Size** section, add -150 Pixels to the bottom.
      4. In the **Adjust Size** section, add -150 Pixels to the right.
      5. Click on **OK.** This will give you a Brightness/Contrast plug-in floater of 60×60 pixels in size.

   H. Use the Floater Adjuster to move the floater to a location where several different images such as the hand and another floater are underneath it.

   I. Click on the **Floater** icon on the Objects palette to open the Floater List.

   J. Double click on the name of the Brightness/Contrast floater on the Floater List to open the **Brightness/Contrast** dialogue box.

   K. Adjust the **Brightness and Contrast** sliders in the Brightness/Contrast box to create a noticeable effect beneath the floater.

   L. Click on **OK.**

M. Use the Floater Adjuster to move the Brightness/Contrast floater around in the drawing space. Notice that the effect moves to wherever you move the floater.

N. Deselect the floater by clicking in the drawing space somewhere other than on a floater.

O. Save this drawing as a file for working with other plug-in floaters. Be sure that you save it as a .rif file and give it the name of proj5.rif. You can compare the work that you have done to the file exer5.rif on the CD-ROM.

There are a number of plug-in floaters that create other kinds of special effects. The Burn plug-in floater creates a burn effect at the edge of a selected image floater. The Tear plug-in floater applies a torn-paper effect to the edge of an image floater. The Bevel World plug-in floater creates 3-D bevel effects to the edge of an image floater. The Equalize plug-in floater changes the contrast of images beneath it. The Glass Distortion plug-in floater creates a distortion effect on images underneath. The Kaleidoscope plug-in floater creates a kaleidoscope effect on the images beneath it. The Liquid Lens plug-in floater smears and distorts the imagery underneath. The Liquid Metal plug-in floater lets you paint with liquids and metals that distort the images beneath it. The Posterize plug-in floater reduces the number of colors in the imagery underneath.

It will take you a good deal of time and experimentation to explore all of the possibilities available by using plug-in floaters. The chapter on plug-in floaters in the *Painter Users Guide* will give you a good place to start in exploring these options.

USING IMAGE EFFECTS

You have already learned to perform some operations such as rotate, scale, flip, etc. using the Effects menu in Painter. This section will cover other of the effects available such as adding lighting, sharpening, softening, and electronic retouching. Most effects are applied to a selection or an image floater. If you apply an effect to a shape, plug-in floater, or reference floater, Painter will automatically convert that object into an image floater. If you do not make a selection before applying an effect then Painter will apply that effect to the entire canvas.

You should open the Art Materials palette before applying any effects. Most of the effects can or sometimes have to be used with the Art Materials palette, but it must be opened before activating the effect.

Another useful command with effects is the Edit/Fade command. This command lets you control the percentage of the effect so that you can apply just as much or as little of it as you would like.

ORIENTATION EFFECTS

The orientation effects control the shape, size, and attitude (angle and rotation) of the selection or floater to which it is applied. You can use the **Effects/ Orientation/Free Transform** option to rotate, resize, and skew an image, or you can individually select the **Rotate**, **Scale**, **Distort**, **Flip Horizontal**, or **Flip Vertical** options.

TONAL CONTROL EFFECTS

The tonal control effects let you work with the colors in an image. Options available here include **Correct Colors**, **Adjust Colors**, **Adjust Selected Colors**, **Brightness/Contrast**, **Equalize**, **Negative**, and **Posterize**.

SURFACE CONTROL EFFECTS

The surface control effects let you work with the paper, color, and light to create a variety of effects. These include **Apply Lighting**, **Apply Screen**, **Apply Surface Texture**, **Color Overlay**, **Dye Concentration**, and **Express Texture**.

FOCUS EFFECTS

The focus effects let you sharpen, soften, blur, and distort the image. The effects available here are **Camera Motion Blur**, **Depth of Field**, **Glass Distortion**, **Motion Blur**, **Sharpen**, **Soften**, **Super Soften**, and **Zoom Blur**.

ESOTERICA EFFECTS

The esoterica effects combine a number of very different effects into one general category. Some of the effects available here include **Marbling**, **Auto Clone**, **Auto Van Gogh**, **Blobs**, **Custom Tile**, **Grid Paper**, **Growth**, **Highpass**, **Maze**, **Place Elements**, and **Pop Art Fill**.

OBJECT EFFECTS

The object effects are **Drop Shadow**, with which you should already be familiar, and **Align**.

Exercise No. 6: Working with Effects

There is a large number of different kinds of effects that are available in Painter. The following exercise will work you through the use of some of them, giving you the basic idea of how to use effects. When you are finished with the exercise, you should explore the rest of the effects in which you might be interested on your own. If you do run into difficulties with one that isn't covered in the exercise, examine the section of the *Painter Users Guide* on image effects for assistance. Orientation effects were covered in the earlier exercise on shapes if you feel that you need a review of how they work.

Part 1: Preparing a Drawing Space

1. Click on **File/New** and create a drawing space 5 inches × 5 inches.
2. Open the following palettes if they are not already open: **Tools, Brushes, Art Materials, Controls,** and **Objects**. On the Objects palette, activate the Floater List.
3. Place a paper texture in the drawing space.
   A. In the Art Materials palette, click on the **Paper** icon.
   B. Select **Handmade** paper.
   C. Give it a scale of **400%**. You may need to use the **Min/Max** button to open this part of the palette.
4. Create some floaters: You can apply the effects commands to a floater, a selection, or the entire drawing space. If nothing is selected, then the effect will be applied to the entire drawing space. In this exercise you'll work with all three.
   A. On the Objects palette pull down menu, click on **Floater/Floaters Portfolio** to open the Floaters Portfolio.
      1. Drag the **FDC Stamp** into the drawing space.
      2. Drag the **X2** floater into the drawing space. You created and saved this floater in the floater exercise.
      3. Drag the **Hand** into the drawing space.
      4. Close the Floaters Portfolio by clicking on the X in the upper right-hand corner.
   B. Click on **Brush** on the Tools palette.
   C. In the Brushes palette, select the **500 lb. Pencil**.
   D. In the Color palette, select a saturated color such as a blue.
   E. Draw a donut in the drawing space.
   F. Click on the **Rectangular Selection** tool in the Tools palette.
   G. Click and drag with the tool to select an area surrounding the donut.
   H. Move the cursor inside the selected area. Notice that it has changed to a pointing-finger symbol like the Floater Selection tool.
   I. Click and drag inside the selected area. The selected area converts to a floater and appears on the Floater List.
   J. Rename the floater that you just created to **Donut**.

K. Click on the **Floater Selector** on the Tools palette.

L. Click in the drawing space outside of all of the floaters to deselect all floaters.

5. Create a brush stroke to be turned into a selection later:

A. Click on the **Brush** on the Tools palette.

B. In the Brushes palette, select the **500 lb. Pencil**.

C. In the Color palette, select a saturated red color.

D. Draw a red splotch in the drawing space that can easily be selected using the Rectangular Selection tool.

6. If you want to work on this exercise over time and need to save it, be sure that you save it as it as an .rif file so that the floaters will remain floaters.

Part 2: Tonal Control Effects

Correct Colors

The **Correct Colors** command can be very useful for improving the color of a washed-out image or for creating unusual color effects.

1. Select the **Hand** floater.

2. On the main pull down menu, click on **Effects/Tonal Control/Correct Colors**.

3. The **Color Correction** box appears. You may need to move it off to the side slightly so that you can see the FDC Stamp image.

    Color corrections are made by adjusting the curve that you see in the graphed area of the box—it's a straight line right now. The red, green, blue, and Master (grey) buttons let you select which color you would like to adjust. Master adjusts all three colors together. Click on the button for the color that you would like to adjust. To the left of the color selection buttons is a pop-up where you can choose one of four different methods of adjusting the color: **Contrast and Brightness**, **Curve**, **Freehand**, or **Advanced**.

4. Select the **Master** button. Select the **Contrast and Brightness** pop-up.

A. Move the **Contrast** slider back and forth to see its effect.

B. Move the **Brightness** slider back and forth to see its effect.

C. Click on the **Reset** button to remove the effects.

5. Select the red button.

A. Move the **Contrast** slider back and forth to see its effect.

B. Move the **Brightness** slider back and forth to see its effect.

C. Click on the **Reset** button to remove the effects.

6. Select the blue button.

A. Move the **Contrast** slider back and forth to see its effect.

   B. Move the Brightness slider back and forth to see its effect.

   C. Click on the Reset button to remove the effects.

7. The Curve, Freehand, and Advanced pop-ups offer more complex methods of adjusting the color curve. If you are interested in these, examine the section in the *Painter Users Guide* on the Correct Colors command.

8. Close the box by clicking on OK if you want to save the changes or on Cancel if you want to remove them.

9. Click on the Floater Adjuster on the Tools palette.

10. Click anywhere in the drawing space other than on a floater to deselect the Hand floater.

Adjust Colors

The Adjust Colors command controls the hue, saturation, and value of the entire image.

1. Click on the Rectangular Selection tool on the Tools palette.

2. Click and drag to form a selection that encloses the red splotch.

3. Click on Effects/Tonal Control/Adjust Colors. The Adjust Color box opens.

4. The Using: pop-up lets you choose where the color adjustment is applied. Uniform Color applies colors equally. Paper uses the grain of the paper underneath to control color adjustment. Masks uses the mask of the selection or floater to adjust color. If you paint a black-white gradation in the mask or visibility mask, you can create a gradation in the color adjustment. Image Luminance makes greater adjustments to areas of greater luminance. Original Luminance works with a clone.

5. Select Paper in the pop-up.

6. Move the Hue Shift, Saturation, and Value sliders back and forth to see their effects. You can use the Reset button at any time to restore the original settings. The changes will appear in the preview window. If you got a preview that you liked, you would click on the OK button to transfer it to the selection in the drawing space.

7. Click on the Cancel button to cancel any changes.

8. On the main pull down menu, click on Select/None to deselect the rectangle.

Negative

The Negative command reverses black and white on part or all of your image.

1. Select the Donut floater.

2. Click on Effects/Tonal Control/Negative. The white parts of the floater become black.

3. Click on Effects/Tonal Control/Negative. The black parts of the floater become white.

4. Use the Floater Adjuster to deselect the Donut floater.

Posterize

The Posterize command adjusts the number of colors in an image. You will see that this effect only works in the downward direction—you cannot increase the number of colors, only decrease them.

1. Select the Hand floater.

2. Click on Effects/Tonal Control/Posterize. The Posterize box opens.

3. Change the number in the Levels: window to 10, then to 5, then to 3. The lower the number of levels, the more dramatic the effect. You will see the changes in the preview window.

4. Click on Cancel to escape the command box.

5. Use the Floater Adjuster to deselect the Hand floater.

6. Save your work as proj6a.rif to a floppy disk or your hard drive. You can compare it to Exer6a.rif on the CD-ROM.

Part 3: Surface Control Effects

Apply Lighting

The Apply Lighting command lets you create lighting effects on an image. You can either apply lighting effects from a library or create your own that can be saved if you like. In this part of the exercise you will work with the entire drawing space as well as a selection and a floater. Save your proj6a.rif as proj6b.rif or open exer6a.rif from the CD-ROM and save it as proj6b.rif.

1. Using the Lighting Library:

A. Click on Effects/Surface Control/Apply Lighting. The Apply Lighting dialogue box appears.

B. Underneath the word Preview you will see three windows that have a scroller beneath. These represent the effects currently available in the Lighting library. Move the scroller back and forth to view the options.

C. Click in one of the three windows to see that effect applied in the larger preview window above.

D. Click on several of the effects available in the library and view the effect in the larger preview window.

E. You should notice that none of the floaters appear in the larger preview window. If you are applying lighting to a drawing, the floaters will only be affected if they are selected. To apply lighting to the entire drawing including all floaters, the floaters would have to be dropped beforehand so that they were no longer floaters. You can, however, apply lighting to just a floater or to just a selection.

1. Click on the Cancel button.
2. Select the Hand floater.
3. Click on Effects/Surface Control/Apply Lighting.
4. Use the library windows to preview several of the lighting effects on the Hand floater.
5. Click on the Cancel button.
6. Deselect the Hand floater with the Floater Adjuster tool.
7. Use the Rectangular Selection tool to select the red splotch.
8. Click on Effects/Surface Control/Apply Lighting.
9. Use the library windows to preview several of the lighting effects on the selection.
10. Click on the Cancel button.
11. Click on Select/None to deselect the red splotch.
12. If you had wanted to apply any of the previewed lighting effects to the drawing space, selection, or floater, you would have clicked on OK instead of Cancel in the above sequences.

2. Creating your own lighting:

A. Select the Hand floater.

B. Click on Effects/Surface Control/Apply Lighting. The Apply Lighting dialogue box appears.

C. Choose the Plain Light option from the library windows. This will give you a very simple setup from which to work. You can add, adjust, or delete lights from the larger preview window. The lighting instrument is represented in the window as a large circle and a small circle connected by two lines. Right now there is only one lighting instrument in the window. At this point you will learn how to manipulate the instruments.

1. Click and drag on the large circle to change the position of the lighting instrument.
2. Click and drag on the small circle to change the direction in which the instrument is pointed.
3. The sliders to the right of the preview window let you control the light coming from the instrument.
   a. The Brightness slider is like a dimmer. Move it back and forth to change the intensity.
   b. The Distance slider controls the distance of the light from the image. Move it back and forth to position the instrument closer to or further away from the image.
   c. The Elevation slider controls the angle of the instrument to the image. Move it back and forth to control shadows.

   d. The Spread slider controls the field angle of your instrument. For nonlighting designers, that means how wide or narrow the beam of light is. Move it back and forth to change the spread of the beam of light coming from the instrument.

   e. The Exposure and Ambient sliders are concerned with the overall lighting level of the image rather than the light coming from a particular lighting instrument. Exposure increases or decreases the brightness of the image as a whole. Ambient controls what might be thought of as a floodlight that lights up the entire image uniformly.

      1. Decrease the Brightness slider to 0.
      2. Increase the Ambient slider to .75.
      3. Increase the Exposure slider to 2.
      4. Restore the brightness to .5, the ambient to .33, and the exposure to 1.

4. The Light Color box lets you change the color of the lighting instrument. Click in it. The Color box opens. Select a color for your lighting instrument. You can choose one of the basic colors by clicking in the box for it. You can choose a hue by clicking in the large rainbow-colored window and then select a value and saturation by moving the slider next to the small vertical rectangle displaying values and saturations for the hue chosen. You can also change colors by changing the numbers in the Hue, Sat., and Lum. or the Red, Green, and Blue boxes. Remember that this is light and you are dealing with additive color mixing. If you create a color that you would like to save, you can do so by clicking on the Add to Custom Colors bar. When you have a color in the preview window that you would like to try out on the instrument, click on OK.

5. The Ambient Light Color box lets you change the color of the ambient light in the scene. It works just like the Light Color box.

6. Adding lighting instruments to the scene:

   a. Click in the preview window anywhere that you would like to add a new lighting instrument. The new lighting instrument will have the same properties and color as the one that is currently selected.

   b. Click and drag on the large circle to move it around.

   c. Click and drag on the small circle to aim it.

   d. Use the sliders to control the light that it produces and the Light Color box to change its color.

   e. Add a couple of new lighting instruments, adjusting each of them after they are added.

       7. Changing the settings of lighting instruments:

         a. Click on a lighting instrument to select it.

         b. Click and drag on one of the circles to move it or aim it.

         c. Use the sliders to control the light it produces and the Light Color box to change its color.

       8. Deleting a lighting instrument:

         a. Click on a lighting instrument to select it.

         b. Use the Backspace/Delete key on the keyboard to delete it.

    D. Create a lighting setup for the hand using the Apply Lighting box. Do **not** click on the OK button to apply it to the Hand floater in the drawing space.

3. Saving a lighting setup: If you have created a lighting setup that you would like to save for later use, click on the Save button in the Apply Lighting box. This will save it to the current Lighting library.

    A. Click on the Save button.

    B. The Save Lighting box opens.

       1. Give it a name in the Save As: window.

       2. Click on OK.

    C. This saves the lighting setup for later use.

    D. Give the lighting setup the name of Test1 and click on OK. Click on OK to apply it to the Hand floater.

    E. Deselect the Hand floater.

    F. Use the Rectangular Selection tool to select the red splotch.

    G. Click on Effects/Surface Control/Apply Lighting. The Apply Lighting dialogue box appears.

    H. Click on the library window for the lighting that you just saved—Test1—to view how it will look on the selection in the preview window.

    I. Click on OK to apply it to the red splotch.

    J. Click on Select/None to deselect the red splotch.

Apply Surface Texture

The Apply Surface Texture command lets you add texture to your entire drawing, a selection, or a floater. You could, for example, texture a single brush stroke. Remember that if no selection is made, the surface texture will be applied to the whole drawing space, but not to the floaters. If you want to texture everything including the floaters, then it is best to wait until the drawing is completed, drop the floaters, and then apply the texture. In the following exercise you will be applying surface texture to a floater using different methods including paper, so you will need to select the paper before using the command. The Apply Surface Texture command lets you apply only the texture to your drawing. If you want to apply texture and color together, you will need to use the Apply Color Overlay command.

1. In the Art Materials palette, click on the Paper icon and select Handmade paper. Give it a scale of 400%.
2. Select the X2 floater.
3. Click on Effects/Surface Control/Apply Surface Texture. The Apply Surface Texture box opens.
4. In the Using: pop-up you have several choices for how the texture will be applied. Click on each of them in turn to see the effect in the preview window.
   A. Click on Paper to pull up the paper texture you selected earlier.
   B. Click on 3D Brush Strokes to see an oil paint brush stroke effect.
   C. Click on Image Luminance to apply a texture based on the values of the image.
   D. Click on Original Luminance to apply a texture based on the clone of the image.
   E. Click on X2 Floater Mask to apply a texture based on the mask of the image. With a floater such as the one selected, this will create texture around the edges of the image.
   F. Click on 3D Brush Strokes.
      1. You can soften the brush strokes by using the Softness slider. Move it back and forth to see the effect, but return it to 0.
      2. Click on the box next to Inverted. This inverts the highs and lows of the brush strokes.
5. The Material sliders let you vary the qualities of the texture.
   A. Adjust the Amount slider up and down.
   B. Adjust the Picture slider up and down.
   C. Adjust the Shine slider up and down.
   D. Adjust the Reflection slider up and down.
6. Texture will, of course, only be revealed through the shadows cast by light, so the rest of the box is concerned with controlling the lighting, which will in turn control the appearance of the texture.
   A. In the Sphere area to the left there is a circle that represents the lighting instrument.
      1. Use the Brightness, Conc, and Exposure sliders to control the light coming from the instrument.
      2. Change the direction of the light by clicking in one of the Light Direction dots or by clicking and dragging on the circle in the Sphere area.

3. Add a lighting instrument by clicking in the Sphere area. You can then change the brightness, concentration, and exposure for that instrument, move it around the area by clicking and dragging, or delete it by using the Backspace/Delete key.

B. The color of the lighting instrument selected can be changed by clicking on the Light Color box.

7. When you have all the changes made to the texture that you would like, click on OK.

8. Deselect the X2 floater.

9. There are a number of other kinds of effects that can also be applied using the Surface Texture command. Examine the section in the *Painter Users Guide* for more information on the command.

Color Overlay

The Color Overlay command lets you apply texture and color together to the drawing, a selection, or a floater. The color must be selected before activating the command. If you are going to be using a paper texture, that also must be selected before activating the command. Remember that these will not be applied to any floaters unless the floaters are selected or have been dropped.

1. In the Art Materials palette, click on the Paper icon and select Basic Paper and give it a scale of about 200%.

2. In the Color palette, select a light tan or cream color.

3. Click on Effects/Surface Control/Color Overlay. The Color Overlay box opens.

4. The Using: pop-up lets you select how the overlay will be applied.

A. Preview the effect of the various options available.

B. Finally, select the Paper option.

5. The Opacity slider lets you control the intensity of the color. Move it back and forth to see the effect, but leave it set at 100%.

6. Dye Concentration and Hiding Power are two options that affect how the texture and color will be applied to the drawing space. Dye concentration works as though the color is a part of the paper. Hiding power means that the color will partially cover paint that is on top of the paper.

A. Click on the circle next to Hiding Power and then click on OK. Notice that the red splotch is partially covered by the color.

B. Click on Edit/Undo Color Overlay.

C. Click on Effects/Surface Control/Color Overlay. In the Color Overlay box, click on the dot next to Dye Concentration and then click on OK.

1. Notice that the red splotch is on top of the texture and color.

2. Notice that with either dye concentration or hiding power, the floaters are still floating above the texture and color.

Dye Concentration

The **Dye Concentration** effect applies a preselected color and texture by adjusting the values of the pigments. If you want to use a paper texture, it must be selected before the command. The color must also be selected before the command. Since you have already selected a paper and color for the last part of the exercise, you can work with them.

1. Click on Effects/Surface Control/Dye Concentration. The Dye Concentration box opens.
2. Preview the effects of the various Using: options in the pop-up. Select Paper.
3. Move the Maximum and Minimum sliders to control the values of the color.
4. When you have something that you like, click on OK.

Express Texture

The name of this command is somewhat deceptive, since what it really does is create a greyscale halftone version of the image.

1. Select the FDC Stamp floater.
2. Click on Effects/Surface Control/Express Texture. The Express Texture box opens.
3. Click on the various options available in the Using: pop-up to see their effects, but finally select Paper.
4. Move the Grey Threshold, Grain, and Contrast sliders to create the greyscale halftone. The Grey Threshold and Grain sliders are very sensitive. You will find that there is a very narrow range on these that will produce a usable image.
5. Click on OK.
6. Click on Edit/Undo Express Texture.
7. Deselect the FDC Stamp floater.

Image Warp

The **Image Warp** command lets you distort the surface of the image.

1. Select the Donut floater.
2. Click on Effects/Surface Control/Image Warp. The Image Warp box opens. There are three different styles of distortions available: Linear, Cubic, and Sphere. The Size slider controls the size of the area affected by the distortion.
3. Click on the dot next to Linear. Click and drag in the preview window. The circle that appears shows the area of the image that will be affected. When you release the mouse button, the distortion effect will be created.

Drag the cursor several times to see the kinds of distortions that you can create.

4. Click on Cancel. Click on Effects/Surface Control/Image Warp.

5. Click on the dot next to Cubic. Click and drag to create a different style of distortion.

6. Click on Cancel. Click on Effects/Surface Control/Image Warp.

7. Click on the dot next to Sphere. Click and drag to create another style of distortion.

8. Click on Cancel.

Quick Warp

The Quick Warp command is a way to quickly create a number of different kinds of distortions.

1. Leave the Donut floater selected.

2. Click on Effects/Surface Control/Quick Warp. The Quick Warp box opens.

3. Select Sphere, Bump, Valley, Swirl, and Ripple in turn and then adjust the sliders for each to create different distortion effects. You will see the result of each action in the preview window.

4. Click on Cancel.

5. Deselect the Donut floater.

6. Save your work to a floppy disk or to the hard drive as proj6b.rif. You can compare it to exer6b.rif in the Painter folder on the CD-ROM.

Part 4: Focus Effects

Glass Distortion

The Glass Distortion command offers some other distortion techniques. It can work with a selected paper texture, 3D Brush Strokes, the Mask, Image Luminance, or Original Luminance effects. In this part of the exercise you'll use a paper texture to create a distortion.

1. Open your file proj6b.rif or the file exer6b.rif from the CD-ROM. Save it to a floppy disk or your hard drive as proj6c.rif.

2. In the Art Materials palette, click on the Paper icon and select a texture of Hatching.

3. Select the Hand floater.

4. Click on Effects/Focus/Glass Distortion. The Glass Distortion box opens.

5. First set the Softness slider to 0 so that you will be able to see the distortion effects more clearly. Later you can adjust it to create softer effects.

6. In the Using: pop-up, try out the 3D Brush Strokes, Image Luminance, Original Luminance, and Hand Mask options so that you can see their effects. Select the Paper option.

7. In the Map: pop-up, try out the Vector Displacement and Angle Displacement options so that you can see their effects. Select the Refraction option.

8. Select Good in the Quality: pop-up.

9. Move the Amount, Variance, and Direction sliders to control the distortion.

10. Check the Inverted box to change the highlights and lowlights.

11. Click on OK to apply the effects to the hand.

Sharpen

The Sharpen command intensifies highlights and lowlights to create a sharper contrast effect.

1. Deselect any floater by clicking in the drawing space with the Floater Adjuster tool. This will adjust the background that you created earlier without affecting the floaters.

2. Click on Effects/Focus/Sharpen. The Sharpen box opens.

3. The Radius slider controls how much of an edge of contrast is affected. Move it to 100.

4. The Highlight slider determines the brightness of the light-colored areas. Move it to 100%.

5. The Shadow slider determines the darkness of the dark-colored areas. Move it to 100%.

6. These settings will give you maximum contrast.

7. Click on OK. It will take a while for the image to sharpen.

Soften

The Soften command quickly softens an image so that all detail is lost.

1. Leave all floaters unselected. You will still be working with the background.

2. Move the Radius slider to soften the image that appears in the preview window. You will see that this is a very sensitive slider. It doesn't take much movement to lose all detail in the image.

3. Set the Radius slider at 1.5. Click OK.

4. The Super Soften command is a stronger version of Soften.

5. Save the work that you have done as proj6c.rif. You can compare it with exer6c.rif on the CD-ROM.

Part 5: Esoterica Effects

Blobs and Marbling

In this part of the exercise you will work with two different effects—**Blobs** and **Marbling**—to create a marbled texture. The Blobs effect lets you put blobs of color randomly around the drawing space. The Marbling effect will then turn those blobs of color into a marbled texture. Before you start the exercise, think about the colors that you would like to have in your marbling. Choose a background color and three marbling colors in your mind. You will first create a drawing space with the background color and then place blobs in it in the three marbling colors.

1. Open your file **proj6b.rif** or the file **exer6b.rif** from the CD-ROM. Save it as proj6cd.rif.

2. Create a new drawing space. Do not close the old one. Click on **File/New** and create a new drawing space that is 2 inches × 2 inches in size.

3. In the **Color** palette, select the color that you want to use for the background in the marbling effect.
   A. Click on **Effects/Surface Control/Color Overlay**. The **Color Overlay** box opens.
   B. In the **Using:** pop-up, select **Uniform Color**.
   C. Click on the **Hiding Power** option.
   D. Click on **OK**. The background color that you have chosen fills the drawing space.

4. In the **Color** palette, select the first of the three colors that you want to use for the texture of the marbling.

5. Click on **Effects/Esoterica/Blobs**. The **Blobs** box opens. The **Number of Blobs** value controls how many blobs will be created. The **Minimum Size** value determines the size of the smallest blob. The **Maximum Size** value determines the size of the largest blob. The **Subsample** value determines the number of steps between the smallest and largest blobs. The **Fill Blobs With** pop-up lets you choose the color to be used. The **Seed Number** comes from a random number generator and is changed each time that you open the Blobs box. You can also enter a number here if you like.
   A. Enter **10** for the number of blobs.
   B. Enter a minimum size of **20 pixels**.
   C. Enter a maximum size of **30 pixels**.
   D. Enter a subsample of **8**.
   E. Select **Fill Blobs With: Current Color**.
   F. Click on **OK**. The first set of blobs appears in the drawing space.

6. In the Color palette, select the second of the three colors that you want to use for the texture of the marbling.

7. Click on Effects/Esoterica/Blobs.

   A. Enter 15 for the number of blobs.

   B. Enter a minimum size of 15 pixels.

   C. Enter a maximum size of 25 pixels.

   D. Enter a subsample of 10.

   E. Select Fill Blobs With: Current Color.

   F. Click on OK. The second set of blobs appears in the drawing space.

8. In the Color palette, select the third of the three colors that you want to use for the texture of the marbling.

   A. Enter 20 for the number of blobs.

   B. Enter a minimum size of 10 pixels.

   C. Enter a maximum size of 20 pixels.

   D. Enter a subsample of 15.

   E. Select Fill Blobs With: Current Color.

   F. Click on OK. The third set of blobs appears in the drawing space.

9. Click on Effects/Esoterica/Apply Marbling. The Apply Marbling box opens. Think of marbling as if you were drawing a rake across the drawing that will drag the color along with it. This will help you understand the settings in the Marbling box.

   A. In the Direction: dots area, click on each of the options to see how they run. Select the one that you would like.

   B. The sliders will define the kind of rake that you are using and the path that it will take. Adjust each of these to get the effect that you would like to create.

      1. Spacing determines how many teeth the rake has.

      2. Offset moves the rake perpendicular to the path that it will take. This determines where the teeth will draw through the picture.

      3. Waviness determines how high the waves are.

      4. Wavelength determines the distance between the peaks of waves.

      5. Phase moves the wave in the direction that the rake will be moving. This lets you determine where along its path the rake will begin moving.

      6. Pull determines how much distortion will occur. Lower values create thin and short effects. Higher values create wider and longer effects.

      7. Quality controls how smooth the marbled image is. Lower values create rougher effects. Higher values create smoother effects.

Remember that if you're not sure about some of these settings you can always click on Edit/Undo Apply Marbling after it has been applied and try again.

C. Click on OK. Click on Edit/Undo Apply Marbling.
   1. Reset the sliders to different settings.
   2. Now take a look at the buttons on the right side of the box. These let you add additional steps or rake strokes to the marbling. The sliders that you just set are for step 1 of 1. If you would like to add an additional step, click on the Add Step button. Reset the sliders for the new step. After you have reset them, click on the Replace button to update the current step. You can use the << and >> buttons to move between the different steps of the effect to make changes. Anytime that you make a change in a step, click on the Replace button to update the current step. The Reset button will clear the current slider settings so that you can start from scratch.

D. Create some new marbling effects of your own and try them out. Click on Edit/Undo after each one to remove the effect.

E. If you would like to save a marbling effect, click on the Save button. A box will open where you must name the effect. Give it a name and click on OK.

F. After you have saved a marbling effect you can replay it by clicking on the Load button. This will display a list of marbling effects. There are also some preset marbling effects that you can try out. Select the one that you want and click on OK. Try out some of the preset marbling effects available under the Load button. Click on Edit/Undo after each one to remove the effect.

10. When you have finished experimenting with the marbling, click on the X in the upper right-hand corner of the new drawing space to close it. You do not have to save it unless you want to for some other use.

Auto VanGogh

The Auto Van Gogh effect turns an image into an impressionistic version. It works with the Clone command and the Auto Van Gogh variant of the Artists brush. This effect works in the entire drawing space including any floaters after you have cloned the space.

1. The file proj6c.rif should still be open. If it is not, open it. Deselect any floaters that might be selected.

2. Click on File/Clone to create a clone of the drawing. Notice that an entirely new drawing space has opened that is titled: Clone of proj6c.rif. Click on the Brush in the Tools palette.

3. In the Brushes palette, select the Artists brush and the Auto Van Gogh variant.

4. Open the Color palette. You may need to click on the Min/Max button to reveal the Color Variability scales for H, S, and V.

   A. You can change the H, S, and V sliders to control these scales in the Auto Van Gogh process.

   B. Try settings of 5% for each.

   C. Move the brush across the drawing space to see the effect.

5. Click on Effects/Esoterica/Auto VanGogh. The Auto VanGogh effect will be applied to the entire cloned canvas.

6. Click on the X in the upper right-hand corner of the Clone of proj6c.rif drawing space to close it. Do *not* save it. The old drawing space that was underneath the cloned drawing space will reappear.

Custom Tile

The Custom Tile effect can be applied to a selection, a floater, or the entire image. It translates the image into a series of single color tiles.

1. Select the Hand floater.

2. Click on Effects/Esoterica/Custom Tile. The Custom Tile box opens.

3. In the Using: pop-up, you can select a variety of tiling styles. Select Brick.

4. Use the Brick Width and Brick Height sliders to control the size of the bricks. Set a width of 2 and a height of 5.

5. The Thickness slider controls the size of the grout between the tiles. Set a thickness of 1.

6. Blur Radius mixes more of the tile color into the grout, decreasing the sharpness of definition between the two. Set a blur radius of 4.

7. Blur Passes increases the mixing between the tile color and the grout, decreasing the sharpness of definition even further. Set blur passes of 2.

8. Click on the Color box to reset the grout color.

9. Click on OK to apply the tiling to the image.

10. Save your work as proj6d.rif. You can compare it to exer6d.rif on the CD-ROM.

If you would like to experiment with other methods of applying the effects with which you have already worked, go ahead and use the drawing space and floaters that you have created. You might also want to try out some of the other effects that were not covered in this exercise. Refer to the effects section of the *Painter Users Guide* for instructions.

CLONING AND TRACING

Cloning and tracing are features of Painter that let you work more easily and quickly. They are especially important when you are importing images from other sources such as AutoCAD, 3D Studio MAX, or Poser. Cloning works by taking an image from a source and duplicating it in a destination. The source and destination may be in different documents or in the same one. Cloning method brush variants are one method of bringing up an image from a source into its destination. These brushes "filter" from the source into the destination drawing the image in the style that you chose. Tracing paper is another method to work with a clone. You can draw over the image onto the tracing paper and create a new drawing that is as stylized or detailed as you would like. There are also a number of techniques that will allow you to modify the image during the cloning process rather than making those modifications later. While you are working in a destination, the source must remain open.

Cloning and tracing are easy ways to take a figure from Poser and build a costume rendering on top of it. The figure can be in the background as an anatomical reference and never appear in your final rendering, or you can bring just part of it forward, such as the head, hands, and feet. Similarly, you can bring a 3-D model of a set into Painter from either AutoCAD or 3D Studio MAX and use it to give you a quick reference for perspective and key points on your set. Then you can create your set rendering with or without bringing any of the model into the rendering. You could then also bring a costume rendering of a figure into the set rendering as a floater and have a combined set and costume rendering. The lighting options of both 3D Studio MAX and Poser can serve as guides to your use of shadow and color in the Painter rendering as well. Because Painter works so much like traditional painting and rendering, you will be using all of the skills that you have worked to develop as an artist, but many other options that might have been more difficult or time-consuming on a real canvas will be available to you on the computer as well.

Cloning is not the same as copying or moving a floater from one file into another. It is a little more complicated to understand but offers many more options than either of those two techniques. The steps in the cloning and tracing process are outlined in the following exercise.

Exercise No. 7: Working with Cloning and Tracing—Working with Files from Other Programs

This exercise will show you some of the basics of cloning, tracing, and how to go about using these techniques to create renderings in combination with elements brought in from AutoCAD, 3D Studio MAX, Poser, and other programs.

Cloning an Image and Using Tracing Paper

1. Open the Tools, Brushes, Art Materials, and Controls palettes if they are not already open.
2. Click on File/Open and open the file Exer7.tif from the CD-ROM that accompanies this book. This is a rendering of a 3-D model done in 3D Studio MAX and then saved as a .tif file. The basic technique that you are about to go through would also work for a figure exported from Poser in a .tif format, a print of a set model from AutoCAD that had been scanned into a file, a digital photograph of an actor, or any other image as long as it is in one of the formats that Painter will accept.
3. Clone the image:
    A. Click on File/Clone.
    B. Another drawing space of the same size appears on top of the previous one. The new one is titled Clone of Exer7.tif.
4. Lay a sheet of tracing paper on top of the cloned image:
    A. Click on Select/All.
    B. Hit the Backspace/Delete key to clear the canvas.
    C. Click on Canvas/Tracing Paper.
    D. A 50 percent ghost of the image appears under the tracing paper.
5. Save the image as a new file in .rif format. This will allow you to work on the rendering at your leisure, come back to it at a later time, and still have all of the options of Painter such as floaters, shapes, etc. in full working order. If you saved the file in another format at this point, you would lose any special Painter techniques or options whenever you closed the file. After you have finished your rendering, you can save it in whatever format you would like for use in other programs.
    A. Click on File/Save As. The Save Image As box opens.
    B. Give it a name in the File Name: area followed by .rif: name it proj7.rif.
    C. Select RIFF Files in the Save as Type: area.
    D. Choose the location that you want to save it to on your hard drive or floppy disk in the Save In: area.
    E. Click on Save.

Working with the Cloning Brushes on Tracing Paper

Working with the clone on tracing paper allows you to use not just the brushes and tools that you have already learned about in Painter but also all of the cloning brushes that you are about to discover. The cloning brushes let you bring up part or all of the image underneath the tracing paper onto the paper itself. There are also specialized cloning brushes that let you transfer the underneath image through a "filter" of techniques. Anything that you can do in a regular Painter drawing space can also be done when you are working on tracing paper such as using the wet layer for watercolors, creating a paper texture, using the Paper palette, creating selections, floaters, and shapes, etc.

1. Drawing over the image with a regular brush:
   A. Click on **Brush** on the **Tools** palette.
   B. Select a brush in the **Brushes** palette.
   C. Select a color in the **Color** palette.
   D. Draw a stroke on the tracing paper. The stroke that you drew appears in the drawing space in 50 percent opacity. To see what you have drawn in 100 percent opacity without the underneath image, turn off the tracing paper by clicking on the **Tracing Paper** button on the border of the drawing space. It is the button outlined in brown just underneath the upper right-hand corner of the blue bar at the top of the border. Click on it again, and the image underneath the tracing paper will reappear. This lets you quickly switch from a view with the underneath image to a view without the underneath image. You can also make this switch using the keyboard by hitting the **Ctrl+T/Command+T** keys.
   E. You can draw over the top of the image using whatever brushes and other Painter techniques that you would like. If you were creating a costume rendering over a Poser image, for example, you could use the Poser figure as a guide without it appearing in your rendering. You might also want to bring just parts of the image such as the head or hands into the rendering. This is where the cloning brushes come into use. For a set or lighting rendering, you could also bring just the parts of the image underneath that you want up onto the tracing paper using the cloning brushes.

2. Using the cloning brushes: The cloning brushes bring the underneath area onto the tracing paper.
   A. The **Straight Cloner** gives you the exact image that is underneath the tracing paper.
      1. Click on **Brush** on the **Tools** palette.
      2. Select the **Cloners** brush type in the **Brushes** palette and the **Straight Cloner** variant.
      3. Choose the size, opacity, and grain that you would like in the **Controls** palette.
      4. Stroke over the top of the part of the image that you want to bring up such as a glass on the table.
         a. Remember that you can zoom in to the part of the figure that you are working on using the **Magnifier** on the Tools palette and then zoom back using the **Zoom Level** pop-up in the Controls palette.

b. The Grabber tool lets you move the canvas around inside the drawing space to get the view that you would like at the zoom level you have chosen.

c. Click on the Tracing Paper button on the border of the drawing space to check the work that you have done without the image underneath and use the Edit/Undo command to erase mistakes. You can also use the eraser brushes to remove, bleach, etc. strokes that you make with the cloning brushes.

B. The Soft Cloner variant gives you a lower opacity and soft edges in cloning.

1. Select the Cloners brush type and the Soft Cloner variant.

2. Choose the size, opacity, and grain that you would like in the Controls palette.

3. Stroke over the top of the part of the image that you would like to bring up such as the light over the table.

C. Try out the other variants on the Cloners brush such as the Chalk Cloner, Driving Rain Cloner, Van Gogh Cloner, etc. After trying out each one, remove the strokes that you made using the Edit/Undo command.

3. Using the Auto Clone feature: You can select an area of the canvas or use the Auto Clone feature on the entire canvas. Auto Clone fills the area automatically.

A. Use the Magnifier to zoom down to one of the bottles on the table.

B. Click on the Lasso tool on the Tools palette. You can use any of the selection tools for this purpose. If you do not select an area, Auto Clone will fill the entire canvas.

C. Select the bottle that you have zoomed down to by drawing a line around it with the Lasso tool.

D. Choose a cloning brush in the Brushes palette such as Straight Cloner.

E. Click on Effects/Esoterica/Auto Clone. The Auto Cloner will fill the selected area with the underneath image in a series of random strokes. Let it go through several strokes. It continues to apply paint to the area until you tell it to stop. Click anywhere in the drawing space to stop the Auto Clone process. Some cloning brushes such as Felt Pen Cloner can take the area all the way to black if you don't stop the Auto Clone process soon enough.

F. Click on Select/None to deselect the area that you just filled.

4. Turning any brush into a cloning brush: Any brush can be turned into a cloning brush by clicking on the Clone Color option in the Color palette.

A. Click on Brush on the Tools palette.

B. Select a brush type and variant in the Brushes palette.

     C. Click on the box next to **Clone Color** in the **Color** palette.

     D. Adjust the size, opacity, and grain in the Controls Palette.

     E. Make a stroke with the brush in the drawing space.

     F. Use the **Edit/Undo** command to remove the stroke.

     G. Try out several other brush types and variants and then use the **Edit/Undo** command after each one to remove the strokes.

     H. Remove the **X** from the Clone Color box.

5. Closing and reopening a cloned document and its source: Remember that for you to clone, both the destination and the source must be open. If you want to stop work in the middle of the cloning process you will need to follow these procedures to begin work again. This is only possible if the document in which you are working—the destination—has been saved as a .rif file.

     A. Save **Proj7.rif** by clicking on **File/Save**.

     B. Close **Proj7.rif** by clicking on the X in the upper right-hand corner of its border.

     C. Close **Exer7.tif** by clicking on the X in the upper right-hand corner of its border.

6. Now reopen the source and destination documents so that you can work in the destination again:

     A. Click on **File/Open** and open the source: **exer7.tif**.

     B. Click on **File/Open** and open the destination: **proj7.rif**.

     C. Designate the clone source: Click on **File/Clone Source/Exer7.tif**.

     D. Click on the **Tracing Paper** button on the Proj7.rif border to see the clone source underneath the tracing paper.

Note: There is a peculiarity in Painter that you have to watch out for at this point. If a cloning brush is selected in the Brushes palette when you try to turn on the tracing paper, you may not be able to see the clone source underneath the tracing paper. You will have to select a brush other than a cloning brush. Then you will be able to turn on the tracing paper. After you have turned on the tracing paper, you can select a cloning brush and continue cloning.

7. Point-to-point cloning: Cloning within and between documents: You can use cloning without tracing paper. So far in this exercise you have been using it with tracing paper because this is a technique that can be extremely helpful when creating renderings in files from other sources such as 3D Studio MAX, AutoCAD, and Poser. However, you can also clone parts of a drawing to another area of the same drawing and clone parts of a drawing into a different drawing.

A. Close Proj7.rif by clicking on the X in the upper right-hand corner of its border.

B. Now let's clone the bottle in Exer7.tif to create another bottle.
1. Use the **Magnifier** to zoom in to the tabletop.
2. Click on **Brush** on the Tools palette and choose a cloning brush such as **Straight Cloner**.
3. In the **Controls** palette, take the size down to about **2 pixels**.
4. Holding down the **Shift/Control** key, click at a point on the bottom of the bottle. This becomes the source point for the cloning.
5. Release the **Shift/Control** key and move the brush to where you want to clone the bottle. Start drawing, and the bottle will appear in the new area.

   Warning: When you use this method, you have to control your brush strokes carefully because you will also get the area around the bottle if you don't. With this method you could clone the entire picture if you kept stroking with the brush. Also notice that as you click and drag with the brush, a + appears over in the area of the source bottle. You can use this + to help guide you in the cloning process. Work carefully and use the **Undo** command if you make a mistake.

C. Turn off the point-to-point cloning by selecting a brush other than a cloning brush.

D. Cloning from one document into another: You can also use point-to-point cloning for cloning between documents.
1. Click on the **Magnifier** and use the **Zoom Level** pop-up in the **Controls** palette to go back to **100%**.
2. Center the image using the **Grabber** tool.
3. Click on **File/Open** and open the file **Clonefig.tif** from the CD-ROM that accompanies this book. This is an image of a male figure that was created in and exported from Poser. You are going to clone this figure into the Exer7.tif drawing.
4. Click on **Brush** on the Tools palette and select the **Straight Cloner** variant of the Cloners brush.
5. In the **Controls** palette, change the size to around **2 to 3 pixels**.
6. Hold down the **Shift/Control** key.
7. Select the source point in the source document by clicking at the top of the figure's head.
8. Release the **Shift/Control** key.
9. Click on the grey bar on the top of the Exer7.tif drawing space. It will turn blue.

10. Move the cursor to the point in the drawing where you want to create the figure, and start drawing. The figure will appear. You'll also notice that it is almost impossible to get just the figure into the drawing and not also get the blue background. Try to bring the figure into the drawing in less than five strokes so that you can undo the strokes to remove the figure. Cloning can be a useful technique, but often in Painter there can be better ways to do things. Next we'll bring the Poser figure into the 3D Studio MAX drawing using a method other than cloning.

11. Click on Edit/Undo to remove the figure from the drawing. If it took you more than five strokes to get the figure into the drawing you will not be able to undo the whole figure. If this is the case, you should close Exer7.tif without saving it. Then open it again before proceeding to the next section.

12. Select a brush other than a cloner brush to escape from point-to-point cloning.

Moving Parts of Drawings Between Drawings

In this part of the exercise you will move the figure from the Poser drawing into the 3D Studio MAX drawing using Select, Copy, and Paste commands. This offers some advantages over the cloning method outlined above but also some disadvantages. Think about the kinds of places where you might want to use point-to-point cloning and the kinds of places where you might want to use the method in the next section of the exercise.

1. Open the file Clonefig.tif from the Painter folder of the CD-ROM.

2. You may need to move the Exer7.tif drawing space to the side. You will need access to both drawing spaces and the Controls and Tools palettes.

3. With the Exer7.tif drawing space active, click on the Magic Wand selection tool on the Tools palette.

4. In the Controls palette, set Tolerance at 1 and Feather at 0 and make sure there is no X in the Anti-Alias box.

5. Click in the light blue background area of the Clonefig.tif drawing space to select it.

6. Click on Select/Invert.

7. Click on Edit/Copy.

8. Click on the grey bar at the top of the Exer7.tif drawing space to activate that drawing space. The bar should turn blue.

9. Click on Edit/Paste/Normal. The figure will appear in the drawing space as a floater. You can use the Floater Selector to move it around in the drawing space to where you would like it to be placed. Move it to that location, but do not drop it to the canvas yet.

10. You will notice that you still have a little bit of the blue background around the figure. Use the Magnifier tool to zoom in to just the head of the figure.

11. Now you'll do some touch-up work.

12. Use the Dropper tool to select the color next to the figure's head and right beside the little bit of blue background in the drawing space. You are going to use this color to cover the small bit of blue background around that part of the figure that is the same color as the color you selected. You will need to have the floater still selected to paint on the floater.

13. Select the Brush tool and the Single Pixel Scribbler variant of pencil. Change the brush method to Cover. Change the Opacity to 100% in the Controls palette.

14. Use the Single Pixel Scribbler to cover the blue background with the color next to it on the background.

15. When you get to an area of a different background color, you will have to select a new color with the Dropper tool and then use that with the Single Pixel Scribbler until you have gone completely around the figure.

16. Click outside of the figure with the Floater Adjuster to deselect it.

17. Save your work as Proj7b.tif. Compare it to Exer7b.tif on the CD-ROM.

You could use basically this same touch-up method to cover your mistakes in point-to-point cloning as well, except that you would not be working in a floater. No matter which method you use you will have to do some touch-up work, but it is still quicker than having to draw the whole figure into the background from scratch.

USING LIBRARIES AND MOVERS

A library is a collection of tools, materials, brushes, etc. that can be saved and recalled as you have need of it. Painter comes with already created libraries for paper textures, patterns, gradations, weaves, brushes, brush looks, nozzles, floaters, selections, lighting, and scripts. You can add to these libraries at any time you would like. The particular process for adding to each library will vary with the type of library. Check the section on the particular resource—paper, weave, etc.—for information on how it is done. You can also create your own new libraries that contain collections that you have created or often use together.

Movers are used to move tools, textures, etc. from one library to another as well as to create new libraries. While you may create as many libraries as you want, only one library of a particular type may be loaded at a time. Large libraries, however, occupy a lot of RAM and can actually slow down the operation of commands in Painter. Careful thought should be given to the creation and organization of libraries after you have become more familiar with your own particular methods of working in Painter. Striking the proper balance between a large number of small libraries and a small number of large libraries will help you to work more efficiently and at top program speed. MetaCreations' Web site also has additional libraries that you can download from *http://www.metacreations.com/.* You can even launch your Web browser directly from Painter 5 by clicking on Help/Fractal Design Online or Help/MetaCreations Online—depending upon the date of purchase—on the pull down menu.

The following exercise will take you through the basic techniques of working with libraries and movers. Except for the creation of new resources, all libraries and movers work alike.

Exercise No. 8: Working with Libraries and Movers

In this exercise you will create a new weave, create a new weave library, move the new weave into the new weave library, copy an item between libraries, delete an item from a library, change the name of an item in a library, and delete a library.

Creating a New Weave

The method for creating a new item will vary with the type of item such as a pattern, a brush, etc., but it will always immediately be placed in the library for that type of item that is open at the time.

1. Click on the Weave icon on the Art Materials palette to open the Weave palette.

2. Select the Standard weave from the Weave pop-up.

3. Open the Weave Parameters section of the Weave palette by clicking on the drawer pushbar or on the Min/Max button. This section will display an enlarged sample of the weave along with a Fiber Type box and sliders for the horizontal scale, vertical scale, and the thickness.

4. Click on Weave/Edit Weave on the pull down menu on the Art Materials palette. This opens the Edit Weave box.

    A. In the Tieup box in the upper right-hand section of the Edit Weave box, click on the squares to create a new weave. Clicking on a square will change its color.

    B. When you have a new weave that you like, click on OK.

5. The new weave is displayed in the Weave Parameters section of the Weave palette.

6. You can change the fiber type from open to tight by clicking in the Fiber Type box.

7. You can change the horizontal scale, vertical scale, and thickness by working with the appropriate sliders.

8. When you have the new weave the way that you want, save it by clicking on Weave/Save Weave on the Art Materials pull down menu.

   A. The Save Weave box opens. You can type a new name in the space provided. In this case use Test1.

   B. Click on OK.

9. You have just created a new weave and added it to the existing and already loaded weave library.

Creating a New Library

1. Click on Weave/Weave Mover on the Art Materials palette pull down menu. This opens the Weave Mover.

2. Click on the New button. The New Weave Library box opens.

3. You can now give the new library a name that ends with the .wev extension for a weave library in the File Name: area. For this exercise, call it Weave2.wev.

4. Select a location for the new library in the Save In: sections. For now it doesn't matter where you save it as long as you remember the location so that you can delete it later in this exercise. Go ahead and use the Tutorial folder, which is usually the default here unless someone else has already created a weave library and saved it elsewhere.

5. Save the new library by clicking on the Save button.

6. You are returned to the Weave Mover box. The right-hand section will now be titled Weave2.wev and represents the new library that you created. Right now it is empty. The next step is to move things over from other libraries. The left-hand section, titled PAINTER.SET, is the currently loaded weave library.

Moving Items Between Libraries

1. To move items between libraries, you must have the library that you want to move an item from on one side of the mover and the library that you want to move an item to on the other side of the mover. If they are not there, you can click on the Close button under the library that you want to close. An Open button will replace the Close button. Click on it to open the Open Weave Library File box and select the library that you desire.

For now, though, you should have the two available weave libraries already open.

2. In the PAINTER.SET library on the left, locate the new weave that you created: Test1. Scroll the scroll bar up and down until you think that you see the icon for the new weave. Click on that icon. The name of the weave will appear in the middle under Current Weave:. When you have the name Test1 in the middle under Current Weave:, you have selected that weave.

3. Copy the weave into the new library by clicking on its icon and dragging it into the new library.

Renaming an Item in a Library

1. Select the Test1 weave in the Weave2.wev library by clicking on it. It will be outlined in red and its name will appear under Current Weave: in the middle of the Weave Mover.

2. Click on the Change Name button in the Weave Mover.

3. The Change Weave Name box opens.

  A. Change the name of the weave to Test2.

  B. Click on OK.

Deleting an Item from a Library

1. Click on the icon for the Test2 weave in the Weave2.WEV library.

2. Its name will appear in the middle under Current Weave:.

3. Click on the Delete button.

4. If you do not want to save the Test1 weave in the PAINTER.SET library, delete it using the same method.

Deleting a Library

To delete a library, you must know the name of the library and where it is located on your hard drive. In a Mac, you delete the file from the desktop. In Windows, you must use Windows Explorer or My Computer to locate the file and then delete it. *Be very careful not to delete any of the Painter default libraries.* The program needs them for start-up.

PRINTING IN PAINTER

Painter can be set up to print in a variety of ways on commercial printers as well as standard printers. If you are using one of the standard printers that are readily available from HP, Canon, etc. then setting up for printing from Painter will be very simple. All of the following instructions assume that your printer is already connected to the computer, has had its drivers installed, and is ready to print.

1. Select the drawing space for the image that you want to print if there is more than one image open on the screen.

2. Click on File/Print Setup or File/Page Setup. The Setup box opens. This is where you will be making some basic choices about how you want the print to look. There could be several different options available here depending upon the particular type of printer that you are using.

   A. Name: Be sure that the name of the printer that you are using is selected here.

   B. Orientation: Here you can decide whether you want the paper oriented vertically—Portrait—or horizontally—Landscape.

   C. Paper Size: Select the proper size for the paper you will be using here.

   D. Source: If your printer has more than one paper feed device, select the one that you are using here.

   E. Other options: There could be a number of different options besides the ones given above depending upon the printer that you are using. You could have a choice of color versus black and white printing, printing separations, etc. Look over the options available carefully and try to select the ones that apply. When in doubt it is usually safer the first time to go with the default options preselected by the program.

3. Click on OK. The box will close.

4. Click on File/Print. The Print dialogue box opens. Now there are a different set of options available to you. These will once again vary with the particular printer that you are using, but will usually include at least the following:

   A. Print Type:

      1. GDI Printing/Color Quickdraw: This is the option that you would select for most color jet-type printers such as an HP DeskJet, an OfficeJet, a Canon BubbleJet, an Epson Stylus, etc. These are examples of nonpostscript printers. They will not do color separations. These are the most common type of printers available today.

      2. Color Postscript: Color postscript printers are usually found in commercial establishments. Examples would be a QMS ColorScript or a Tektronix color thermal printer.

      3. Separation: If you have a color postscript printer, you can choose this option to do a separation in which it will print out four separate pages: one each for cyan, magenta, yellow, and black.

      4. B & W Postscript: Check this option to print to a black and white postscript printer such as a laser printer.

   B. Number of Copies: Enter the number of copies that you want to print in this box.

    C. Other options: Depending upon the printer type, there may be other options available. Select the ones that seem to apply to what you are trying to do, and when in doubt, go with the default.

5. Click on **OK**. The program will send the printing information to your printer.

IMPORTING AND EXPORTING WITH PAINTER

Painter can be used in a variety of ways with the other programs in this book and its companion. While working through the exercises, you already learned about one of the most useful applications of Painter, namely creating your own style of renderings using tracing paper over the top of a cloned file from Poser, 3D Studio MAX, or AutoCAD. This will allow you to do a set rendering using a printout from AutoCAD that has been scanned into a file, a set rendering using a rendering file from 3D Studio MAX, a costume rendering using a Poser rendering that has been exported, and a costume or set rendering using a file from a digital camera. You may also begin working from any sketch, drawing, or other material that has been scanned into a file. A file from any of these sources must be capable of being opened in Painter. The following four file types can all be opened in Painter. They will be the ones that you will work with most of the time when using the other programs in this volume and the AutoCAD volume.

Tiff File (*.tif): This file type can be created with most scanners. It can be exported from Poser. It can be created as a rendering file in 3D Studio MAX. It can be created in most other drawing programs such a Corel8, Adobe Illustrator, Adobe Photoshop, etc. This format is not used in most digital cameras.

Bitmap File (*.bmp): This file type can be created with some scanners. It can be exported from Poser. It can be created as a rendering file in 3D Studio MAX. It can be created in some drawing programs. This format is not used in most digital cameras.

JPEG File (*.jpg): This file type can be created with many scanners. It can be created as a rendering file in 3D Studio MAX. It is the most common format used in digital cameras. It can be created in most drawing programs. It cannot be exported from Poser.

Targa File (*.tga): This file type can be created with many scanners. It is used as a texture or bitmap file in 3D Studio MAX. It can be created in most drawing programs. This format is not used in most digital cameras.

    Painter can also be used for other purposes besides creating renderings. You can create and/or modify bump and texture maps for Poser by using

Painter with .tif or .bmp files. You can create and/or modify texture and bitmaps for 3D Studio MAX using Painter with .tif or .tga files. Look in the importing and exporting section for each of the other programs in this book for specific instructions on how to use Painter files in that particular program.

You can take a number of different file types that you acquire from the World Wide Web, digital cameras, sources such as Judy Juracek's *Surfaces* book, etc. and convert them into file types that can be used in the other programs with or without modifications. If, for example, you have a texture that you want to use in 3D Studio MAX that you have located on a building or fabric somewhere, you could photograph it with a digital camera or photograph it using a regular camera and then scan that photo. Once it has been converted into a file that can be opened in Painter, that file can be modified using Painter to give you the exact look that you want and saved as a different file type that could be used as a texture in 3D Studio MAX or Poser. The following is a list of file types that can be opened and saved in Painter. You can use Painter to convert from one of these file types to any of the others. You could, for example, convert a digital photograph of a texture from .jpg format to .tif format.

Painter File Types

.rif	.gif
.tif	.jpg
.psd	.pct
.bmp	.frm
.pcx	.pyr
.tga	.avi

Importing a File into Painter

Files don't have to be "imported" into Painter in the way that they do in many of the other programs in this book. They can simply be opened by clicking on File/Open and then locating the file in the Look In: section of the Select Image box, as long as they are in one of the formats given above.

Exporting a File from Painter

Once again, files do not have to be "exported" from Painter. You simply use the File/Save As command to save the file as a particular type by selecting the format that you want in the Save As Type: section of the Save Image As box. There is, however, one file type that has to be exported from Painter: an Adobe Illustrator file. You can use the Export command to save a shape as an Adobe Illustrator file. This only works with shapes, however, not with any other part of an image.

Using Advanced Techniques

As with all of the other chapters, this chapter is intended as an introduction to Painter, not as the definitive work on every aspect of the program's use. There are a number of other techniques available in Painter that you might find worth exploring. The use of mosaics and the image hose was covered as a simple case. There are a large number of further options available using each of these techniques. The digital video and animation techniques available with Painter have not even been touched on and may be of interest to you as well. Scripts are another area that can be worth exploring. Scripts will let you overcome the five-step undo limit of Painter by literally recording every step of a detailed drawing process. These scripts can then be recorded, played back using different brushes and art materials to create different effects, and edited to save you a good deal of time in reproducing a complex technique. I also highly recommend dropping by MetaCreations' Web site at *http://www.metacreations.com/products/painter/resources*, where you can expand Painter's libraries, download new plug-ins, and pick up lots of advanced tips on using the program.

Painter 5.5

If you have the latest upgrade on Painter, you will find that everything described in this book works exactly the same way for it as it does for Painter 5.0. Painter 5.5, or the "Web Edition," as it is described, has a number of options that make Painter easier to use for creating images for the Web. If you are interested in working on Web images, the following techniques would be worthwhile for you to investigate:

Dynamic Text: The dynamic text options in Painter 5.5 are certainly worth exploring for theatrical applications. With dynamic text, you can add text to your images and then much more easily edit that text than text in earlier versions.

Slicing Images and Rollovers: Image slicing lets you divide a larger image into smaller parts and write the HTML necessary for creating clickable navigation maps. JavaScript rollover effects also are based on image slicing to define the rollover area.

Image Mapping: An image map is a feature of HTML that allows the user to jump to different locations by clicking on parts of a larger image.

Web Backgrounds: Painter 5.5 lets you create seamless, tiled background effects much more easily than you could with earlier editions. This is another area that you may find valuable with theatrical applications.

Web Buttons: Creating buttons for Web pages is very simple with this version.

Transparent .gifs: Creating .gif files with transparent backgrounds is now possible in Painter. This feature was not available in earlier versions.

Web Colors and Brushes: The upgrade includes a World Wide Web color set option and a group of new brushes that are especially useful for Web work.

APPENDIX A

INTEGRATION: SHARING, MOVING, IMPORTING, AND EXPORTING PROGRAM FILES

This is one of the most important sections of these two volumes. All of the information contained in this section is also found in a variety of locations in the two volumes of this work, but in this Appendix, I have gathered all the instructions for sharing, moving, importing, and exporting files together in one location for easier reference. Here is the basic information that you will need to integrate the four programs: what the different file types are and how they work, how to export the different file types from the programs involved, and how to import them into the other programs. This is where you will start learning how to go about sharing the files between programs and thus also with your fellow designers and technicians. Most of this information is also included in the text on the specific programs, but it is summarized in this section for easier access.

As I stated at the beginning of this volume, programmers have yet to devote the time and effort that it would take to arrive at the one program that will do everything that we in the theatre would desire on a completely integrated basis. Until that time arrives we will have to make the best use possible of the already available programs. These two volumes in general and this section in particular were written toward that end: to show you how to integrate these four programs as completely as you can.

File Types

The first step in the integration process is understanding the different file types that are involved in the four programs. Before you can move a file from one program to another, you need to know whether it is compatible and what are some of its more important characteristics. This is a listing of all of the file types that can be created by the programs, detailing which are compatible with which other programs and describing some of their major characteristics.

AutoCAD File Types and Extensions

AutoCAD Internal Files

These file types are used by AutoCAD in creating its drawings. Some of them are usable in other programs as well.

DWG File (*.dwg): This is the basic AutoCAD drawing format. The same extension is used for all three releases, but R14 files cannot be read by R12 or R13. R13 files can be read by R14, but not by R12. R12 files can be read by both R13 and R14. R14, however, can save files in either an R12 or R13 format. 3D Studio MAX claims to be able to read a .dwg file, but unless you are using R14, I don't recommend trying to use one in 3D Studio MAX. DXF files work much better.

Drawing Template File (*.dwt): This file type is only used in R14. It is used internally to save a template that can be used to set up later drawings.

AutoCAD Export and Import Files

These file types can be used as 3-D files in other programs.

DXF File (*.dxf): This is a drawing export file. This type is used by AutoCAD and other programs as a general export format. These files can be exported from all releases. They can be opened in R14 or imported into R12 and R13. They can be imported in to 3D Studio MAX. They can be imported into Poser as props.

3D Studio Mesh File (*.3ds): This file type can be exported only from AutoCAD R14. It can be imported into 3D Studio MAX or Poser. It can be imported into AutoCAD R13. It can be inserted into AutoCAD R14.

AutoCAD Rendering Files

These file types are 2-D file types that you can get from AutoCAD. They can be used in Painter and many other drawing programs. Some of them can also be used as texture or bitmap files in 3D Studio MAX and Poser.

TIFF Image File (*.tif): This is a popular graphics file format with commercial printers. These files have a large file size, but excellent detail. They can be created in all releases of AutoCAD. They can be read in Painter and Adobe Photoshop. They can be used as texture files in 3D Studio MAX and Poser. They can be used as background files in Poser.

GIF File (*.gif): This is the most common graphic file type used on the World Wide Web. These files are compact in size. They can be created in all releases of AutoCAD. They cannot be opened in Photoshop, but they can be created there. GIF files can be opened in Painter, and other file types can be saved as GIF files.

Targa Image File (*.tga): Originally developed for video, this is a widely used commercial graphics file type. These are relatively large files, but they have good detail. They can be created in all releases of AutoCAD. They can be created in Painter, but not in Adobe Photoshop. Other file types can be converted to this type in Painter.

BMP Image File (*.bmp): This file type is often referred to as a "bitmap" file. A BMP file is a type of graphic file used for display on computer monitors. Most of the icons that you see on your computer screen are BMP files. BMP files are large in size. They can be created in all releases of AutoCAD. They can be used as background files in Poser.

Encapsulated Postscript File (*.eps, *.ps): Used by many commercial printers, this file type cannot be opened in Painter, but it can be opened in Adobe Photoshop. It cannot be read in Poser or 3D Studio MAX. It can be exported from all releases of AutoCAD.

3D STUDIO MAX FILE TYPES AND EXTENSIONS

3D Studio MAX Internal Files

This file type is what is created when you save or save as in the program.

MAX File (*.max): 3D Studio MAX uses this file type to create its 3-D scenes. However, this type cannot be used in any other of the four programs in this volume.

3D Studio MAX Export Files

These are the file types that you can use to export 3-D objects or scenes to AutoCAD for making technical drawings or to Poser to be used as props.

3D Studio Mesh File (*.3ds): This file type can be exported from 3D Studio MAX. It can be inserted into AutoCAD R14 or imported into AutoCAD R13. It cannot be used in AutoCAD R12. It can be imported into Poser as a prop.

DWG File (*.dwg): This is the standard AutoCAD drawing format. It can be exported from 3D Studio MAX and used in AutoCAD R12, R13, and R14.

DXF File (*.dxf): This is an export format that is used by many programs besides AutoCAD and 3D Studio MAX. It can be opened in AutoCAD R14. It can be imported into AutoCAD R12 and R13. It can be imported into Poser as a prop.

3D Studio MAX Texture and Bitmap Files

These are the file types that can be used by 3D Studio MAX as materials, textures, and bitmaps after being brought in through the Material/Map Browser.

TIFF Image File (*.tif): A popular graphics file format with commercial printers, this type has a large file size, but excellent detail. These files can be created in Painter and Adobe Photoshop. They can be created in AutoCAD. They can be created with many scanners. Other file types can be converted to this type in Painter.

Targa Image File (*.tga): Originally developed for video, this is a widely used commercial graphics file type. These are relatively large files, but they have good detail. They can be created in Painter, but not in Adobe Photoshop. They can be created in AutoCAD. Other file types can be converted to this type in Painter.

JPEG File (*.jpg): This is a widely used compact graphic format. It can be created in Painter, Adobe Photoshop, and many other graphic programs. It is the most popular format used in digital cameras. Other file types can be converted to this type in Painter.

GIF File (*.gif): This is the most common graphic file type used on the World Wide Web. These files are compact in size. They cannot be opened in Photoshop, but they can be created there. They can be created in AutoCAD. GIF files can be opened in Painter and other file types can be saved as GIF files.

RLA File (*.rla): This format lets you include separate channels for different elements of the graphics. The files cannot be opened in Painter or Adobe Photoshop.

AutoDesk Flic Image File (*.flc, *.fli, *.cel): This file type is used by AutoDesk for several of its animator programs. Unless you have one of these programs you will probably not want to use this file type.

Image File List File (*.ifl): IFL files are actually text files that are a list of image files. They can be used in animation to switch or change the texture, bitmap, etc. on an object during the course of the animation. This can create such effects as changing the color of the surface of an object.

3D Studio MAX Rendering Files

These are file types that can be created in 3D Studio MAX to save the renderings of scenes. Do not confuse these file types with the object file types that are used in 3D Studio MAX to save objects or whole 3-D scenes such as .max, .dxf, .dwg, or .3ds.

JPEG File (*.jpg): This is a widely used compact graphic format. These files can be opened in Painter, Adobe Photoshop, and many other graphic programs.

This is a good choice for exporting a file to Painter or another graphics program. These files cannot be used in Poser.

TIFF Image File (*.tif): A popular graphics file format with commercial printers, this type has a large file size, but excellent detail. These files can be opened in Painter and Adobe Photoshop. They can be used as a background file in Poser.

BMP Image File (*.bmp): This file type is often referred to as a "bitmap" file. Do not confuse this use of the term with the way that 3D Studio MAX uses the term *bitmap* to refer to any file type that can be applied to an object as a texture. A BMP file is a type of graphic file used for display on computer monitors. Most of the icons that you see on your computer screen are BMP files. BMP files are large in size. They can be opened in Painter, but not in Adobe Photoshop. They can be used as background files in Poser.

Targa Image File (*.tga): Originally developed for video, this is a widely used commercial graphics file type. These are relatively large files, but they have good detail. They can be opened in Painter, but not in Adobe Photoshop. They cannot be used in Poser.

AVI File (*. avi): This is one of the most common file types used in animation viewers. If you are creating an animation, this is the file type you will most likely use. Single AVI files can also be opened in Painter, but not in Adobe Photoshop.

AutoDesk Flic Image File (*.flc, *.fli, *.cel): AutoDesk uses this file type for several of its animator programs. Unless you have one of these programs you will probably not want to use this file type.

Encapsulated Postscript File (*.eps, *.ps): This file type is used by many commercial printers. This type cannot be opened in Painter, but it can be opened in Adobe Photoshop.

PNG Image File (*.png): This is a compact graphics file type that is intended to supplant the GIF file type. So far it has not found widespread use in spite of its advantages. These files cannot be opened in Painter, Adobe Photoshop, or many other graphics programs.

RLA Image File (*.rla): This format lets you include separate channels for different elements of the graphics. It cannot be opened in Painter or Adobe Photoshop.

PAINTER FILE TYPES AND EXTENSIONS

These are file types that can be created in Painter or brought into Painter from other sources.

RIFF File (*.rif): RIFF files are exclusive to Painter. If you save a file as a RIFF file you will not be able to use it in any of the other programs in this book and its companion. If, however, you are going to use it just in Painter or you are going to store it on a floppy disk there are a number of advantages to using a RIFF file. It is a highly detailed file type, but still compact. If you need to save space it might be a good idea to save the file as a RIFF file and then convert it to another file type in Painter before you use it in another program. If you are just going to be using the file in Painter then this would be an excellent choice for the file type. There are a number of special techniques used in Painter such as Floaters that will only be saved if the file is saved as a RIFF file.

TIFF File (*.tif): TIFF files are large, detailed files that can be imported into a wide variety of other programs. TIFF files can be imported into Poser for use as backgrounds, bump maps, and texture maps. They can also be used in 3D Studio MAX as textures and bitmaps. TIFF files can be created from renderings in 3D Studio MAX. TIFF files can also be created in AutoCAD. They can be opened in Adobe Photoshop as well. This format is not used in most digital cameras. It is a format that is often used in scanners. Scanned files may first appear in this format and then be converted to other formats in Painter. TIFF files can be opened in Painter and other files can be saved as TIFF files.

JPEG File (*.jpg): This graphic file type is often used on the World Wide Web. These files are compact in size. They can be used as textures or bitmaps in 3D Studio MAX. They can be created as rendering files from 3D Studio MAX. They cannot be used in Poser. They can be opened in Photoshop. They can be created with some scanners. This is the most common format used in digital cameras. JPEG files can be opened in Painter and other files can be saved as JPEG files.

Targa File (*.tga): This is another relatively large file type that is used in many graphics programs. These files can be used as textures or bitmaps in 3D Studio MAX. They can be created as rendering files in 3D Studio MAX. They can be created in AutoCAD. They cannot be used in Poser. They can be opened in Photoshop. They can be created with some scanners. This format is not used in digital cameras. Targa files can be opened in Painter and other files can be saved as Targa files.

Bitmap File (*.bmp): This is a large file type often used on computer screen graphics. These files can be used as backgrounds, bump maps, and texture maps in Poser, but they cannot be used in 3D Studio MAX. They can be created as rendering files from 3D Studio MAX. They can be exported from AutoCAD R13 or R14 and can be created by using the Tools/Save Image pull down menu in AutoCAD R14. They cannot be opened in Photoshop. They can be created with some scanners. This format is not used in digital cameras. Bitmap files can be opened in Painter and other files can be saved as Bitmap files.

Video for Windows File (*.avi): This is one of the most common file types used in animation viewers. If you are creating an animation, this is the file type you will most likely use. These file can be created as rendering files in 3D Studio MAX. Single AVI files can also be opened in Painter, but not in Adobe Photoshop. Other file types cannot be saved as AVI files by Painter.

PICT File (*.pct): This file type is common to Macs. These files can be opened in Adobe Photoshop, but they cannot be used in Poser or 3D Studio MAX. PICT files can be opened in Painter and other files can be saved as PICT files.

Photoshop File (*.psd): This is an Adobe Photoshop file type. These files cannot be opened in Poser or 3D Studio MAX. Photoshop files can be opened in Painter and other files can be saved as Photoshop files.

PC Paintbrush File (*.pcx): This file type is common in PC graphics programs. These files cannot be used in Poser, 3D Studio MAX, or Photoshop. PC Paintbrush files can be opened in Painter and other file types can be saved as PC Paintbrush files.

GIF File (*.gif): This is the most common graphic file type used on the World Wide Web. These files are compact in size. They can be used as textures or bitmaps in 3D Studio MAX. They can be created in AutoCAD. They cannot be used in Poser. They cannot be opened in Photoshop, but they can be created there. GIF files can be opened in Painter and other file types can be saved as GIF files.

Pyramid Image File (*.pyr): Pyramid Images are very large, highly detailed files sometimes used in commercial printing. They cannot be used in any of the other programs in these volumes. They can be opened in Painter and other file types can be saved as Pyramid Images.

Frame Stack File (*.frm): Frame Stack files are also commonly used in animation. They cannot be used in any of the other programs in these volumes. Frame Stack files can be opened in Painter, but other file types cannot be saved as Frame Stack files.

Postscript File (*.eps): This file type is often used in commercial graphics. These files cannot be used in Poser or 3D Studio MAX. They can be opened in Photoshop. Postscript files cannot be opened in Painter, but other file types can be saved as Postscript files.

Adobe Illustrator File (*.ai): This file type was developed for the Adobe Illustrator program. These files cannot be used in any of the four programs covered in these volumes. They can be opened in Photoshop. They can be exported from Painter.

POSER FILE TYPES AND EXTENSIONS

Poser Internal File Types

These file types are used to save the work that you have done so that it can be worked on again in Poser. They cannot be used directly in any of the other programs in these volumes.

POZ (*.poz): This is the Poser 1 file type. It can also be opened in Poser 2 or Poser 3.

PZR (*.pzr): This is the Poser 2 file type. It can be opened in Poser 3, but not Poser 1.

PZ3 (*.pz3): This is the poser 3 file type. It cannot be opened in Poser 1 or Poser 2.

Poser 3-D Image Export File Types

These are file types that can be exported from Poser so that they can be used in other programs as 3-D images of figures.

3D Studio Mesh File (*.3ds): This is the easiest format to use with either AutoCAD or 3D Studio MAX. It can be imported into AutoCAD R12 and R13 or 3D Studio MAX and can be inserted in AutoCAD R14.

DXF File (*.dxf): This is a drawing export file. These files can be imported into AutoCAD R12, R13, and 3D Studio MAX. They can be opened in AutoCAD R14. They cannot be used in Painter or most other drawing programs.

Poser 2-D Image Export File Types

These are file types that can be exported from Poser and then used in other programs as 2-D representations of figures. Both of these file types can be used in Painter to create renderings.

TIFF File (*.tif): When exported from Poser, this file type can be opened in Painter. This image can then be manipulated in any way you would like in Painter. These files are usually smaller in size than BMP files. See "Painter File Types" for more description.

Bitmap File (*.bmp): When exported from Poser, this file type can be opened in Painter. This image can then be manipulated in any way you would like in Painter. See "Painter File Types" for more description.

Poser Import File Types

These file types can be imported into Poser for use as backgrounds, props, and bump and texture maps.

Background Files

These file types can be used by Poser to create backgrounds behind the figures.

TIFF File (*.tif): This file type can be created in Painter or saved from a rendering in 3D Studio MAX. These files can be brought in from a scanned image. They can also be created in AutoCAD. They can also be created by taking a digital photo and then converting the image from JPEG into TIFF in Painter.

Bitmap File (*.bmp): This file type can be created in Painter or saved from a rendering in 3D Studio MAX. The files can also be exported from AutoCAD R13 and R14. They can also be brought in from scanned images or created by taking digital photos and then converting the images from JPEG to BMP files in Painter.

Bump or Texture Map Files

These file types can be used by Poser to create bump or texture maps for the figures.

TIFF File (*.tif): This file type can be created in Painter or brought in from a scanned image. Another file type can be converted to a TIFF file in Painter.

Bitmap File (*.bmp): This file type can be created in Painter or brought in from a scanned image. Another file type can be converted to a BMP file in Painter.

Prop Files

These file types can be brought into Poser and used as props along with the figures.

3D Studio Mesh File (*.3ds): Three-dimensional objects created in 3D Studio MAX can be exported from that program as .3ds files and then imported into Poser as props. This format can also be exported from AutoCAD R13 and R14.

DXF File (*.dxf): Three-dimensional objects created in AutoCAD can be exported from that program in DXF format and then imported into Poser as Props. **Note:** DXF files do not work as well as .3ds files in Poser. If you have an option, go for a .3ds file instead of a DXF file. See the section on importing into Poser (see page 338).

Importing and Exporting Files from the Programs

This section will provide you with a quick summary of how to import and export the various file types out of each of the programs covered in these volumes. If you need more details on dealing with a specific program, that information is available in the text on the program.

AUTOCAD

Exporting 3-D Image Files

These files can be used as 3-D objects or figures in other programs.

DXF Files (*.dxf): These files can be brought into 3D Studio MAX as objects or into Poser as props. They are created in all releases of AutoCAD by clicking on File/Export on the pull down menu.

3D Studio Mesh Files (*.3ds): These files can be used in 3D Studio MAX as objects or in Poser as props. They can only be created in AutoCAD R14. Click on File/Export on the pull down menu.

Exporting 2-D Image Files

These files can be used as 2-D backgrounds, images, or the basis of renderings.

TIFF Image Files (*.tif), GIF Image Files (*.gif), and Targa Image Files (*.tga): All of these file types can be opened in Painter. TIFF files can be used as backgrounds and texture maps in Poser and as textures in 3D Studio MAX. In R12, click on Render/Files/Save Image on the pull down menu. In R13, click on Tools/Image/Save. In R14, click on Tools/Display Image/Save.

BMP Image Files (*.bmp): These files can be opened in Painter. They can be used as backgrounds and texture maps in Poser and as textures in 3D Studio MAX. In AutoCAD R12, click on File/Save As. In R13 and R14, click on File/Export.

Encapsulated Postscript Files (*.eps, *.ps): These files cannot be used in any of the other programs in these volumes. In all releases, click on File/Export.

Importing Files

These are files that can be brought into AutoCAD to create drawings.

DXF Files (*.dxf) : After being created in another program such as 3D Studio MAX these files can be brought into AutoCAD. For R12 and R13, click on File/Import. For R14, click on File/Open.

3D Studio Mesh Files (*.3ds): These files cannot be brought into R12. For R13, click on File/Import. For R14, click on Insert/3D Studio.

3D STUDIO MAX

Exporting 3-D Image Files

These are file types that can be used in other programs as objects or to create accurate technical drawings.

3D Studio Mesh Files (*.3ds): These files can be used in AutoCAD R13 and R14, but not R12. They can be used in Poser as props. To create, click on File/Export.

DWG Files (*.dwg): These files can be used in all versions of AutoCAD. To create, click on File/Export.

DXF Files (*.dxf): These can be imported into all versions of AutoCAD. They can also be imported into Poser as props. To create, click on File/Export.

Exporting Rendering Files

These are files that are created from 3D Studio MAX renderings and can be saved for use in rendering programs such as Painter or as backgrounds in Poser.

JPEG (*.jpg), TIFF (*.tif), BMP (*.bmp), Targa (*.tga), AVI (*.avi), FLIC (*.flc), EPS (*.eps), PNG (*.png), and RLA (*.rla) Files:

1. To save to one of these formats after the rendering has already been created, click on the icon above the rendering window that looks like a 3.5-inch disk.

2. To save to one of these formats before the rendering is created:
   A. Click on the Render Scene button.
   B. In the Render Scene box:
      1. Click on Single under Time Output.
      2. Select output size desired.
      3. Click on the File button under Render Output.
         a. Select the drive and folder where you want to save the file.
         b. Select the file type that you desire.
         c. Enter a file name and extension.
         d. Click on OK. You are returned to the Render Scene box.
      4. Be sure there is a check next to Save File under Render Output.
      5. Click on the Render button.

Importing 3-D Image Files

These are the files that can be brought into 3D Studio MAX as objects or entire scenes.

3D Studio Mesh Files (*.3ds): These files can be created in Poser and AutoCAD R14. To bring one into 3D Studio MAX click on File/Import on the pull down menu.

DWG Files (*.dwg): These files can be created in all releases of AutoCAD. To bring one into 3D Studio MAX, click on File/Import on the pull down menu. You may experience some difficulties importing this file type into 3D Studio MAX. If so, use a DXF file instead.

DXF Files (*.dxf): These files can be created in Poser and all releases of AutoCAD. To bring one into 3D Studio MAX click on **File/Import** on the pull down menu.

Importing Texture and Bitmap Files

These file types can be used by 3D Studio MAX as materials, textures, and bitmaps to be applied to objects. They can be created in a variety of sources such as Painter and by using scanners and digital cameras.

TIFF (*.tif), Targa (*.tga), JPEG (*.jpg), GIF (*.gif), RLA (*.rla), AutoDesk Image (*.flc), and Image File List (*.ifl) Files:

1. Open the **Material Editor** and select a **Sample Slot**.
2. Under the **Maps** bar click on the **None** bar to the right of the diffuse spinner.
3. The **Material/Map Browser** opens.
   A. In the **Browse From** section, click on **New**.
   B. Click on **Bitmap** in the large window.
   C. Click on **OK**.
4. You are returned to the Material Editor.
5. Click on the blank bar next to **Bitmap** in the **Bitmap Parameters** section.
6. The **Select Bitmap Image** file box opens.
   A. Choose the drive and folder where the file is located.
   B. Click on the file name that you want to use.
   C. Click on **OK**.
7. The file will appear in the sample slot that you have selected in step 1.
8. You can now assign that material to a selected object in the program.

Importing Files to Use with Lighting Instruments

These file types can be used by 3D Studio MAX with target spots and directional spots in their projector option. They will then act like patterns, templates, gobos, or projected images. They can be created in a variety of sources such as Painter and by using scanners and digital cameras.

TIFF (*.tif), Targa (*.tga), JPEG (*.jpg), GIF (*.gif), RLA (*.rla), AutoDesk Image (*.flc), and Image File List (*.ifl) Files:

1. In the **Spotlight Parameters** area of the lighting instrument's **Modify Parameters** section, click on the box next to **Projector**.
2. Click on the **Assign** button.
3. The **Material/Map Browser** opens. Click on **New** in the **Browse from:** section. Click on **Bitmap** in the large box on the right-hand side. Click on **OK**.

4. Back in the Spotlight Parameters area, click on the button next to Map:. The Put to Material Editor box opens. Select a slot # and click on OK.

5. Open the Material Editor. The slot number that you selected in the last step is black. Click on this slot to select it. In the Bitmap Parameters section of the Material Editor, click on the large blank button next to Bitmap.

6. The Select Bitmap Image File box opens.

   A. Find the file that you desire in whichever drive it is located.

   B. Be sure that the name of the file appears in the File name: window.

   C. Click on OK.

7. You are returned to the Material Editor. The file that you selected appears in the slot previously selected.

8. Close the Material Editor and do a quick render to see the result.

PAINTER

The following file types can all be opened (File/Open) in Painter. Once they have been opened they can be saved as (File/Save As) any of the other file types. For more information on the various file types, see the part of this section dealing with file types. To bring a file into Painter, it must be in one of these formats:

RIFF files (*.rif)	TIFF files (*.tif)
JPEG files (*.jpg)	Targa files (*.tga)
Bitmap files (*.bmp)	GIF files (*.gif)
PICT files (*.pct)	Photoshop files (*.psd)
PC Paintbrush files (*.pcx)	Video for Windows files (*.avi)
Pyramid Image files (*.pyr)	Frame Stack files (*.frm)
Postscript files (*.eps)	

There is one file type that cannot be opened in Painter, but can be exported from Painter. That is an Adobe Illustrator file (*.ai). To save another file type as an .ai file, click on File/Export.

POSER

Exporting Files

To export a file from Poser you click on File/Export/Name of the Filetype on the pull down menu. 3D Studio Mesh files (*.3ds) and DXF files (*.dxf) export as 3-D figures and can be used in AutoCAD and 3D Studio MAX. TIFF (*.tif) and Bitmap (*.bmp) files export as 2-D views of figures and can be opened in Painter as the beginning of a rendering.

Importing Files

Background Files

TIFF (*.tif) and Bitmap (*.bmp) files can be brought into Poser to use as backgrounds behind the figures. To import one of these file types to use as a background, click on File/Import/Background Picture on the pull down menu. After you have imported the background you must still tell the program to use it in the rendering. Click on Render/Render Options. This opens the Render Options box. In the Render Over section, select Background Picture and click on OK.

Bump and Texture Map Files

TIFF (*.tif) and Bitmap (*.bmp) files can be brought into Poser to use as bump and texture maps for the figures. These files are loaded in the following manner after a figure type and pose has been selected:

1. Click on Render/Surface Material on the pull down menu.
2. Click on Load in either the Bump Map or Texture Map area, depending upon which kind you want to load into the program.
3. The Open box appears.
   A. Locate the file that you want and click on it so that its name appears in the File Name window.
   B. Click on Open.
4. If you are loading a bump map you will be prompted to convert it to a .bum file. Convert it into a .bum file.
5. Click on the arrow button under Bump or Texture Map, depending upon which kind you are loading, and select the file that you just loaded.
6. Click on the OK button to exit the Surface Materials box.

Prop Files

3D Studio Mesh (*.3ds) or DXF (*.dxf) files can be brought into Poser and used as props along with the figures. A prop can also be substituted for a part of a figure. To import one of these files as a prop:

1. Click on File/Import/Name of the filetype for either 3D Studio or DXF.
2. Locate the file that you want to import and click on it so that its name appears in the File Name window.
3. Click on Open.
4. The Prop Import Options box opens. Here you will make choices about the prop's size relative to the figure and location. Click on OK.
5. The prop will appear in the scene. It is already selected when it appears and has been given a name such as OBJ_IMPORT_1. You can move it around as you desire.
6. You can color the prop using the Render/Surface Material.

APPENDIX B

BIBLIOGRAPHY

Bertol, D. 1994. *Visualizing with CAD: An AutoCAD Exploration of Geometric and Architectural Forms*. Santa Clara, CA: TELOS.

Bertoline, G. R. 1994. *The Essential AutoCAD*. New York: Maxwell Macmillan International.

Billing, K. W., et al. 1993. *AutoCAD—The Professional Reference*. Carmel, IN: New Riders Publishers.

Busch, D. D. 1999. *Painting Amazing Web Images with Fractal Design Painter 5*. Orlando, FL: Academic Press Inc.

Dix, M. 1989. *Discovering AutoCAD*. Englewood Cliffs, NJ: Prentice Hall.

Hood, J. D. 1988. *Easy AutoCAD*. New York: McGraw-Hill.

Juracek, J. A. 1996. *Surfaces: Visual Research for Artists, Architects, and Designers*. New York: W. W. Norton.

Karaiskos, P. 1995. *AutoCAD for Mechanical Engineers and Designers*. New York: Wiley.

Kirsher, L. 1997. *Painter 5: Users Guide*. Santa Clara, CA: Citation Press.

London, S. 1997. *Fractal Design Painter*. Research Triangle Park, NC: Ventana Communications Group Inc.

Love, L. 1997. *Painter 5: Tutorial*. Santa Clara, CA: Citation Press.

Martier, S. 1998. *MetaCreations Poser 3 Handbook*. Rockland, MD: Charles River Media.

Matossian, M. 1998. *Teach Yourself 3D Studio Max in 14 Days*. Indianapolis: Sams.

———. 1999. *3D StudioMax: Visual Quick Start Guide*. Berkeley: Peachpit Press.

Miller, P. 1997. *Inside 3D Studio Max*. Indianapolis: New Riders Publishers.

Omura, G., and B. R. Callori. 1993. *AutoCAD Release 12 for Windows—Instant Reference*. Alameda, CA: SYBEX Inc.

Payne, D. R. 1994. *Computer Scenographics*. Carbondale, IL: Southern Illinois University Press.

Pinnell, W. H. 1996. *Perspective Rendering for the Theatre*. Carbondale, IL: Southern Illinois University Press.

Potts, F., and D. H. Freidel Jr. 1996. *3D Studio Max Design Guide*. Scottsdale, AZ: Coriolis Group.

Raker, D. 1976. *Inside AutoCAD: A Teaching Guide to the AutoCAD Microcomputer Design and Drafting Program*. Thousand Oaks, CA: New Riders Publishers.

Rose, R. 1990. *AutoCAD Onstage: A Computer-Aided Design Handbook for Theater, Film and Television*. White Hall, VA: Betterway Publications.

Sanchez, L. 1994. *Fallingwater in 3d Studio: A Case Study and Tutorial*. Sante Fe, NM: On Word Press.

Schaefer, A. T. 1988. *The AutoCAD Productivity Book: Tapping the Hidden Power of AutoCAD*. Chapel Hill, NC: Ventana Press.

Sperling, K. 1997. *Fractal Design: Painter 5 Complete*. Indianapolis: IDG Books Worldwide.

Sutton, J. 1996. *Fractal Design: Painter Creative Techniques*. Indianapolis: Hayden.

————. 1996. *Tutorials, 3D Studio Max*. Kinetix, AutoDesk.

Vera, E., and L. Kirsher. 1998. *Poser 3: The Remarkable Figure Design and Animation Tool: Users Guide*. MetaCreations Corp.

INDEX

3D STUDIO MAX

PAINTER

POSER

About the CD-ROM

CD Contents

- Sample files are included on this CD to use for following exercises outlined in the book. Files are included for AutoCAD, 3D Studio MAX, Painter, and Poser.
- Note: The CD-ROM contains only samples files, NOT the applications used to create them.

System Requirements

Windows:

- Windows 95 or higher
- 200 mHZ Pentium II Processor (or higher)
- Minimum 32 MB of application RAM (more recommended)
- Color Display (24-bit recommended)
- CD-ROM Drive

Macintosh:

- System 7.5 (or higher)
- 200 mHZ Power PC Processor (or higher)
- Minimum 32 MB of application RAM (more recommended)
- Color Display (24-bit recommended)
- CD-ROM Drive
- Poser 3 requires System 8.0

These system requirements need to be met in order to run the applications associated with the sample files included on this disk.

Have a question about any of our electronic products? Call or e-mail our tech support hotline at (800) 793-2154 or techsupport@heinemann.com

R12 AND READ ONLY FILES

If you are working in AutoCAD R12 you may experience some problems opening a file from the CD-ROM. This is because R12 must have a different file location for temporary files. Any file that has a "Read Only" property such as any file on a CD-ROM would cause this difficulty in R12. If you find that you cannot open a file in R12 you will have to reconfigure the program to send temporary files to a new location. The procedure is as follows:

When you attempt to open the file from the CD-ROM you will receive the following error message: To access files in a read-only directory you must configure a temporary file location other than "DRAWING". Click on OK. This returns you to the Open Drawing Box. Click on Cancel. Now you must reconfigure for a new temporary file location.

Click on File/Configure to begin reconfiguration. Hit Enter (Return) twice to get to the Configuration Menu list. Once you are in the Configuration Menu list type in the number for Configure Operating Parameters and hit Enter. You should now be in the Configure Operating Parameters list. Type in the number for Placement of Temporary Files and hit Enter.

The prompt on the screen will read: Enter directory name for temporary files, or DRAWING to place them in the same directory as the drawing being edited <DRAWING>. Now you will have to give AutoCAD a folder (directory) on your hard drive in which it can place these temporary files. Type in the letter that identifies your hard drive followed by :\ (colon backslash) and the name of the folder (directory). It does not matter what folder on your hard drive you select. For example, say that all of your AutoCAD files are in a folder named ACAD and the letter that designates your hard drive is C. Then at this prompt you could type in C:\ACAD. Hit Enter and you will be returned to the Configure Operating Parameters list. If this is not a valid folder on your hard drive AutoCAD will tell you so and you will have to try again. When you are returned to the Configure Operating Parameters list hit Enter again to select <0> Exit to configuration menu. You will be returned to the Configure Menu List. Hit Enter again to select <0> Exit to drawing editor. You will be prompted for whether you want to keep the configuration changes. Hit Enter again to select <Y> Keep configuration changes. You will be returned to the drawing editor.

Now you can open the file on the CD-ROM or any other Read Only file. When you attempt to do so you will see a message on the screen that reads: Unable to write to that directory. Do you want to continue? Click on Yes and the file will open.